W9-CMQ-117

TECHNICAL COLLEGE OF THE LOWCOUNTRY
LEARNING RESOURCES CENTER
POST OFFICE BOX 1288
BEAUFORT, SOUTH CAROLINA 29901-1288

Contemporary American
Ethnic Poets

TECHNICAL COLLEGE OF THE LOWCOUNTRY
LEARNING RESOURCES CENTER
POST OFFICE BOX 1288
BEAUFORT, SOUTH CAROLINA 29901-1288

Contemporary American Ethnic Poets

Lives, Works, Sources

Edited by Linda Cullum

GREENWOOD PRESS
Westport, Connecticut • London

TECHNICAL COLLEGE OF THE LOWCOUNTRY
LEARNING RESOURCES CENTER
POST OFFICE BOX 1288
BEAUFORT, SOUTH CAROLINA 29901-1288

Library of Congress Cataloging-in-Publication Data

Cullum, Linda, 1947–
    Contemporary American ethnic poets : lives, works, sources / by Linda Cullum.
        p.   cm.
    Includes bibliographical references and index.
    ISBN 0–313–32484–0 (alk. paper)
    1. American poetry—Minority authors—Bio-bibliography—Dictionaries. 2. Poets,
American—21st century—Biography—Dictionaries. 3. Poets, American—20th century—
Biography—Dictionaries. 4. Ethnic groups in literature—Dictionaries. 5. Minorities in
literature—Dictionaries. 6. Ethnicity in literature—Dictionaries. I. Title.
PS153.M56L56   2004
811′.5409920693′04—dc22   2003064258

British Library Cataloguing in Publication Data is available.

Copyright © 2004 by Linda Cullum

All rights reserved. No portion of this book may be
reproduced, by any process or technique, without the
express written consent of the publisher.

Library of Congress Catalog Card Number: 2003064258
ISBN: 0–313–32484–0

First published in 2004

Greenwood Press, 88 Post Road West, Westport, CT 06881
An imprint of Greenwood Publishing Group, Inc.
www.greenwood.com

Printed in the United States of America

The paper used in this book complies with the
Permanent Paper Standard issued by the National
Information Standards Organization (Z39.48–1984).

10 9 8 7 6 5 4 3 2 1

Contents

List of Poets

List of Poets by Ethnicity

AFRICAN AMERICAN

Maya Angelou
Amiri Baraka
Gwendolyn Brooks
Lucille Clifton
Wanda Coleman
Rita Dove
Mari Evans
Nikki Giovanni
June Jordan
Etheridge Knight
Yusef Komunyakaa
Marilyn Nelson
Quincy Troupe
Ishmael Reed
Sonia Sanchez

AMERICAN INDIAN

Sherman Alexie
Paula Gunn Allen
Beth Brant
Joseph Bruchac
Diane Glancy
Joy Harjo
Linda Hogan
Maurice Kenny
N. (Navarre) Scott Momaday
Duane Niatum
Simon J. Ortiz
Wendy Rose

Leslie Marmon Silko
Mary TallMountain
Luci Tapahonso

ASIAN AMERICAN

Ai
Nick Carbó
Diana Chang
Marilyn Chin
Jessica Hagedorn
Garrett Kaoru Hongo
Lawson Fusao Inada
Li-Young Lee
Shirley Geok-lin Lim
James Matseo Mitsui
Janice Mirikitani
David Mura
Cathy Song
José García Villa
Mitsuye Yamada

EAST INDIAN AMERICAN

Chitra Banerjee Divakaruni

IRISH AMERICAN

Eamon Grennan
Galway Kinnell
Paul Muldoon

ITALIAN AMERICAN

Dana Gioia

JEWISH AMERICAN

Marjorie Agosín
Enid Dame
Irena Klepfisz
Linda Pastan
Marge Piercy
Gerald Stern

LATINO/LATINA

Marjorie Agosín
Jack Agüeros
Julia Alvarez
Gloria Anzaldúa
Jimmy Santiago Baca
Lorna Dee Cervantes
Sandra Cisneros
Judith Ortiz Cofer
Victor Hernández Cruz
Martín Espada
Tato Laviera
Pat Mora
Leroy V. Quintana
Alberto Alvaro Ríos
Gary Soto

PALESTINIAN AMERICAN

Suheir Hammad
Naomi Shihab Nye

POLISH AMERICAN

Irena Klepfisz
Czeslaw Milosz

SLAVIC AMERICAN

Charles Simic

WEST INDIAN AMERICAN

Derek Walcott

List of Poets by Theme

All of the poets represented in this volume share certain similar concerns. All, for example, look and actively work for cultural healing—in their poetry and their other work. Most have a political agenda in their writing as well: they speak out on social issues in their works and decry racism and discrimination in all forms. However, within that broad framework, there are certain points of departure, and this list is designed to give readers a sense of general areas of focus for each poet.

AGING/ILLNESS/MORTALITY

Julia Alvarez
Dana Gioia
Eamon Grennan
Galway Kinnell
Li-Young Lee
Czeslaw Milosz
N. (Navarre) Scott Momaday
Mary TallMountain

ALCOHOLISM/DRUG ADDICTION

Sherman Alexie
Etheridge Knight

ANCESTRY

Sherman Alexie
Paula Gunn Allen
Beth Brant
Lucille Clifton
Rita Dove
Garrett Kaoru Hongo
Maurice Kenny

N. (Navarre) Scott Momaday
Alberto Alvaro Ríos
Wendy Rose
Sonia Sanchez
Leslie Marmon Silko
Cathy Song

ART/PHOTOGRAPHY

Diana Chang
Chitra Banerjee Divakaruni
Li-Young Lee
James Matseo Mitsui
Wendy Rose
Cathy Song

BICULTURAL/MUTICULTURAL IDENTITY

Ai
Paula Gunn Allen
Gloria Anzaldúa
Jimmy Santiago Baca
Beth Brant
Lorna Dee Cervantes
Diana Chang
Judith Ortiz Cofer
Dana Gioia
Diane Glancy
Linda Hogan
Shirley Geok-lin Lim
N. (Navarre) Scott Momaday
Pat Mora
Naomi Shihab Nye
Alberto Alvaro Ríos
Wendy Rose
Mary TallMountain

BIOGRAPHICAL/HISTORICAL NARRATIVE

Ai
Sherman Alexie
Gloria Anzaldúa
Beth Brant
Lorna Dee Cervantes
Rita Dove

Dana Gioia
Joy Harjo
Maurice Kenny
Marilyn Nelson
Duane Niatum
Simon Ortiz

BLACK ARTS MOVEMENT (BLACK AESTHETIC)

Amiri Baraka
Gwendolyn Brooks
Mari Evans
Nikki Giovanni
Ishmael Reed
Sonia Sanchez

BORDERS AND BORDER LIFE

Gloria Anzaldúa
Lorna Dee Cervantes
Judith Ortiz Cofer
Pat Mora
Alberto Alvaro Ríos

THE CARIBBEAN

Victor Hernández Cruz
Derek Walcott

CHILDREN'S/YOUNG ADULT LITERATURE

Jack Agüeros
Julia Alvarez
Maya Angelou
Gloria Anzaldúa
Joseph Bruchac
Sandra Cisneros
Chitra Banerjee Divakaruni
Mari Evans
Nikki Giovanni
Suheir Hammad
Lawson Fusao Inada
Joy Harjo
June Jordan

Pat Mora
Marilyn Nelson
Simon Ortiz
Gary Soto

CREATION STORIES AND LEGENDS

Beth Brant
Joseph Bruchac
Joy Harjo
Leslie Marmon Silko

FAMILY AND COMMUNITY

Julia Alvarez
Lucille Clifton
Chitra Banerjee Divakaruni
Nikki Giovanni
Li-Young Lee
Shirley Geok-lin Lim
James Matseo Mitsui
Pat Mora
Paul Muldoon
Marilyn Nelson
Simon Ortiz
Linda Pastan
Cathy Song
Gary Soto
Luci Tapahonso

HAWAII

Garrett Kaoru Hongo
Cathy Song

HUMOR

Sherman Alexie
Sandra Cisneros
Nikki Giovanni
Yusef Komunyakaa
Marilyn Nelson
Charles Simic
Gary Soto

IMMIGRATION AND ASSIMILATION

Julia Alvarez
Diana Chang
Marilyn Chin
Victor Hernández Cruz
Chitra Banerjee Divakaruni
Suheir Hammad
Garrett Kaoru Hongo
Shirley Geok-lin Lim

IMPRISONMENT

Jimmy Santiago Baca
Etheridge Knight

JAPANESE INTERNMENT

Garrett Kaoru Hongo
Lawson Fusao Inada
Janice Mirikitani
James Matseo Mitsui
David Mura
Mitsuye Yamada

JARGON AND VERNACULAR

Amiri Baraka
Victor Hernández Cruz
June Jordan
Tato Laviera
Sonia Sanchez

JEWISH IDENTITY

Marjorie Agosín
Enid Dame
Irena Klepfisz
Gerald Stern

LESBIAN IDENTITY

Paula Gunn Allen
Gloria Anzaldúa

POLITICAL ISSUES/SOCIAL PROTEST

Wanda Coleman
Martín Espada
Mari Evans
Nikki Giovanni
Suheir Hammad
June Jordan
Galway Kinnell
Paul Muldoon
Naomi Shihab Nye
Ishmael Reed
Derek Walcott

POPULAR CULTURE

Sherman Alexie
Nick Carbó
Jessica Hagedorn

RELIGION

Paula Gunn Allen
Judith Ortiz Cofer
Enid Dame
Marilyn Nelson
Charles Simic
Mary TallMountain
José García Villa

RESERVATION LIFE

Sherman Alexie
Paula Gunn Allen
Beth Brant
Linda Hogan
Wendy Rose

SEPTEMBER 11, 2001

Enid Dame
Nikki Giovanni
Diane Glancy
Joy Harjo
Suheir Hammad
Naomi Shihab Nye

SEXUALITY/RELATIONSHIPS

Maya Angelou
Sandra Cisneros
Rita Dove
Simon Ortiz
Linda Pastan
Gary Soto

THE SOUTHWEST LANDSCAPE

Paula Gunn Allen
Joy Harjo
Simon Ortiz
Leroy V. Quintana
Alberto Alvaro Ríos
Luci Tapahonso

SPORTS

Sherman Alexie
Lucille Clifton
Martín Espada
Galway Kinnell
Yusef Komunyakaa
James Matseo Mitsui
Linda Pastan
Marge Piercy
Gary Soto
Quincy Troupe

URBAN LIFE

Jack Agüeros
Jimmy Santiago Baca
Gwendolyn Brooks
Sandra Cisneros
Wanda Coleman
Victor Hernández Cruz
Nikki Giovanni
Joy Harjo

VIETNAM WAR

Yusef Komunyakaa
Simon Ortiz
Marge Piercy

WOMEN'S RIGHTS

Paula Gunn Allen
Maya Angelou
Lorna Dee Cervantes
Marilyn Chin
Lucille Clifton
Judith Ortiz Cofer
Wanda Coleman
Chitra Banerjee Divakaruni
Suheir Hammad
Irena Klepfisz
Shirley Geok-lin Lim
Janice Mirikitani
Marge Piercy
Sonia Sanchez
Luci Tapahonso
Mitsuye Yamada

WORDPLAY/EXPERIMENTATION WITH LANGUAGE

Jack Agüeros
Gloria Anzaldúa
Amiri Baraka
Dana Gioia
Irena Klepfisz
Etheridge Knight
N. (Navarre) Scott Momaday
David Mura
Leroy V. Quintana
Charles Simic
Gerald Stern
José García Villa

WORKING-CLASS LIFE

Sandra Cisneros
Gary Soto

WORLD WAR II/HOLOCAUST/BOMBING OF HIROSHIMA

Marjorie Agosín
Irena Klepfisz
Czeslaw Milosz
Janice Mirikitani

Acknowledgments

This sourcebook is truly a collective accomplishment that owes its existence to so many. First of all, let me thank my friend and department chair at Kutztown University, Guiyou Huang, for trusting me to take over his course in ethnic literature and then recommending me to edit this volume. Thanks also go to my advising editor at Greenwood Press, Lynn Araujo (formerly Lynn Malloy), and to photography editor Liz Kincaid, for their unfailing guidance, support, and good cheer.

I was aided in this project by four exceedingly accomplished women who used their specific expertise to advise me on poet selection and to write some, and edit all, entries in their respective fields. They are Cecilia Rodríguez Milanés, who supervised all of the Latino/Latina entries; Veronica Watson, who was in charge of the African American entries; Alice Trupe, who handled all of the Asian American entries; and Jennifer McNamara Dressler, who coordinated the entries of poets of Irish, Italian, Jewish, Palestinian, Czech, Polish, and East and West Indian origin. Information about each of these scholars is available at the conclusion of this volume. I thank them for their knowledge, their reliability, their willingness to stick by me regardless of the crisis of the day, and above all, their friendship.

Thanks also go to all those who contributed individual entries, with a special acknowledgment to Sue Czerny, who was first onboard with this project and who kept writing until the end, filling in gaps and picking up projects abandoned by others. Megwitch, Sue. And, of course, thanks to my students in the ethnic American literature course at Kutztown University of Pennsylvania. As they sit amid the farmlands of eastern Pennsylvania, their willingness to open their hearts and minds to make connections with the course material is an ongoing inspiration.

Finally, I want to acknowledge the less tangible but no less essential contributions of my family. Thanks go to my parents, for their love and pride; to my daughters, Lauren, Annie, and Katie—who hardly ever complained about my constant state of distraction and who provided materials, insights, renewed energy, and faith in the future; and especially to my husband and my ultimate resource, Charlie.

Acknowledgments

As always, any positive contributions that this collection makes are owed to the many persons involved with the project. Any errors or oversights are mine alone.

Introduction

Poetry is not a luxury.
—Audre Lorde

Poetry is the language of affirmation.
—Joseph Bruchac

OVERVIEW

Poetry can thrill us with its intensity and emotion, delight us with its sounds and rhythms, and lead us on a path toward discovering our own truths and learning of the realities of others. The poetic word is powerful, indeed, and the poetry of the seventy-five writers explored in this volume stands as testament to this power. These poets have produced works that display the range of human experience and expression, but with an added intensity as well, for they are poets who are generally regarded as both American and as ethnic. This identification has left them, in varying degrees, to function within an American cultural framework—which can be seen as largely European and patriarchal—even as they retain, explore, and celebrate their own unique heritage.

Until fairly recently, most of these poets—and their unique stories—would have gone unread and unheeded by most of America. Historically, those in the majority, primarily white, European American males, were in the position to select what got taught in the schools, what was reproduced in literary anthologies, and which poets were published by the mainstream American presses, thus institutionalizing literary tastes and ratifying the perspectives of those already in control. As Jann Pataray-Ching, assistant professor of Language and Literacy Studies at University of Nebraska–Lincoln, has observed, building on the work of anthropologist James Clifford, institutions and texts came to function as "bordered spaces . . . becoming sites of struggle for power and representation" (Ching and Pataray-Ching, p. 24), all too often to the exclusion of more marginalized Americans.

Happily, these borders have begun to expand and even collapse, and the era ushered in by the end of World War II has seen, if not the emergence, then at least the promise, of a true American multiculture. There are many reasons for this fortunate development, both in education and in the larger culture. For example, between the 1950s and the 1980s, enrollment in higher education increased 400 percent, with the proportion of high school students going on to college rising from 25 to 60 percent (*Strong Foundations,* p. 22). Thus more of every segment of the population has become literate and better educated, often due to the GI Bill and other government initiatives.

In addition, the 1960s and 1970s saw the rise of a number of various Civil Rights organizations, including the Student Nonviolent Coordinating Committee (SNCC), Students for a Democratic Society (SDS), the Congress on Racial Equality (CORE), the American Indian Movement (AIM), and the United Farm Workers of America, as well as major legislation such as the Civil Rights Act of 1964 and the more recent Civil Liberties Act of 1988, which made reparations to the Japanese Americans interned during World War II. Oppressed groups continue to fight for, and win, their civil rights, allowing a deeper American consciousness to be formed. Ongoing immigration to this country and increased globalization have also sparked greater interest in other cultures, even as they suggest that Western thought is but one perspective, not the exclusive standard bearer of ideas and tastes. For students of literature, this is all very good news, since our contemporary poetic world is developing into one of rich tapestry and deep texture, one where we can discover the experiences of so many others even as we find ourselves—and our own infinite variety—represented.

The poets represented here are varied, portraying a wide range of views, experiences, perspectives, and exposure. They are Americans with roots in African, Asian, Native, and Latino cultures, and with Irish, Italian, Jewish, Arabic, Polish, Czech, and West Indian heritages. Most are still actively writing, although untimely deaths have visited several, such as June Jordan, Mary TallMountain, and Gwendolyn Brooks. Some are widely lauded, including Nobel Prize winner Derek Walcott and national treasure Maya Angelou, while many are still emerging writers, yet to be fully discovered by a general readership. Some are professors around the country; others devote themselves full-time to their craft. Some lecture, some sit on national boards, some do charitable works, run publishing houses, and raise families. Most also work in other genres, ranging from literary criticism to screenplays, from Web sites to novels, and everywhere in between.

Despite their diversity, these poets do stand on some common ground. They all share the ability to give to their readers a sense of themselves, their experiences as Americans, and their reality as ethnicized Americans—a designation they may not have sought but now choose to recognize, to explore, and to celebrate. All use poetry as a means of discovering these realities, displaying anger but also hope, despair but also a good dose of humor. They can grapple with contemporary issues as well as the classic questions of existence and meaning. They establish differences but can also cut across borders.

Specific themes and concerns of the individual artists are considered within each bio-bibliographical entry in this volume. However, there are some general issues surrounding the experience of being an ethnic American that bear exploring in these introductory comments. For example, the importance of giving voice both to personal experiences *and* to cultural and historical realities is stressed repeatedly in the poetry of these disparate writers. As peoples all too familiar with cultural silencing know, language is often used as an antidote to suppression and invisibility, creating what Brian Swann calls a "poetry of historical witness . . . , grow[ing] out of a past that is very much a present" (p. xvii). Heeding Cuban American anthropologist Ruth Behar's admonition that the only real death is the "death of memory" (quoted in Ching and Pataray-Ching, p. 25), they often use their poetic voices to celebrate their heritage while ensuring that their readers do not forget the injustices that their people—which is to say our people, since we are all members of the same human race—have experienced in America. These voices also frequently long for their homelands, both geographic and metaphorical, as they ratify and gain sustenance from their ancestral links.

Linked to these concepts is an extraordinary appreciation of aspects of life that have often been undervalued in American thought, based as it has been on autonomy, the "self-made man," and success in the marketplace. Replacing these public, highly individualistic notions, we often find other aspects of life celebrated: nature, community, the personal and spiritual, and families, both past and present. Time and space, too, often become more broadly interpreted. In addition to the here and now, there is also a before and an after; horizontal motion joins linearity. In these ways, realities expand, interdependencies are forged, and borders blur.

One more common thread deserves mention here. Many of the ethnic poets represented in this volume speak of a moment of recognition—usually after years of being exposed to European and European American authors only—a moment when they saw their life in the words of others for the first time and realized that they too had a contribution to make. In an interview done with Random House AudioBooks, Sandra Cisneros describes that moment when she discovered her "spoken voice, the voice of an American Mexican":

> One time or another, we all have felt Other. When I teach writing, I tell the story of the moment of discovering and naming my Otherness. It is not enough to simply sense it; it has to be named and then written about from there. Once I could name it I ceased being ashamed and silent. I could speak up and celebrate my Otherness as a woman, as a working class person, as an American of Mexican descent. When I recognized the places where I departed from my neighbors, my classmates, my family, my town, my brothers, when I discovered what I knew that no one else in the room knew, I spoke it in a voice that was my voice. . . . [W]hen I could

give myself permission to speak from that intimate space, then I could I could talk like myself, not like me trying to sound like someone I wasn't, then I could speak, shout, laugh from a place that was uniquely mine, no one else's in the universe, that would never be anyone else's.

Similarly, Sherman Alexie (Spokane/Coeur d'Alene) tells an interviewer on the audiocassette of his novel *Indian Killer* about the first time that he read literature wherein he could recognize his own experiences in the printed word. The book was Joseph Bruchac's anthology *Songs from This Earth on Turtle's Back*, and Alexie was twenty-two years old:

In this book I found all of these incredible Native American writers—Simon Ortiz, Leslie Marmon Silko, Joy Harjo, Adrian Louis, Linda Hogan. All these writers of very diverse tribal backgrounds writing in very diverse ways but telling stories that I recognized. I think it was amazing to read a poet such as Adrian Louis . . . where I saw myself in literature for the very first time as a Native American, as a Spokane/Coeur d'Alene.

As are so many other writers throughout America, the seventy-five poets discussed in this volume are pioneers, every one. They search through their poetry and other genres for identity, for recognition, for justice, for peace. Their influences are far-reaching and varied, coming from popular culture and from ancient myth; their muses are courage and frustration, optimism and despair. And yet, as Michelle Cliff, writer and literary critic, reminds us, even while poems "may originate in . . . common experience . . . may need that experience to exist in the first place, [this] does not mean that the poet does not possess a distinctive voice, and does not mean that each member of the group . . . does not remain an individual" (p. 33); there is nothing essential about an ethnic voice.

There may be some who question the very existence of "segregated" anthologies and sourcebooks that focus on one or another group. But as Brian Swann notes, these *are* necessary, at least until all vestiges of "tokenism and parochialism" (p. xvii) are eradicated from our canon, our classrooms, our minds. We aren't there yet, but we do stand on a threshold—a liminal state—of full representation. This will not be an inclusivity designed to pretend difference away—for that would be no more than a return to that misguided Eurocentric attempt to create a "melting pot"—but rather one that celebrates and grows from it, one that would contribute to a positive, restorative vision of society. African American writer and critic bell hooks articulates this vision as that of "beloved community," one that "is formed not by the eradication of difference but by its affirmation, by each of us claiming the identities and cultural legacies that shape who we are and how we live in the world" (p. 265).

This volume stands as a contribution to this idea of "beloved community" by lifting up many worlds of poetry—not to marginalize but to expand and to push apart all of those bordered spaces.

It seems fitting to conclude this introduction with the words of a poet represented in this volume, the woman whose works introduced me to the world of ethnic American writers. In a 1993 essay titled "Giveaway," Beth Brant writes:

> I come to the place where past, present, and future speak. An Indian place. A place to call myself and to call the spirits. Being a Native lesbian is like living in the eye of the hurricane—terrible, beautiful, filled with sounds and silences, the music of life-affirmation and the disharmony of life-despising. To balance, to create in this midst is a gift of honor and respect. (p. 944)

We should not presume to know in what particular "hurricane's eye" each of these poets resides. But we can certainly appreciate what they are "giving away" to all of us through their efforts to balance, create, and make for themselves their own "place" out of words. In doing so, they enable all of us to share in their stories and to learn about them—and ourselves—in honor and respect. What finer gift could there be?

SCOPE AND ARRANGEMENT OF THE BOOK

The seventy-five poets were selected using several criteria. As the book's title asserts, each is considered a contemporary writer who has published, and often continues to publish, poetry in the past several decades. All are being read to varying degrees in high schools and colleges across the country, and all have, to some extent, been included in anthologies aimed at those audiences. Poets are arranged alphabetically by last name, and while many authors contributed to this text, each entry follows a similar format. This format features a biographical section followed by a thematic overview. Concluding each entry is a bibliographical section with four components. First is a listing of poetry collections—both those published in traditional formats or those published as chapbooks, which are generally small, less formally bound, and printed by private presses. This is followed by a listing of selected anthologies where individual poems by the poet can be found. These lists are not intended to be exclusive but focus generally on anthologies that feature writings by ethnic Americans; thus the myriad of American poetry and literature anthologies that are in print have generally been omitted in favor of more specialized ones to give readers a sense of the breadth of anthologies that exist of late. Some Web sites for individual poets have also been listed; bear in mind, however, that Web sites can often have limited life spans. This is followed by a list of selected additional works by the poet, since almost every poet represented in this volume has written in at least one other genre. Finally, a list of selected resources for further reference—usually the most recent in the field—is given. Following the bibliographical lists, each entry is attributed to its contributor, a brief biographical description of whom can be found at the end of this volume.

In addition, several supplemental lists appear in this book. In the first list, poets are grouped according to their primary ethnic allegiance. This ethnicity list has the potential to be of great use, for example, to librarians helping patrons find poets of certain backgrounds or for school assignments that ask students to research a poet from their own ancestry. Second is a thematic guide to the poets, designed to enable the reader to easily access the writers whose works focus on subject matter of particular interest. Teachers selecting poetry assignments or preparing classroom presentations on thematic units will find this list a useful way to explore the biocritical entries. It is also helpful for comparing and contrasting the themes and concerns of various poets. The third list, of additional poets, acknowledges that, happily, the seventy-five contemporary ethnic American poets represented in this volume are just the beginning. By offering a representative sampling, organized by ethnicity, of the many other ethnic voices that can be heard today, this list encourages readers to further explore their interests.

GENERAL REFERENCES FOR FURTHER STUDY

The list of selected resources that concludes each entry features essays, books, and interviews that focus on the individual poet. In addition, more and more poets have their own Homepages on the Internet, and these are excellent places to begin one's research. There are also a number of reference sources—both hardcopy and electronic—that focus on more general biographical information. Further, access to the spoken word has never been easier, and the Internet has made it possible to hear many poets reading their own poetry. The best sites as of summer 2003 are included in the following list. While this list is not exhaustive, it is a good starting point for research.

Academy of American Poets. Online. www.poets.org.
Bookmark. Online. www.startribune.com/stonline/html/books/podium/bookmark/html.
A Celebration of Women Writers. Online. www.literati.net.
Contemporary Authors. Detroit, MI: Gale Research, 1964– . Also available online as part of *Gale's Biography Resource Center.*
Contemporary Poets. 6th ed. Detroit, MI: St. James Press, 1996.
Current Biography. New York: Wilson, 1940– .
Dictionary of Literary Biography. Detroit, MI: Gale, 1982– . See especially: *American Poets since World War II* (vols. 41, 120, 165, 169, 193); *Chicano Writers of the United States* (vols. 122, 209); *Native American Writers of the United States* (vol. 175 and others).

Gale's Biography Resource Center. Gale Group. Online. www.galegroup.com.
Internet Poetry Archive. Online. www.ibiblio.org.
Internet Public Library. Online. www.ipl.org.
Modern American Poetry Project. Online. www.english.uiuc.edu.
National Endowment for the Arts. Online. www.arts.endow.gov/explore.
Online Poetry Classroom. Online. www.onlinepoetryclassroom.org.
The Open Poetry Project. Online. www.openpoetry.com.
Salmon Poetry. Online. www.salmonpoetry.com.
Storytellers: Native American Authors Online. www.hanksville.org/storytellers/
    index.html.
Voices from the Gaps (Women Writers of Color). Online. www.voices.cla.umn.edu.
www.poems.com.
www.poetryhunter.com.

WORKS CITED

Alexie, Sherman. *Indian Killer.* San Bruno, CA: Audio Literature, 1996.
Brant, Beth. "Giveaway: Native Lesbian Writers." *Signs: Journal of Women in Culture and Society* 18 (Summer 1993): 944–947.
Bruchac, Joseph. *Survival This Way: Interviews with American Indian Poets.* Tucson: University of Arizona Press, 1987.
Ching, Stuart, and Jann Pataray-Ching. "Memory as Travel in Asian American Children's Literature." *The New Advocate* 15.1 (2002): 23–34.
Cisneros, Sandra. *The House on Mango Street.* New York: Random House AudioBooks, 1998.
Cliff, Michelle. "Poetry Is a Way of Reaching Out to What Is Reaching for You." *American Poetry Review* 24.4 (July–August 1995): 29–35.
hooks, bell. *Killing Rage: Ending Racism.* New York: Holt, 1995.
Lannan Foundation. *Readings & Conversations.* Online. www.lannan.org/readings/ dove.
Strong Foundations: Twelve Principles for Effective General Education Programs. Washington, DC: Association of American Colleges, 1994.
Swann, Brian. Introduction to *Harper's Anthology of 20th Century Native American Poetry.* Ed. Duane Niatum. San Francisco, CA: HarperSanFrancisco, 1988.

Linda Cullum

Contemporary American
Ethnic Poets

Marjorie Agosín

(1955–)

Chilean American

Photo by Ted Polumbaum, courtesy of Wellesley College.

BIOGRAPHY

Born in Bethesda, Maryland, while her father was working as a scientist in the United States, Marjorie Agosín and her family returned to Chile, her native land, when she was three months old. The fair-skinned and blue-eyed middle child of a Jewish family who were economically comfortable, Agosín describes the "privilege" of having indigenous nannies sing to her and tell her stories. She was deeply influenced by the stories of her relatives, Jews of the European Diaspora, absorbing the rich culture and sad historical legacies. Saying that her formative years had been spent under a dictator's control, she and her family exiled themselves to the United States again, finally to Georgia, where her father worked at the University of Georgia–Athens, while Agosín was in her teens.

An internationally known and honored human rights activist and author of more than forty books, Agosín is the most prolific contemporary Latina writer, publishing in both English and Spanish, although she says that Spanish is her literary tongue. She has published sixteen of books of poetry, five books of fiction, four memoirs, and a dozen books of criticism, has edited eighteen anthologies, and has written three plays. She earned a B.A. in philosophy and Spanish literature from the University of Georgia in 1976, an M.A. in Spanish literature in 1977 from Indiana University, and a Ph.D. in Spanish American literature in 1982, also from Indiana University. She is professor of Spanish at Wellesley University and has held over a dozen distinguished teaching positions, including the Hilliard Professorship at the University of Nevada–Reno, Distinguished Visiting Artist at the University of Georgia, the Cesar Chavez–Martin Luther King–Rosa Parks Distinguished Professorship at the University of Michigan, the Green Professorship at Texas Christian University, and the Hanes Willis Distinguished Professorship in the Humanities at the University of North Carolina–Chapel Hill.

She has received many awards, prizes, and accolades for her own writing as well as for her editing and translating work. These include a National Endowment for the Arts grant, two National Endowment for the Humanities grants,

First Prize for Poetry from Letras de Oro, the 1995 Latino Literature Prize, the American Association of Literary Translations Award for *Circles of Madness,* a New England Foundation grant, and the 1995 Mexican Cultural Institute Prize. She was recently awarded the Gabriela Mistral Medal of Honor by the government of Chile as a tribute for lifetime achievements; she was also named a member of Chile's Academia Chilena de la Lengua. In addition, Agosín has been recognized internationally as a human rights activist, earning the United Nations Leadership Award in Human Rights, the Judith Trolnick Award for Social Change, the Henrietta Zolds Award, the Jeannete Rankin Award for Achievement in Human Rights, and the Good Neighbor Award from the National Association of Christians and Jews. She lives in Massachusetts with her husband, son, and daughter.

THEMES AND CONCERNS

Marjorie Agosín's poetic imagination is as vast as it is brilliant. A glance at her extensive bibliography will serve to give readers a sense of her creativity and concerns. Her native land, its geography, culture, and inhabitants, is a constant source of inspiration, although her works are often set elsewhere, particularly in other troubled lands of Latin America. Much of her work is also concerned with life in the United States. She is absorbed by the plight of the powerless—women, children, the oppressed, regardless of color or background. For example, *Dear Anne Frank* (1997) is a remarkable collection of poems dedicated to the mythic holocaust icon. Agosín brings Anne close, corresponding with her to create an intimacy often removed from discussions of horror and genocide. She writes *to* Anne as well as *of* her to bring the reader to the moment of deep connection and empathy.

Agosín's themes range from the ills of imperialism, torture, rape, poverty, and voicelessness to the splendor of nature, love, solidarity, justice, and hope. As a Latin American poet, her work is influenced by her compatriot—the great Pablo Neruda—but she has surpassed any debt to the master and established her own distinct voice. As a female poet, she is inspired by many internationally admired women, including Gabriela Mistral (the first woman to win a Nobel Prize for literature—also from Chile), Sor Juana de la Cruz (called the foremother of Latin American women's letters), Maria Luisa Bombal, Adrienne Rich, and other contemporary American women writers. In *Máscaras,* she describes Gabriela Mistral as a voice that was "calm and never grandiloquent" (p. 105). Agosín also states that she only writes "honestly about myself and about others" and that her active work "in poetry and human rights is the most essential aspect of my life's work and myself" (p. 101). Wide availability of Agosín's works translated into English or published in *face-en-face* editions (bilingual collections where the two different languages face each other) is facilitating regular inclusion of her writing in ethnic American literature courses, and her international literary and activist reputation has made her a mainstay in women's studies curricula.

POETRY COLLECTIONS

Brujas y Algo Más. Pittsburgh, PA: Latin American Literary Review Press, 1984.
Women of Smoke. Pittsburgh, PA: Latin American Literary Review Press, 1987.
Hogueras/Bonfires. Tempe, AZ: Bilingual Review Press, 1990.
Circles of Madness. Fredonia, NY: White Pine Press, 1992.
Sargasso. Fredonia, NY: White Pine Press, 1993.
Towards the Splendid City. Tempe, AZ: Bilingual Review Press, 1994.
Starry Night. Fredonia, NY: White Pine Press, 1996.
Las Chicas Desobedientes. Madrid: Ediciones Toerremozas, 1997.
The Council of the Fairies. Falls Church, VA: Azul Editions, 1997.
Dear Anne Frank. Reissued ed. Brandeis Series on European Jewry. Hanover, NH: University Press of New England, 1997.
An Absence of Shadows. Fredonia, NY: White Pine Press, 1998.
Melodious Women. Pittsburgh, PA: Latin American Literary Review Press, 1998.
Desert Rain/Lluvia en el desierto. New Mexico: Sherman Asher, 1999.
The Angel of Memory. San Antonio, TX: Wings Press, 2001.
In the Threshold of Memory: Selected Works. Fredonia, NY: White Pine Press, 2003.

SELECTED ANTHOLOGIES WHERE POETRY APPEARS

Fernandez, Roberta, ed. *Other Words*. Houston, TX: Arte Público Press, 1994.
Fernandez Olmos, Margarite, ed. *El Placer de la Palabra: Literature Erótico Femenina*. English version. New York: Penguin Books, 1994.
Flattley, Kerru, and Chris Wallace, eds. *From the Republic of Conscience: An International Anthology of Poetry*. Melbourne, Australia: Aird Books in association with Amnesty International, 1993.
Kelly, Bill, ed. *Violence to Non-Violence: An Anthology*. The Netherlands: Hardwood Academic, 1993.
Milligan, Bryce, et al., eds. *Daughters of the Fifth Sun: A Collection of Latina Fiction and Poetry*. New York: Riverhead Books, 1995.
———. *Floricanto Sí! A Collection of Latina Poetry*. New York: Penguin/Putnam, 1998.
Pffeifer, Erna, ed. *Torturada*. Vienna, Austria: Goldman Verlag, 1994.
Reyes, Sandra, ed. *One More Stripe to the Tiger: A Selection of Contemporary Chilean Poetry and Fiction*. Fayetteville: University of Arkansas Press, 1989.

SELECTED MEMOIR, FICTION, AND NONFICTION

Happiness. Fredonia, NY: White Pine Press, 1993.
A Cross and a Star: Memoirs of a Jewish Girl in Chile. Albuquerque: University of New Mexico Press, 1995.
Furniture Dreams. Reno: Black Rock Press of the University of Nevada Reno, 1995.
Women in Disguise. Falls Church, VA: Azul Editions, 1996.
Always from Somewhere Else: My Jewish Father. New York: Feminist Press, 1998.
The Alphabet of My Hands. New Brunswick, NJ: Rutgers University Press, 1999.
Amigas. With Emma Sepúlveda. Austin: University of Texas Press, 2000.

SELECTED EDITED COLLECTIONS

A Gabriela Mistral Reader. Fredonia, NY: White Pine Press, 1993.

Landscapes of a New Land: Short Stories by Latin American Women Writers. Fredonia, NY: White Pine Press, 1993.

These Are Not the Sweet Girls: 20th Century Latin American Women Poets. Fredonia, NY: White Pine Press, 1993.

A Dream of Light and Shadow: Portraits of Latin American Women Writers. Vol. 1. Albuquerque: University of New Mexico Press, 1996.

A Necklace of Words: Mexican Women Writers. With Nancy Hall. Fredonia, NY: White Pine Press, 1997.

The House of Memory: Jewish Stories from Jewish Women of Latin America. New York: Feminist Press, 1999.

A Map of Hope: Women Writers and Human Rights. New Brunswick, NJ: Rutgers University Press, 1999.

Uncertain Travelers: Jewish Women Emigrants to the Americas. Hanover, NH: University Press of New England, 1999.

Taking Root: Narratives of Jewish Women in Latin American. Athens: Ohio University Press, 2002.

To Mend the World: Essays on September 11th. With Betty Jean Craige. Fredonia, NY: White Pine Press, 2002.

Memory, Resistance, and Oblivion: Jewish Culture in Latin America. Austin: University of Texas Press, 2003.

SELECTED RESOURCES FOR FURTHER REFERENCE

"A Dream of Shadows: Writing, Speaking, Becoming." In *Máscaras.* Ed. Lucha Corpi. Berkeley, CA: Third Woman Press, 1997, 99–110.

Hirsh, Mariana. "Projected Memory: Holocaust Photographs in Personal and Public Fantasy." In *Acts of Memory: Cultural Recall in the Present.* Eds. Mieke Bal, Jonathan Crewe, and Leo Spitzer. Hanover, NH: University of New England Press, 1999, 3–23.

Muslea, Rahel. "A Profile of Marjorie Agosín." *Hadassah,* September 2002.

Scott, Nina. "Marjorie Agosín as Latina Writer." In *Breaking Boundaries: Latina Writings and Critical Readings.* Ed. Asuncion Horno-Delgado. Amherst: University of Massachusetts Press, 1989, 235–249.

Stavans, Ilan. "Marjorie Agosín: Judaism and Latin American Literature." *Bloomsbury Review,* Fall 1995.

Cecilia Rodríguez Milanés

Jack Agüeros

(1934–)

Puerto Rican

BIOGRAPHY

Born in East Harlem, Jack Agüeros has published three volumes of original poetry, has translated and edited a major bilingual edition of Puerto Rican writer Julia de Burgos's poetry, and has written prolifically in every conceivable genre. His parents, Joaquin Agüeros and the former Carmen Diaz, both emigrated from Puerto Rico. In his memoir essay "Halfway to Dick and Jane," Agüeros describes a childhood shaped by working-class parents—Carmen was a seamstress and Joaquin did a variety of jobs in the restaurant business—who provided a culturally rich home environment filled with books, music, stories, and food.

A graduate of Brooklyn College, where he majored in speech and minored in English, Agüeros showed an early interest in poetry, drama, and essays. He was only one course away from completing an M.F.A. in script writing at Hunter College and was the first Latino writer to have a television drama appear on a major network (*He Can't Even Read Spanish* was broadcast by NBC on May 8, 1971), but Agüeros felt the influence of political activism in the late 1960s and early 1970s and traveled to Los Angeles, where he earned a master's degree in urban planning from Occidental College. The turn to social engagement is evident in Agüeros's writing from this period, which features journalism, sociological studies, television scripts for training and voter education pieces, and in his 1976 appointment to the directorship of El Museo del Barrio in East Harlem. Agüeros held this position for ten years, during which time he developed the museum's collection and programming, and succeeded in having it included as part of New York's fabled "museum mile." Such responsibilities left little time for creative writing apart from some children's fiction.

Agüeros made a serious return to literary pursuits in the mid-1980s, and since then his poetry has regularly appeared in journals such as *Massachusetts Review, Revista Chicano-Riqueña, The Rican, Parnassus,* and *The Progressive,* and in anthologies such as *El Coro* and *Borinquen: An Anthology of Puerto Rican Literature.* Agüeros has published fiction in journals including *Callaloo, Sombra,* and *African Voices.* Readings of his plays, including *The News from Puerto Rico, No More Flat World, MY DOG!!!, Ye Tragicale Historie of Doctor*

Albizu-Campos, and *Kari and the Ice Cream Cone,* have been presented throughout New York. Now a downtown resident, Agüeros is a regular part of the New York poetry scene.

THEMES AND CONCERNS

Agüeros's principal concern in his poetry and other writings is to reveal the contours of the Puerto Rican experience in New York City. His poems celebrate Puerto Rican language, family relations, work experiences, food, and music. They also protest against the poverty, discrimination, crime, and addiction suffered by Puerto Ricans in New York. Agüeros explores the difference between migrants who seek to return home and ultimately remain in an island state of mind, and those Puerto Ricans born in New York who are intimate with both U.S. and island cultures but never truly at home in either. The pressure to embrace assimilation and the fight to resist it are experiences faced by islanders and New Yorkers alike in Agüeros's poetry. He further complicates Puerto Ricanness by evoking unique, individual experiences within the group history. Personas like the philosophical speaker of his psalms and the emotionally tortured speaker of the love sonnets, and characters such as cabbies, godmothers, junkies, painters, dancers, boxers, warehouse clerks, and gamblers shatter the limiting mirror of Latino stereotypes into a multitude of glittering pieces. Finally, at the edges of his Puerto Rican tapestry, Agüeros fosters stimulating interethnic dialogue, particularly with African American themes and experiences.

Correspondence Between the Stonehaulers (1991), Agüeros's first published book, offers perhaps the best introduction to the range of themes and styles that characterize his poetry. Two groupings of "Sonnets from the Puerto Rican" express elements of social document and protest. The first nine poems are called psalms and raise philosophical and theological concerns, but after that the author abandons the psalm label. Using a first-person persona, Agüeros announces an imaginary dialogue between two workers separated by time and space but united by the experience of erecting stone monuments in Egypt and the Andes region. Presented as an epistolary exchange of postcards between the stonehaulers, we see the workers begin to rise above their condition of drudge labor. Agüeros emphasizes the dignity and creativity of everyday people, as fellow poet and critic Martín Espada notes in his foreword to Agüeros's book, and underscores the historical basis of Latin American identity in African and Indian labor.

Agüeros's two most recent collections, *Sonnets from the Puerto Rican* (1996) and *Lord, Is This a Psalm?* (2002), confirm the sonnet and the psalm as his preferred verse forms. Clearly aware of the history of the sonnet from the Renaissance down to the present moment, Agüeros experiments with the form and writes in a free style that mixes traditional four-line stanzas with single lines and even the occasional single-word line. While the deep structure of his sonnets gestures toward the twelve-syllable line common in Spanish poetry, he forces recognition of the sonnet as a cross-cultural form with a history in romance languages.

Thematically, Agüeros applies traditional concerns of politics, religion, emotions, and epigrams dedicated to important public figures to his interest in contemporary Puerto Rican life. "Landscapes" and "Portraits" are sections that expand the social critique to include commentary on ecological issues, homelessness, war, colonialism, and racial politics. The section "Five Sonnets for the Happy Land Social Club Fire" memorializes the victims of a 1990 fire that Agüeros describes as a mass murder. The poems in "Sonnets for the Four Horsemen of the Apocalypse: Long Time Among Us," meanwhile, argue that apocalyptic experiences are not looming in the future but rather have already occurred for victims of the slave trade and colonialism. In the long cycle of poems titled "Love . . ." Agüeros uses the love sonnet as a platform for wrestling with cowardice, heart disease, creative malaise, and emotional paralysis before breaking through to erotic renewal.

Even when they engage in social protest, Agüeros's sonnets evince a lyricism and gravitas that contrast sharply with the skepticism, secularism, and irreverence of his book of psalms. Indeed, the title of his most recent volume, *Lord, Is This a Psalm?*, captures perfectly the tension running throughout a body of verse that directly addresses the deity while simultaneously questioning not only its own status as praise song but the accessibility and even existence of God. Agüeros delivers a series of Job-like laments for a world staggering under the hammer-blows of poverty, violence, racism, consumerism, the death penalty, homophobia, and draped over it all, a veil of church-sponsored hypocrisy. While the dominant tone is accusatory, Agüeros also has a strong countercurrent of celebratory psalms that sing the praises of women, Spanish language, and especially Puerto Rican delicacies such as pasteles, tostones, rice and beans, bacalao, and coquito. In their capacity to question authority while respecting the language of tradition, and to address universal concerns while speaking from a core Puerto Rican experience, Jack Agüeros's psalms exemplify his writing as a whole.

POETRY COLLECTIONS

Correspondence Between the Stonehaulers. Brooklyn, NY: Hanging Loose Press, 1991.
Song of the Simple Truth: The Complete Poems of Julia de Burgos. Willimantic, CT: Curbstone Press, 1996.
Sonnets from the Puerto Rican. Brooklyn, NY: Hanging Loose Press, 1996.
Lord, Is This a Psalm? Brooklyn, NY: Hanging Loose Press, 2002.

SELECTED ANTHOLOGIES WHERE POETRY APPEARS

Babín, Maria Teresa, and Stan Steiner, eds. *Borinquen: An Anthology of Puerto Rican Literature.* New York: Knopf, 1974.

De Jesús, Joy L., ed. *Growing Up Puerto Rican: An Anthology.* New York: Morrow, 1997.

Espada, Martín, ed. *El Coro: A Chorus of Latino Latina Poetry.* Amherst: University of Massachusetts Press, 1997.

Moramarco, Fred, and Al Zolynas, eds. *Men of Our Time: An Anthology of Male Poetry in Contemporary America.* Athens: University of Georgia Press, 1992.

SELECTED FICTION, NONFICTION, AND CHILDREN'S FICTION

"Halfway to Dick and Jane." In *The Immigrant Experience.* Ed. Thomas C. Wheeler. New York: Dial, 1971, 85–105.

"Pito y La Maraca." *Nuestro Magazine,* December 1977.

"Cheo y Los Reyes Magos." *Nuestro Magazine,* December 1978.

Otra Caja. Hispanic Policy Development Project for the New York City Board of Education, 1991.

"Beyond the Crust." In *Daily Fare: Essays from the Multicultural Experience.* Ed. Kathleen Aguero. Athens: University of Georgia Press, 1993, 216–227.

Dominoes and Other Stories. Willimantic, CT: Curbstone Press, 1993.

SELECTED RESOURCES FOR FURTHER REFERENCE

Espada, Martín. "Jack Agüeros." *Boston Review* 18.3 (June–August 1993). Online. http://bostonreview.mit.edu/br18.3/espada.html.

Inez, Collette. "Short Takes." *Parnassus: Poetry in Review* 20.1–2 (1995): 453–457.

"An Interview With Jack Agüeros." Online. www.curbstone.org/ainterview.cfm.

"Jack Agüeros." In *Puerto Rican Voices in English.* Ed. Carmen Dolores Hernández. Westport, CT: Praeger, 1997, 18–32.

Kevin Meehan

Ai (aka Florence Anthony, Florence Ogawa)

(1947–)

Japanese American, African American, American Indian (Choctaw and Cheyenne)

BIOGRAPHY

Born Florence Anthony in Albany, Texas, Ai grew up in several cities around the West

Photo by Christopher Felver/CORBIS.

and Southwest, including San Francisco, Las Vegas, and Tucson. The child of her mother's scandalous affair with a Japanese man, Ai did not know anything of her father's identity for years. Thus she chooses to be known exclusively through her self-given first name, declining to tie her identity to that of a man she never met. Because she is a woman of mixed ancestry, Ai's identity remains fluid. She is variously anthologized as a woman poet, as an Asian American poet, as an African American poet, as a poet of the Southwest, as an American poet, as a Jazz poet. Similarly, she identifies herself differently in each interview she gives. In some cases, Ai is "simply," if one can use that term, Japanese American, African American, and American Indian. But in some cases, she adds black Dutch or Irish into the mix. Sometimes she mentions growing up in Tucson. At other times, she mentions Las Vegas. Sometimes she adds a Mexican Catholic identity from her time spent in a Catholic school in Los Angeles.

This willingness to take on different identities at different moments funnels into Ai's poetry, in which she assumes the roles of many different people. Ai started writing poetry at age fourteen in response to a poster for a poetry contest focusing on a historical figure. She seems to have taken that theme and run with it over the entirety of her career to date. Ai found that writing poetry provided an escape from the realities of her childhood, when, she says, bad times eclipsed the good.

When Ai attended the University of Arizona, majoring in Japanese, she met Galway Kinnell, then a professor at New York University, when he came to give a reading. Kinnell became a mentor and urged Ai to attend the writing program at the University of California at Irvine, which she did. During her second year there, Kinnell took Ai's thesis to an editor at Houghton Mifflin, who decided to publish it; this became Ai's 1973 volume of poetry, *Cruelty*. Following upon its heels came a series of fellowships and visiting professorships, including both a Bunting and a Guggenheim fellowship in 1975, the Massachusetts Arts and Humanities fellowship in 1976, a National Endowment for the Arts fellowship in 1978 and a second in 1985, and a position as visiting poet at Wayne State University.

Her second volume of poetry, *Killing Floor*, appeared in 1979. Shortly thereafter, she received the Ingram Merrill Award (1983) and a St. Botolph Foundation grant (1986). She has published five additional volumes of poetry since. In 1987 she received the American Book Award for *Sin*, and in 1999 received the National Book Award for *Vice*, a collection of previously published and new poems. The award led to a visiting professorship at Oklahoma State University in Stillwater, which turned into a full professorship, giving Ai financial security for the first time. It also provided the freedom to begin research on her Oklahoma Choctaw and Cheyenne ancestors for the autobiographical poems that would be published in *Dread*, published in 2003. Ai held the Mitte Chair in Creative Writing at Oklahoma State for 2002–2003.

THEMES AND CONCERNS

Ai's poetry relies on the dramatic monologue to tackle themes of loss and desperation. She adopts the personae of either the underrepresented—an anonymous murderer, a woman who makes love to her dead husband's murderer, the child beater—or the icon—J. Edgar Hoover or Marilyn Monroe— and gives voice to the individuals who lie beneath our blanket assumptions or beyond our comprehension. She succeeds in personalizing the political this way, giving explanations for events in the world around us.

Though readers may initially feel distanced from this cast of criminals and public figures, Ai seems to hope that we may glimpse ourselves in them. She says of *Cruelty* that she wrote with the intent that people would be able to see the pain they inflict upon themselves and others. Her use of simple and accessible language that stands outside of the speech patterns and dialects of the individual enables the reader to form a connection to the speaker more easily. However, Ai has been criticized for this consistency of tone. As an actor, for that is the way Ai describes her role, is she failing if she does not personalize the voice or speech in individual poems? On the other hand, this equity gives the reader equal access to all personalities, refusing to reinforce our tendencies to romanticize the famous and look down upon the criminal. Furthermore, this simplicity of language has contributed to her success with a popular audience.

Ai's use of the narrative poem is unique in that, until her most recent poems, she does not use the poem as a vehicle to write about her own life. She once started readings with a disclaimer that she had never had an abortion or committed murder. Instead, she truly uses the poem to express the voice of its speaker, often reading biographies to gain deeper understanding and to get into character.

Some critics have faulted Ai's tendency to represent the male point of view. Ai, however, resists the idea that as a woman she has an obligation to write about women and believes that anyone is allowed to speak in her poems. This contention also addresses criticisms that she fails to represent African American experience and reinforces her claim that, as a woman of many identities, Ai has no obligation to any one identity.

Ai's 2003 volume, *Dread,* marks a shift in that Ai writes some of the poems from her own experience. However, she still gives voice to a cast of characters besides her own persona. This time her cast of characters is drawn from her family. She tries to understand her mother's shame about Ai's father and Ai herself, the bastard daughter, and the mistreatment of her female (Choctaw) ancestors at the hands of their (white) husbands in poems in which her grandfather and great-grandfather speak. She also, more unusually for her, speaks from her own childhood to understand the abuse she experienced.

POETRY COLLECTIONS

Cruelty: Poems. Boston, MA: Houghton Mifflin, 1973.
Killing Floor: Poems. Boston, MA: Houghton Mifflin, 1979.
Sin: Poems. Boston, MA: Houghton Mifflin, 1986.
Fate. Boston, MA: Houghton Mifflin, 1991.
Greed. New York: W. W. Norton, 1993.
Vice: New and Selected Poems. New York: W. W. Norton, 1999.
Dread: Poems. New York: W. W. Norton, 2003.

SELECTED ANTHOLOGIES WHERE POETRY APPEARS

Barnstone, William, and Aliki, eds. *A Book of Women Poets from Antiquity to Now.* New York: Schocken Books, 1992.
Chester, Laura, ed. *Deep Down: The New Sensual Writing by Women.* Boston, MA: Faber & Faber, 1989.
Christopher, Nicholas, ed. *Walk on the Wild Side; Urban American Poetry Since 1975.* Toronto: Collier Books, 1994.
Deming, Alison Hawthorne, ed. *Poetry of the American West.* New York: Columbia University Press, 1996.
Feinstein, Sascha, and Yusef Komunyakaa, eds. *The Second Set: The Jazz Poetry Anthology.* Vol. 2. Bloomington: Indiana University Press, 1996.
Howe, Florence. *No More Masks! An Anthology of Twentieth-Century American Women Poets.* New York: Harper Perennial, 1993.
Major, Clarence. *The Garden Thrives: Twentieth-Century African-American Poetry.* New York: Harper Perennial, 1996.
Olsen, Tillie. *Mother to Daughter, Daughter to Mother: Mothers on Mothering.* Old Westbury, NY: Feminist Press, 1985.

Parker, Alan Michael, and Mark Willhardt. *The Routledge Anthology of Cross-Gendered Verse*. New York: Routledge, 1996.

Piercy, Marge. *Early Ripening: American Women's Poetry Now*. New York: Pandora Press, 1990.

Shinder, Jason. *First Light: Mother and Son Poems*. San Diego, CA: Harcourt Brace Jovanovich, 1992.

Webster, Catherine, and Catherine L. Maraconi. *Handspan of Red Earth: An Anthology of American Farm Poems*. Iowa City: University of Iowa Press, 1991.

SELECTED ADDITIONAL WORK

Black Blood. New York: W. W. Norton, 1997. (novel)

SELECTED RESOURCES FOR FURTHER REFERENCE

"Ai." *Gale Literary Databases: Contemporary Authors*. Online. www.galegroup.com.

Hueving, Jeanne. "Divesting Social Register: Ai's Sensational Portraiture of the Renowned and Infamous." *Critical Survey* 9.2 (May 1997): 126–127.

Ingram, Claudia. "Writing the Crises: The Deployment of Abjection in Ai's Dramatic Monologues." *LIT: Literature Interpretation Theory* 8.2 (October 1987): 173–192.

Kearney, Lawrence, and Michael Cuddihy. "Interview with Ai." In *American Poetry Observed: Poets on Their Work*. Ed. Joe David Bellamy. Bloomington: University of Illinois Press, 1984, 1–8.

Mintz, Susannah B. "A 'Descent Toward the Unknown' in the Poetry of Ai." *SAGE: A Scholarly Journal on Black Women* 9.2 (Summer 1995): 36–47.

Mary Tasillo

Sherman Alexie

(1966–)

American Indian (Spokane/ Coeur d'Alene)

Photo by Rex Rystedt/SeattlePhoto.com, courtesy of the Sherman Alexie.

BIOGRAPHY

No one attending Sherman Alexie's birth on October 7, 1966, on the Spokane Indian Reservation in Wellpinit, Washington, could have predicted his eventual success. The son of Sherman Joseph Alexie Sr., a Coeur d'Alene Indian, and Lillian Agnes Cox Alexie, who is Spokane and white, Alexie was born hydrocephalic (a condition commonly termed as having "water on the brain"). He was not expected to survive the brain operation he underwent at the age of six months, and when he did, the doctors predicted that he would have severe mental retardation. It turned out to be just the opposite, though; Alexie was always very bright and an early, avid reader, devouring everything he could find in the reservation library.

A self-described "geek," Alexie was ostracized by his peers on the reservation. All of this changed, however, when he transferred to a white high school in Reardan, Washington—thirty-two miles away—to get a better education than the one afforded to students on the reservation. As Alexie says on his Homepage (www.fallsapart.com), at Reardan he was the "only Indian . . . except for the school mascot." He found acceptance there, becoming a star player on the basketball team—the Reardon Indians—the senior class president, and even prom king. He also excelled academically and earned a scholarship to Gonzaga University in Spokane. Two years later he transferred to Washington State University in Pullman. Although he left there in 1991 three credits short of his B.A. in American studies, the university awarded him the degree, along with an Alumni achievement award, in 1995.

Alexie's inspiration to become a writer came in 1989, when he enrolled in a poetry workshop at Washington State University taught by Alex Kuo, himself a talented poet. Alexie often speaks of that moment of recognition—after years of reading only European writers—when he was given the chance to read contemporary Indian poetry (the anthology the class used was Joseph Bruchac's *Song's from This Earth on Turtle's Back*). Kuo required his students to submit their poems to literary magazines, and Alexie chose Hanging Loose. His first book, a collection of forty poems and five short stories titled *The Business of Fancydancing,* grew out of this assignment and was published by Hanging Loose Press in 1992. *I Would Steal Horses,* a limited-edition chapbook of poems, was also published that year. These achievements were crucial to Alexie for another reason as well. He had developed a dependence on alcohol in college, but as soon as he learned that Hanging Loose Press was to publish his work, he quit drinking (at age twenty-three) to devote himself to building a career as a writer. He has been sober ever since.

These first publications began a creative career that is both prolific and varied. Although Alexie remains a poet, he is also a writer of short fiction, nonfiction essays, novels, songs, and screenplays and often mixes genres with ease. From the beginning, his work has been recognized with numerous honors and awards. For example, in 1991, Alexie received a Washington State Commission poetry fellowship, followed in 1992 by a National Endowment for the Arts poetry fellowship. Also in 1992, *The Business of Fancydancing* was named one of the *New York Times Book Review*'s Notable Books of the Year, while *I Would Steal Horses* won the Slipstream Press annual chapbook contest. In 1993, his first collection of short stories, *The Lone Ranger and Tonto Fistfight in Heaven,* won the PEN/Hemingway Award for Best First Book of Fiction, and in 1994 Alexie was awarded the Lila Wallace–Reader's Digest Writers' Award. His first novel, *Reservation Blues,* won the 1996 American Book Award, while in 1999 his film *Smoke Signals* garnered awards at the Sundance Film Festival. In 2001, Alexie retired as the undefeated champion of the Poetry Bouts.

The *New Yorker* has acknowledged Alexie as one of the top writers for the twenty-first century, and this certainly seems to be true. His creative outpouring shows no signs of abating, as he continues to publish poetry and fiction, contribute to periodicals and Web sites, and give countless interviews and readings across the country. Always growing and experimenting, Alexie has also recorded (with Jim Colville) an album based on the songs that begin each chapter of *Reservation Blues;* he has just released the movie *The Business of Fancydancing* (2002), which he wrote and directed; and he has begun doing stand-up comedy. Sherman Alexie lives with wife and two sons in Seattle, Washington.

THEMES AND CONCERNS

While the images and forms in Alexie's poetry continue to expand and evolve, the basic premise of his poetry, as with all of his creative work, is to chronicle the life of contemporary American Indians, especially those living on the reservation. Stories abound in Alexie's poetry, which is characterized by a strong narrative thread and features a broad range of characters who also appear in his fiction and films. They are stories of reservation life, and its attendant poverty, commodity food, depression, despair, and alcoholism, but also humor and perseverance. Since Alexie spent most of his life living on the Spokane reservation, with a hardworking mother and an alcoholic father, and has struggled with alcoholism himself, it is a life he knows well.

In all of Alexie's poetry, there is enormous anger at and confrontation of the devastating effects on the Indian people of more than 500 years of oppression and colonization. Prose poems such as "Postcard to Columbus" (*Old Shirts & New Skins*) and "My Heroes Have Never Been Cowboys" (*First Indian on the Moon*) evoke this sense of sadness and indignation, of historical awareness and personal loss. However, there is also a recurring sense of survival, as in "War All the Time" (*The Business of Fancydancing*) and "The Game Between the Jews and the Indians Is Tied" (*First Indian on the Moon*), plus a growing emphasis on hopefulness and a willingness to forgive—an aspect of his work that Alexie attributes to the fact that he is no longer drinking.

There are a number of other ideas and images that recur in Alexie's poetry. One of the most prominent is fire, which can bring about either destruction or resolution (see, for example, "Fire Storm" in *First Indian on the Moon* and "Fire as Verb and Noun" in *The Summer of Black Widows*). Another central image—captured so movingly in poems such as "Inside Dachau" (*The Summer of Black Widows*) and "Split Decisions" (a poem about Muhammed Ali, in *First Indian on the Moon*)—is that of waiting, which functions as a metaphor for broken promises, betrayal, and unrealized dreams.

Humor is almost always present in his work as well. While sometimes it is dark and highly ironic (as in the Crazy Horse poems), often it captures the joy of everyday life. This aspect of Alexie's poetry is especially welcome, since the humor of modern Native life is seldom caught in print. Many of Alexie's funniest poems, including "Things for an Indian to do in New York (City)" and "The Sasquatch Poems" (*The Summer of Black Widows*) also contain multiple references to pop culture. As Alexie has said on several occasions, he is an Indian and an American, so how could popular American culture not affect him?

Sherman Alexie's far-reaching talent, tireless public appearances, humor, intelligence, and honesty have brought him fame and critical acclaim. In return, he presents a compelling and always honest portrait of reservation America. It is this honesty that Alexie sees as part of his and other Indian writers' cultural responsibility because of their history of being misrepresented and misunderstood.

POETRY COLLECTIONS

The Business of Fancydancing: Stories and Poems. Brooklyn, NY: Hanging Loose Press, 1992.
First Indian on the Moon. Brooklyn, NY: Hanging Loose Press, 1993.
Old Shirts & New Skins. Los Angeles: American Indian Studies Center, UCLA, 1993.
The Summer of Black Widows. Brooklyn, NY: Hanging Loose Press, 1996.
One Stick Song. Brooklyn, NY: Hanging Loose Press, 2000.

TECHNICAL COLLEGE OF THE LOWCOUNTRY
LEARNING RESOURCES CENTER
POST OFFICE BOX 1288
BEAUFORT, SOUTH CAROLINA 29901-1288

LIMITED EDITION POETRY CHAPBOOKS

I Would Steal Horses. Niagara Falls, NY: Slipstream Press, 1992.
Seven Mourning Songs for the Cedar Flute I Have Yet to Learn to Play. Walla Walla, WA: Whitman College Book Arts Lab, 1994.
Water Flowing Home. Boise, ID: Limberlost Press, 1995.
The Man Who Loves Salmon. 1998.

SELECTED ANTHOLOGIES WHERE POETRY APPEARS

Collins, Billy, ed. *Poetry 180: A Turning Back to Poetry.* New York: Random House, 2003.
Ramazani, Jahan, ed. *The Norton Anthology of Modern and Contemporary Poetry.* New York: W. W. Norton, 2003.
Smelcer, John E., D. L. Birchfield, and Duane Niatum, eds. *Durable Breath: Contemporary Native American Poetry.* Chugiak, AK: Salmon Run, 1994.
Suarez, Virgil, and Ryan G. Van Cleave, eds. *American Diaspora: Poetry of Displacement.* Ames: University of Iowa Press, 2001.

SELECTED FICTION AND SCREENPLAYS

The Lone Ranger and Tonto Fistfight in Heaven. New York: Perennial, 1994.
Reservation Blues. New York: Warner Books, 1994.
Indian Killer. New York: Atlantic Monthly Press, 1996.
Smoke Signals. With Chris Ayres. 1999. (screenplay)
The Toughest Indian in the World. New York: Atlantic Monthly Press, 2000.
The Business of Fancydancing. 2002. (screenplay, written and directed)
Ten Little Indians. New York: Grove/Atlantic, 2003.

SELECTED RESOURCES FOR FURTHER REFERENCE

Brill de Ramirez, Susan Berry. "Fancy Dancer: A Profile of Sherman Alexie." *Poets and Writers* 27.1 (January–February 1999): 54–59.
Fast, Robin Riley. *The Heart as a Drum: Continuance and Resistance in American Indian Poetry.* Ann Arbor: University of Michigan Press, 1999.
Gillan, Jennifer. "Reservation Home Movies: Sherman Alexie's Poetry." *American Literature* 68 (March 1996): 91–110.
Kincaid, James R. "Who Gets to Tell Their Stories?" *New York Times Book Review,* May 3, 1992, pp. 1, 24–29.
Official Sherman Alexie Homepage. Online. www.fallsapart.com.
60 Minutes II. CBS. March 20, 2001. Interview with Vickie Mawbrey.

Linda Cullum

Paula Gunn Allen

(1939–)

American Indian (Laguna/Sioux)

BIOGRAPHY

Paula Gunn Allen is an artist inspired by the "Cubist" style of Gertrude Stein, she is a poet who says her lyrical rhythms mimic those of Mozart and Tchaikovsky, and she is a multicultural woman who, for most of her life, "fit nowhere." Born on October 24, 1939, in Albuquerque, New Mexico, Paula Gunn Allen was the product of a multiracial heritage; her mother was a mix of Laguna Pueblo and Scottish, while her father was a full-blooded Lebanese who was raised in the Catholic faith. She faced external conflict as a youth, attending Catholic boarding school, an institution that as a whole elevated European exploration above the cultural devastation of the natives of America. Gunn Allen describes the experience as unconscionable European indoctrination. In "Where I Come from Is Like This," she recalls her Roman Catholic upbringing, a curriculum that emphasized the destructive influence of the missionaries on her native ancestors. She admits that as an adolescent, she believed the European propaganda of her schooling.

As an independent adult, realizing the monomania of her schooling, she rebelled against the established rhetoric of literature and history, earning her M.F.A. in 1968 at the University of Oregon and later her Ph.D. at the University of New Mexico in 1976, and blazing a trail for American Indian literary analysis and criticism. However, for many years of her life, she attempted to fit in by "being just one thing," an extension of the monomania of her youth that made her suicidal (Foss, Foss, and Griffin, p. 191). After years of self-denial and a succession of failed marriages, she embraced her inherent diversity and wove her multicolored threads into that of a poet, novelist, and respected literary critic active in feminist, lesbian/bisexual, and antiwar organizations.

Gunn Allen's teaching credits include a position at the University of California, Berkeley, where she held a postdoctoral fellowship to study oral tradition in Native American literature. She later became a professor of English at the University of California, Los Angeles, a post from which she retired in 1999. She has received numerous awards and grants throughout her career, including a writing fellowship from the National Endowment for the Arts in

1978. Her novel *Spider Woman's Granddaughters: Traditional Tales and Contemporary Writing* won the American Book Award from the Before Columbus Foundation in 1990, as well as the Susan Koppelman Award from the Popular and American Culture Associations and the Native American Prize for Literature. She received the Lifetime Achievement Award from the Native Writers' Circle of the Americas in 2001.

THEMES AND CONCERNS

The reader experiences a wide range of themes in the works of Paula Gunn Allen. Her work explores the deracination of the Laguna Pueblo people as well as the celebratory cultural traditions of her ancestors. As do her contemporaries Linda Hogan and Leslie Marmon Silko, Gunn Allen decries the alienation and homelessness of her people. In poems such as "Answering the Deer," Gunn Allen refers to herself and her ancestors as shapeless, formless, and invisible, not silent, but not heard either. However, her defense against her history is her celebration of womanhood. Born of a culture that embraces the woman as a figure of reverence, Gunn Allen incorporates the image of the Laguna Pueblo woman in her works, a figure more advanced than women in American society, where females have only gained veneration within the last century.

Similarly, in "Who Is Your Mother? Red Roots of White Feminism" Gunn Allen further explores the disparity between Laguna Pueblo and American culture. She cites immigrants and their haste to accept assimilation into American standards of living. Seeing these immigrants as ashamed of their own heritage, Gunn Allen attributes the American habit of overlooking the consequences of history on American society to this encouraged rejection of culture (p. 14). By embracing American culture and rejecting their own, the assimilated shed the oppression of their past and forget, often participating in the same oppression in cyclical fashion. Paula Gunn Allen recognizes this trait and perpetuates her native culture in her works.

POETRY COLLECTIONS

Blind Lion. Berkeley, CA: Thorp Springs Press, 1974.

Coyote's Daylight Trip. Albuquerque, NM: La Confluencia, 1978.

A Cannon Between My Knees. New York: Strawberry Hill Press, 1981.

Star Child. Marvin, SD: Blue Cloud Quarterly Press, 1981.

Shadow Country. Los Angeles: University of California American Indian Studies Center, 1982.

Wyrds. San Francisco, CA: Taurean Horn Press, 1987.

Skin and Bones: Poems, 1979–1987. Albuquerque: University of New Mexico Press, 1988.

Life Is a Fatal Disease: Collected Poems 1962–1995. Albuquerque: University of New Mexico Press, 1996.

SELECTED ANTHOLOGIES WHERE POETRY APPEARS

Audio Literature Presents A Circle of Nations: Voices and Visions of American Indians (The Earthsong Collection). Read by Joy Harjo and Simon Ortiz. Hillsboro, OR: Beyond Words Publications, 1993.

Green, Rayna, ed. *That's What She Said: Contemporary Poetry and Fiction by Native American Women.* Bloomington: Indiana University Press, 1984.

Newman, Leslea, ed. *My Lover Is a Woman: Contemporary Lesbian Love Poems.* New York: Ballantine Books, 1999.

Niatum, Duane, ed. *Harper's Anthology of 20th Century Native American Poetry.* San Francisco, CA: Harper and Row, 1988.

SELECTED ADDITIONAL WORKS

From the Center: A Folio—Native American Art and Poetry. Editor. New York: Strawberry Hill Press, 1981.

Studies in American Indian Literature: Critical Essays and Course Designs. Editor. New York: Modern Language Association of America, 1983.

The Woman Who Owned the Shadows. San Francisco, CA: Aunt Lute Books, 1984.

"Answering the Deer: Genocide and Continuance in American Indian Women's Poetry." In *Coming to Light: American Women Poets in the Twentieth Century.* Eds. Diane Wood Middlebrook and Marilyn Yalom. Ann Arbor: University of Michigan Press, 1985, 223–232.

"Who Is Your Mother? Red Roots of White Feminism." In *The Graywolf Annual Five: Multicultural Literacy.* Ed. Rick Simonson and Scott Walker. St. Paul, MN: Graywolf Press, 1988, 13–27.

Spider Woman's Granddaughters: Traditional Tales and Contemporary Writing by Native American Women. Editor. New York: Fawcett Books, 1990.

Grandmothers of the Light: A Medicine Woman's Sourcebook. Boston, MA: Beacon Press, 1992.

The Sacred Hoop: Recovering the Feminine in American Indian Traditions. Boston, MA: Beacon Press, 1992.

Gossips, Gorgons, and Crones: The Fates of the Earth. With Jane Caputi. Santa Fe, NM: Bear, 1993.

"'Border' Studies: The Intersection of Gender and Color." In *The Ethnic Canon: Histories, Institutions, and Interventions.* Ed. David Palumbo-Liu. Minneapolis: University of Minnesota Press, 1995, 31–47.

Voice of the Turtle: American Indian Literature 1900–1970. Editor. New York: Ballantine Books, 1995.

Women in American Indian Mythology. Santa Barbara, CA: ABC-CLIO, 1995.

"Where I Come from Is Like This." In *Daughters of the Revolution: Classic Essays by Women.* Ed. James D. Lester. Lincolnwood, IL: NTC, 1996, 130–138.

Off the Reservation: Reflections on Boundary-Busting, Border-Crossing Loose Canons. Boston, MA: Beacon Press, 1999.

Song of the Turtle: American Indian Fiction 1974–1994. Editor. New York: Ballantine Books, 1999.

Hozho—Walking in Beauty: Native American Stories of Inspiration, Humor, and Life. Editor, with Carolyn Dunn. Chicago, IL: Contemporary Books, 2001.

The Paula Gunn Allen American Indian Poets Series. Editor. San Pedro: That Painted Horse Press, 2002.

SELECTED RESOURCES FOR FURTHER REFERENCE

Bruchac, Joseph. *Survival This Way: Interviews with American Indian Poets.* Tucson: University of Arizona Press, 1987, 1–22.

Foss, Karen, Sonja K. Foss, and Cindy L. Griffin. *Feminist Rhetorical Theories.* Thousand Oaks, CA: Sage, 1999.

Keating, AnaLouise. *Women Reading Women Writing: Self-Invention in Paula Gunn Allen, Gloria Anzaldúa, and Audre Lorde.* Philadelphia: Temple University Press, 1996.

Nelson, Emmanuel S. *Critical Essays: Gay and Lesbian Writers of Color.* Binghamton, NY: Harrington Park Press, 1994.

"Paula Gunn Allen." In *Backtalk: Women Writers Speak Out.* Ed. Donna Marie Perry. New Brunswick, NJ: Rutgers University Press, 1993, 1–18.

Purdy, John. "And Then, Twenty Years Later . . . : A Conversation with Paula Gunn Allen." *Studies in American Indian Literatures* 9.1 (Fall 1997): 5–16.

St. Clair, Janet. "Uneasy Ethnocentrism: Recent Works of Allen, Silko, and Hogan." *Studies in American Indian Literatures* 6.1 (Spring 1994): 83–98.

Van Dyke, Annette. "The Journey Back to Female Roots: A Laguna Pueblo Model." In *Lesbian Texts and Contexts: Radical Revisions.* Ed. Karla Jay and Joanne Glasgow. New York: New York University Press, 1990, 339–354.

Weaver, Jace. *Other Words: American Indian Literature, Law, and Culture.* Norman: University of Oklahoma Press, 2001.

———. *That the People Might Live: Native American Literatures and Native American Community.* New York: Oxford University Press, 1997.

Alice D'Amore

Julia Alvarez

(1950–)

Dominican American

BIOGRAPHY

Julia Alvarez claims to have been born "by accident" in New York City, since her homeland and the place where she was reared until ten years of age is the Dominican Republic. Moving to the United States in 1960 with her four sisters and parents when her father's involvement in the movement against the dictator Trujillo endangered all of their lives, Alvarez was educated in American public and private boarding schools. Alvarez writes on her Middlebury College Homepage that the "radical uprooting from my culture, my native language, my country" is the reason she began writing and that "English, not the United States, was where I landed and sunk deep roots." She attended Connecticut College and earned a B.A. with honors (summa cum laude) from Middlebury College in 1971. She received an M.F.A. from Syracuse University in 1975 and attended the Bread Loaf School of English from 1979 to 1980. Early in her career, Alvarez served as a Poet-in-the-Schools in Kentucky, Delaware, and North Carolina; she also traveled extensively and taught at several schools including the University of Illinois at Urbana, George Washington University, and Middlebury College, where she has been a faculty member since 1988. In 2000, Alvarez decided to forgo tenure for the freedom and flexibility of teaching a reduced load and having more time to write. She is involved in activist endeavors in the United States and also in her native Dominican Republic, including an organic coffee farm in the mountains that she helps promote with her husband, biologist Bill Eichner.

Alvarez began her distinguished writing career with the publication of her poetry—*The Housekeeping Book* in 1984 followed by *Homecoming: New and Collected Poems* in 1986 and then two other volumes of poetry, *The Other Side/ El Otro Lado* in 1995 and *Seven Trees* in 1998. Alvarez has also published four well-received novels and a collection of essays and has begun writing children's books. Among her innumerable awards, honors, and tributes to her work, Alvarez has received the Benjamin T. Marshall Poetry Prize, the American Academy of Poetry Prize, the La Reina Creative Writing Award for Poetry, a National Endowment for the Arts grant, and the Jessica Nobel-Maxwell Poetry Prize. She has also been named a John Atherton Scholar in Poetry and a

Robert Frost Fellow in Poetry. Her poetry has been widely anthologized, appearing in over sixty publications including prestigious literary journals such as *Callaloo, Ploughshares, The American Poetry Review,* and *The Kenyon Review.*

THEMES AND CONCERNS

Primarily known as a novelist, Julia Alvarez once admitted to an audience at the 1997 Bread Loaf Writers' Retreat that she was a "wannabe poet." Much of Alvarez's work deals with immigrant, and specifically Latina, life in the United States—issues of acculturation/assimilation, language difficulties, and citizenship are evident. Her poetry often highlights the tension that an unsteady voice will provoke, regardless of the speaker's command of the language or status in society. In an interview with Juanita Heredia, Alvarez speaks of the Czeslaw Milosz quotation about language being the only homeland serving as an epigraph to her first book: "The page is where I've learned to put together my different worlds . . . the world of the imagination is the one I feel most at home in" (p. 32).

In the early "Housekeeping" poems of *Homecoming,* Alvarez mines the territory of domesticity from the perspective of the dutiful daughter, helping her mother clean, launder, cook—the day-to-day undervalued work of the world—making a home for her sisters, her father, and herself. In the later poems of the "Heroines" section, the speaker is a grown woman coming to power, wrestling with the expectations of women within her native culture in contrast to those of the more liberal and liberated North American women. The forty-one sonnets in the second part of the collection range in topic, including love (from lust to loss), aging, friendship, and restricted cultural expectations for a Latin American woman such as herself.

Alvarez's *The Other Side/El Otro Lado* reveals a poetic voice that is confident and confidential while still questioning; she begins the collection with her "Bilingual Sestina," a much-anthologized poem revealing both the pleasure and the tension discernible in Alvarez's use of language. This poem prepares the reader for the at times nostalgic, at once conflicted, and most often insightful narrator of the poems to follow. She describes being there, in the Dominican Republic, then about being *from* there and being *here* without the cultural touchstones to guide her, making her journey to artistic freedom precarious. Themes of privilege and North American standards of living surface in contrast to Dominican village life. Throughout her poems Alvarez highlights the power and delicacy of language. For her, language offers a safety net when rough terrain endangers not just artistic expression but even the articulation of "reality," as shown in her closing poem, "Estel." Words comfort, draw one near, and soothe, while the world distances and silences.

POETRY COLLECTIONS

The Housekeeping Book. Burlington, VT: C.E.S. MacDonald, 1984.
The Other Side/El Otro Lado. New York: Dutton, 1995.
Homecoming: New and Collected Poems. New York: Plume 1996.
Seven Trees. North Andover, MA: Kat Ran Press, 1998. (poetry and art)

SELECTED ANTHOLOGIES WHERE POETRY APPEARS

Cavalieri, Grace, ed. *WPFW 89.3 Poetry Anthology.* Washington, DC: Crocodile Press, 1992.
Coco De Filippes, Daisy, and E. J. Robinett, eds. *Poems of Exile and Other Concerns: Poetry by Dominicans in the United States.* New York: Ediciones Alcance, 1988.
Cruz, Victor Hernández, Leroy Quintana, and Virgil Suarez, eds. *Paper Dance: 55 Latino Poets.* New York: Persea Books, 1995.
Espada, Martín, ed. *El Coro: A Chorus of Latino and Latina Poetry.* Amherst: University of Massachusetts Press, 1997.
Finch, Annie, ed. *A Formal Feeling Comes: Poems in Form by Contemporary Women.* Brownsville: Story Line Press, 1994.
Gemin, Pamela, and Paula Sergi, eds. *Boomer Girls: Poems by Women from the Baby Boom Generation.* Iowa City: University of Iowa Press, 1999.
Jarman, Mark, and David Mason, eds. *Rebel Angels: 25 Poets of the New Formalism.* Ashland, OR: Story Line Press, 1996.
Jordan, June, ed. *Soulscript: An Anthology.* New York: Doubleday, 1970.
Milligan, Bryce, et al., eds. *Daughters of the Fifth Sun: A Collection of Latina Fiction and Poetry.* New York: Riverhead Books, 1995.
———. *¡Floricanto Sí! A Collection of Latina Poetry.* New York: Penguin/Putnam, 1998.
Pack, Robert, and Jay Parini, eds. *American Identities: Contemporary Multicultural Voices.* Hanover, NH: University Press of New England, 1994.
———. *Poems for a Small Planet: Contemporary American Nature Poetry.* Hanover, NH: Middlebury College Press, 1993.
Strand, Mark, ed. *The Best American Poetry 1991.* New York: Charles Scribner's Sons, 1991.

SELECTED FICTION, NONFICTION, AND FILM ADAPTATION

Old Age Ain't for Sissies. Editor. Sanford: Crane Creek Press, 1979.
My English. Chapel Hill, NC: Algonquin Books, 1990.
How the García Girls Lost Their Accents. Chapel Hill, NC: Algonquin Books, 1991.
In the Time of the Butterflies. Chapel Hill, NC: Algonquin Books, 1994.
¡Yo! Chapel Hill, NC: Algonquin Books, 1996.
"An Unlikely Beginning for a Writer." In *Máscaras.* Ed. Lucha Corpi. Berkeley, CA: Third Woman Press, 1997, 189–199.
Something to Declare. Chapel Hill, NC: Algonquin Books, 1998.
In the Name of Salomé. Chapel Hill, NC: Algonquin Books, 2000.
The Secret Footprints. New York: Knopf, 2000.

A Cafecito Story. With Bill Eichner. White River Junction, VT: Chelsea Green, 2001.
How Tía Lola Came to Stay. New York: Knopf, 2001.
In the Time of Butterflies. Dir. Mariano Barroso. MGM, 2001. (film)
Before We Were Free. New York: Knopf, 2002.

SELECTED RESOURCES FOR FURTHER REFERENCE

Heredia, Juanita. "Citizen of the World: An Interview with Julia Alvarez." In *Latina Self-Portraits: Interviews with Contemporary Women Writers.* Ed. Bridget Kevane and Juanita Heredia. Albuquerque: University of New Mexico Press, 2000, 19–32.

"Julia Alvarez." In *The Hand of the Poet: Poems and Papers in Manuscript.* Ed. Rodney Phillips et al., with essays by Dana Gioia. New York: Rizzoli, 1997.

Julia Alvarez Homepage. Online. www.middlebury.edu/~english/alvarez.

Muratori, Fred. "Traditional Form and the Living, Breathing American Poet." *New England Review and Bread Loaf Quarterly* 9.2 (Winter 1986): 231–232.

Umpierre, Luzma. "From Protest to Creation: Latina Women Writers in the U.S.A." *Cultural Times* (Spring 2000): 54–58.

Varnes, Kathrine. "'Practicing for the Real Me': Form and Authenticity in the Poetry of Julia Alvarez." *Antípodas: Journal of Hispanic and Galician Studies* 10 (1998): 67–77.

Vela, Richard. "Daughter of Invention: The Poetry of Julia Alvarez." *Postscript: Publication of the Philological Association of the Carolinas* 16 (1999): 33–42.

Cecilia Rodríguez Milanés

Maya Angelou

(1928–)

African American

BIOGRAPHY

Author, actress, producer, and educator Maya Angelou was born Marguerite Johnson in St. Louis, Missouri, on April 4, 1928. Her parents, Bailey and Vivian Baxter Johnson, divorced when she was about three years old, and she was sent to live with her grandmother in rural Stamps, Arkansas. At one point, she and her brother, Bailey, went to live with their mother in Chicago, but when, at age eight, Angelou was the victim of a sexual assault, they were sent back to Arkansas. For four years after the assault, Angelou spoke only to her brother. Eventually, they moved to San Francisco to live again with their mother, and Angelou attended high school briefly before dropping out to work as the first black cable car conductor in San Francisco. In 1945 she graduated from high school and at sixteen years of age became a single mother to her son, Guy Johnson. To support herself and her son, she worked a number of jobs around San Francisco, including prostitute, nightclub dancer, and tour member with the Everyman's Opera Company production of *Porgy and Bess.* While dancing at San Francisco nightclub the Purple Onion, she adopted the name Maya Angelou.

In 1959, Angelou moved to Brooklyn, New York, to join the Harlem Writer's Guild. She directed and performed in *Cabaret for Freedom,* a play she cowrote with actor Godfrey Cambridge. She also became active in the Civil Rights Movement, becoming the northeastern regional coordinator for the Southern Christian Leadership Conference (SCLC) and meeting both Martin Luther King Jr. and Malcolm X. In 1960 she married South African freedom fighter Vusumi Make and moved to Africa, living first in Cairo, Egypt, and working as an associate editor for the *Arab Observer.* In 1963 she moved to Ghana, working at different times at the University of Ghana, the *African Review,* the *Ghanaian Times,* and the Ghanaian Broadcasting Company. While in Ghana, she researched her African ancestral roots. She has continued to travel throughout her life and is fluent in French, Spanish, Italian, Arabic, and West African Fanti.

After returning to the United States in the late 1960s, she produced a television series titled *Black, Blues, Black,* which explored African traditions in

American life, and began work on her first autobiographical novel, *I Know Why the Caged Bird Sings* (1970), which was nominated for a National Book Award. Angelou has continued to be involved in theater, film, and television. She wrote and produced a Pulitzer Prize–nominated screenplay, *Georgia, Georgia,* in 1972, and received a Tony Award for her performance in *Look Away* in 1973. She also wrote one of the first television dramas to feature an African American cast, *Sister, Sister.* In 1977 she was nominated for an Emmy Award for her performance in *Roots,* and she won the Golden Eagle Award for her documentary *Afro-Americans in the Arts.*

She published her first volume of poetry, *Just Give Me a Cool Drink of Water 'Fore I Diie,* in 1971, and followed this by thirteen more collections of poetry, including her two best-known volumes, *And Still I Rise* (1978) and *Phenomenal Woman* (1995). When President Clinton asked her to write and deliver a poem for the 1993 presidential inauguration, she became only the second African American poet to have this honor. Due to her bestselling books of poetry and prose and her ever-growing celebrity status, Angelou is "probably the most widely recognized embodiment of the figure of the poet in contemporary U.S. culture" (Burr, p. 1).

In 1981, Angelou was appointed to a lifetime position as the Reynolds Professor of American Studies at Wake Forest University in Winston-Salem, North Carolina. She has received numerous honors and awards, including over fifty honorary degrees, the *Ladies' Home Journal* Woman of the Year Award (1976), the *Essence* Woman of the Year Award (1982), the American Academy of Achievement's Golden Plate Award (1990), the Distinguished Woman of North Carolina Award (1992), the Alston/Jones International Civil & Human Rights Award (1998), and the Presidential Medal of Arts (2000). In 1995 she won a Grammy Award for Best Spoken-Word Album for her production of *Phenomenal Woman,* and in 2003 she won her third Grammy for her production of *A Song Flung Up to Heaven.* She remains a highly sought-after public speaker.

THEMES AND CONCERNS

Maya Angelou is perhaps best known for writing poetry and prose that stems directly from her experience. Her first book, *I Know Why the Caged Bird Sings* (the first volume of her autobiography), was published in 1970 and established Angelou as a writer who translates her tumultuous life experiences into lyrical, earthy, and dramatic reflections upon what it means to be a black woman in the twentieth century. Her poetry builds on her autobiographical experiences by drawing connections between her life and the larger cultural context in which she and her readers exist. Angelou tries to live what she calls a "poetic existence," in which she "take[s] responsibility for the air I breathe and the space I take up" (Tate, p. 4), and her poetry reflects this effort to underscore the poetic within everyday lived experience.

Angelou's poetry often recalls the style of black spirituals and the cadence of black preachers, using repetition, alliteration, and rhythm to create poems that are much like songs or speeches. They are performative texts, and many of those who praise Angelou write that her poetry sings and speaks. No doubt her long career as a singer, dancer, and actor contributes to the theatricality of her poetry and other writing. In fact, her poetry has been set to music in several theatrical productions, including *And Still I Rise* (1977) and Mamarra McKinney's *Roots of Rap: Poetry* (1992). Her poetry has also been featured in films such as 1993's *Poetic Justice*.

When Angelou read her poem "On the Pulse of the Morning" at Bill Clinton's inaugural celebration, she read it slowly, forcefully, and in a sonorous voice that matched the gravity of the event. The poem asks Americans to learn from their own history, especially in healing the scars of racism and violence and ultimately is hopeful about America's future. It emphasizes that as with the dawn of every new day, America is at the dawn of a new moment in history in which a peaceful future can be written. As in many of her other works, including her most famous poem, "Still I Rise," the overriding theme is hope.

POETRY COLLECTIONS

Just Give Me a Cool Drink of Water 'Fore I Diie. New York: Random House, 1971.
Oh Pray My Wings Are Gonna Fit Me Well. New York: Random House, 1975.
And Still I Rise. New York: Random House, 1978.
Shaker, Why Don't You Sing? New York: Random House, 1983.
Now Sheba Sings the Song. New York: E. P. Dutton, 1987.
I Shall Not Be Moved. New York: Bantam Books, 1990.
On the Pulse of the Morning. New York: Random House, 1993.
The Complete Collected Poems of Maya Angelou. New York: Random House, 1994.
Phenomenal Woman: Four Poems for Women. New York: Random House, 1995.
Black Pearls: The Poetry of Maya Angelou. New York: Wea/Atlantic/Rhino, 1998. (audio CD)
Life Doesn't Frighten Me. New York: Stuart Tabori & Chang, 1998.
Maya Angelou Poetry Collection. New York: Random House, 1999. (audiobook)

SELECTED ANTHOLOGIES WHERE POETRY APPEARS

Bell-Scott, Patricia. *Double Stitch: Black Women Write About Mothers & Daughters.* Boston, MA: Beacon Press, 1991.
Gates, Henry Louis, Jr., and Nellie Y. McKay, eds. *The Norton Anthology of African American Literature.* New York: W. W. Norton, 1996.
Hill, Patricia Liggins, et al., eds. *Call and Response: The Riverside Anthology of the African American Tradition.* New York: Houghton Mifflin, 1998.
Linthwaite, Illona, ed. *Ain't I a Woman! A Book of Women's Poetry from Around the World.* New York: Wings Books, 1993.

SELECTED ADDITIONAL WORKS

The Poetry of Maya Angelou. New York: GWP Records, 1969. (spoken-word album)
I Know Why the Caged Bird Sings. New York: Bantam Books, 1970.
Gather Together in My Name. New York: Random House, 1974. (autobiography)
And Still I Rise. 1976. (play)
Singin' and Swinging' and Getting' Merry Like Christmas. New York: Random House, 1976. (autobiography)
The Heart of a Woman. New York: Random House, 1981. (autobiography)
All God's Children Need Traveling Shoes. New York: Random House, 1986. (autobiography)
On the Pulse of the Morning. New York: Random House Audio, 1993. (spoken-word album)
Wouldn't Take Nothing for My Journey Now. New York: Random House, 1993. (autobiography)
My Painted House, My Friendly Chicken, and Me. New York: Crown, 1994. (children's book)
Phenomenal Woman. New York: Random House Audio, 1995. (spoken-word album)
Even the Stars Look Lonesome. New York: Random House, 1997. (essays)
A Song Flung Up to Heaven. New York: Random House, 2002. (autobiography and spoken-word album)
Kofi and His Magic. New York: Knopf, 2003. (children's book)

SELECTED RESOURCES FOR FURTHER REFERENCE

Braham, Jeanne. *Crucial Conversations: Interpreting Contemporary American Literary Autobiographies by Women.* New York: Teachers College Press, Columbia University, 1995.
Burr, Zofia. *The Reception of Maya Angelou's Poetry.* Online. http://english.rutgers.eduangelou.htm.
Courtney-Clark, Margaret. *Maya Angelou: The Poetry of Living.* New York: Clarkson Potter, 1999.
Hagen, Lyman. *Heart of a Woman, Mind of a Writer, and Soul of a Poet: A Critical Analysis of the Writings of Maya Angelou.* Lanham, MD: University Press of America, 1997.
Maya Angelou. Los Angeles, CA: Pacific Arts, 1993. (film)
McPherson, Dolly Aimee. *Order Out of Chaos: The Autobiographical Works of Maya Angelou.* New York: Virago Press, 1991.
Tate, Claudia. *Black Women Writers at Work.* New York: Continuum, 1983.

Rachael Groner

Gloria Anzaldúa

(1942–)

Chicana/Mexican American

BIOGRAPHY

Gloria Anzaldúa is a seventh-generation American of Mexican roots. She was born on September 26, 1942, and grew up on a ranch settlement in the Valley of South Texas, near the Mexican border. As migrant workers, Anzaldúa's family constantly moved from ranch to ranch in search of work, until her father decided to migrate on his own so that the children could attend school regularly in Hargill, Texas. After graduating from the eighth grade, Anzaldúa was bussed to a school in Edinburgh, Texas, but she continued working in the fields of her home in the valley even through college, until she earned her B.A. from Pan American University in 1969. Out of these early life experiences, Anzaldúa gained a deep appreciation and respect for migrant workers and Chicana/Chicano (Mexican American) culture. Many aspects of her work are an effort to build a place for Chicana/Chicano culture in the American consciousness.

After receiving her M.A. in English from the University of Texas at Austin in 1973, Anzaldúa began teaching high school in communities with large numbers of migrant children. She became a liaison between the migrant camps and the school system, which led to a position as the bilingual and migrant education director for the state of Indiana. During this early part of her teaching career, Anzaldúa also worked with emotionally and mentally challenged children, as well as gifted children, and taught high school literature classes, working with students of every ethnicity and background. Anzaldúa went on to earn her Ph.D. in history of consciousness at University of California at Santa Cruz. She has taught creative writing, Chicano studies, and feminist studies at the University of Texas, San Francisco State University, Vermont College of Norwich University, and at University of California at Santa Cruz, among others. Her books have won awards throughout the art world, including those presented by the Before Columbus Foundation, the National Endowment for the Arts, *Library Journal, Hungry Minds Review,* and *Utne Reader.*

THEMES AND CONCERNS

Anzaldúa claims many identities, which she feels compose the strongest, most dynamic idea of who she is. Poet, critic, activist, teacher, Chicana, lesbian, women-of-color feminist, and new mestiza are just some of the titles she has claimed throughout her writing career. The books she has written and edited often deal with the intersection of these different identities and her encounters with exclusion, oppression, and abuse in the United States as consequences of difference itself.

Although Anzaldúa has received a great deal of recognition for anthologies of Chicana and feminist writing that she has initiated and edited or co-edited, such as the groundbreaking *This Bridge Called My Back: Writings by Radical Women of Color* (1981) and its more comprehensive follow-up, *Making Faces, Making Soul: Haciendo Caras* (1990), the prose and poetry in her original landmark work, *Borderlands/La Frontera: The New Mestiza* (1987), contains some of her most revealing, impassioned, and concise reflections on American culture. *Borderlands* also contains the largest collection of her poetry printed to date. Bilingual, freeformed, and image-driven, her poems use intimate moments as well as historical events to open sites of resistance and understanding for America's "others."

Mestizaje is the Spanish term for the mixing of Native American and Spanish blood. In *Borderlands,* Anzaldúa illustrates the ways in which mestiza culture exists between the Mexican and the American worlds, creating double or multiple identities. This splitting of identity is compounded by the experiences of being a woman in a male-dominated society and of being a homosexual in a homophobic world. Anzaldúa takes these psychic contradictions and balances them within what she calls a new mestiza consciousness. *Borderlands* reflects this multiplicity in its structure by using English/Spanish and prose/poetry interchangeably. The new mestiza consciousness is thus a new way to examine the linguistic, cultural, and creative contradictions of Anzaldúa's Chicana world.

POETRY COLLECTIONS

Borderlands/La Frontera: The New Mestiza. San Francisco, CA: Aunt Lute, 1987.

SELECTED ANTHOLOGIES WHERE POETRY APPEARS

Gilbert, Sandra M., and Susan Gubar, eds. *The Norton Anthology of Women's Literature*. New York: W. W. Norton, 1996.

Gillan, Maria M., and Jennifer Gillan, eds. *Unsettling America: Anthology of Contemporary American Ethnic Poetry*. New York: Penguin, 1994.

Milligan, Bryce, et al., eds. *Daughters of the Fifth Sun: A Collection of Latina Fiction and Poetry*. New York: Riverhead Books, 1995.

———. *¡Floricanto Sí! A Collection of Latina Poetry*. New York: Penguin/Putnam, 1998.

Singer, Bennett L., ed. *Growing Up Gay: A Literary Anthology*. New York: New Press, W. W. Norton, 1993.

SELECTED FICTION AND NONFICTION

This Bridge Called My Back: Writings by Radical Women of Color. Editor, with Cherríe Moraga. Watertown, MA: Persephone Press, 1981.

Cuentos: Stories by Latinas. Editor, with Alma Gomez et al. New York: Kitchen Table/ Women of Color, 1983.

Making Face, Making Soul/Haciendo Caras: Creative And Critical Perspectives by Women of Color. Editor, with Melanie Kaye Kantrowitz. San Francisco, CA: Aunt Lute, 1990.

Prietita Has a Friend. San Francisco, CA: Children's Book Press, 1991.

Friends from the Other Side. San Francisco, CA: Children's Book Press, 1993.

Lloronas, Women Who Howl: Autohistorias-Teorías and the Productions of Writing, Knowledge, and Identity. San Francisco, CA: Aunt Lute, 1996.

Prietita y La Llorona. San Francisco, CA: Children's Book Press, 1996.

La Prieta. San Francisco, CA: Spinsters/Aunt Lute, 1997.

Interviews/Entrevistas. Editor, with AnaLouise Keating. New York: Routledge, 2000.

This Bridge We Call Home: Radical Visions for Transformation. Editor, with AnaLouise Keating. New York: Routledge, 2002.

SELECTED RESOURCES FOR FURTHER REFERENCE

Barnard, Ian. "Gloria Anzaldúa's Queer Mestisaje." *MELUS: The Journal of the Society for the Study of the Multi-Ethnic Literature of the United States* 22 (Spring 1997): 35–53.

Blom, Gerdien. "Divine Individuals, Cultural Identities: Post-Identitarian Representations and Two Chicana/o Texts." *Thamyris: Mythmaking from Past to Present* 4.2 (Autumn 1997): 295–324.

Concannon, Kevin. "The Contemporary Space of the Border: Gloria Anzaldúa's Borderlands and William Gibson's Neuromancer." *Textual Practice* 12.3 (Winter 1998): 429–442.

Freedman, Diane P. *An Alchemy of Genres: Cross-Genre Writing by American Feminist Poet-Critics*. Charlottesville: University of Virginia Press, 1992.

Hedley, Jane. "Nepantilist Poetics: Narrative and Cultural Identity in the Mixed Language Writings of Irena Klepfisz and Gloria Anzaldúa." *Narrative* 4 (January 1996): 36–54.

Ikas, Karin Rosa. *Chicana Ways: Conversations with Ten Chicana Writers*. Reno: University of Nevada Press, 2002.

Kantrowitz, Melanie Kaye. "Crossover Dreams." *Village Voice* 33 (June 28, 1988): 60, 62.

Keating, AnaLouise. *Women Reading Women Writing: Self-Invention in Paula Gunn Allen, Gloria Anzaldúa, and Audre Lorde*. Philadelphia, PA: Temple University Press, 1996.

Lugones, Maria. "On Borderlands/La Frontera: An Interpretive Essay." *Hypatia* 7.4 (1992): 31–37.

Murphy, Patrick. "Grandmother Borderland: Placing Identity and Ethnicity." *Isle: Interdisciplinary Studies in Literature and Environment* 1 (June 1993): 35–41.

Steele, Cassie Premo. *We Heal from Memory: Sexton, Lorde, Anzaldúa, and the Poetry of Witness.* New York: Palgrave, 2000.

Yarbro-Bejarano, Yvonne. "Gloria Anzaldúa's *Borderlands/La Frontera:* Cultural Studies, 'Difference,' and the Non-Unitary Subject." *Cultural Critique* 28 (Fall 1994): 5–28.

Roy Pérez

Jimmy Santiago Baca

(1952–)

Chicano/Mexican American, American Indian (Apache)

Photo by Kent Barker, courtesy of Jimmy Santiago Baca.

BIOGRAPHY

Poetry and personal experience are inextricably linked, one to the other. While this is true for most poets, Baca's past, perhaps more than that of any other poet before him, must be known to fully comprehend the magnitude of his work and the miracle of his accomplishments. Baca began his tumultuous life on January 2, 1952, as a child of Chicano and Apache Indian decent. His parents' marriage ended when he was only two, and they abandoned him to the custody of a grandparent. By age five, Baca was living in a New Mexico orphanage, his father was dead of alcoholism, and his mother was married to a second husband who would eventually murder her. Baca often fled from the orphanage to hide in the barrio or to live with his relatives, only to eventually become homeless and live on the streets. By the time he was twenty, he was abusing alcohol and drugs and had been convicted of drug possession. Baca was sentenced to several years in a maximum-security prison in Arizona, ultimately spending four years in solitary confinement, and received electroshock treatments for his combative nature. He spent a total of six years in jail. Baca's life changed in many ways toward the end of his prison sentence. He gained acclaim in the literary world, but also found further happiness and normalcy with his marriage to Beatrice and the birth of their two children, Antonio and Gabriel.

Baca developed a depth and spirituality while in prison that infused his writing with emotional honesty and beauty. Rather than reacting with anger or self-pity at his circumstances, Baca found an intellectual zeal and taught himself to read and write, completed his G.E.D., and began writing poetry. Encouraged by a fellow inmate, Baca sent his works to the periodical *Mother Jones,* where poetry editor and poet Denise Levertov read and printed his poems. She later corresponded with Baca during his prison term and found a publisher for his first book. This book was published just one year after the end of his prison term and was met with rave reviews from critics and poetry magazines. In the years following his release from prison, Baca received his B.A. in English from University of New Mexico in 1984, and recently graduated with his Ph.D. in literature from the same university in 2003.

With the publication of his third book of poetry, *Martin and Meditations on the South Valley* (1987), Baca earned the American Book Award for Poetry. This success brought international attention and he found himself in demand for teaching positions and poetry readings. With the publication of his next book in 1989, *Black Mesa Poems,* Baca expressed the feelings of a return to normalcy and mainstream living through his marriage and the birth of two children. It is in this book that Baca's spiritual harmony shines through the brightest.

Baca received a National Endowment for the Arts grant for poetry and won the Ludwig Vogelstein Award for Poetry in 1987. He also received the American Book Award as well as the Pushcart Prize in 1988 and the International Hispanic Heritage Award in 1990. In 1989 and 1990 respectively, Baca was awarded the Berkeley Regent's Fellowship and the Wallace Stevens Fellowship from Yale University. Baca received the Southwest Book Award in 1993 and the Endowed Hulbert Chair in Southwest Studies from Colorado College in 1995, won the World Champion Poetry Bout in Taos, New Mexico, in 1996 and 1997, was awarded the Humanitarian Award from the City of Albuquerque in 1997, and is the recipient of the Barnes and Noble Discover Award for his memoir *A Place to Stand.* Baca also founded Black Mesa Enterprises in Albuquerque to offer young people an alternative to violence through a community centered around language. He has been poet in residence at both Berkeley and Yale universities, and his poems often appear in such periodicals as *Mother Jones, Ironwood, Bilingual Review, Harbor Review, Confluencia, Las Americas, New Kauri, Quarterly West,* and *Puerto del Sol.* He also maintains an active online presence; his official Jimmy Santiago Baca Web site features poetry, interactive discussions, and a variety of other information about himself. Currently Baca resides in and writes from his home in Albuquerque, New Mexico.

THEMES AND CONCERNS

Baca's miraculous life change from homelessness and illiterate convict to award-winning poet is reflected in his poignant, observant, and emotionally honest writings. Unlike a growing number of "prison writers" who infuse their work with rage and desolation, Baca writes poems dealing with spiritual rebirth and triumph over tragedy. Inspired by his tumultuous life experiences, his poetry is marked by recurrent themes of transformation, self-actualization, and metamorphosis. His writing is attuned to real-life circumstances of Chicano and Mestizo people, prisoners, drug addicts, and people on the fringes of society. Baca gives a voice to the racial oppression, exploitation of laborers, which first inspired him to educate himself, and horrors of prison life.

While Baca offers a voice for his people, much of his poetry is directly auto-biographical and reflects the acceptance of his earlier life. In "Bells" from *Black Mesa Poems,* Baca recounts the experience of his birth with a voice of forgive-ness and compassion for his parents. As with his prison sentence, his work relating to his childhood is noticeably devoid of blame or bitterness. In other poems he details his feelings of abandonment and displacement, but shows their resolution within the work. Although he has overcome much personal turmoil, Baca maintains the attitude of humility, which is manifest through-out his work, from prison sentence to the present. His poetry still speaks from his heart to the people of the barrio, Chicano Mestizo people, and those searching for a compassionate voice for their own challenges.

POETRY COLLECTIONS

Jimmy Santiago Baca. Santa Barbara, CA: Rock Bottom, 1978.
Immigrants in Our Own Land: Poems. Baton Rouge: Louisiana State University, 1979.
Swords of Darkness. San Jose, CA: Mango, 1981.
What's Happening. Willimantic, CT: Curbstone Press, 1982.
Poems Taken from My Yard. Fulton, MO: Timberline, 1986.
Martin and Meditations on the South Valley. New York: New Directions, 1987.
Black Mesa Poems. New York: New Directions. 1989.
In the Way of the Sun. New York: Grove Press, 1997.
Set This Book on Fire. San Diego, CA: Cedar Hill Publications, 1999.
Healing Earthquakes. New York: Grove Atlantic, 2001.
C-Train and 13 Mexicans. New York: Grove Atlantic, 2002.

SELECTED ANTHOLOGIES WHERE POETRY APPEARS

Forche, Carolyn, ed. *Against Forgetting: Twentieth-Century Poets of Witness.* New York: W. W. Norton, 1993.
Gillan, Maria, and Jennifer Gillan, eds. *Unsettling America: An Anthology of Contemporary Multicultural Poetry.* New York: Penguin, 1994.
Gonzalez, Ray, ed. *After Aztlan: Latino Poets of the Nineties.* Boston: D. R. Godine, 1992.
Harris, Marie, and Kathleen Aguero, eds. *An Ear to the Ground: An Anthology of Contemporary American Poetry.* Athens: University of Georgia Press, 1989.
Henderson, Bill, ed. *The Pushcart Prize XIV.* New York: Penguin, 1989.
Moramarco, Fred, and Al Zolynas, eds. *Men of Our Time: An Anthology of Male Poetry in Contemporary America.* Athens: University of Georgia Press, 1992.

SELECTED ADDITIONAL WORKS

Aftershock: Poems and Prose from the Vietnam War. Introduction. El Paso, TX: Cinco Puntos Press, 1991.
Los Tres Hijos de Julia. First produced at Los Angeles Theatre Center, Spring 1991. (play)

Working in the Dark: Reflections of a Poet of the Barrio. Santa Fe, NM: Red Crane Books, 1992. (stories and essays)
Bound by Honor. Hollywood Pictures, 1993. (screenplay)
The Lone Wolf—The Story of Pancho Gonzalez. HBO Productions, 2000. (film)
A Place to Stand. New York: Grove Atlantic, 2001. (memoir)
A Glass of Water. Independent Film Production, 2003.
Jesse's Journey. Independent Film Production, 2003.
Wash Up. Independent Film Production, 2003.

SELECTED RESOURCES FOR FURTHER REFERENCE

Balassi, William, John F. Crawford, and Annie E. Eysturoy, eds. *This Is about Vision: Interviews with Southwestern Writers.* Albuquerque: University of New Mexico Press, 1990.

Krier, Beth Ann. "Baca: A Poet Emerges from Prison of His Past." *Los Angeles Times,* February 15, 1989, pp. V5–V7.

Levertov, Denise. Afterword to *What's Happening.* Willimantic, CT: Curbstone, 1982.

———. Introduction to *Martin and Meditations on the South Valley.* New York: New Directions, 1987.

The Official Jimmy Santiago Baca Site. Online. www.jimmysantiagobaca.com.

Olivares, Julián. "Two Contemporary Chicano Verse Chronicles." *Americas Review* 16 (Fall–Winter 1988): 214–231.

Rector, Liam. "The Documentary of What Is." *Hudson Review* 41 (Summer 1989): 393–400.

Bronwen West

Amiri Baraka (aka LeRoi Jones, Imamu Amiri Baraka)

(1934–)

African American

Photo by AP/Wide World Photos.

BIOGRAPHY

Amiri Baraka, a poet, playwright, essayist, fiction writer, and activist, was born on October 7, 1934 in Newark, New Jersey. Born Everett LeRoy Jones, the son of Coyt LeRoy Jones, a supervisor for the U.S. Post Office, and Anna Lois (Russ) Jones, a social worker, he comes from a middle-class family. He attended both Rutgers University and Howard University, but did not do well at either institution. After Howard, he served in the U.S. Air Force for three years but was dishonorably discharged.

In 1957 he moved to Manhattan, where he began writing actively and became a central figure in the Beat Movement. Known as LeRoi Jones during this period, he was prominent in a loosely knit group of Greenwich Village artists, musicians, and intellectuals. In 1958 he married Hettie Cohen, a middle-class Jewish woman, and together they founded and coedited the avant-garde Beat literary magazine *Yugen,* which published writers such as Allen Ginsberg, Charles Olson, and Jack Kerouac. Baraka's work was greatly influenced by these writers; like them, he believed that poetry should be open in form and essentially exploratory in nature. Baraka's literary career began to flourish in 1961 with the publication of his well-received volume of poetry *Preface to a Twenty Volume Suicide Note.*

Largely as a result of Baraka's growing commitment to the necessity of politicized art and his changing cultural views, he moved to Harlem after the 1965 assassination of Malcolm X, divorced his wife, and began a period of Black Nationalism, a movement that held that the liberation of African nations from colonial powers provided an exemplary model of black self-determination. Baraka's intensified interest in racial issues can be seen most easily in his Obie Award–winning play *Dutchman* (1964), a powerful indictment of white American racism that set the tone for much black activism in the 1960s. In 1968, ideological and professional transition complete, he adopted the Muslim name

Imamu Amiri Baraka and married African American poet Amina Baraka, formerly Sylvia Robinson.

Baraka was instrumental in the Black Arts Movement of the 1960s, the literary outgrowth of the political Black Power Movement. His move to Harlem reveals the depth of Baraka's political commitment, since it recentered his artistic energy in a geographically black community rather than in the more lucrative locations of Broadway and Greenwich Village. During this period, Baraka created works that both embodied a black aesthetic and reflected a racially conscious politics, often employing black vernacular language and black oral modes and expressing revolutionary political themes. This poetry, collected in *Black Magic: Collected Poetry, 1961–1967* (1969), *It's Nation Time* (1970), and *In Our Terribleness* (1970), was enormously influential to a generation of African American writers that includes Haki Madhubuti, Nikki Giovanni, and Sonia Sanchez.

Black Nationalism advocated the violent rejection of, and resistance to, white society as a way to purge internalized feelings of inferiority in black Americans. While this was a necessary step in the process of black political liberation, Baraka does not see it as the final step, and in 1974 he rejected Black Nationalism as racist, dropped the spiritual title "Imamu" from his name, and published the manifesto "Towards Ideological Clarity," which announced his adoption of Marxist-Leninist perspectives. In *Hard Facts* (1975), *Poetry for the Advanced* (1979), and *Daggers and Javelins* (1984), he fuses elements of Marxist thought with aspects of cultural nationalism.

Baraka has also been an influential publisher and editor during his career. He founded Totem Press and has edited or coedited a number of anthologies, including *Confirmation: An Anthology of African-American Women* (1983), which won an American Book Award from the Before Columbus Foundation. The quality and volume of Baraka's work has led to honors that include fellowships from the Guggenheim Foundation and the National Endowment for the Arts. He also has received the PEN/Faulkner Award, the Rockefeller Foundation Award for Drama, and the Langston Hughes Award from the City College of New York. In May 2002 Baraka was appointed to a two-year term as Poet Laureate of New Jersey.

Baraka's commitment to social transformation has led him to be a teacher and an active developer of community and political organizations. He cofounded, with Diane di Prima, the American Theater for Poets in 1961, which was followed in 1965 by the Black Arts Repertory Theatre/School (BART/S), a model for the black theaters across the country. In 1966 he founded Spirit House, a black repertory theater and cultural center in Newark, New Jersey, and he organized the Black Community Development and Defense Organization to serve the African American community in Newark. In the early 1970s Baraka was instrumental in organizing the Pan African Congress of African Peoples in Atlanta and the National Black

Political Convention in Gary, Indiana. In 1979 he began teaching in the Department of Africana Studies at the State University of New York in Stony Brook and retired from that institution after twenty years. Currently he is codirector, with his wife, of Kimako's Blues People, a community arts space in Newark. A frequent speaker at colleges and universities, Baraka continues to write, create art, and compose.

THEMES AND CONCERNS

Baraka's literary work is generally regarded as having four distinct periods: the Beat Period (1957–1962), the Transitional Period (1963–1965), the Black Nationalist Period (1965–1974), and the Third World Marxist Period (1974–present). His use of free-verse style and sarcasm reflect his immersion in the Beat Movement. For instance, his free-verse poem "In Memory of Radio" implies that America has blurred the distinction between entertainment and religion, both through the reverence paid to the material world as reflected in entertainment media and through the use of media by religious figures.

Baraka's use of experimental form also developed in response to the Beat influence. His fictional work "Answers in Progress" can be read as poetry more easily than as fiction. Like other Beat writers, he is interested in exploring divinity as a nebulous reality rather than as prescribed conventions. The experimental form of "Answers in Progress" reflects this perception. Unlike other Beat writers, however, social and political consciousness is always present in Baraka's thought and work. For instance, "Hymn for Lannie Poo" moves beyond a satire of empty middle-class values to touch on the effect of those values on black Americans.

One of Baraka's primary concerns since the mid-1960s has been the creation of a consciousness in black Americans that affirms the value of African American history, culture, and language and replaces cultural self-doubt with an acceptance of African American heritage. Poems such as "Afrikan Revolution" exemplify the global perspective of the Black Nationalist Movement. This overarching concern informs Baraka's poetic aesthetic and explains his commitment to using black language and culture in the creation of art. The use of sound and image in Baraka's poetry is essential to understanding its meaning.

Throughout his career, Baraka has searched for the means to have a self-determined concept of identity for African Americans. During his Beat Period he sought to use the prevailing artistic forms of the Beat counterculture to achieve this end. During the Black Nationalist Period he sought total isolation of the black community to ensure the possibility of an entirely self-determined African American culture. Finally, he currently seeks to use Marxist theory to further the political aspirations of black liberation.

POETRY COLLECTIONS

Preface to a Twenty Volume Suicide Note. New York: Totem Press, 1961.
The Dead Lecturer. New York: Grove Press, 1964.
Black Art. Newark, NJ: Jihad, 1967.
Black Magic: Collected Poetry 1961–1967. Indianapolis, IN: Bobs-Merrill, 1969.
In Our Terribleness. Indianapolis, IN: Bobs-Merrill, 1970.
It's Nation Time. Chicago, IL: Third World Press, 1970.
Spirit Reach. Newark, NJ: Jihad, 1972.
Hard Facts. Newark, NJ: Congress of Afrikan People, 1975.
Selected Poetry of Amiri Baraka/LeRoi Jones. New York: William Morrow, 1978.
Reggae or Not! New York: Contact II, 1981.
The LeRoi Jones/Amiri Baraka Reader. Ed. William J. Harris in collaboration with
        Amiri Baraka. New York: Thunder's Mouth Press, 1991.
Transbluesency: The Selected Poems of Amiri Baraka/LeRoi Jones. New York: Marsilio,
        1995.
Wise, Why's Y's. Chicago, IL: Third World Press, 1995.
Funk Lore: New Poems. Los Angeles, CA: Litoral Books, 1996.

SELECTED ANTHOLOGIES WHERE POETRY APPEARS

Forche, Caroline, ed. *Against Forgetting: Twentieth Century Poets of Witness.* New
        York: W. W. Norton, 1993.
Gates, Henry, and Nellie McKay, eds. *The Norton Anthology of African-American
        Literature, Best American Poetry.* New York: W. W. Norton, 1997.
Gilbert, Derrick I. M., ed. *Catch the Fire!!! A Cross-Generational Anthology of
        Contemporary African-American Poetry.* New York: Riverhead Books, 1998.
Harper, Michael S., and Anthony Walton, eds. *Every Shut Eye Ain't Asleep: An An-
        thology of Poetry by African Americans Since 1945.* New York: Little, Brown,
        1994.
Hill, Patricia Liggins, ed. *Call & Response: The Riverside Anthology of the African
        American Literary Tradition.* Boston: Houghton Mifflin, 1998.
Medina, Tony, ed. *Bum Rush the Page: A Def Poetry Jam.* New York: Three Rivers
        Press, 2001.
Miller, E. Ethelbert, ed. *In Search of Color Everywhere: A Collection of African
        American Poetry.* New York: Stewart, Tabori, and Chang, 1996.
Randall, Dudley, ed. *Black Poets.* New York: Bantam Books, 1971.

SELECTED ADDITIONAL WORKS

Raise, Race, Rays, Raze: Essays Since 1965. New York: Random House, 1971.
The Motion of History and Other Plays. New York: Morrow, 1978.
Selected Plays and Prose of Amiri Baraka. New York: Morrow, 1979.
Confirmation: An Anthology of African-American Women. Comps. Amiri Baraka and
        Amina Baraka. New York: Morrow, 1983.
The Autobiography of LeRoi Jones/Amiri Baraka. New York: Freundlich Books, 1984.
Daggers and Javelins: Essays, 1974–1979. New York: Morrow, 1984.
The Fiction of Leroi Jones/Amiri Baraka. Chicago: Lawrence Hill Books, 2000.

SELECTED RESOURCES FOR FURTHER REFERENCE

Andrews, W.D.E. "'All Is Permitted': The Poetry of LeRoi Jones/Amiri Baraka." *Southwest Review* 67.2 (Spring 1982): 197–221.

Benston, Kimberly W. *Baraka: The Renegade and the Mask.* New Haven, CT: Yale University Press, 1976.

———, ed. *Imamu Amiri Baraka (Leroi Jones): A Collection of Critical Essays.* Englewood Cliffs, NJ: Prentice Hall, 1978.

Berry, Jay R., Jr. "Poetic Style in Amiri Baraka's Black Art." *College Language Association Journal* 32.2 (December 1988): 225–234.

Brown, Lloyd W. *Amiri Baraka.* Boston: Twayne, 1980.

Freydberg, Elizabeth H. "The Concealed Dependence upon White Culture in Baraka's 1969 Aesthetic." *Black American Literature Forum* 17.1 (Spring 1983): 27–29.

Harris, William J. *The Poetry and Poetics of Amiri Baraka: The Jazz Aesthetic.* Columbia: University of Missouri Press, 1986.

Hudson, Theodore R. *From LeRoi Jones to Amiri Baraka: The Literary Works.* Durham, NC: Duke University Press, 1973.

Lacey, Henry C. "Baraka's 'AMTRAK': Everybody's Coltrane Poem." *Obsidian II* 1.1–2 (Spring–Summer 1986): 12–21.

Reilly, Charlie, ed. *Conversations with Amiri Baraka.* Jackson: University Press of Mississippi, 1994.

Shannon, Sandra G. "Manipulating Myth, Magic, and Legend: Amiri Baraka's Black Mass." *College Language Association Journal* 39.3 (March 1996): 357–368.

Joseph Register

Beth Brant (aka Degonwadonti)

(1941–)

American Indian (Bay of Quinte Mohawk)

BIOGRAPHY

Beth Brant, a poet, fiction writer, and essayist, was born on May 6, 1941, in Detroit, Michigan. The daughter of a Native father and Irish/Scots mother—and the descendant of tribal leaders Molly Brant and Chief Joseph Brant—she is a Bay of Quinte Mohawk from the Tyendinaga Reserve in Deseronto, Ontario. Her paternal grandparents moved to the Detroit area with the hope that their children, of which there were nine, would find more opportunities away from the reservation. Along with her parents, Joseph and Hazel Brant, brother, and sister, Brant grew up in her grandparents' house in Detroit, where her father worked first in an automobile factory and later as a teacher. Brant dropped out of high school and married at seventeen; she had three daughters from this marriage: Kim, Jennifer, and Jill. When she divorced, she worked as a waitress, salesclerk, cleaning woman, and at other unskilled jobs in order to support herself and her children.

It wasn't until 1981, when Brant was forty years old, that she began her life as a writer. She traces the origins of this decision to a motor trip through the Mohawk Valley that she took with her partner, Denise Dorsz. As she describes in the afterword to *Mohawk Trail,* "a Bald Eagle flew in front of my car, sat in a tree, and instructed me to write." She has been writing steadily since this time, displaying a style that ranges from humorously lighthearted—particularly in her recollections of her family—to angry, intense, and spiritual.

Her first book-length publication was *Mohawk Trail* (1985), a miscellany of poems and stories, both fiction and autobiographical. Brant gained national recognition with her next publication, *A Gathering of Spirit: A Collection by North American Women* (1988). Originally appearing as a special issue of the periodical *Sinister Wisdom* before being published in book form, it was the first anthology of contemporary Indian women's art, poetry, and short fiction. Striving to present a representative compilation, Brant not only solicited entries from established writers, but also advertised for contributions in tribal newspapers and in women's prisons; the work of Native lesbians is featured as well. Groundbreaking in conception and scope, the work has enjoyed four printings and remains an important collection. In 1991, Brant published

Food & Spirits, a collection of short stories featuring protagonists who are on the margins of society. Her most recent book-length works are titled *Writing and Witness: Essays and Talk* (1994) and *I'll Sing 'til the Day I Die: Conversations with Tyendinaga Elders* (1995), a collection of interviews done while she was writer-in-residence at the Kainite Library on the Tending Mohawk Reserve in Canada in 1993. Brant's poetry, stories, and essays continue to be published extensively in anthologies and periodicals, particularly those with Native, feminist, and/or lesbian perspectives.

Teaching and mentoring have also played a significant role in Brant's life. She was a lecturer at the University of British Columbia in 1989 and 1990, has been a guest lecturer in women's studies and Native studies at the New College of the University of Toronto, and lectures and gives readings at universities and cultural centers throughout North America. Brant has also contributed to a number of creative writing workshops, such as the Women of Color Writing Workshop held in Vancouver in 1991, the 1991 Michigan Festival of Writers in East Lansing, the International Feminist Book Fair held in Amsterdam in 1992, and the Flight of the Mind Writing Workshop in Eugene, Oregon in 1992. In addition, she has formed creative writing workshops for groups of Indian women, women in prison, and high school students. Always seeking ways to help others express themselves, Brant has participated in a project called Returning the Gift, which was designed to create new opportunities for Native writers to share their work. The project included a 1992 meeting of 250 writers in Norman, Oklahoma, various outreach programs, and the formation of an organization known as the Native Writers' Circle of the Americas.

Brant has spearheaded other projects as well. In 1982 she cofounded Turtle Grandmother, a clearinghouse for manuscripts by Native American women and a source of information about Native women, an endeavor that lasted until 1987. She is also an AIDS activist, working for People with AIDS (PWA) and giving AIDS education workshops throughout the Indian community. Her many talents have received such recognition as the Creative Writing Award from the Michigan Council for the Arts (1984 and 1986), an award from the National Endowment for the Arts in 1991, and the Canada Council Award in Creative Writing in 1992. She and Denise Dorsz, her partner of more than two decades, divide their time between Michigan and Ontario.

THEMES AND CONCERNS

Brant identifies herself as Mohawk, lesbian, mother, grandmother, writer, mentor, activist, editor, speaker, and storyteller. Her writing is equally multifaceted, including poetry, short fiction, essays, and critical reviews. However, regardless of the genre, poetry is often at its heart. For example, her book of short stories *Food & Spirits* is introduced by the long narrative poem "Telling." Describing three silenced victims of the white patriarchy—a sexually abused young girl, a little boy removed from a violent home, and a murdered Indian woman—it establishes the general theme of the collection. Similarly, her short story "A Simple Act" is intricately framed with poetic passages that connect its various strands (*Mohawk Trail*). And while the fictive elements of this story warn again of the destructiveness of imposed silences—speaking both of those forced on Native individuals and on the entire American Indian community—the poetic passages offer hope and celebration of the power of language to keep their heritage and their individual voices strong and enabling.

The celebration of the power of language to restore and empower is a central theme in Brant's poetry. Not coming to writing and public speaking herself until middle age, Brant understands the fundamental necessity of being able to tell one's own story. Other dominant themes that appear throughout her work include her love of her family and of the Mohawk people; her interest in women's relationships, both sexual and platonic; and the depiction of the suffering and alienation experienced by those outside the mainstream of the dominant culture. "Her Name Is Helen" (*Mohawk Trail*) offers one such poetic sketch of a Native woman co-opted and ultimately destroyed by white society.

Central metaphors that establish and enrich these themes include the image of hair, which has been shorn at the hands of the powerful but must be woven together in reaffirmation, and the grandmother, who connects past, present, and future and safeguards the heritage of the Native people. These two images come together beautifully in "For All My Grandmothers" (*Mohawk Trail*), an optimistic expression of Brant's belief that, with love and patience, words can be recovered and fashioned together again.

In *New Voices from the Longhouse,* Brant observes that "economic realities, Indian invisibility, the lack of 'formal, Euroamerican education' have taken their toll" (quoted in Bruchac, p. 56). And yet she acknowledges that these same struggles have shaped her artistry: "These things have made me the kind of writer I am. I like to think I am continuing the long journey of being a storyteller that my people first began" (p. 56). Brant's many contributions continue to make her a positive force in American Indian poetry and an inspiration for all of us to discover the words and stories within.

POETRY COLLECTIONS

Mohawk Trail. Ithaca, NY: Firebrand Books, 1985. (poetry and fiction)
A Gathering of Spirit: A Collection by North American Women. Editor. Ithaca, NY: Firebrand Books, 1988. (poetry, fiction, and art)

SELECTED ANTHOLOGIES WHERE POETRY APPEARS

Barrington, Judith, ed. *An Intimate Wilderness: Lesbian Writers on Sexuality*. Portland, OR: Eighth Mountain Press, 1991.

Bruchac, Joseph, ed. *New Voices from the Longhouse: An Anthology of Contemporary Iroquois Writing*. Greenfield Center, NY: Greenfield Review Press, 1989.

————. *Songs from This Earth on Turtle's Back: Contemporary American Indian Poetry*. Greenfield Center, NY: Greenfield Review Press, 1983.

Dykewords: An Anthology of Lesbian Writing. Ed. Lesbian Writing and Publishing Collective. Toronto: Women's Press, 1990.

Piercy, Marge, ed. *Early Ripening: Poetry by Women*. New York, Pandora Books, 1987.

Roscoe, Will, ed. *Living the Spirit: A Gay American Indian Anthology*. New York: St. Martin's Press, 1988.

SELECTED ADDITIONAL WORKS

"Grandmothers of a New World." *Women of Power* 16 (Spring 1990): 40–47.

Food & Spirits. Ithaca, NY: Firebrand Books, 1991.

"Giveaway: Native Lesbian Writers." *Signs: Journal of Women in Culture and Society* 18 (Summer 1993): 944–947.

"The Good Red Road." *American Indian Culture and Research Journal* 21.1 (1997): 193–206.

Writing as Witness: Essay and Talk. Toronto: Women's Press, 1994.

I'll Sing 'til the Day I Die: Conversations with Tyendinaga Elders. Toronto: McGilligan Books, 1995.

SELECTED RESOURCES FOR FURTHER REFERENCE

Bruchac, Carol, Linda Hogan, and Judith McDaniel. *The Stories We Hold Secret: Tales of Women's Spiritual Development*. Greenfield Center, NY: Greenfield Review Press, 1986.

Cullum, Linda. "Survival's Song: Beth Brant and the Power of the Word." *MELUS: The Journal of the Society for the Study of the Multi-Ethnic Literature of the United States* 24.3 (Fall 1999): 129–140.

Feminist Writers. Toronto: St. James Press, 1996.

Petrone, Penny. *Native Literature in Canada: From the Oral Tradition to the Present*. Toronto: Oxford University Press, 1990.

Smoke Rising: The Native North American Literary Companion. Ed. Janet Witalec and Sharon Malinowski. Detroit, MI: Visible Ink Press, 1995.

Linda Cullum

Gwendolyn Brooks

(1917–2000)

African American

BIOGRAPHY

Gwendolyn Brooks, activist, novelist, editor, and author of more than twenty collections of poetry, was born to David and Keziah Wims Brooks in Topeka, Kansas, on June 17, 1917. She was raised in Chicago and even though she traveled widely and spent long periods of time elsewhere, Brooks always actively maintained her association with Chicago's South Side.

Brooks was a creative child, and by the age of thirteen she had her first poem published in *American Childhood Magazine*. Her parents encouraged her poetic ability, taking her to meet James Weldon Johnson and Langston Hughes whenever they lectured at churches in and around Chicago. She attended Hyde Park High School, the leading white high school in the Chicago, but transferred to the all-black Wendell Phillips for a short time before finally attending and graduating from the racially integrated Englewood High School. Her experiences at these various schools impacted her view of education and urban racial dynamics, and this view influenced her poetry throughout her career. She graduated from Wilson Junior College in 1936. Brooks married Henry Blakely, a fellow South Side writer, and had two children: Henry Jr. in 1940 and Nora in 1951.

Brooks became a regular contributor to the *Chicago Defender*, and by 1934 she had published almost 100 of her poems in the *Defender*'s weekly poetry column. In 1937, when Brooks was twenty, her work had already appeared in several anthologies. In 1943, as a result of the support she received from a group of writers working with *Poetry: A Magazine of Verse,* she won the Midwestern Writers Conference Poetry Award. Two years later, she gained sudden fame after publishing her first volume of poetry, *A Street in Bronzeville* (1945). Her second book of poems, *Annie Allen* (1949), won *Poetry* magazine's Eunice Tietjens Prize and garnered Brooks her first Guggenheim Fellowship and the honor of becoming the first African American to win a Pulitzer Prize for poetry when she received the award in 1950 for this collection.

As her reputation grew, she began to review books for the major Chicago newspapers. In 1962, President Kennedy invited her to read at a Library of

Congress poetry festival, and in 1963 she began teaching a poetry workshop at Chicago's Columbia College. Brooks taught at a variety of institutions throughout her career, including Northeastern Illinois University, Columbia University (New York), and the University of Wisconsin. During this time, she also began receiving the first of what were to be more than fifty honorary doctorates.

During the 1950s and 1960s, while maintaining an active writing and lecturing schedule, Brooks became involved with the Civil Rights Movement and became a leading voice in the development of the Black Arts Movement. This was a turning point in her career, for although Brooks's poetry had already focused on social protest and the black experience, she was inspired to begin publishing with small black publishers instead of major publishing houses and to advocate for the academic theories of Black Aesthetics. She also began a poetry workshop with members of a Chicago teen gang, the Blackstone Rangers. In 1968, Brooks was appointed to succeed Carl Sandburg as Poet Laureate of Illinois, and in 1970, Western Illinois University opened the Gwendolyn Brooks Cultural Center. She and her husband separated in 1969, in part due to their differing political beliefs, but they reconciled in 1973. Although Brooks had health problems beginning in her forties, she maintained an active writing and lecturing schedule up until her death from cancer in 2000 at the age of eighty-three. She published volumes of poetry throughout the 1980s in particular, and her last published volume of poetry was *Children Coming Home* (1991).

A number of impressive events occurred during the last two decades of her life. These included an invitation to read at the White House in 1980, an appointment to the Presidential Commission on the National Agenda for the Eighties, and her visit to the Soviet Union in 1982. Brooks was also named a Consultant in Poetry to the Library of Congress (1985–1986), she received a lifetime achievement award from the National Endowment for the Arts (1989), and she was selected by the National Endowment for the Humanities as the 1994 Jefferson Lecturer, the highest award in the humanities given by the federal government.

THEMES AND CONCERNS

Gwendolyn Brooks's poetry consists of local and intimate portraits of urban life. The characters she creates are not important in and of themselves—Satin-Legs Smith, Annie Allen, Maud Martha, Afrika, the young pool players in "We Real Cool," Rudolph Reed—but exist as elements of a collage of African American experiences. *A Street in Bronzeville,* for example, features a series of vignettes that not only use detail to explain the way things look and smell, but also speak to the emotional quality of being in Bronzeville and of maintaining dignity within urban poverty. In doing so, she contributes the characters, stories, words, emotions, and images of everyday African American life to the mainstream of American poetry, which had previously ignored their existence or worth as poetic material.

Brooks is a complicated poet to categorize, and many critics choose to emphasize her range and the evolution of her style and content over the course of her career. For example, Brooks writes in a variety of poetic forms, both traditional and experimental, including sonnets, ballads, epic poetry, street language, and jazz and blues rhythms, and these forms are interspersed throughout her books of poetry. Her primary influences are Langston Hughes, James Weldon Johnson, and Paul Laurence Dunbar, but the influences of writers such as T. S. Eliot, Gertrude Stein, and John Donne are also present in her work. In the 1960s, after her shift toward the Black Arts Movement and smaller, black-owned publishing houses, her poetry took on a slightly more radical feel, but the elements of social protest and struggle were in her writing from the beginning of her career.

Many critics regard Brooks as one of the most undervalued American poets of the twentieth century, which may be due to the difficulty that critics face in categorizing her poetry. Throughout her career, Brooks continued to experiment and reach out to her audience, particularly her African American readers and students. Her work with the Blackstone Rangers, for example, indicates her refusal to see poetry and everyday life as separate endeavors. In working to empower her readers and by being so visible as a public figure, especially after the 1960s, Brooks challenges literary historians who would label her an integrationist poet and asks us to rethink the purpose and meaning of categories and labels.

POETRY COLLECTIONS

A Street in Bronzeville. New York: Harper & Row, 1945.
Annie Allen. New York: Harper & Row, 1949.
Bronzeville Boys and Girls. New York: Harper & Row, 1956.
The Bean Eaters. New York: Harper & Row, 1960.
Selected Poems. New York: Harper & Row, 1963.
We Real Cool. Detroit, MI: Broadside Press, 1966.
The Wall. Detroit, MI: Broadside Press, 1967.
In the Mecca. New York: Harper & Row, 1968.
Riot. Detroit, MI: Broadside Press, 1969.
Family Pictures. Detroit, MI: Broadside Press, 1970.
Aloneness. Detroit, MI: Broadside Press, 1971.
Black Steel: Jo Frazier and Muhammad Ali. Detroit, MI: Broadside Press, 1971.
Report from Part One. Detroit, MI: Broadside Press, 1972.
Beckonings. Detroit, MI: Broadside Press, 1975.
Young Poet's Primer. Chicago, IL: Brooks Press, 1980.
To Disembark. Chicago, IL: Third World Press, 1981.
Black Love. Chicago, IL: Black Position Press, 1982.
Very Young Poets. Chicago, IL: Brooks Press, 1983.

The Near-Johannesburg Boy and Other Poems. Chicago, IL: Third World Press, 1986.
Blacks. Chicago, IL: Third World Press, 1987, 1991.
Winnie. Chicago, IL: Third World Press, 1988, 1991.
Gottschallk and the Grande Tarantelle. Chicago, IL: Third World Press, 1989, 1991.

SELECTED ANTHOLOGIES WHERE POETRY APPEARS

Gates, Henry Louis, Jr., and Nellie Y. McKay, eds. *The Norton Anthology of African American Literature.* New York: W. W. Norton, 1996.

Hill, Herbert, ed. *Soon, One Morning: New Writing by American Negroes, 1940–1962.* New York: Alfred A. Knopf, 1963.

Hill, Patricia Liggins, et al., eds. *Call and Response: The Riverside Anthology of the African American Tradition.* New York: Houghton Mifflin, 1998.

Hughes, Langston, and Arna Bontemps, eds. *The Poetry of the Negro, 1746–1949.* Garden City, NY: Doubleday, 1949.

Seaver, Edwin, ed. *Cross-Section 1945: A Collection of New American Writing.* New York: L. B. Fischer, 1945.

SELECTED ADDITIONAL WORKS

Maud Martha. New York: Harper & Row, 1953.
Jump Bad: A New Chicago Anthology. Editor. Detroit: Broadside Press, 1971.
The World of Gwendolyn Brooks. New York: Harper & Row, 1971.
The Tiger Who Wore White Gloves, or What You Are You Really Are. Chicago, IL: Third World Press, 1974.
Primer for Blacks. Chicago, MI: Black Position Press, 1980.
Report from Part Two. Chicago, MI: Third World Press, 1996.

SELECTED RESOURCES FOR FURTHER REFERENCE

Horvath, Brooke K. "The Satisfactions of What's Difficult in Gwendolyn Brooks's Poetry." *American Literature* 62.4 (December 1990): 606–616.

Kent, George E. *A Life of Gwendolyn Brooks.* Lexington: University Press of Kentucky, 1990.

Madhubuti, Haki R., ed. *Say That the River Turns: The Impact of Gwendolyn Brooks.* Chicago, IL: Third World Press, 1987.

Melhem, D. H. *Gwendolyn Brooks: Poetry and the Heroic Voice.* Lexington: University Press of Kentucky, 1987.

Mootry, Maria K., and Gary Smith. *A Life Distilled: Gwendolyn Brooks, Her Poetry and Fiction.* Urbana: University Press of Illinois, 1987.

Shaw, Harry B. *Gwendolyn Brooks.* Boston, MA: Twayne, 1980.

Wright, Stephen Caldwell. *On Gwendolyn Brooks: Reliant Contemplation.* Ann Arbor: University of Michigan Press, 1996.

Rachael Groner

Photo by Carol Bruchac, courtesy of Joseph Bruchac.

Joseph Bruchac

(1942–)

American Indian (Abenaki Nation)

BIOGRAPHY

Joseph Bruchac is a poet, author, storyteller, musician, educator, editor, publisher, and recording artist. He is a member of Abenaki Indian tribe through his grandfather, and his ancestors were also of English and Slovak descent. Born on October 16, 1942, in Sarasota Springs, New York, Bruchac spent his childhood in New York State and was raised by his mother's parents. They did not discuss his American Indian heritage with him for fear that it would negatively affect the way people treated them. Today, he still lives in the Adirondack mountain foothills in the town of Greenfield Center, in the house built by his grandfather, Jesse Bowman.

Joseph Bruchac received a B.A. in 1965 from Cornell University, where he majored in English with a minor in zoology. He earned an M.A. in creative writing in 1966 from Syracuse University, and in 1975 was granted a Ph.D. in comparative literature from the Union Institute of Ohio. In 1966, Bruchac and his wife, Carol, joined the Peace Corps and lived in the West African country of Ghana until 1969. As their assignment, they taught English and literature at the Keta secondary school. Their contact with the local culture reinforced for them the importance of community and a sense of pride in their roots. More important, their contact with the people of Ghana helped the Bruchacs to form a plan for their lives when they returned to the United States. Upon returning to New York in 1969, Joseph and Carol Bruchac founded the family business, the Greenfield Review Literary Center, and Joseph became the editor of the Greenfield Review Press.

No discussion of Joseph Bruchac would be complete without mentioning his work as a mentor and promoter of new American Indian writers and poets. He is considered an important supporter and advocate for many of the poets of the Native American Renaissance. The mission of the Greenfield Review Literary Center is to promote multicultural literature and especially to bring forward the work of new poets and authors who would not normally be published by larger publishers. In addition, Joseph Bruchac has edited two of the most significant Native American anthologies in the last part of the twentieth century. *Songs from the Earth on Turtle's Back,* published in 1983, is a compilation of the work of fifty-two Native American poets, many of whom are now famous. He also edited the book *Survival This Way,* a collection of interviews with Native American poets. In addition, the Greenfield Press has also published poetry written by Asian Americans and prisoners.

Most of Bruchac's recent work is devoted to acquainting young children with the Native American culture by recounting for them, through books and storytelling, the tales and legends of many different Indian tribes. He firmly believes that the children are the future, and coupled with his sense of urgency to save the planet as we know it, he strives to quietly teach children through his storytelling many of the same lessons he teaches adults through his poetry and fiction. He accomplishes this by bringing to children the tales and poems of many American Indian tribes in both the written and the spoken word. In addition to being an award-winning poet and author, Bruchac is also an award-winning storyteller and has stated his belief that storytelling helps restore harmony and balance to the world.

For the past thirty years, Joseph Bruchac has also been a participant in the Poetry in the Schools program. Today, he works with his sister Margaret and his sons James and Jesse to promote the culture and contributions of Native Americans through storytelling at schools and for special events. They also have formed a singing group, the Dawn Land Singers, and have recorded their first CD of Native American music, titled *Alnobak.*

Joseph Bruchac has received many awards, including the American Book Award from the Before Columbus Foundation (1984), the Cherokee Nation Prose Award (1986), the Mountain & Plains Award (1995), a National Endowment for the Arts writing fellowship for poetry (1974), the Publishers Marketing Association Person of the Year Award (1993), and the Wordcraft Circle of Native Writers and Storytellers: Storyteller of the Year Award (1998). A prolific writer, Joseph Bruchac has published over 600 articles and poems and has written over 100 books.

THEMES AND CONCERNS

Joseph Bruchac believes that poetry "is as much a part of human beings as breath—and that, like breath, poetry links us to all other living things and is meant to be shared" ("Joseph Bruchac, III"). His work centers on several key themes. One is American Indian folklore, and Bruchac often uses this folklore in his poetry, making frequent references to Indian legends and beliefs and especially to legendary animals familiar to his ancestors, such as bears, wolves, and buffaloes. He also stresses humankind's need to respect and preserve nature, while observing and listening to the world around us. In a *MELUS* interview with Meredith Ricker, Bruchac states his optimistic belief that "this natural harmony, this understanding of nature around us and family that's part of us, is something for which we all long. . . . When we learn to see ourselves as members of a community, we will move toward the gentleness of change" (p. 178).

Another of Joseph Bruchac's key concerns is humanity's destruction of the environment. Throughout his poetry, he subtly calls for the reader to respect the Earth, nature, and animals as ancestral Native Americans did. In many of his poems, there is a sense of urgency that the world needs saving because Western attitudes and civilization are at odds with the natural environment. He also strives to preserve American Indian mythology and folklore through his poetry. He often incorporates words and phrases from Abenaki and other American Indian languages in his works. In conjunction with the American Indian culture, his poetry often stresses the interconnectedness of all things on the planet. He takes everyday experiences and finds meaning by connecting them to the practices, beliefs, and culture of his American Indian heritage.

A fourth theme in Bruchac's work is listening. He encourages his readers to listen to nature, observe animals, and derive lessons from the destruction that humankind is still bringing upon the Earth. Listening leads to remembering, and Bruchac's poetry often reminds the reader of the importance of cultural memory. Listening also leads to compassion for the Earth and its creatures.

Despite such serious themes as habitat destruction and loss of the natural world, Bruchac's poetry is optimistic in content. This optimism is a quality that Bruchac himself attributes to the grandparents who raised him, and he is careful to preserve that optimism. The reader is left with the hope that the wrongs can be made right, that physical and spiritual balances can be restored, and that humankind can learn to live in harmony with the rest of the planet. Despite his grave concerns and his belief in the need for immediate action, Joseph Bruchac's poetry neither chides nor preaches to the reader. Rather, by giving the reader positive images and quiet explanations, Bruchac allows his audience to discover problems and reach conclusions on its own.

POETRY COLLECTIONS

Indian Mountain and Other Poems. Ithaca, NY: Ithaca House, 1971.
Flow. Austin, TX: Cold Mountain Press, 1975.
Road to Black Mountain. Berkeley, CA: Thorp Springs Press, 1977.
Tracking. Memphis, TN: Ion Books, 1986.
Near the Mountains. Fredonia, NY: White Pine Press, 1987.
Walking with My Sons and Other Poems. Bangor, ME: Landlocked Press, 1987.
Translator's Son. Merrick, NY: Cross-Cultural Press, 1989.
No Borders. Duluth, MN: Holy Cow! Press, 1999.

SELECTED ANTHOLOGIES WHERE POETRY APPEARS

Fitzharris, Tim, ed. *Soaring with Ravens Visions of the Native American Landscape.* San Francisco, CA: HarperCollins, 1995.

Harris, Marie, and Kathleen Aguero, eds. *An Ear to the Ground: An Anthology of Contemporary American Poetry.* Athens: University of Georgia Press, 1989.

Moramarco, Fred, and Al Zolynas, eds. *Men of Our Time: An Anthology of Male Poetry in Contemporary America.* Athens: University of Georgia Press, 1992.

SELECTED ADDITIONAL WORKS

Aftermath: An Anthology of Poems in English from Africa, Asia, and the Caribbean. Greenfield Center, NY: Greenfield Review Press, 1977.

Breaking Silence: An Anthology of Contemporary Asian American Poets. Editor. Greenfield Center, NY: Greenfield Review Press, 1983.

Songs from This Earth on Turtle's Back. Editor. Greenfield Center, NY: Greenfield Review Press, 1983.

Survival This Way: Interviews with American Indian Poets. Tucson: University of Arizona Press, 1987.

Keepers of the Earth. With Joseph A. Caduto. Golden, CO: Fulcrum Press, 1989.

New Voices from the Longhouse. Editor. Greenfield Center, NY: Greenfield Review Press, 1989.

Keepers of the Animals. With Joseph A. Caduto. Golden, CO: Fulcrum Press, 1990.

Four Ancestors: Stories, Songs, and Poems from Native North America. Editor. New Jersey: Bridgewater Books, 1996. (children's anthology)

Sacajawea: *The Story of Bird Woman and the Lewis and Clark Expedition.* New York, NY: Scholastic, 2003. (young adult)

AUDIOTAPES AND CDS

Many of Joseph Bruchac's books have accompanying audiotapes or CDs. His music recordings are listed below.

Iroquois Stories. 1988.

Boy Who Lived with Bears. 1990.

Gluskabe Stories. 1990.

Keepers of the Earth. 1991.

Keepers of the Animals. 1993.

Keepers of Life. 1994.

SELECTED RESOURCES FOR FURTHER REFERENCE

Alderdice, Kit. "Joseph Bruchac: Sharing a Native-American Heritage." *Publishers' Weekly,* February 19, 1996, pp. 191–192.

Dresang, Eliza J. "An Interview with Joseph Bruchac." CCBC-net. Online. www. soemadison.wisc.edu/ccbc/bruchac.htm.

"Joseph Bruchac, Interview with the Author." *Read Across America.* Online. www. nea.org/readacross/multi/jbruchac.html.

"Joseph Bruchac, III." *Contemporary Authors Online.* http://galenet. galegroup.com.

Joseph Bruchac Homepage. Online. www.josephbruchac.com.

Ricker, Meredith. "A MELUS Interview: Joseph Bruchac." *MELUS: The Journal of the Society for the Study of the Multi-Ethnic Literature of the United States* 21.3 (Fall 1996): 159–178.

Rodia, Becky. "The Good Mind of Joseph Bruchac." *Teaching Prek-8* 32.4 (2002): 56–58.

Wiget, Andrew, ed. *Dictionary of Native American Literature.* New York: Garland, 1994.

Sue Czerny

Nick Carbó

(1964–)

Filipino American

Photo by Denise Duhamel, courtesy of Coffee House Press.

BIOGRAPHY

Nick Carbó was born in 1964 in Legazpi, Albay, Philippines, and grew up in Manila. Adopted by a Spanish couple, he became a citizen of Spain. A relative newcomer to the United States, he came to attend St. Mary's University, where he earned a B.A. in English in 1990. He received his M.F.A. from Sarah Lawrence College (New York) in 1992.

After discovering a chapbook by poet Denise Duhamel in Bucknell University's library, where he was a resident poet, Carbó wrote her a fan letter, thus initiating a two-year correspondence. They finally met after Duhamel completed her M.F.A. at Sarah Lawrence. The couple married in 1992 and lived in Manhattan for several years, where Carbó was active in the Asian American Writers' Workshop.

Carbó has published two books of poetry to date: *El Grupo Mcdonald's* (1995) and *Secret Asian Man* (2000), which won the Asian American Literary Prize. He has also edited or coedited several volumes of Filipino and Filipino-American poetry. These are *Returning a Borrowed Tongue* (1996), *Babaylan: An Anthology of Filipina and Filipina American Writers,* with poet and scholar Eileen Tabios (2000), and *Sweet Jesus: Poems About the Ultimate Icon,* with Denise Duhamel (2002).

Carbó's work is widely published on the Internet and in periodicals that include *Asian Pacific American Journal, DisOrient, Indiana Review, MELUS, Poetry, TriQuarterly,* and *Western Humanities Review.* He continues to be a member of the Asian American Writers' Workshop and frequently gives public readings from his work, often with Duhamel. His awards include grants from the National Endowment for the Arts and the New York Foundation for the Arts. He has held poetry residencies at the MacDowell Colony, Yaddo, Fundación Valparaiso (Spain), and Le Chateau de Lavigny (Switzerland). He has been resident poet at Bucknell University and writer-in-residence at American University in Washington, DC. Carbó is currently on the faculty of the University of Miami and lives in Miami with his wife. He is at work on a third volume of poetry and a memoir.

THEMES AND CONCERNS

Nick Carbó's poems convey a postcolonial worldview of cultural hybridization and cultural clash. Ranging in tone from the serious to the satiric to the comic, his poems comment on Philippine politics, media portrayals of Filipinos, and the impact of Western culture on the Philippines. He juxtaposes phrases in Tagalog and Spanish with the English in his poems and by doing so evokes strong sensual images, including tastes and smells with sights and sounds.

Much of Carbó's poetry is rooted in popular culture. In *Secret Asian Man,* he explores the perceptions of "Ang Tunay Na Lalaki" (Tagalog for "the Real Man," a macho, bare-chested character from Philippine advertising) as this commercial representation of Philippine sex appeal finds his way around New York City. It was Carbó's intention to "bring this character to New York City and have him interact with new cultural surroundings," he writes in *The Literary Review* (p. 115), explaining the origins of his poem "Ang Tunay Na Lalaki Visits His Favorite Painting." In the Metropolitan Museum of Art, a vividly rendered scene depicted by Winslow Homer in 1898 reminds Ang Tunay Na Lalaki of his tropical island home and, further, reminds him of the domination of the Philippines by Americans since that significant year when the Spanish were displaced. As Carbó notes, "The language of Emerson, Thoreau, and Whitman invaded the islands and became the lingua franca for more than a century. This is the postcolonial legacy that Ang Tunay Na Lalaki confronts in his walks around New York City" (p. 115).

Ang Tunay Na Lalaki pays attention to billboards, commercials, and his reflection in shop windows, thinking about media images of masculinity and Asians and about encounters with women. Carbó's poem "Ang Tunay Na Lalaki Meets Barbie at the Shark Bar" makes sly allusion to Duhamel's book of Barbie doll poems, *Kinky,* and notes that the Barbie doll, like Ang Tunay Na Lalaki himself, was made in the Philippines. The poem is entertaining but calls attention to Barbie's production by "exploited laborers," her composition of "petroleum based plastic," and her anger at being addressed as "doll" rather than "Barbie." Carbó focuses on media portrayals of the "Little Brown Brother" in the poem by that name and in Ang Tunay Na Lalaki's comparison of himself to Tonto in "Ang Tunay Na Lalaki Stalks in the Streets of New York."

References to the "high" culture of painting also appear in work other than the "Ang Tunay Na Lalaki" poems. For instance, in the poem "Sign Language," which appeared in *ASHA,* the publication of the American Speech-Language-Hearing Association, the speaker likens signing hands to the hands of painters Matisse, Renoir, and Rousseau. Carbó's preoccupation with language takes a playful bent in "Grammarotics," in which he uses grammatical and poetic terminology to describe a sexual encounter.

Carbó's playfulness is further illustrated by his experimental "cube dice poem," which can be found online in *xPress(ed)* (www.xpressed.org/title.html). Lines of poetry are displayed in colored squares linked so that they can be made into cubes, and the reader is directed to cut out the cube, paste it together as a cube, and roll it with other cubes to read the resulting poem.

Carbó's perspective is fresh, and the density of his cultural allusions is frequently dazzling. His editorial work and promotion of Filipino and Filipino-American writing, as well, have contributed to his forceful impact on the Asian American literary scene.

POETRY COLLECTIONS

El Grupo McDonald's. Chicago, IL: Tia Chucha Press, 1995.
Secret Asian Man. Chicago, IL: Tia Chucha Press, 2000.

SELECTED ANTHOLOGIES AND WEB SITES WHERE POETRY APPEARS

Cabico, Regie, and Todd Swift, eds. *Poetry Nation: The North American Anthology of Fusion Poetry*. Montreal: Vehicule Press, 1998.
Collier, Michael, ed. *The New American Poets: A Bread Loaf Anthology*. Hanover, NH: University Press of New England, 2000.
Costanzo, Gerald, and Jim Daniels, eds. *American Poetry: The Next Generation*. Pittsburgh, PA: Carnegie Mellon University Press, 2000.
Francia, Luis, and Eric Gamalinda, eds. *Flippin': Filipinos on America*. New York: Asian American Writers' Workshop, 1998.
Lim, Shirley Geok-lin, and Cheng Lok Chua, eds. *Tilting the Continent: An Anthology of Southeast Asian American Writing*. St. Paul, MN: New Rivers Press, 2000.
Oldpoetry.com. Online. www.oldpoetry.com/author/nick%20carbó.
Prufer, Kevin, ed. *The New Young American Poets: An Anthology*. Carbondale: Southern Illinois University Press, 2000.
"Rising from Your Book." *xPress(ed)*, Summer 2003. Online. www.xpressed.org/title.html.

OTHER WORKS

Returning a Borrowed Tongue: An Anthology of Contemporary Filipino and Filipino-American Poetry. Editor. Minneapolis, MN: Coffee House Press, 1996.
"Manuel Viray." *Heritage* 11.2 (Summer 1997): 29–30.
Babaylan: An Anthology of Filipina and Filipina-American Writers. Editor, with Eileen Tabios. San Francisco, CA: Aunt Lute Books, 2000.
"Sources." *The Literary Review* 44.1 (Fall 2000): 115.
Sweet Jesus: An Anthology of Poems about the Ultimate Icon. Editor, with Denise Duhamel. Los Angeles, CA: Anthology Press, 2002.

SELECTED RESOURCES FOR FURTHER REFERENCE

Cabusao, Jeffrey Arellano. "*Babaylan*" (book review). *Amerasia Journal* 27.2 (August 2001): 206–212.

"Nick Carbó 1964– ." *Contemporary Authors Online*. Gale Group, 2003. www.galegroup.com.

Trelles, Emma. "Tell-tale Hearts." *Miami Herald,* April 11, 2003. Online. www.miami.com/mld/streetmiami.

Alice Trupe

Lorna Dee Cervantes

(1954–)

Chicana/Mexican American, American Indian (Chumash)

Photo © Arte Público Press.

BIOGRAPHY

Lorna Dee Cervantes's cultural heritage is firmly rooted in the North and Central American landscape. The poet, educator, and activist was born on August 6, 1954, in the Mission District of San Francisco. Her mother's ancestors were of Mexican and Chumash Indian descent, while her paternal lineage follows the Tarascan Indians of Michoacán, Mexico. She and her brother, musician Steve Cervantes, grew up in a barrio of mostly Chicano and Mexican working-class families. Spanish was not allowed in Cervantes's childhood home, but she acquired the language by proximity in the barrio and through study later in life.

Cervantes's poems are economic and lyrical, profound and direct. Her style stems from her childhood: she became acquainted with Shakespeare and the Romantic poets and was writing her own poetry by the time she was eight years old. In her late teens she accompanied her brother in a *teatro* group that performed in the *Quinto Festival de los Teatros Chicanos* in Mexico City in 1974. At this event, she gave a bilingual performance of her poem "Barco de Refugiados/Refugee Ship" (*Emplumada,* pp. 40–41), which later appeared in Mexico City's *El Heraldo* and became her first major publication.

After graduating from high school in 1972, Cervantes dedicated her time to writing, editing, and publishing. In 1974, Cervantes taught herself how to operate a printing press, and soon she was editing and publishing the work of other ethnic writers in two journals that she founded—*Mango* and, later, *Red Dirt.* After establishing herself as a voice in Chicana literature, she returned to school in 1982 to study toward a B.A. in creative arts at San Jose State University. She then attended the University of California at Santa Cruz in 1990, where she received her Ph.D.

Even before the publication of her two collections—*Emplumada* in 1981 and *From the Cables of Genocide: Poems on Love and Hunger* in 1989—Cervantes's refined, well-crafted poetry began gaining national recognition with appearances in journals and anthologies. A significant aspect of her work is her ability to make insightful and important connections between art and the real-life circumstances of Chicanos/Chicanas in the United States. Such a synthesis of the personal and the political, combined with her consistently well-crafted aesthetic style, has marked her as one of the most important rising artists of the Chicano/Chicana movement and American literature.

The social and literary impact of Cervantes's work has been recognized by such honors as two fellowships from the National Endowment for the Arts (1978, 1993), a visiting scholar fellowship from the University of Houston's Mexican American studies program, and the prize of Outstanding Chicana Scholar by the National Association of Chicana Scholars (1993), among others. She uses the grants she receives for her writing to fund community projects throughout the western United States, and is working on more than one manuscript for future publication. She is currently director of the creative writing program at the University of Colorado, Boulder.

THEMES AND CONCERNS

Cervantes's poetry speaks for the disenfranchised, the dominated, and the abused. Her polemical style gives voice to American Indians, women, and even nature. Her compassionate awareness of cultural conflict stems from her experience as a Chicana contending with social prejudice. She believes that the distance between her two homelands is artificial—"that imaginary boundary" (Ikas, p. 30) between the southwestern United States and Mexico. She identifies herself as a *Chicana* writer, because the word emphasizes her American belonging and contrasts with the masculine word *Chicano*.

A central theme in Cervantes's writing is humankind's abuse of power over women and the land. However, she does not dwell on ideas of subjugation and destruction so much as she explores the possibility of regeneration and survival. In *Emplumada,* Cervantes often uses birds to evoke freedom through images of flight and a return to nature. The title is itself a Spanish pun on the power of flight and implies a means of resistance—*emplumado* means "feathered," and *plumada* "a flourish of the pen." In "Crow," the speaker is likened to the resourceful bird and learning to use tools and repair the home reflect the crow's crucial ingenuity, while in "This Morning" lively robins are given mystical authority over the land but are observed, warped and distant, through the captive speaker's windowpane. Poems such as "Starfish," "Spiders," and "Beetles" emphasize the importance of returning to nature by bestowing nobility and the power of healing to the land.

Many of the poems contain more direct social messages. In "Poem for the Young White Man Who Asked Me How I, an Intelligent, Well-Read Person Could Believe in the War Between the Races," the speaker argues that though dominant society can ignore race issues in their everyday lives, there are those *others* who are incessantly reminded of prejudice by the color of their skin.

The poem describes the idea of being American but excluded from the American ideal, a theme that surfaces again in the poem "Visions of Mexico While at a Writing Symposium in Port Townsend, Washington." Both poems depict the speaker questioning where she belongs by contrasting cultural images to illustrate contradictions that are part of her identity.

From the Cables of Genocide is a different kind of collection that focuses more intensely on the personal by exploring issues such as love, desire, and depression. The challenging nature of the book is a reflection of the complicated dynamics of human emotion and how dark forces often motivate those who hold power. The social causes introduced in *Emplumada* become the speakers' intimate problems in *From the Cables of Genocide*. "Litost" and "Macho" reflect this idea of the personal as part of history, and Cervantes herself states: "For my poetry and me, a differentiation between passionate and political writing does not exist, as both merge in my work" (Ikas, p. 43).

Cervantes's writing is an effort to revise the telling of history, because she believes that the accuracy of history depends on the inclusion of personal experience. As such, her poetry works to document her own life and thus make its themes part of a new American consciousness. Her form and style challenge stereotypes applied to Chicana artists, proving that political and social reform can be incited even while achieving artistic transcendence and engaging in intellectual discourse. Hers is a voice that will thrive both in American literature and as an advocate of the cultural outsider.

POETRY COLLECTIONS

Emplumada. Pittsburgh, PA: University of Pittsburgh Press, 1981.
From the Cables of Genocide: Poems on Love and Hunger. Houston, TX: Arte Público Press, 1989.

SELECTED ANTHOLOGIES WHERE POETRY APPEARS

de Hoyos, Angela, Bryce Milligan, and Mary Guerro Milligan, eds. *Daughters of the Fifth Sun: A Collection of Latina Fiction and Poetry.* New York: Riverhead Books, 1995.
Deming, Alison, ed. *Poetry of the American West: A Columbia Anthology.* New York: Columbia University Press, 1996.
Fernandez, Roberta, ed. *In Other Words: Literature by Latinas of the United States.* Houston, TX: Arte Público Press, 1994.
Flores, Lauro, ed. *The Floating Borderlands: Twenty-five Years of U.S. Hispanic Literature.* Seattle: University of Washington Press, 1998.
Gilbert, Sandra M., and Susan Gubar, eds. *The Norton Anthology of Literature by Women.* 2nd ed. New York: W. W. Norton, 1996.
Gillan, Maria M., and Jennifer Gillan, eds. *Unsettling America: Anthology of Contemporary American Ethnic Poetry.* New York: Penguin, 1994.
Gonzalez, Ray, ed. *Touching the Fire: Fifteen Poets of Today's Latino Renaissance.* New York: Doubleday, 1998.

Herrera-Sobek, Maria, ed. *Chicana Creativity & Criticism*. Albuquerque: University of New Mexico Press, 1996.

Howe, Florence, ed. *No More Masks! An Anthology of Twentieth-Century American Women Poets*. New York: Harper Perennial, 1993.

Kanellos, Nicolas, ed. *The Hispanic Literary Companion*. Detroit, MI: Visible Ink Press, 1997.

Madison, D. Soyini, ed. *The Woman That I Am: The Literature and Culture of Contemporary Women of Color*. New York: St. Martin's, 1995.

McKenna, Teresa, ed. *Migrant Song: Politics and Process in Contemporary Chicano Literature*. Austin: University of Texas Press, 1997.

Ochester, Ed, and Peter Oresick, eds. *The Pittsburgh Book of Contemporary American Poetry*. Pittsburgh, PA: University of Pittsburgh Press, 1992.

Oresick, Peter, and Nicholas Coles, eds. *Working Classics: Poems on Industrial Life*. Chicago: University of Illinois Press, 1990.

Phillips, J. J., Ishmael Reed, and Gundar Strads, eds. *The Before Columbus Foundation Poetry Anthology*. New York: W. W. Norton, 1992.

Rebolledo, Tey D., and Eliana S. Rivero, eds. *Infinite Divisions: An Anthology of Chicana Literature*. Tucson: University of Arizona Press, 1992.

SELECTED RESOURCES FOR FURTHER REFERENCE

Candelaria, Cordelia. *Chicano Poetry: A Critical Introduction*. Westport, CT: Greenwood Press, 1986.

Ikas, Karin Rosa. *Chicana Ways: Conversations with Ten Chicana Writers*. Reno: University of Nevada Press, 2002.

Madsen, Deborah L. *Understanding Contemporary Chicana Literature*. Columbia: University of South Carolina Press, 2000.

Sánchez, Marta. *Contemporary Chicana Poetry: A Critical Approach to an Emerging Literature*. Berkeley: University of California Press, 1985.

Seator, Lynette. "*Emplumada:* Chicana Rites-of-Passage." *MELUS: The Journal of the Society for the Study of the Multi-Ethnic Literature of the United States* 11.1 (Summer 1984): 23–38.

Roy Pérez

Diana Chang

(1934–)

Chinese American

BIOGRAPHY

Diana Chang, poet, novelist, short story writer, and painter, was born in New York City in 1934 to a Chinese father and Eurasian mother. As an infant, Chang moved to China, where she spent her early years in Beijing and Shanghai before the family returned to New York in the wake of the Communist Revolution. Chang attended Barnard College, graduating with a B.A. in 1955.

Chang's father, an architect, wrote poetry in English, and her mother took piano lessons and played Western classical music in their home. The earliest ambition that Chang recalls was to be a ballet dancer. Yet writing would bring her success at a young age. Three of her poems were published in *Poetry* magazine while she was still an undergraduate, and her first novel, *Frontiers of Love* (1956), brought her critical acclaim. She published five more novels before her first volume of poetry, *The Horizon Is Definitely Speaking* (1982), which was followed by *What Matisse Is After* (1984) and *Earth, Water, Light: Landscape Poems Celebrating the East End of Long Island* (1991). Chang has received a National Endowment for the Arts grant, and her poems have appeared in *Chelsea, New York Quarterly, The Nation, American Scholar,* and *Montserrat Review,* and other periodicals.

Chang worked as an editor after graduating from college, but she found it challenging to write while working on other people's manuscripts, so she quit her job "with $200 in the bank" (Hamalian, p. 42) and did some freelance copyediting, at one point supplementing her writing income by working for a telephone answering service from 11:00 P.M. to 9:00 A.M. two nights a week. She also began teaching creative writing at Barnard College in New York City. Invited to teach while novelist and critic Elizabeth Hardwick took a year off, Chang found she enjoyed teaching and continued as an adjunct instructor at Barnard. It was her teaching that led her to practicing the short story form. Chang has served as the editor of *The American Pen,* a journal published by the international writers' association PEN.

Chang is perhaps better known as a writer of fiction than as a poet. *Frontiers of Love* was well received upon its publication in the mid-1950s, when little fiction by Chinese Americans was being published. In her introduction to the reissued edition (1994), Shirley Geok-lin Lim notes that this "formidable first novel . . . is one of the earliest transgressors of canonical frontiers" because it raised questions about "categories of identity—national, racial, class, and gender" when such questions were being raised by few and heard by even fewer Americans, and hence the novel's "themes, characters, actions, and stylistic textures appear strikingly contemporary" (p. v).

While Chang has drawn upon her Chinese American background in two of her novels and sometimes refers to the Chinese appearance of her body in poems, she has adopted a range of voices in both fiction and poetry. "Being a Chinese-American woman is an elusive identity and a confusing one, even to myself. I feel that I am a minority person, but as a writer I know that sometimes I don't write 'ethnic' work, that often my imagination takes me to other situations, themes and voices," she stated in a 1995 interview with Leo Hamalian (p. 30). In the introduction to her poems in the anthology *Chinese American Poetry*, Chang notes that, "I feel I'm an American writer whose background is mostly Chinese" (quoted in Wang and Zhao, p. 18). She explained further in her interview with Hamalian, "There are many kinds of Chinese-Americans" (p. 30).

A painter who works in oils, pastels, acrylics, and watercolors, Chang has exhibited in both solo and group shows. Her 1974 novel *Eye to Eye* features a white, male visual artist as protagonist. Chang's dual identity as artist and writer is perhaps as significant for her writing as is her ethnic identity as a Chinese American, and her interest in the visual and the world of the arts is acknowledged in the titles of her second and third collections of poems, *What Matisse Is After* and *Earth, Water, Light: Landscape Poems Celebrating the East End of Long Island*.

THEMES AND CONCERNS

Important themes in Diana Chang's poems are the natural landscape, the visual arts, perception, and creativity in general. Critics have noted her subtlety, her elusiveness, and her understatement. Contrasting her concerns in her fiction with those in her poems, Chang has said, "While my main concerns in my novels seem to be in character, emotion and being, in my poetry I often write of the land, the ocean, the moon" (quoted in Bruchac, p. 18). The title poem of *The Horizon Is Definitely Speaking*, for example, describes the movement of clouds and of geese against the stationary hill and the fragmented reflection of water at the speaker's feet.

Her own sense of her poetry is that it is "imagistic" (quoted in Wang and Zhao, p. 18), concerned with the concrete, and she has noted that her narrative impulse is expressed in her fiction rather than her poetry. Thus, Chang addresses her concrete, physical being as a Chinese American in several poems, such as "An Appearance of Being Chinese," "Second Nature," and the frequently anthologized "Saying Yes," in which the speaker is asked by an unnamed questioner whether or not she is Chinese, thus bringing out in dialogue the duality of her identity. The speaker then reflects on her sense of home, establishing her American identity as weighing equally with her Chineseness.

Other poems, like "The Personality of Chairs," focus on everyday objects. Chairs are highly suggestive and have fascinated Chang, she has said, because of "their innate characteristic of waiting, waiting to be filled" (Hamalian, p. 40). An earlier poem, "Once and Future," noted the Chinese custom of providing chairs for ancestral ghosts.

Chang has identified Emily Dickinson as an early influence on her poetry, and Chang's ability to draw complex metaphorical meaning from simple images, rendered in spare, quiet language, seems to confirm this. The influence of her painting is suggested both in subject matter (the naming of painters in a number of poems) and in her emphasis on subtleties of geometric shapes and light. The importance of line, and its ability to define spaces, is emphasized in her poem "What Matisse Is After." Chang also notes the perspective and perception of the viewer in many of her poems.

POETRY COLLECTIONS

The Horizon Is Definitely Speaking. Port Jefferson, NY: Backstreet Editions, 1982.
What Matisse Is After. New York: Contact II, 1984.
Earth, Water, Light: Landscape Poems Celebrating the East End of Long Island. New York: Birnham Wood Graphics, 1991.

SELECTED ANTHOLOGIES WHERE POETRY APPEARS

Bruchac, Joseph, ed. *Breaking Silence: An Anthology of Contemporary Asian American Poets.* Greenfield Center, NY: Greenfield Review Press, 1983.
Chang, Julia, ed. *Quiet Fire: A Historical Anthology of Asian American Poetry, 1892–1970.* Philadelphia: Temple University Press, 1998.
Hurt, James, ed. *Literature: A Contemporary Introduction.* New York: Prentice-Hall, 1994.
Lim, Shirley Geok-lin, Mayumi Tsutakawa, and Margarita Donnelly, eds. *The Forbidden Stitch: An Asian American Women's Anthology.* Corvallis, OR: Calyx Books, 1989.
Wang, L. Ling-chi, and Henry Yiheng Zhao, eds. *Chinese American Poetry: An Anthology.* Santa Barbara, CA: Asian American Voices. Dist. Seattle: University of Washington Press, 1991.

SELECTED FICTION

The Frontiers of Love. 1956. Reissue with introduction by Shirley Geok-lin Lim. Seattle: University of Washington Press, 1994.
A Woman of Thirty. New York: Random House, 1959.

A Passion for Life. New York: Random House, 1961.
The Only Game in Town. New York: Signet, 1963.
Eye to Eye. New York: Harper & Row, 1974.
A Perfect Love. New York: Jove Books/Harcourt Brace Jovanovich, 1978.

SELECTED RESOURCES FOR FURTHER REFERENCE

Davidson, Cathy N., Linda Wagner-Martin, et al., eds. *The Oxford Companion to Women's Writing in the United States.* New York: Oxford University Press, 1995.

"Diana Chang." *Eurasian American Literature.* Online. www.lone-crow.com/eurasianlit.

Fink, Thomas. "*Chang's 'Plunging into View.*'" *The Explicator* 55 (March 1997): 175.

Fisher, Dexter, ed. *The Third Woman: Minority Women Writers of the United States.* Boston, MA: Houghton Mifflin, 1980.

Grice, Helena. *Negotiating Identities: An Introduction to Asian American Women's Writing.* Manchester: Manchester University Press, 2002.

Hamalian, Leo. "A MELUS Interview: Diana Chang (Maskers and Tricksters)." *MELUS: The Journal of the Society for the Study of the Multi-Ethnic Literature of the United States* 20.4 (Winter 1995): 29–43.

Lim, Shirley Geok-lin. Introduction to *The Frontiers of Love,* by Diana Chang. Seattle: University of Washington Press, 1994.

Ling, Amy. "Writer in the Hyphenated Condition: Diana Chang." *MELUS: The Journal of the Society for the Study of the Multi-Ethnic Literature of the United States* 7.4 (Winter 1980): 69–83.

Trudeau, Lawrence J. "Diana Chang." In *Asian American Literature: Reviews and Criticism of Works by American Writers of Asian Descent.* Detroit, MI: Gale, 1999, 17–32.

Alice Trupe

Marilyn Chin

(1955–)

Chinese American

BIOGRAPHY

Marilyn Chin, a poet and translator, was born in Hong Kong in 1955 but grew up in Portland, Oregon. Her immigration was marked by her father's changing her name from Mei Ling to Marilyn. She earned a B.A. in Chinese literature from the Univer-

Photo by Niki Berg, courtesy of Marilyn Chin and Milkweed Editions.

sity of Massachusetts, Amherst, in 1977, and an M.F.A. from the University of Iowa in 1981. She studied classical Chinese literature further in Taiwan and at Stanford University as a Stegner Fellow.

Chin's career has revolved around editing, translating Chinese poetry, and teaching creative writing as well as writing poetry. In the late 1970s and early 1980s, Chin translated, edited, and taught in the international writing program at the University of Iowa. Major translating projects, in which she acted as cotranslator, include Gozo Yoshimasu's poems, *Devil's Wind: A Thousand Steps or More* (1980), and *The Selected Poems of Ai Qing* (1982).

Dwarf Bamboo (1987), Chin's first book of poems, was nominated for the Bay Area Book Reviewers Award. She won the PEN Josephine Miles Award for her second volume of poems, *The Phoenix Gone, the Terrace Empty* (1994). Her third volume, *Rhapsody in Plain Yellow* (2002), was also extremely well received. Among Chin's many awards are a Mary Roberts Rinehart Award, two National Endowment for the Arts grants, several Pushcart Prizes, inclusion in *Best American Poetry 1996,* and a Lannan Foundation residency fellowship.

Chin has coedited an anthology of Asian American writing with fellow University of Iowa graduate David Wong Louie. A short story, "Moon," appeared in *Charlie Chan Is Dead: An Anthology of Contemporary Asian American Fiction* (1993), and recently she has focused on a volume of short stories, not yet published. Her play *The Love Palace* (2002) is being produced by the Core Assembly.

Chin teaches in San Diego State University's M.F.A. program and has taught in a number of other creative writing programs as a visiting professor or summer faculty member. Among them are the National Donghwa University,

Taiwan; the University of Hawaii; the University of Technology, Sydney, Australia; and the University of Iowa's Writers' Workshop.

THEMES AND CONCERNS

Marilyn Chin's work has focused on issues of personal and ethnic identity, specifically Asian American acculturation, and she explores the complex balance and tensions among Chinese, Chinese American, and Asian American elements of her identity. The content of many of her poems attests to her concern with Chinese Americans' assimilation. For example, her poem "How I Got That Name," which explains her name change from Mei Ling to Marilyn as a response to Marilyn Monroe's status as a cultural icon, is subtitled "An Essay on Assimilation." Foregrounding her own experience in the "I" of her poems, she explores Chinese American experience rather than focusing solely on personal feelings. Adrienne McCormick calls such poems "feminist acts of theorizing," while Zhou Xiaojing attributes much of the ironic, mocking tone of her voice to Daoist humor (p. 73).

Concerned not to lose her rich cultural heritage and Chinese language, Chin has formally studied classical and contemporary Chinese writings and Chinese history. This knowledge brings a unique blending of Eastern and Western traditions, the latter at the heart of her American education, to her own poetic sense, which she describes as experimental. In "What Is American about American Poetry?" Chin says, "My poetry both laments and celebrates my 'hyphenated' identity. I believe that my work is very ambitious in thematic scope and form and is both a delicate and apocalyptic melding of east and west. Sometimes this may mean breeding hybrid forms."

Another important theme is the place of women within a patriarchy. For example, the complex poem "The Phoenix Gone, The Terrace Empty" links images of women's status in the past, typified by their bound feet, with her parents' and grandparents' experiences and her own identity in America. Her third volume, *Rhapsody in Plain Yellow,* is dedicated to her mother, who died in 1994, and her grandmother, who died in 1996.

Critics focus the passion and intensity of Chin's voice as well as the devotion to craft that marks her work. Diction, rhythm, and poetic form absorb her attention. Chin attests to these concerns in the headnote to her poems in Wang and Zhao's 1991 anthology, *Chinese American Poetry:*

> A poet, certainly, has her work cut out for her. She may spend days contemplating on the next sentence, or on the next image, or on something as abstract or ambitious as an idea. . . . I believe that the most formidable challenge is that presented by the art itself. . . . My eternal struggle as a poet is to perfect my craft, to strive for excellence, to "learn my trade." (p. 30)

She pays close attention to the theme and the cohesiveness of each book of poems she publishes, as well:

> I take the "integrity" of "the book" very seriously. . . . It usually takes me five–six years to complete a book of poems, because I am very finicky about constructing a holistic experience for the reader. Once again, each book has its own individual personality and yearns to be presented in its own particular way that would set itself apart from the others. (quoted in "What Imagination Calls For")

The titles of her books convey complex allusive meanings. *Dwarf Bamboo,* for example, alludes to Tang Dynasty poet Po Chu-yi's poem "Planting Bamboo" and refers the young poet herself, as well as Chinese American literary history, still young and small (Xiaojing, p. 73).

Referring to Chin's most recent volume, *Rhapsody in Plain Yellow* (2002), Adrienne Rich writes that Chin's poems "are unmistakable evidence of the universal reach of the particular—when the art is powerful, uncompromised, and unerring as hers" (quoted in "WSUI").

POETRY COLLECTIONS

Dwarf Bamboo. Greenfield Center, NY: Greenfield Review Press, 1987.
The Phoenix Gone, the Terrace Empty. Minneapolis, MN: Milkweed Editions, 1994.
Rhapsody in Plain Yellow: Poems. New York: W. W. Norton, 2002.

SELECTED ADDITIONAL WORKS

Devil's Wind: A Thousand Steps or More. By Gozo Yoshimasu. Translator, with the author. Rochester, MI: Oakland University Press, 1980.
Selected Poems of Ai Qing. Ed. Eugene Eoyang. Translator, with Eugene Eoyang and Peng Wenlan. Bloomington: Indiana University Press, 1982.
Writing from the World, II. Editor. Iowa City: University of Iowa Press, 1985.
Dissident Song: A Contemporary Asian American Anthology. Editor, with David Wong Louie Santa Cruz, CA: Quarry West, 1991.
"Moon." In *Charlie Chan Is Dead: An Anthology of Contemporary Asian American Fiction.* Ed. Jessica Hagedorn. New York: Penguin, 1993, 87–90.
"Translating Self: Stealing from Wang Wei, Kowtowing to Hughes, Hooking Up with Keats, Undone by Donne." In *After Confession: Poetry as Autobiography.* Ed. Kate Sontag and David Graham. St. Paul, MN: Graywolf Press, 2001, 305–316.
"What Is American about American Poetry?" *Poetry Society of America.* Online. www.poetrysociety.org/chin.html.

SELECTED ANTHOLOGIES WHERE POETRY APPEARS

Axel, Brett, ed. *Will Work for Peace: New Political Poems.* Trenton, NJ: Zeropanik Press, 1999.

Belieu, Erin, and Susan Aizenberg, eds. *The Columbia Anthology of Women's Poetry.* New York: Columbia University Press, 2000.

Bruchac, Joseph, ed. *Breaking Silence: An Anthology of Contemporary Asian American Poets.* Greenfield Center, NY: Greenfield Review Press, 1983.

Hongo, Garrett, ed. *The Open Boat: Poems from Asian America.* New York: Doubleday/ Anchor, 1993.

Lim, Shirley Geok-lin, Mayumi Tsutakawa, and Margarita Donnelly, eds. *The Forbidden Stitch: An Asian American Women's Anthology.* Corvallis, OR: Calyx, 1989.

Ray, David, ed. *Two Hundred Contemporary Poets.* Athens, OH: Swallow Press, 1981.

Rich, Adrienne, ed. *The Best American Poetry 1996.* New York: Scribner's, 1996.

Wang, L. Ling-chi, and Henry Yihang Zhao, eds. *Chinese American Poetry: An Anthology.* Santa Barbara, CA: Asian American Voices, 1991.

Wong, Shawn, ed. *Asian American Literature: A Brief Introduction and Anthology.* New York: HarperCollins, 1996.

SELECTED RESOURCES FOR FURTHER REFERENCE

Hong, Yunah, dir. *Between the Lines: Asian American Women's Poetry.* (video-recording)

Lim, Shirley Geok-lin, and Amy Ling, eds. *Reading the Literatures of Asian America.* Philadelphia: Temple University Press, 1992.

"Marilyn Chin." Indiana University Writers' Conference, February 10, 2003. Online. www.indiana.edu/~writecon/chin.html.

McCormick, Adrienne. "'Being Without': Marilyn Chin's Poems as Feminist Acts of Theorizing." *Hitting Critical Mass* 6.2 (Spring 2000). Reprinted at *Modern American Poetry.* Online. www.english.uiuc.edu/maps/poets/a_f/chin/mccormick.htm.

Moyers, Bill. *The Language of Life: A Festival of Poets.* New York: Doubleday, 1995.

Shelton, Pamela L., ed. *Contemporary Women Poets.* Detroit, MI: St. James Press, 1998.

Slowik, Mary. "Beyond Lot's Wife: The Immigration Poems of Marilyn Chin, Garrett Hongo, Li-Young Lee, and David Mura." *MELUS: The Journal of the Society for the Study of the Multi-Ethnic Literature of the United States* 25.3–4 (Fall–Winter 2000): 221–231.

Tabios, Eileen. *Black Lightning: Poetry-in-Progress.* New York: Asian American Writers' Workshop, 1998, 280–312.

"What Imagination Calls For." *The DOJ, Drexel Online Journal.* www.drexel.edu/doj/artsands/marilynchin_interview.asp.

"WSUI 'Live from Prairie Lights' Series Adds Final Summer Reading." University of Iowa News Release, July 16, 2003. Online. www.uiowa.edu/~ournews/2003/july/071603prairie-lights.html.

Xiaojing, Zhou. "Marilyn Mei Ling Chin (1955–)." In *Asian American Poets: A Bio-Bibliographical Critical Sourcebook.* Ed. Guiyou Huang. Westport, CT: Greenwood Press, 2002, 71–82.

Alice Trupe

Sandra Cisneros

(1954–)

Mexican American

Photo by AP/Wide World Photos.

BIOGRAPHY

Born in Chicago's South Side to a working-class Mexican father and Chicana mother as the only daughter among six brothers, Sandra Cisneros had to break free from the traditional female role that her family and culture imposed on her. During her childhood her brothers attempted to control her and she often felt that she had "seven fathers." The attitudes of the men in her family forced Cisneros to spend time alone, and in Miriam-Goldberg's book-length study of her poetry, she credits this period in her life as one that formed her future: "that aloneness, that loneliness was good for a would-be writer—it allowed me time to think and think, to imagine, to read and prepare myself" (p. 24).

As an adolescent she wrote poetry and short stories, but it was not until after she graduated from Loyola University of Chicago with a B.A. in English in 1976 that she found her literary voice. Cisneros received a scholarship to attend a prestigious creative writing program, the University of Iowa Writers' Workshop; there she realized that her experiences as a Chicana woman were vastly different from those of her wealthy white American classmates. She then decided to write about the cultural and social concerns that emerged from growing up Latina in Chicago, issues such as alienation, poverty, cultural suppression, identity, gender ideology, and sexuality.

After completing the workshop, Cisneros returned to Chicago and started teaching at the Latino Youth Alternative High School. She began to write more about her experiences and those of her students, who also faced poverty and hopelessness. During this time she began reading her poetry in local coffeehouses, which led to an opportunity with the Chicago Transit Authority's new poetry project. Her poetry was chosen by the Poetry Society of America to be featured on posters in the buses and subways throughout the city. This recognition led to the publishing of her first book by the small Latino company Mango Publications. *Bad Boys,* published in 1980, is one in a series of Chicano chapbooks; it contains seven poems that detail the aspects of life in the barrio.

Cisneros then began working as a college recruiter and counselor for minority students at Loyola University of Chicago; this experience propelled her to write her most well-known work of fiction, a volume of vignettes titled *The House of Mango Street* (1984). In 1987 she published a collection of sixty poems that dealt with the conflicting issues of exploring her sexual identity and her Catholic upbringing, titled *My Wicked, Wicked Ways*. In 1994 Cisneros followed that collection of poetry with another volume titled *Loose Woman*, for which she won the Mountains & Plains Booksellers Association's 1995 Regional Book Award in the category of adult poetry. She has published two other novels and a children's book, all of which have been well received by both the literary world and mainstream audiences.

Cisneros has been widely recognized for her unique writing style and has received two National Endowment for the Arts fellowships for fiction and poetry (1982 and 1988) and the Paisano Dobie fellowship in 1986. She was awarded the American Book Award from the Before Columbus Foundation in 1985 for *The House on Mango Street* and won the Lannan Foundation Literary Award in 1991. In 1995 she received a prestigious fellowship from the MacArthur Foundation, a highly coveted grant given in the fields of arts and sciences to people of remarkable talent. The $225,000 grant was awarded to Cisneros with "no strings attached" for her creative contributions, not for a specific project. Other awards have included an honorary Doctor of Letters from the State University of New York at Purchase in 1993, and an honorary Doctor of Humane Letters from Loyola University in 2002. During her writing career she has also served as an artist in residence at the Foundation Michael Karolyi in Vence, France, and as a literature director for the Guadalupe Cultural Arts Center in San Antonio, Texas. She has also been a guest professor at a variety of universities. Cisneros is a member of PEN (a major association of writers, whose acronym stands for "Poets, Playwrights, Essayists, Editors, and Novelists") and Mujeres por la Paz, a women's peace group. She currently resides in San Antonio, Texas, where she has lived on and off for the past fifteen years.

THEMES AND CONCERNS

Sandra Cisneros has defined poetry as "the art of telling the truth" (Miriam-Goldberg, p. 95), and she embodies that definition with her honest and humorous way of writing about her unique life experiences as a Chicana woman. The poems in *My Wicked, Wicked Ways* are a journey from her role as the "bad girl" in her conservative family to her discovery of independence, sex, and love as an adult woman. Her voice is refreshingly sassy and playful as she seamlessly switches her tone from innocent to seductive, sometimes within the same poem. This volume of her poetry reveals a yearning for freedom from her family's ideals, from a patriarchal culture that encourages male domination, and from her own sexual guilt as a result of her strict upbringing. She begins her journey with poems such as "Sir James Southside" and "Joe," which provide realistic portrayals of the people in the barrio and are rife with social commentary without losing the whimsicality and charisma of Cisneros's voice. Her journey takes her throughout Europe as she chronicles the adulterous escapades that take her from a "bad girl" to a defiant woman.

In her third collection of poetry, *Loose Woman,* Cisneros writes from the perspective of a woman who is exerting her independence and has found the internal freedom that she once longed for. In "You Bring Out the Mexican in Me" she reclaims the stereotypes and labels imposed upon her for being a Mexican American woman by reappropriating them and proudly displaying them in her poetry to reveal her raw sexuality and recklessness. "The Heart Rounds up the Usual Suspects" deals with the fear of a single woman who must grapple with either being alone or settling for whatever man is around. Cisneros's use of saucy language and sharp-tongued humor offsets the serious issues at the heart of her poetry. Her narrative poems read more like short stories because Cisneros forgoes the structural devices of traditional poetry to convey her livelier and spirited tone. By focusing on her heritage and life experience, Cisneros has articulated a distinct, audacious, and accessible voice drawing an extensive and worldwide audience to her poetry and fiction.

POETRY COLLECTIONS

Bad Boys. San Jose, CA: Mango, 1980.
My Wicked, Wicked Ways. Bloomington, IL: Third Woman Press, 1987.
Loose Woman. New York: Alfred A. Knopf, 1994.

SELECTED ANTHOLOGIES WHERE POETRY APPEARS

Aguero, Kathleen, and Marie Harris, eds. *An Ear to the Ground: An Anthology of Contemporary American Poets.* Athens: University of Georgia Press, 1989.
Cumpian, Carlos, ed. *Emergency Tacos: Seven Poets Con Picante.* Chicago, IL: March/ABRAZO Press, 1989.
Espada, Martín, ed. *El Coro: A Chorus of Latino and Latina Poetry.* Amherst: University of Massachusetts Press, 1997.
Milligan, Bryce, et al., eds. *Daughters of the Fifth Sun: A Collection of Latina Fiction and Poetry.* New York: Riverhead Books, 1995.
———. *¡Floricanto Sí! A Collection of Latina Poetry.* New York: Penguin/Putnam, 1998.
Tatum, Charles M., ed. *Mexican American Literature.* Orlando, FL: Harcourt Brace Jovanovich, 1990.

SELECTED FICTION AND NONFICTION

The House on Mango Street. New York: Random House, 1984.
Women Hollering Creek and Other Stories. New York: Random House, 1991.

Hairs: Pelitos. New York: Alfred A. Knopf, 1994.
"Only Daughter." In *Máscaras.* Ed. Lucha Corpi. Berkeley, CA: Third Woman Press, 1997, 120–123.
Caramelo. New York: Alfred A. Knopf, 2002.

SELECTED RESOURCES FOR FURTHER REFERENCE

Kevane, Bridget, and Juanita Heredia. "A Home in the Heart." In *Latina Self-Portraits: Interviews with Contemporary Women Writers.* Ed. Bridget Kevane and Juanita Heredia. Albuquerque: University of New Mexico Press, 2000, 45–58.
McCraken, Ellen. "Sandra Cisneros' *The House on Mango Street:* Community-Oriented Introspection and the Demystification of Patriarchal Violence." In *Breaking Boundaries: Latina Writings and Critical Readings.* Ed. Asuncion Horno-Delgado and Eliana Ortega. Amherst: University of Massachusetts Press, 1989.
Miriam-Goldberg, Caryn. *Sandra Cisneros: Latina Writer and Activist.* Springfield, NJ: Enslow, 1998.
Telgen, Diane, and Jim Kamp, eds. *Latinas! Women of Achievement.* Detroit, MI: Visible Ink Press, 1996.

Tatiana Bido

Lucille Clifton

(1936–)

African American

Photo by AP/Wide World Photos.

BIOGRAPHY

Award-winning African American poet Lucille Clifton has been described as a modest poet who does not much care for the limelight. While she has been a prolific and critically acclaimed poet for over twenty years, it does seem true that Clifton has not gained the public presence of other African American poets of her stature. Perhaps this is because Clifton understands herself as a political poet who restores the missing or lost parts of American history, which is not always a popular undertaking. She states that her early writings are part of a movement that "brought American Literature a long missing part of itself" (Rowell, p. 67).

Currently a Distinguished Professor of Humanities at St. Mary's College of Maryland, Thelma Lucille Sayles was born in Depew, New York, on June 27, 1936, and grew up with a strong love of the South, from which her family originated. She was raised with two half sisters and a brother, and Clifton's parents, Samuel and Thelma Moore Sayles, instilled in her a love for books and learning, which she capitalized on by entering college early, at age sixteen. She attended Howard University in Washington, DC, and Fredonia State Teachers College, but decided she wanted to write before graduating from either institution. However, her college years were anything but fruitless. While at Howard she associated with intellectuals such as Sterling Brown, LeRoi Jones (Amiri Baraka), A. B. Spellman, and Chloe Wofford (now Toni Morrison), the latter of whom edited Clifton's writing for Random House. She also met her future husband, Fred Clifton, while at Howard.

Clifton's first collection of poems, *Good Times* (1969), was heralded as one of the best books of the year by the *New York Times,* and accolades for her writing have not waned since then. Of the ten collections of poetry she has published to date, *Two-Headed Woman* (1980) and *Good Woman: Poems and a Memoir, 1969–1980* (1987) were both nominated for Pulitzer Prizes, while *Two-Headed Woman* went on to win the University of Massachusetts Press

Juniper Prize. Her collection *The Terrible Stories* (1995) was nominated for the National Book Award, and in 2000 *Blessing the Boats: New and Selected Poems 1988–2000* won the prestigious award. Additionally, Clifton has won a Lannan Literary Award, the YM-YWHA Poetry Center Discovery Award, the Shelley Memorial Award, and two fellowships from the National Endowment for Arts. She was elected chancellor of the Academy of American Poets and is a past Poet Laureate for the state of Maryland.

Clifton is also a well-known author of children's stories and has published nineteen such books. She resides in Columbia, Maryland, and is the mother of six children.

THEMES AND CONCERNS

Clifton's poems are suffused with a need to know about the lives, feelings, and histories of African ancestors who were brought to America. Thus the subject of slavery is addressed directly and intensely. Issues of racism, human suffering, endurance, and survival are also themes and concerns in her work.

Clifton's love for family is very strong. Her memoir, *Generations,* delves into and delineates her family roots from her father's side—the Sayles family. Her connectedness to African roots is established through the family matriarch, Mammy Ca'line (Clifton's great-grandmother, Caroline Donald), who comes from Dahomey, a West African country that is now known as Benin and was famous for the Amazon armies that resisted French colonialism. Another female foremother, Lucille, is described as the first black woman to be legally hanged in Virginia for killing the white man who fathered her son. These portraits also introduce the themes of black women and their resolve to fight against and survive the injustice of a racist and sexist world. These are strong and determined women who inspire Clifton in her own life and work today.

Clifton's interest in memorializing and invoking the lives of African ancestors, known and unknown, is evident in the poem "at the cemetery." Clifton shows us a picture of the slaves' suffering and their dignified resolve to live and survive in horrific conditions. Her remembrances present them as human beings whose lives counted, and she mourns the unknown slaves even as her writing expresses love toward those forgotten people. Her use of imagination confers dignity on a humiliated and despised group in America. Clifton also hints at the impossibility of ever erasing the memory of black slaves when she boldly states that even the tools they used stand as silent witnesses to their lives. Hope is thereby infused into this poem: hope that these slaves will no longer be forgotten, which the act of writing about them ensures.

Political critiques of African Americans are also implicit in Clifton's poetry. Of particular concern to her are the ways in which black people treat each other. In "move," from *The Book of Light* (which is based on actual events in Philadelphia in 1985), Clifton remembers an obscure group of blacks who lived their lives in an attempt to epitomize and celebrate their African roots.

Contradictions and irony abound in the situation where a black mayor orders the destruction of an African-oriented group. Clifton indicates in "move" that this is the highest form of betrayal—a betrayal of Africa and, by implication, the mayor's own self. These paradoxes are intensified by the fact that black neighbors complain about this Afro-based group because they find its presence disturbing. The poem exposes the community's resistance to difference even when the group members basically mind their own business. The poem also hints at a brainwashed/whitewashed black community who not only want to distance themselves from everything African but to obliterate their African identity as well. The poem notes that the twofold tragedy of these events: the group members lose their lives and the community loses its self-identity, cultural pride, and cohesiveness. The issue of identity and black people's pressure to conform to whiteness is manifest.

Throughout all of Clifton's work, her commitment to self-discovery and expression, ethnic/racial pride, the narration of personal and public histories, and the continuing development of race and gender consciousness are evident and central to her poetic aesthetic.

POETRY COLLECTIONS

Good Times. New York: Random House, 1969.
Good News about the Earth. New York: Random House, 1972.
An Ordinary Woman. New York: Random House, 1974.
Two-Headed Woman. Amherst: University of Massachusetts Press, 1980.
Good Woman: Poems and a Memoir, 1969–1980. Brockport, NY: BOA Editions, 1987.
Next: New Poems. Brockport, NY: BOA Editions, 1987.
Ten Oxherding Pictures. Santa Cruz, CA: Moving Parts Press, 1988.
Quilting: Poems 1987–1990. Brockport, NY: BOA Editions, 1991.
The Book of Light. Port Townsend, WA: Copper Canyon Press, 1993.
The Terrible Stories. Berkeley, CA: Small Press Distribution, 1995.
Blessing the Boats: New and Selected Poems 1988–2000. Brockport, NY: BOA Editions, 2000.

SELECTED ANTHOLOGIES WHERE POETRY APPEARS

Berg, Stephen, David Bonanno, and Arthur Vogelsang, eds. *The Body Electric: America's Best Poetry from the American Poetry Review.* New York: W. W. Norton, 2000.
Collins, Billy, ed. *Poetry 180: A Turning Back to Poetry.* New York: Random House, 2003.
Gilbert, Sandra M., and Susan Gubar, eds. *The Norton Anthology: Literature by Women.* New York: W. W. Norton, 1996.
Harper, Michael, and Anthony Walton, eds. *Every Shut Eye Ain't Asleep: An Anthology of Poetry by African Americans Since 1945.* New York: Little, Brown, 1994.
Hill, Patricia Liggins. *Call & Response: The Riverside Anthology of the African American Literary Tradition.* Boston: Houghton Mifflin, 1998.

Quashie, Kevin, R. Joyce Lausch, and Keith D. Miller. *New Bones: Contemporary Black Writers in America*. Upper Saddle River, NJ: Prentice Hall, 2001.

SELECTED ADDITIONAL FICTION, NONFICTION, AND CHILDREN'S LITERATURE

Everett Anderson's Christmas Coming. New York: Holt, Rinehart, and Winston, 1971.
All Us Come Cross the Water. New York: Henry Holt, 1973.
Don't You Remember. New York: E. P. Dutton, 1973.
Good, Says Jerome. New York: E. P. Dutton, 1973.
All of Us Are All of Us. Detroit, MI: Broadside Press, 1974.
My Brother Fine with Me. New York: Henry Holt, 1975.
Generations: A Memoir. New York: Random House, 1976.
Amifika. New York: E. P. Dutton, 1978.
Everett Anderson's Nine Month Long. New York: Henry Holt, 1978.
The Lucky Stone. New York: Delacorte Press, 1979.
My Friend Jacob. New York: E. P. Dutton, 1980.
Sonora Beautiful. New York: E. P. Dutton, 1981.
Everett Anderson's Goodbye. New York: Holt, Rinehart, and Winston, 1983.
Some of the Days of Everett Anderson. New York: Henry Holt, 1987.
Everett Anderson's Christmas Coming. New York: Henry Holt, 1991.
The Boy Who Didn't Believe in Spring. New York: E. P. Dutton, 1992.
Everett Anderson's Year. New York: Henry Holt, 1992.
One of the Problems of Everett Anderson. New York: Henry Holt, 2001.
The Times They Used to Be. New York: Yearling, 2002.

SELECTED RESOURCES FOR FURTHER REFERENCE

Davis, Elsa. "Lucille Clifton and Sonia Sanchez: A Conversation." *Callaloo* 25.4 (2002): 1038–1074.
Glaser, Michael S. "I'd Like Not to Be a Stranger in the World: A Conversation/ Interview with Lucille Clifton." *Antioch Review* 58.3 (2000): 310–328.
Holladay, Hilary. "Black Names in White Space: Lucille Clifton's South." *Southern Literary Journal* 34.2 (2002): 120–133.
Ostriker, Alicia. "Kin and Kin: The Poetry of Lucille Clifton." *American Poetry Review* 22.6 (November–December 1993): 41–48.
Rowell, Charles H. "An Interview with Lucille Clifton." *Callaloo* 2.1 (1999): 56–72.
Somers-Willet, Susan B. "A Music in Language: A Conversation with Lucille Clifton." *American Voice* 49 (Summer 1999): 73–92.
Wall, Cheryl A. "Sifting Legacies in Lucille Clifton's *Generations*." *Contemporary Literature* 40.4 (1999): 552–574.
Whitley, Edward. "A Long Missing Part of Itself: Bringing Lucille Clifton's Generations into American Literature." *MELUS: The Journal of the Society for the Study of the Multi-Ethnic Literature of the United States* 26.2 (2001): 47–64.

Augustina Edem Dzregah

Judith Ortiz Cofer

(1952–)

Puerto Rican

Photo by Rick O'Quinn, © Arte Público Press.

BIOGRAPHY

When Cofer was young, her father joined the American Navy and moved the family from Puerto Rico to New York. As his tours of duty took him away from the family for months at a time, she, her mother, and her brother would often return to Puerto Rico. These many trips and separations had a profound impact on her; she became adept at handling both cultures, learning to speak English quickly and often aiding her mother in making the transition from the island to the mainland. This constant travel back and forth also profoundly affected Cofer's developing sense of identity and self. She writes in "The Story of My Body" that she was "born a white girl in Puerto Rico but became a brown girl when I came to live in the United States" *(The Latin Deli*, p. 135). Her struggles to assimilate and find her place in American culture led her to seek shelter in reading, and writing poetry became a passion and a refuge as a result.

Cofer's first collection of poetry, *Peregrina,* won first place in the Riverstone International Chapbook Competition in 1985. Its subsequent publication by Riverstone Press in 1986 launched her career as a poet. *Terms of Survival* and *Reaching for the Mainland* followed in 1987. A PEN/Martha Albrand Special Citation in Nonfiction followed the publication of her autobiographical memoir, *Silent Dancing: A Partial Remembrance of a Puerto Rican Childhood,* in 1990. *The Latin Deli* (1993), *An Island Like You: Stories of the Barrio* (1998), and *The Year of Our Revolution: Selected and New Prose and Poetry* (1998) followed, bringing her more awards and recognition for her writing. Judith Ortiz Cofer resides in Georgia with her husband, and they have a daughter who has recently completed graduate work. Cofer is currently the Franklin Professor of English and Creative Writing at the University of Georgia.

THEMES AND CONCERNS

Judith Ortiz Cofer's bicultural background, Catholicism, strong family storytelling tradition, the role of women in society, and the experience of

American assimilation are the most prominent themes in her writing. The constant movement between the U.S. mainland and the island features prominently in her work, such as in the poem "Nothing Wasted" (*The Latin Deli*). Here, she focuses on the childhood memory of her mother starting a new avocado tree from a seed in a jar of water on her kitchen windowsill every time her father received a navy order to move. Much of her work, both poetry and prose, resonates with the challenge of shifting notions of "home," although in *Máscaras* she states that "I have never abandoned the island of my birth, or perhaps that obsession called 'the island' has never left me" ("And Are You a Latina Writer?" p. 11).

Cofer's poetry became a way for her to work through all the difficulties of being constantly displaced and in the perpetual motion of movement between cultures. For example, in "The Habit of Movement" (*Silent Dancing*), she writes about the losses and dispossession she felt as a result of constantly being uprooted by her parents' lifestyle. But in this poem and others, she also displays a method of learning to cope with this pattern. This theme also appears in her essays and memoir writings. In "The Paterson Public Library" *ensayo* (essay) in *The Latin Deli*, Cofer relates the experience of being menaced by an African American girl she was assigned to tutor and finding refuge in the local public library from the girl's taunts of violence. Here, Cofer relates how being smart and new in the neighborhood targeted her for injustice from her peers, and how language and words became her method of escape. Her essay also conveys the reality that even the very young can become painfully aware of racial injustice, making it more applicable to those who experienced the same feelings.

In the past, critics have been anxious to apply labels to Cofer's work, categories that she steadfastly refuses. As she notes in her essay "And Are You a Latina Writer?" her writing is personal and comes from a place of wanting to capture "moments of being," rather than conforming to any type of agenda or wider applicability to human experience. She views her work as "a process of discovery," which she says entails "[re-envisioning] scenes of my youth and [transforming] them through my imagination, attempting to synthesize the collective yearnings of these souls into a collage that means Puerto Rican to me, that gives shape to my individual vision" (p. 17). When viewed through this lens, Cofer's poetry and other writings become intensely personal visions of life that work to illuminate aspects of the human experience not seen and heard by others. The beauty of her work is that it resonates across the vast divides of our differences, connecting us through the powerful and beautiful bond of language.

POETRY COLLECTIONS

Peregrina. Golden, CO: Riverstone Press, 1986.
Reaching for the Mainland. Tempe, AZ: Bilingual Review Press, 1987.
Terms of Survival. Houston, TX: Arte Público Press, 1987.

Silent Dancing: A Partial Remembrance of a Puerto Rican Childhood. Houston, TX: Arte Público Press, 1990.

The Latin Deli: Prose and Poetry. Athens: University of Georgia Press, 1993.

The Year of Our Revolution: Selected and New Prose and Poetry. Houston, TX: Arte Público Press, 1998.

SELECTED ANTHOLOGIES WHERE POETRY APPEARS

Aizenberg, Susan, and Erin Belieu, eds. *The Extraordinary Tide: New Poetry by American Women*. New York: Columbia University Press, 2001.

Daly, Patricia, and Paula Hooper Mayhew, eds. *Envisioning the New Adam: Empathic Portraits of Men by American Women Writers*. Westport, CT: Greenwood Press, 1995.

Gilbert, Sandra M., Susan Gubar, and Diana O'Hehir, eds. *Mothersongs: Poems for, by, and about Mothers*. New York: W. W. Norton, 1995.

Gillan, María, et al., eds. *Unsettling America: Race and Ethnicity in Contemporary American Poetry*. New York: Viking Penguin, 1994.

Gonzalez, Ray, ed. *After Aztlan: Latino Poets in the Nineties*. Boston, MA: David Godine, 1998.

Heyck, Denis Lynn Daly. *Barrios and Borderlands: Cultures of Latinos and Latinas in the United States*. New York: Routledge, 1994, 328–330.

Keller, Gary D., and Francisco Jimenez. *Hispanics in the United States: An Anthology of Creative Literature*. Ypsilanti, MI: Bilingual Press, 1997.

Latino Caribbean Literature. Paramus, NJ: Globe Fearon, 1999.

Madison, D. Soyini, ed. *The Woman That I Am: The Literature and Culture of Contemporary Women of Color*. New York: St. Martin's, 1997.

Milligan, Bryce, et al., eds. *Daughters of the Fifth Sun: A Collection of Latina Fiction and Poetry*. New York: Riverhead Books, 1995.

———. *¡Floricanto Sí! A Collection of Latina Poetry*. New York: Penguin/Putnam, 1998.

Seely, Virginia, ed. *Latino Poetry*. Paramus, NJ: Globe Fearon, 1994.

Shinder, Jason, ed. *More Light: Father & Daughter Poems*. New York: Harcourt Brace, 1993.

Tashlik, Phyllis, ed. *Hispanic, Female, and Young*. Houston, TX: Piñata Books, 1994.

Turner, Faythe, ed. *Puerto Rican Writers at Home in the U.S.A.* Seattle, WA: Open Hand, 1991.

Vigil, Evangelina, ed. *Woman of Her Word: Hispanic Women Write*. Houston, TX: Arte Público Press, 1987.

SELECTED FICTION AND NONFICTION

The Line of the Sun. Athens: University of Georgia Press, 1989.

"And Are You a Latina Writer?" In *Mascaras*. Ed. Lucha Corpi. Berkeley, CA: Third Woman Press, 1997, 11–20.

An Island Like You: Stories of the Barrio. New York: Troll Books, Penguin, 1998.

Sleeping with One Eye Open: Women Writers and the Art of Survival. Editor, with Marilyn Kallet. Athens: University of Georgia Press, 1999.

Woman in Front of the Sun: On Becoming a Writer. Athens: University of Georgia Press, 2000.

SELECTED RESOURCES FOR FURTHER REFERENCE

Bruce-Novoa, Juan. "Judith Ortiz Cofer's Rituals of Movement." *Americas Review* 19.3–4 (1991): 88–99.

Grobman, Laurie. "The Cultural Past and Artistic Creation in Sandra Cisneros' *The House on Mango Street* and Judith Ortiz Cofer's *Silent Dancing.*" *Confluencia: Revista Hispanica de Cultura y Literatura* 11.1 (1995): 42–49.

O'Shea, Michael. "Reviews." [*The Latin Deli: Prose and Poetry,* by Judith Ortiz Cofer.] *Studies in Short Fiction* 31.3 (Summer 1994): 502–503.

Piedra, Jose. "His and Her Panics." *Disposito: Revista Americana de Estudios Comparados y Culturales/American Journal of Comparative and Cultural Studies* 16.41 (1991): 71–93.

Rangil, Viviana. "Pro-Claiming a Space: The Poetry of Sandra Cisneros and Judith Ortiz Cofer." *Multicultural Review* 9.3 (2000): 48–51, 54–55.

Lisa Treviño Roy-Davis

Wanda Coleman

(1946–)

African American

Photo by Heather Harris, courtesy of Wanda Coleman.

BIOGRAPHY

Wanda Coleman, a performer, poet, essayist, short story and novel writer, editor, and critic, was born in Los Angeles, California, on November 13, 1946, to George and Lewana Scott Evans. Her mother worked as a seamstress and domestic worker, while her father was in the advertising business. Coleman was married twice before marrying her present husband, poet Austin Straus. Coleman has three children: Anthony, Tunisia, and Ian Wayne Grant.

Despite the fact that Coleman did not like school, she enjoyed writing and published her first poems at age twelve in her local newspapers. But as a wife and mother of two by age twenty, she did not have many opportunities to write professionally. Rather, she worked a number of jobs to support herself and her family, including medical transcriber, insurance billing clerk, recruiter for the Peace Corps, and columnist for the *Los Angeles Times Magazine*.

Between 1975 and 1976, Coleman was a writer for the NBC soap opera *Days of Our Lives,* and in 1976 she won an Emmy for her contributions to the show. In addition to having many of her poems and fictional pieces anthologized, Coleman has published numerous articles and/or reviews and edited two collections of poetry/prose, one collection of short stories (1988), and one novel (1999). But by far Coleman has been most prolific as a poet.

In 1970, Coleman published her first short story, "Watching the Sunset," in *Negro Digest*. Seven years later, Coleman published her first poetry manuscript, *Art in the Court of the Blue Fag*. Since then, she has published nine other books of poetry, including *Imagoes,* which earned her a National Endowment for the Arts grant in 1981 and a Guggenheim poetry fellowship in 1984, and *Bathwater Wine,* for which she was awarded the Lenore Marshall Poetry Prize from the Academy of American Poets in 1999. Coleman's most recent collection of poetry, *Mercurochrome: New Poems,* earned her a position as a finalist for the National Book Award for poetry in 2001.

Coleman extends her talents beyond just the writing of her poems; she prefers to perform the poetry she has written. Part of the recent revival of spoken-word artistry, she has presented hundreds of readings of her works, mostly at colleges and universities, and has recorded several spoken-word albums for Harvey Kubernick's New Alliance releases. She can also be heard reading her poetry at various sites on the Internet. Coleman is the Fletcher Endowed Chair in Literature and Writing at Loyola Marymount University.

THEMES AND CONCERNS

Regardless of what genre Coleman writes in, there are several themes that pervade her work. Primarily rooted in African American experiences, Coleman explores the politics of individual and institutional racism and sexism in black America and considers the status of the black underclass, especially in Los Angeles. In her poem "Drone," for instance, Coleman comments on the callous American health system, noting the disparities in health care opportunities for lower-class African Americans and Hispanics. She is concerned with the dangerous injustices that African Americans have to endure in the United States, and using the language of the street, she gives voice to countless others who are silent and silenced in America. In Coleman's essay "Letter to Jamal," connections are made between the 1965 Watts Riot and 1992 South Central rebellions, demonstrating continued biases and racism in the United States. Coleman's stories in the book *A War of Eyes and Other Stories* all explore how people perceive one other, with the perceptions often giving rise to racial attitudes and actions.

Yet in all of the pain and struggle, Coleman often marks moments of joy and opportunities for resistance and finds ways to encourage her readers. Coleman's celebratory poems, exemplified well by the poem "Doing Battle with the Wolf," often describe the bonds between mothers and daughters or between women. Her work is connected to and grows out of the black oral tradition, a custom that encompasses everything from the African and African American historical preservation of griots (West African storytellers) to blues and rap music. A number of Coleman's poems sound like biblical cadences, namely "Walkin' Paper Blues," "Bottom Out Blues," and "Blues for the Man on Sax." The oral tradition is especially evident in Coleman's work when she performs it in venues like classrooms, community centers, and clubs.

Coleman's works tend to be naturalistic in style, as her characters are condemned to lead lives of poverty and to experience racial oppression. Not only does she confront readers with thought-provoking issues, but does so with straightforward language as well as violent and sexual imagery. The poem "Rape" is the epitome of the sexual and violent imagery, utilized to invoke anger from readers. Poems like "La Dolce Morte" and "Stone Rock Lady" incite anger. When asked about the issues she covers in her work in an interview conducted by Tony Magistrale and Patricia Ferreira, Coleman responded in this way: "As a writer, I feel I best serve my readership when I rehumanize the dehumanized, when I illuminate what is in darkness, when I give blood and bone to statistics that are too easily missed" (p. 492). When asked how she would reply to readers who consider her works too harsh, she said simply, "I have to write about my perceptions, what my grasp on reality is as I move through the fabric of American society, and my responses to it as a woman and as a black woman. It's not pretty" (p. 498).

Coleman's work is inextricably tied to the daily lives and realities of African Americans, and it cries out for social change and demands social justice.

POETRY COLLECTIONS

Art in the Court of the Blue Fag. Santa Barbara, CA: Black Sparrow Press, 1977.
Mad Dog Black Lady. Santa Barbara, CA: Black Sparrow Press, 1979.
Imagoes. Santa Barbara, CA: Black Sparrow Press, 1983.
Women for All Seasons: Poetry and Prose about the Transitions in Women's Lives. Pasadena, CA: Woman's Building, 1988.
Dicksboro Hotel and Other Travels. Ft. Lauderdale, FL: Ambrosia Press, 1989. (poetry and fiction)
African Sleeping Sickness: Stories and Poems. Santa Rosa, CA: Black Sparrow Press, 1990.
Heavy Daughter Blues: Poems and Stories. Santa Rosa, CA: Black Sparrow Press, 1991.
Hand Dance. Santa Rosa, CA: Black Sparrow Press, 1993.
American Sonnets. Kenosha, WI: Light and Dust Books, 1994.
Bathwater Wine. Santa Rosa, CA: Black Sparrow Press, 1998.
Mercurochrome: New Poems. Santa Rosa, CA: Black Sparrow Press, 2001.

SELECTED ANTHOLOGIES AND WEB SITES WHERE POETRY APPEARS

Clark, John, ed. *Ploplop: An "Antholozine" of Poetry, Prose, and Artwork*. Indianapolis, IN: Geekspeak Unique Press, 1997.
Gates, Henry Louis, Jr., and Nellie McKay, eds. *The Norton Anthology of African-American Literature, Best American Poetry*. New York: W. W. Norton, 1997.
Hoover, Paul, ed. *Post Modern American Poetry: A Norton Anthology*. New York: W. W. Norton, 1994.
Iddings, Kathleen, ed. *What She Could Not Name*. La Jolla, CA: La Jolla Poets Press, 1987; Dayton, OH: Bottom Dog Press, 2002.
Salaam, Kalamu, and Kwame Alexander, eds. *360°: A Revolution of Black Poets*. Washington: Black Words, 1998.
Salon.com Online. www.salon.com.

SELECTED FICTION AND NONFICTION

A War of Eyes and Other Stories. Santa Rosa, CA: Black Sparrow Press, 1988.
Earthbound in Betty Grable's Shoes. New York: Chiron Press, 1990.

Native in a Strange Land: Trials and Tremors. Santa Rosa, CA: Black Sparrow Press, 1996. (autobiographical sketches and essays)

Mambo Hips and Make Believe. Santa Rosa, CA: Black Sparrow Press, 1999.

Yefief: Health and Human Rights (A View Along the Running Edge). With English to Chinese Translation. Trans. Xue Di. La Puebla: Images for Media, 2003.

SELECTED RESOURCES FOR FURTHER REFERENCE

Coleman, Wanda. "Black on Black: Fear & Reviewing in Los Angeles." *Konch Magazine,* 2002. Online. www.ishmaelreedpub.com/coleman.html.

Lehrich, Tamar. "Heavy Daughter Blues: Poems and Stories 1968–1986" (book review). *The Nation* 246.8 (1988): 242–244.

Magistrale, Tony. "Doing Battle with the Wolf: A Critical Introduction to Wanda Coleman's Poetry." *African American Review* 23.3 (1989): 539–554.

———. "Hard Times." *African American Review* 26.2 (Summer 1992): 355–357.

Magistrale, Tony, and Patricia Ferreira. "Sweet Mama Wanda Tells Fortunes: An Interview with Wanda Coleman." *Black American Literature Forum* 24.3 (Autumn 1990): 491–507.

McDonnell, Evelyn. "New Poets with a Rock and Roll Attitude: Native Tongues." *Rolling Stone,* August 5, 1993, pp. 20–21.

Stanley, Sandra. "Reviews." *African American Review* 33.2 (Summer 1999): 371.

Alyce Baker

Victor Hernández Cruz

(1949–)

Puerto Rican

Photo by Nestor Barreto,
courtesy of Victor Hernández Cruz.

BIOGRAPHY

Poet, fiction writer, and essayist, Victor Hernández Cruz was born February 6, 1949, in Aguas Buenas, Puerto Rico. Because of economic concerns, he and his family left the small tropical town and moved to New York City when he was six years old. They settled on the Lower East Side of Manhattan, an area populated largely by Caribbean Latinos and African Americans. The family continued to suffer hardships and soon after the move, Cruz's parents were divorced. Cruz's attraction to books and the written word began early, and by the age of fourteen he'd begun to write. By seventeen he'd written his first book of poetry, *Papo Got His Gun!* (1966). Still a student at Benjamin Franklin High School, Cruz mimeographed 500 copies and distributed them to stores to be sold for seventy-five cents each. The book was picked up by the *Evergreen Review,* an avant-garde New York magazine that later ran a seven-page spread featuring Cruz's poems alongside photographs of *el barrio,* the Lower East Side neighborhood.

In 1967, still in his teens, Cruz joined the staff of *Umbra* magazine as an editor. *Umbra,* which grew out of the black revolutionary and literary movement that flourished in the 1960s and 1970s, boasted contributors such as Ishmael Reed, Larry Neal, Quincy Troupe, Amiri Baraka, and others of the Black Arts Movement who became close friends. Soon his work began to appear in anthologies such as *Black Fire: An Anthology of Afro-American Writing.* These successes and their resulting associations enabled Cruz to explore Berkeley, California, and thus began his back-and-forth relationship with the East and West Coasts. There Cruz interacted with other artists and began to read the works of Richard Wright, Ralph Ellison, Franz Fanon, Pablo Neruda, Ernesto Cardinal, Octavio Paz, and others whose poetry ultimately influenced his development. While in Berkeley, he taught briefly at an experimental public school and later, back in New York, he tutored youths in basic education skills through a Columbia University program.

Cruz's first major publication, *Snaps*, was published by Random House in 1969 and received wide critical acclaim. In language that is bold, direct, and colloquial, he expresses his disdain for white American culture, examines death and *espiritismo*, and reveals images of street life and growing up in the Bronx, all to the underlying polyrhythmic beat of the salsa. Cruz's poetry continued to be anthologized during the early 1970s; in addition, it was put to music and performed in 1974 by the London Symphony and later by the Contemporary Music Players at the San Francisco Opera House. Cruz's second book of verse, *Mainland* (1970), has also received many critical accolades.

Cruz earned a grant from New York's Creative Artists Program Service, which enabled him to work on his third volume of poetry, *Tropicalization* (1976). As he gained exposure, his work began to appear in a wider range of anthologies throughout the 1970s. In 1975, Cruz married Elisa Ivette, with whom he had two children. The following year he became a contributing editor of *Revista Chicano Riqueña*, and he moved to San Francisco, where he worked with the San Francisco Neighborhood Arts Program. He published *Tropicalization* in 1976 followed by *By Lingual Wholes* in 1982. After what Cruz called thirty-five years of "exile," he moved back to Aguas Buenas, Puerto Rico, because he wanted "to immerse [himself] in the Spanish of the Caribbean, hear it, smell it, taste it" (Cabanillas, p. 50). *Red Beans* was published in 1991 and also received critical appreciation for its celebration of Caribbean life.

Panoramas, published in 1997, is an engaging memoir of rural Puerto Rico in which Cruz makes connections, bridges between past and present, the island and the mainland, urban and rural, Spanish and English. It is a coming together of many of the concepts he has been scrutinizing throughout his career and he seems to have found a solid perch from his island vantage point. Victor Hernández Cruz is the recipient of numerous awards, including a Guggenheim, a National Endowment for the Arts fellowship, and the New York Poetry Foundation Award.

THEMES AND CONCERNS

While Cruz's early themes centered on urban life and his most recent explore the rural, his most prevailing concerns are the meaning and force of language, identity, and the relationship between one's cultural and historical pasts and how they affect the present. Cruz's poetry exalts the history of the Caribbean, the indigenous people, the Africans, and the Spanish who together created the "tapestry" that is a blended, multicultural, multiracial people. He glories in the use of the rhythm and melodies that have risen out of the African Spanish culture. Yet although Cruz has been mislabeled African American in some texts because he exalts the African heritage in Puerto Rican culture and he has been published in a number of African American anthologies, he would be considered "white Hispanic" by U.S. Census standards because of his straight hair, light skin, and fine features. He himself often self-identifies as a Nuyorican, an individual of Puerto Rican descent who is born and reared in New York City, thereby claiming both islands as his or her cultural legacies.

This confusion is not Cruz's; it belongs to those who seek to interpret his work through a limited spectrum. His work is ultimately an exploration of Puerto Ricanness, which includes his semirural origins on the tropical island and the immigration/migration to the urban metropolises east and west, all filtered through the cadence of his unique language mixtures, Spanish his first language, English his second, and music his primal, the insistent rhythms of the salsa tempered and held together by the drum. In a television interview with Bill Moyers, Cruz himself says, "My poetry is the history of the migrations that I have participated in. I try to see the connections between things, between myself and history."

POETRY COLLECTIONS

Papo Got His Gun! And Other Poems. New York: Calle Once, 1966.
Doing Poetry. Berkeley, CA: Other Ways, 1968.
Snaps. New York: Random House, 1969.
Mainland. New York: Random House, 1973.
Tropicalization. New York: Reed, Canon, & Johnson, 1976.
By Lingual Wholes. San Francisco, CA: Momo's Press, 1982.
Rhythm, Content, and Flavor: New and Selected Poems. Houston, TX: Arte Público Press, 1989.
Red Beans. Minneapolis, MN: Coffee House Press, 1991.
Panoramas. Minneapolis, MN: Coffee House Press, 1997.

SELECTED ANTHOLOGIES WHERE POETRY APPEARS

Adoff, Arnold, ed. *The Poetry of Black America.* New York: Harper & Row, 1973.
Babin, Maria T., and Stan Steiner, eds. *Borinquen: An Anthology of Puerto Rican Literature.* New York: Knopf, 1974.
Breman, Paul, ed. *You Better Believe It: Black Verse in English from Africa, the West Indies, and the United States.* Baltimore, MD: Penguin Books, 1973.
Chapman, Abraham, ed. *New Black Voices: An Anthology of Contemporary Afro-American Literature.* New York: American Library, 1972.
Jones, LeRoi, and Larry Neal, eds. *Black Fire: An Anthology of Afro-American Writing.* New York: Morrow, 1968.
Lomax, Alan, and Raoul Abdul, eds. *3000 Years of Black Poetry.* New York: Dodd, Mead, 1970.
Lowenfels, Walter, ed. *In a Time of Revolution: Poems from Our Third World.* New York: Random House, 1969.
Major, Clarence, ed. *The New Black Poetry.* New York: William Morrow, 1969.
Matilla, Alfredo, and Ivan Silen, eds. *The Puerto Rican Poets: Los Poetas Puertorriquenos.* New York: Bantam Books, 1972.
Miller, Adam David, ed. *Dices or Black Bones.* Boston, MA: Houghton Mifflin, 1970.

Mirikitani, Janice, and Luis Syquia, eds. *Time to Greeze*. San Francisco, CA: Glide, 1975.

Reed, Ishmael. *Necromancers from Now*. Garden City, NJ: Doubleday, 1970.

Troupe, Quincy, and Rainer Schulte, eds. *Giant Talk: Anthology of Third World Writings*. New York: Random House, 1975.

SELECTED ADDITIONAL WORKS

Stuff: A Collection of Poems, Visions, and Imaginative Happenings from Young Writers in Schools Closed. With Herbert Kohl. New York: World, 1970.

"The Champagne of Cocaine" and others. *Yardbird Reader* 1 (1972): 99–102.

"You Gotta Have Your Tips on Fire." *Village Voice*, October 31, 1974, p. 56.

"The Latest Latin Dance Craze" and others. *Revista Chicano Riquena* 3 (Summer 1975): 12–14.

The Low Writings. San Francisco, CA: Lee/Lucas Press, 1980.

"Mountains in the North." *Americas Review* 18.1 (Spring 1990): 110–114.

Paper Dance: 55 Latino Poets. Editor, with Leroy Quintana and Virgil Suárez. New York: Persea, 1995.

SELECTED RESOURCES FOR FURTHER REFERENCE

Aparicio, Frances R. "Salsa, Maracas, and Baile: Latin Popular Music in the Poetry of Victor Hernández Cruz." *MELUS: The Journal of the Society for the Study of the Multi-Ethnic Literature of the United States* 16.1 (1989–1990): 43–58.

Cabanillas, Franciso. "Spanish and English: An Interview with Victor Hernández Cruz." *Latino Studies Journal* 6.1 (1995): 49–61.

Esterrich, Carmelo. "Home and the Ruins of Language: Victor Hernández Cruz and Miguel Algarin's Nuyorican Poetry." *MELUS: The Journal of the Society for the Study of the Multi-Ethnic Literature of the United States* 23.3 (Fall 1998): 43–56.

Mohr, Eugene. *The Nuyorican Experience: Literature of the Puerto Rican Minority*. Westport, CT: Greenwood, 1982.

Moyers, Bill. *The Language of Life with Bill Moyers*. Prod. and dir. David Grubin. PBS, 1995.

Turner, Faythe. *Puerto Rican Writers at Home in the USA: An Anthology*. Seattle, WA: Open Hand, 1991.

Esperanza Cintron

Enid Dame

(1940?–)

Jewish American

BIOGRAPHY

Enid Dame is a poet, writer, and teacher. She grew up in Beaver Falls, Pennsylvania, in the 1940s and early 1950s before she and her parents, who were radical labor activists, moved to Pittsburgh, Pennsylvania. Dame's parents were politically progressive and unconventionally Jewish, and even after the family moved from Beaver Falls, which had a very small Jewish population, to Pittsburgh, the home of a larger Jewish population, Dame experienced a sense of "otherness." She often felt the pressures of living in two distinct cultures. Carrying with her a sensitivity for the marginalized in society, in the 1960s and 1970s Dame participated in groups that supported radical social, economic, and cultural transformation. She has been committed to poetry since the late 1970s.

Dame holds a Ph.D. from Rutgers University, where she has taught creative writing courses, and currently she is a lecturer at the New Jersey Institute of Technology. Dame has also led writing workshops at locations including universities, high schools, libraries, synagogues, and community centers. The New Jersey Council for the Humanities' Religious Diversity Seminars has hosted Dame's presentations on Jewish women poets and midrashic poetry, which expands biblical texts in imaginative ways as poets "engage the Torah and Talmud in ways that had been previously restricted to men" (Schneider, p. 61).

Dame has served on the editorial committees of *Bridges* and *Jewish Women's Literary Annual,* and she coedits the literary tabloid *Home Planet News.* She was awarded the New York State Creative Artist in Public Service poetry fellowship, and her poem "Chagall Exhibit, 1996" was the 1997 cowinner of the Many Mountains Moy competition. Dame currently lives in Brooklyn and High Falls, New York, with her husband, the poet Donald Lev.

THEMES AND CONCERNS

Two themes pervade Enid Dame's poetry: religion and nature. One of the most prominent participants in the midrashic tradition of poetry, Dame has authored a number of works about Lilith, "who, according to an eleventh-century Hebrew text, was created as Adam's equal, but who, when he tried to dominate her, uttered God's secret name and resolutely left Eden" (Dame, Rivlin, and Wenkart, p. xv). Dame's Lilith is unlike the folkloric Lilith, however. Whereas the demonic Lilith of folklore pays visits to men during the night, participates in their sexual dreams, and takes new babies from this life, Dame's Lilith is earthy, sensual, and heroic. She is to be celebrated rather than feared.

Frequently, Dame allows Lilith to speak through her poetry. For example, in "Lilith in a Garden in San Antonio, Texas," or "The Name Game," Lilith mirrors Adam's mission in the Book of Genesis and takes it upon herself to name the various birds and trees that she encounters. As the poem progresses, one senses that she relishes the power that comes with this task, only to be deflated in the piece's final lines by a man who appears and offers his assistance, surmising that she must be lost. Lilith falls silent; the game is over and the clipboard-wielding man is the reader's final image.

Dame's "Lilith" is another poem that describes the impossibility of gender unity. Dame's speaker looks back on a failed relationship and connects her male lover to God, neither of whom, she says, she could live with. There is a sense of impossibility and nostalgia that surrounds the relationship; despite the fact that the man is hardworking and patient, this woman cannot exist with him; too many unspoken differences separate the lovers. She cannot move past the idea that the man holds the power in the relationship.

The poem "Lilith, I Don't Cut My Grass" is another decidedly feminist piece. The speaker mentions her relationship to her mother, the inevitability of reaching menopause, her fear of power, which she engenders as masculine and equates to the Messiah, her connection with nature, and the purity and peacefulness of her own backyard garden, in which she envisions Lilith. Despite the presence of masculine power in the poem, however, the speaker's connection with nature and with Lilith provides a security that is empowering.

In much of Dame's work, nature is a personified and a powerful force that offers a sense of stability in its constancy and persistence. Specifically, Dame writes about gardens full of unruly weeds and stinging insects as well as gardens that bear the mark of human interlopers—rusty bicycles and young boys' chipped teeth. In many places, Dame overtly connects nature to religion; she frequently references the Garden of Eden, and in "The Collier Brothers' Backyard" she notes that the earth is a sort of tabernacle. Generally, Dame views humans' efforts to control and tame plants and weeds both futile and foolish, preferring instead the peaceful chaos of the natural world.

A resident of Brooklyn, New York, Dame was closely affected by the bombing of the World Trade Center towers on September 11, 2001. Her poem "Beach," dated September 14, 2001, again shows Dame turning to nature for solace, with the crumbling city placed literally behind her as she looks out over the water in Brooklyn. She observes a solitary monarch butterfly that reminds her of nature's stability and endurance as the jellyfish on the shore hold down the sand like paperweights. As she does in most of her other works, Dame turns a keen eye toward the natural world, which is perpetually in balance. This piece presents a moving juxtaposition of the balanced natural world in front of the speaker and the crumbling, half-destroyed human-made world behind her.

POETRY COLLECTIONS

Between Revolutions. New York: X-press Press for the Downtown Poets Co-op, 1979.
On the Road to Damascus, Maryland. New York: Downtown Poets, 1980.

SELECTED ANTHOLOGIES AND WEB SITES WHERE POETRY APPEARS

Gillan, Maria M., and Jennifer Gillan, eds. *Unsettling America: An Anthology of Contemporary Multicultural Poetry.* New York: Penguin, 1994.
Wise Woman's Web: A Magazine of Women's Literature. Online. www.users.tellurian.net/ wisewomensweb/dame.html.

SELECTED ADDITIONAL WORKS

Lilith and Her Demons. Merrick, NY: Cross-Cultural Communications, 1989.
Monologhi: Fatti E Fantasie Di Donne Detti Spudoretamente. Trans. Nina Scammacca. Merrick, NY: Cross-Cultural Communications, 1989.
Bridges: A Journal for Jewish Feminists and Our Friends. Editor. 1990. Online. www.bridgesjournal.org/editors.html.
Anything You Don't See. With Denise Bergman. Albuquerque: University of New Mexico Press, 1992.
Which Lilith? Feminist Writers Re-Create the World's First Woman. Editor, with Lilly Rivlin and Henny Wenkart. Northvale, NJ: Jason Aronson, 1998.

SELECTED RESOURCES FOR FURTHER REFERENCE

Collins, Sandra, et al. "Book Reviews: Arts & Humanities." *Library Journal* 123.18 (1998): 92.
Kimmelman, Burt. "The Historical Imperative in Contemporary Jewish American Poetry: Enid Dame, Michael Heller, and Nikki Stiller." *Shofar: An Interdisciplinary Journal of Jewish Studies* 21.1 (2002): 103–110.
Reed, Christine L. "Review: Which Lilith?—Feminist Writers Re-Create the World's First Woman." *Wise Women's Web.* 2000. Online. www.users.tellurian.net/ wisewomensweb.
Schneider, Steven P. "Poetry, Midrash, and Feminism." *Tikkun* 16.4 (2001): 61–65.

Amy C. O'Brien

Courtesy of Doubleday Publishing.

Chitra Banerjee Divakaruni

(1957–)

East Indian American

BIOGRAPHY

Acclaimed poet, short-story writer, and novelist Chitra Banerjee Divakaruni came to creative writing later in life. Born in Calcutta in 1957, she was raised Hindu and attended a convent school in India run by Irish nuns. After earning a bachelor's degree in English from the University of Calcutta, she immigrated to the United States in 1976, at the age of nineteen, to continue her education in English literature. While completing her master's degree at Wright State University in Dayton, Ohio, she met her husband, Murthy, whom she married two years later. Divakaruni earned a Ph.D. at the University of California at Berkeley and settled with her husband and two sons, Abhay and Anand, in northern California, where she still resides.

Only after completing her Ph.D. did Divakaruni begin to write creatively. While her experience with academia enabled her to begin a fulfilling career as a professor, it left her with little desire to write academic nonfiction, which she felt to be disconnected from the realities of life. Furthermore, the recent death of the grandfather had prompted a desire to write to remember—her family, her culture, her country, her experiences. She enrolled in the Berkeley Poets' Co-op and shared her work publicly for the first time. Her early poetry focused almost entirely on intensely personal reflection. Thanks to the feedback of co-op participants, however, Divakaruni learned to move away from poetry as private expression and toward poetry that uses personal experience—her own and others'—as the basis for more universally accessible poems. Her first three books of poetry appeared in fairly rapid succession: *Dark Like a River* was published in 1987, *The Reason for Nasturtiums* in 1990, and *Black Candle* (a volume that earned Divakaruni an honorable mention in the prestigious Pushcart Prize competition in 1992) in 1991. Her most recent volume of poetry, *Leaving Yuba City,* was published in 1997, and poems from the volume have won a Pushcart Prize, an Allen Ginsberg Prize, and a Gerbode Foundation Award.

Once Divakaruni began to write poetry, she also branched out into other artistic forms, particularly short stories and novels, and these endeavors helped to establish her reputation as an important literary voice. Her first short story collection, *Arranged Marriage* (1995), earned the Bay Area Book Reviewers Award for Best Fiction, the PEN Oakland/Josephine Miles Award, and the American Book Award. Her latest short story collection, *The Unknown Errors of Our Lives* (2001), has enjoyed high praise from critics and audiences alike. Similarly, her novels, including *The Mistress of Spices* (1997), *Sister of My Heart* (1999), and its sequel *Vine of Desire* (2002), have placed Divakaruni among the most well respected fiction writers of our time. Divakaruni has also recently published her first children's book, *Neela: A Victory Song* (2002).

While most of her time is dedicated to writing, Divakaruni is also engaged in service to her community, particularly to South Asian immigrant women in the United States, many of whom are trapped in unhealthy or abusive relationships that rely on the laws and customs of their South Asian countries of origin. After hearing these women's stories, Divakaruni began volunteering at battered women's shelters and eventually cofounded Maitri (meaning "friendship"), a free help-line for South Asian women in the San Francisco Bay area. Maitri is run entirely by volunteers who hail from South Asian countries themselves and thus understand both the culture and the languages of the South Asian women they seek to help.

Although Divakaruni today writes mostly fiction rather than poetry, poetry was where Divakaruni found her voice and began to explore the subject matter that would make her such an important voice in today's literary world.

THEMES AND CONCERNS

Divakaruni's poetry is informed by her dual perspective: she recalls in rich detail her Indian childhood and the way of life of the Indian people, and she also speaks from the perspective of an immigrant adapting to a new way of life. This duality is at the heart of much of her poetry, as she depicts life on the Indian subcontinent and the South Asian immigrant experience with equal richness. Her poems are emotionally powerful, covering a broad range of subjects: childhood, love, family, isolation, ethnicity, changing traditions, friendship, loss, fear, and hope. Further, they are deeply sensory-driven, sometimes using paintings or films as inspiration; images, sounds, tastes, smells, and textures permeate her work.

Also at the heart of Divakaruni's poetry is the experience of women, particularly South Asian and Asian American women. In her poetic treatment of these women, Divakaruni illustrates their struggles and triumphs, their suffering and survival. By depicting cultural customs that at once constrain and venerate, abuses that initially victimize but ultimately empower, and relationships that both deplete and fulfill women, Divakaruni's poetry makes clear the paradoxes of women's lives. These images are at times horrifying and haunting, at other times hopeful and inspiring, always emotionally and intellectually engaging.

Despite the prominent focuses on the immigrant experience and the experience of women in her work, Divakaruni bristles at the thought that her work is relevant only to Asian Americans and women. She believes, instead, that her work can be enjoyed by all readers, regardless of their race, sex, creed, or custom. "If your art is good enough," she says, "everyone should be able to get something from it. And if it's good enough it should . . . touch something in people" (quoted in Bauer).

POETRY COLLECTIONS

Dark Like the River. Calcutta: Writers Workshop, 1987.
Black Candle. St. Paul, MN: Consortium Book Sales and Distribution, 1990.
The Reason for Nasturtiums. Berkeley, CA: Berkeley Poets Press, 1990.
Leaving Yuba City: New and Selected Poems. New York: Anchor Books, 1997.

SELECTED ANTHOLOGIES AND WEB SITES WHERE POETRY APPEARS

Bender, Sheila, ed. *The Writer's Journal: 40 Contemporary Writers and Their Journals.* NY: Dell, 1997.
Bold Type: Poems by Chitra Banerjee Divakaruni. Online. www.randomhouse.com/boldtype.
Guth, Hans, and Gabriele Rico, eds. *Discovering Literature.* Compact ed. New York, Prentice Hall, 1999.
Laguardia, Dolores, and Hans Guth, eds. *American Visions: Multicultural Literature for Writers.* New York: McGraw-Hill, 1994.
Lim, Shirley Geok-lin, Mayumi Tsutakawa, and Margarita Donnelly, eds. *The Forbidden Stitch: An Asian American Women's Anthology.* Corvallis, OR: Calyx, 1989.
Skerritt, Joseph T., ed. *Literature, Race, and Ethnicity: Contesting American Identities.* New York: Longman, 2002.

SELECTED ADDITIONAL WORKS

"The Most Beautiful Picture in the World" (translation of a story by Sunil Gangopadhyay). *Chicago Review* 38.1–2 (1992): 61–66.
"A Distinct Flavor." *Amerasia Journal* 20.3 (1994): 35–36.
Multitude: Cross-Cultural Readings for Writers. Editor. Columbus, OH: McGraw Hill, 1996.
Arranged Marriage: Stories. New York: Anchor Books, 1997.
The Mistress of Spices. New York: Anchor Books, 1997.
"My Work with MAITRI." *Bold Type.* 1997. Online. www.randomhouse.com/boldtype.
We, Too, Sing America. Editor. Columbus, OH: McGraw Hill, 1997.
Sister of My Heart. New York: Doubleday, 1999.

"Uncertain Objects of Desire." *Atlantic Monthly* 285.3 (March 2000): 22–25.
"A Mother's Gift." *Good Housekeeping* 232.5 (May 2001): 126–130.
The Unknown Error of Our Lives: Stories. New York: Doubleday, 2001.
"Being Dark-Skinned in a Dark Time." *Good Housekeeping* 234.1 (January 2002): 89–89.
"Christmas with Grandfather." *Good Housekeeping* 135.6 (December 2002): 75–77.
Neela: Victory Song. Middleton, WI: Pleasant, 2002.
Vine of Desire. New York: Doubleday, 2002.

SELECTED RESOURCES FOR FURTHER REFERENCE

Bauer, Erika. "A Discussion with Chitra Divakaruni." May 1993. Online. www.ebstudios.com/homespun/poetry.divakruni.html.
Chitra Banerjee Divakaruni Homepage. Online. www.chitradivakaruni.com.
Clipper-Sethi, Robert. "They Forgive My Fiction: An Interview with Chitra Banerjee Divakaruni." *Little India.* 1999. Online. www.littleindia.com.
Farmanfarmaian, Roxane. "Chitra Banerjee Divakaruni: Writing from a Different Place." *Publishers Weekly* 248.20 (May 2001): 46–47.
Kalamaras, George. "Moments of Grace and Magic and Miracle." *Bloomsbury Review* 18.2 (March–April 1998): 3, 6.
Mehta, Julie. "Arranging One's Life." *Metroactive.* 1996. Online. www.metroactive.org.
Moka-Dias, Brunda. "Chitra Banerjee Divakaruni." In *Asian American Novelists: A Bio-Bibliographical Critical Sourcebook.* Ed. Emmanual S. Nelson. Westport, CT: Greenwood, 2000, 87–92.
Pais, Arthur. "Profile." *SAJA: South Asian Journalists Association.* February 1999. Online. www.saja.org/divakaruni.html.
Rai, Sudha. "Diasporic Location and Matrilineage: The Poetry of Sujata Bhatt, Meena Alexander and Chitra Banerjee Divakaruni." In *Indian Feminisms.* Ed. Jasbir Jain and Avadhesh-Kumar Singh. New Delhi, India: Creative Books, 2001, 176–189.
Rasiah, Dharini. "Chitra Banerjee Divakaruni." In *Words Matter: Conversations with Asian American Writers.* Ed. King-Kok Cheung. Honolulu: University of Hawaii Press, with the UCLA Asian American Studies Center, 2000, 140–153.
Ross, Robert L. "'Dissolving Boundaries': The Woman as Immigrant in the Fiction of Chitra Banerjee Divakaruni." In *Missions of Interdependence: A Literary Directory.* Ed. Gerhard Stilz. Amsterdam, Netherlands: Rodopi, 2002, 247–254.
———. "'Haunting Presence' and 'Broken Identities': The Immigrant Experience in Fiction." *South Asian Review* 18.15 (December 1994): 94–103.
Sarvate, Sarite. "The Mistress of Magical Writing." *San Francisco Review of Books* 22.2 (March–April 1997): 33–36.

Anne M. Dickson

Rita Dove

(1952–)

African American

BIOGRAPHY

Rita Frances Dove was born in Akron, Ohio, in 1952, the daughter of Elvira (Hord) and Ray Dove and the oldest daughter in a family of four. The Doves believed in the power of education, and encouraged their children to excel in this arena. Dove certainly did so, being named a Presidential Scholar in 1970 (an award given to the top 100 high school seniors each year) and entering Miami University in Ohio as a National Achievement Scholar. She graduated summa cum laude from Miami University in 1973, and from 1974 to 1975 she attended the University of Tubingen in West Germany as a Fulbright Scholar. In 1977 she earned her M.F.A. from the Iowa Writers' Workshop. Dove is fluent in German and is a studied musician (her instruments are the cello and viola de gamba).

In addition to three chapbooks (*Ten Poems,* 1977; *The Only Dark Spot in the Sky,* 1980; *The Other Side of the House,* 1988), a collection of short stories (*Fifth Sunday,* 1985), a play (*The Darker Face of Earth,* which has been performed at the Kennedy Center), a novel (*Through the Ivory Gate,* 1992), and a collection of essays (*The Poet's World,* 1995), Dove has published multiple volumes of poetry and her work has been widely translated. Her most noted collections include *Thomas and Beulah* (1986), which earned her the Pulitzer Prize for poetry, and *On the Bus with Rosa Parks* (1999), which was both a finalist for the National Book Critics Circle Award and was named a *New York Times* Notable Book of the Year. In 1993 Dove read her poem at the ceremony commemorating the 200th anniversary of the U.S. Capitol and the restoration of the Freedom Statue on the Capitol's dome. The poem was published as a limited edition the following year, having been commissioned by the University of Virginia Libraries to be its four millionth acquisition.

Dove has earned wide recognition and support for her work. She has been awarded fellowships from the National Endowment for the Arts, the National Endowment for the Humanities, and the Fulbright and Guggenheim Foundations. Among her many awards are the Lavan Younger Poets Award (1986), which she received from the Academy of American Poets, and the NAACP Great American Artist Award (1993). But perhaps the clearest marker of

Dove's prestige as a poet came when she was named Poet Laureate of the United States, a post she held from 1993 to 1995. She was the first African American and youngest person to serve in this position.

Dove is currently Commonwealth Professor of English at the University of Virginia, a position she has held since 1993. She resides in Charlottesville, Virginia, with her husband, German novelist Fred Viebahn, and their daughter, Aviva.

THEMES AND CONCERNS

Dove's poems reveal her engagement with history and her deep interest in language and the ways it can be used for expression and communication. She has written on topics as diverse as South American dictators, aging, art, sexuality, and motherhood, but her themes tend to focus on personal, national, and international history, and the lives of ordinary people, especially those forgotten or disregarded by mainstream history, fascinate Dove. She enters the consciousnesses and experiences of her characters to produce poems that reveal the lives, motivations, and concerns of her subjects without didacticism. In other words, Dove finds many things of interest in her subjects, not just their political relevance as ethnic or raced people.

She also frequently explores issues surrounding slavery. For example, "The House Slave" ushers us into an era where being black meant living in fear and vulnerability, without any rights or means of defense. The poem brings out all these themes and concerns and one experiences an ordinary day in the life of a slave through the voice of a persona who is a slave. The early morning activity of slaves and their families as they prepare to start their daily chores is evoked in the first three lines of the poem. The next stanza makes one aware of the harshness of slave life through the narrator's fear of being whipped if she or he was tardy in waking up. The theme of fear deepens into horror with the knowledge that the narrator's sister always cries for help because she is often the victim of abuse at the hands of either the white master or other white plantation figures. Here is an introduction of the theme of miscegenation that recurs in several of Dove's poems. The narrator feels a sense of rage and impotence because he or she is powerless to go to the sister's defense. As a female, the sister is doubly vulnerable to the rapacity of the white males, some of whom may be related to her—a hint at possible incest in the slave world.

Dove's biographical and autobiographical poems, such as those in *Thomas and Beulah* that chronicle the lives of her grandparents, have long evidenced her interest in the ways that "monumental events of history merge with everyday events so that the reader feels the continuity between the private moment and the public happening" (Gates and McKay, p. 2583). In this collection, her grandparents' experiences are used to portray a generation of black people who experienced the Great Migration between 1900 and 1960, as well as their social, political, and familial concerns. The collections *Grace Notes* and *Mother*

Love are also autobiographical, tracing her experiences as a daughter and a mother, themes and images that recur in Dove's work.

Dove is also respected for her attention to the technical aspects of her craft; she has been called "the most disciplined and technically accomplished poet since Gwendolyn Brooks" (Andrews, p. 226).

POETRY COLLECTIONS

The Yellow House on the Corner. Pittsburgh, PA: Carnegie-Mellon University Press, 1980.
Museum. Pittsburgh, PA: Carnegie-Mellon University Press, 1983.
Thomas and Beulah. Pittsburgh, PA: Carnegie-Mellon Press, 1986.
Die morgenländische Tänzerin (selected poems in German translation). Hamburg: Rowohlt Verlag, 1988.
Die Gläserne Stirn der Gegenwart (selected poems in German translation). Echzell: Heiderhoff Verlag, 1989.
Grace Notes. New York: W. W. Norton, 1989.
Selected Poems. Random House, 1993. (audio book)
Selected Poems. New York: Pantheon/Vintage, 1993.
Lady Freedom among Us. Newark, VT: Janus Press, 1994.
Mother Love. New York: W. W. Norton, 1995.
Det Rosa Er I Oss (selected poems in Norwegian translation). Oslo: Det Norske Samlaget, 1996.
Evening Primrose. City: Minneapolis, MN: TunheimSantrizos, 1998.
On the Bus with Rosa Parks. New York: W. W. Norton, 1999.
Thomas et Beulah (poems—bilingual edition, English and French). Paris: L'Harmattan, 1999.
Breakfast of Champions (selected poems in Hebrew translation). Tel Aviv: Keshev, 2000.

SELECTED ANTHOLOGIES WHERE POETRY APPEARS

Gates, Henry Louis, Jr., and Nellie McKay, eds. *The Norton Anthology of African American Literature.* New York: W. W. Norton, 1997.
Gilbert, Sandra, and Susan Gubar, eds. *The Norton Anthology: Literature by Women.* 2nd ed. New York: Norton, 1996.
Harper, Michael S., and Anthony Walton, eds. *Every Shut Eye Ain't Asleep: An Anthology of Poetry by African Americans Since 1945.* New York: Little, Brown, 1994.
Hill, Patricia Liggins, ed. *Call & Response: The Riverside Anthology of the African American Literary Tradition.* Boston, MA: Houghton Mifflin, 1998.
Miller, E. Ethelbert, ed. *In Search of Color Everywhere: A Collection of African American Poetry.* New York: Stewart, Tabori, and Chang, 1996.

SELECTED ADDITIONAL WORKS

Fifth Sunday. Callaloo Fiction Series no. 1. Charlottesville: University Press of Virginia, 1985. (short stories)

Through the Ivory Gate. New York: Pantheon Books, 1992. (novel)
The Darker Face of the Earth. Ashland, OR: Story Line Press, 1994, 1996, 2000.
    (drama)
The Poet's World. Washington, DC: Library of Congress, 1995.
The Best American Poetry 2000. Editor. New York: Scribner's, 2000.

SELECTED RESOURCES FOR FURTHER REFERENCE

Andrews, William, Frances Smith Foster, and Trudier Harris, eds. *The Oxford Companion to African American Literature.* New York: Oxford University Press, 1997.

Pereira, Malin. "An Interview with Rita Dove." *Contemporary Literature* 40.2 (1999): 182–213.

———. "When Pear Blossoms/Cast Their Pale Faces/On the Darker Face of the Earth: Miscegenation, the Primal Scene, and the Incest Motif of Rita Dove's Work." *African American Review* 36.2 (2002): 195–211.

Rampersad, Arnold. "The Poems of Rita Dove." *Callaloo* 9.1 (1986): 52–60.

Sample, Maxine. "Dove's Thomas and Beulah." *Explicator* 52.4 (1994): 251–252.

Schneider, Steven. "Coming Home: An Interview with Rita Dove." *Iowa Review* 19.3 (1989): 112–123.

Steffen, Therese. "The Darker Face of the Earth: A Conversation with Rita Dove." *Transition* 74 (1998): 104–123.

Wallace, Patricia. "Divided Loyalties: Literal and the Literary in the Poetry of Lorna Dee Cervantes, Cathy Song and Rita Dove." *MELUS: The Journal of the Society for the Study of the Multi-Ethnic Literature of the United States* 18.3 (1993): 3–19.

Augustina Edem Dzregah

Photo by Steve Long, University of Massachusetts
Photo Services.

Martín Espada
(1957–)
Puerto Rican

BIOGRAPHY

Frequently referred to as the most important Latino poet of his generation, Martín Espada was born in Brooklyn, New York, where he grew up surrounded by Puerto Rican activism. The inspiration for Espada's compelling poetic style in which politics and art blend together for mutual support can be found in these movements for civil rights and independence, as well as in influential individuals such as his father, Frank Espada, an organizer-photographer, and long-lived militant Clemente Soto Vélez, an organizer-writer after whom Martín named his own son. In numerous interviews and essays, Espada testifies to the impact of his father's activism, which led to jail time in Mississippi when the senior Espada refused to move to the back of a bus, a weeklong "disappearance" into the city jails of New York after a political demonstration when Espada was five years old, and (after the "disappearance") frequent exposure for the young son to a wide range of meetings, demonstrations, and events. At the same time, Frank Espada pursued photography and eventually found time to exhibit his work in galleries and museums and to collaborate with Martín in publishing projects.

In addition to his literary credentials, Espada also holds a law degree from Northeastern University, and he worked for six years as a tenant lawyer before joining the English faculty at the University of Massachusetts–Amherst in 1993. Additional work experiences include jobs as a bouncer, factory worker, and night desk clerk at a transient hotel. Espada's first volume, *The Immigrant Iceboy's Bolero,* appeared in 1982, and since then he has published seven collections of poetry, two edited anthologies, a translation, and a book of essays. *Rebellion Is the Circle of a Lover's Hands* (1990) received both a PEN/Revson fellowship and the Paterson Poetry Prize.

Espada won an American Book Award for *Imagine the Angels of Bread* (1996), and the edited anthology *El Coro: A Chorus of Latino and Latina Poetry* (1997) earned the Myers Outstanding Book Award. His book of essays,

Zapata's Disciple (1998), was awarded an Independent Publisher Book Award. In addition to these awards, Espada has won two fellowships from the National Endowment for the Humanities and one from the Massachusetts Arts Foundation, and he has been a reader and adjudicator for numerous prestigious competitions. *Alabanza: New and Selected Poems, 1982–2002,* is his latest collection and celebrates two decades of steady achievement. Espada lives with his wife and son in Amherst, Massachusetts.

THEMES AND CONCERNS

Espada is proud to be known as a political poet, and the most striking aspect of his poetic style—the ability to combine lyrical expression with themes of progressive political struggle—is perhaps best understood by recalling (as Espada often does) his legal training and background as a tenant lawyer. In that role, Espada represented society's underdogs in their fight against powerful hostile interests, and this stance is reflected thematically in poems that unveil hunger, poverty, miserable work life, imprisonment, prejudice, and the impact of organized violence from lynch mobs, police, and marauding mercenaries. *Abogado,* the Spanish word for "lawyer," is related to the English word *advocate,* and Espada has characterized his work as a poetry of advocacy. It is often apparent that lawyering has helped define the poet's artistic mission: he feels the necessity and privilege of speaking for those who would otherwise remain voiceless. Espada has also commented on advocacy as responsibility and the similarity between the lawyer's quest for a perfect statement in legal documents or court hearings and the poet's obsession with finding the perfect word.

Numerous commentators have focused on Espada's tendency to concentrate on an individual, a place, or an incident as a way of personalizing and lyricizing political content that might otherwise result in stiff pamphleteering. Still, when writing with intense specificity about himself, his wife, a cousin, his grandfather, a janitor who decides to quit his job and let the mop drag itself across the bathroom floor, a Puerto Rican baseball great denied a tryout with the Yankees, and so on, Espada links particular moments to larger social patterns and forces, particularly the hemispheric sweep of Latin American history and culture.

This larger framework of *latinadad* is significant in at least three ways. First, it allows Espada to expand—not imperialistically but in solidarity—beyond home turf issues so that his poetry takes in the lynching of Mexicans in California, the U.S. government's multipronged war in Central America in the 1980s, African American struggles such as Mumia Abu Jamal's fight against death-row confinement, the antifascist sacrifice of Irish Republican combatants in the Spanish civil war, and more. Second, by affiliating with earlier writers such as Clemente Soto Véles, Ernesto Cardenal, Pablo Neruda, César Vallejo, and others, Espada self-consciously links himself to a global literary tradition that is populist and experimental. Surrealism, with its wild combinations of bodily and spiritual images and its radical agenda to dismantle existing perceptions and reassemble them in freer formats, found some of its greatest adherents among Latin American writers and artists, and this legacy echoes strongly in Espada's poetry. Third, when Espada writes, the Spanish language duets triumphantly with English, announcing cultural hybridity as a sign of health and strength, cementing Latin American cultural history with its documentary force, and perhaps most important, providing injections of piquant humor that balance the choruses of justified anger.

POETRY COLLECTIONS

The Immigrant Iceboy's Bolero. Madison, WI: Ghost Pony Press, 1982.
Trumpets from the Islands of Their Eviction. Tempe, AZ: Bilingual Press, 1987.
Rebellion Is the Circle of a Lover's Hands. Willimantic, CT: Curbstone Press, 1990.
City of Coughing and Dead Radiators. New York: W. W. Norton, 1993.
Imagine the Angels of Bread: Poems. New York: W. W. Norton, 1996.
A Mayan Astronomer in Hell's Kitchen: Poems. New York: W. W. Norton, 2000.
Alabanza: New and Selected Poems, 1982–2002. New York: W. W. Norton, 2003.

SELECTED ANTHOLOGIES WHERE POETRY APPEARS

Axel, Brett, ed. *Will Work for Peace: New Political Poems.* Trenton, NJ: Zeropanik Press, 1999.
Carlson, Lori M., ed. *Cool Salsa: Bilingual Poems on Growing Up Latino in the United States.* New York: Fawcett Juniper, 1995.
Cruz, Victor Hernández, Leroy Quintana, and Virgil Suárez, eds. *Paper Dance: 55 Latino Poets.* New York: Persea, 1995.
Gillan, Maria M., and Jennifer Gillan, eds. *Unsettling America: Anthology of Contemporary American Ethnic Poetry.* New York: Penguin, 1994.
Gonzalez, Ray, ed. *Touching the Fire: Fifteen Poets of Today's Latino Renaissance.* New York: Doubleday, 1998.
Harris, Marie, and Kathleen Aguero, eds. *An Ear to the Ground: An Anthology of Contemporary American Poetry.* Athens: University of Georgia Press, 1989.
Shange, Ntozake. *The Beacon Best of 1999: Creative Writing by Women and Men of All Colors.* Boston, MA: Beacon Press, 2000.

SELECTED ADDITIONAL WORKS

The Blood That Keeps Singing: Selected Poems of Clemente Soto Velez. Translator, with Camilo Perez-Bustillo. Willimantic, CT: Curbstone Press, 1991.
Poetry Like Bread: Poets of the Political Imagination from Curbstone Press. Editor. Willimantic, CT: Curbstone Press, 1994.
El Coro: A Chorus of Latino and Latina Poetry. Editor. Amherst: University of Massachusetts Press, 1997.
Zapata's Disciple: Essays. Cambridge, MA: South End Press, 1998.

SELECTED RESOURCES FOR FURTHER REFERENCE

Browning, Sarah. "Give Politics a Human Face: An Interview with Lawyer-Poet-Professor Martín Espada." *Valley Advocate,* November 18, 1993. Online. www.valleyadvocate.com.

O'Connel, Kathy. "Impassioned Prose from a Passionate Poet." *Valley Advocate,* September 17, 1998. Online. www.valleyadvocate.com.

Ratiner, Steven. "Poetry and the Burden of History: An Interview with Martín Espada." *Giving Their Word: Conversations with Contemporary Poets.* Amherst: University of Massachusetts Press, 2002.

Steptoe, Lamont B. "Poetry, Controversy, and Mumia Abu-Jamal." *Grafico,* April 1997.

Kevin Meehan

Mari Evans

(1923–)

African American

BIOGRAPHY

Born in Toledo, Ohio, on July 16, 1923, Mari Evans is an artist whose gifts have been expressed in many fields and media. She wrote and hosted *The Black Experience,* a program that aired from 1968 to 1973 on prime time on Indianapolis's Channel 4–WTTV, and several of her plays have been produced over the years. These include the musical *Eyes* (1979), an adaptation of Zora Neale Hurston's *Their Eyes Were Watching God,* which was performed at by the renown Karamu Theater of Performing Arts in Cleveland, and her one-woman piece *Boochie,* which was performed at the Billie Holliday Theater in Brooklyn. She has also served as a consultant for the National Endowment for the Arts (1969–1970).

A dramatist, teacher, poet, educator, and musician, Evans's talents were nurtured and encouraged by her father, who raised her after her mother died early in Evans's life. She attended Toledo public schools as well as the University of Toledo. Evans began her own teaching career after she received a Woodrow Wilson grant in 1968. She has been in academia now for over twenty years, teaching at institutions of higher education such as Spelman College, Purdue University, Cornell University, and Indiana University, Bloomington, among others.

Beyond these accomplishments, Evans is greatly acknowledged for her poetry, which has been translated into several languages, including Russian, French, German, Dutch, Norwegian, and Italian. Her work has also appeared in more than 300 anthologies. She received the First Annual Poetry Award from the Black Academy of Arts and Letters in 1970 and was awarded National Endowment for the Arts grant in 1981. In 1997 she was honored by the East African country of Uganda, which celebrated her achievements by producing a stamp with her picture on it. She is also a children's book author, often publishing with Just Us Books, an important press that focuses on books of "black interest" for young people.

Evans is divorced and has two children. She resides in Indianapolis.

THEMES AND CONCERNS

As a writer who was influenced by and contributed to the Black Arts Movement, Evans believes that black writers have a responsibility to use language as a political tool. Her poetry reflects this commitment, as many of her works have overtly political aims, which are cogently presented through the use of black history/realities and precise, moving language. The collection *I Am a Black Woman* (1970) marked the beginning of critical attention to her work, and evidences Evans's use of black history to make the case that revolution is needed to eradicate racial oppression and inequity. As one is taken through the different scenarios of the Middle Passage, Nat Turner's rebellion, and other painful incidents in black history, Evans imaginatively puts the reader in the shoes of the suffering and oppressed to show the connectedness between contemporary African Americans and the slave and free ancestors who fought to overcome racial and gendered oppression. Beyond the history of suffering, though, she stresses the themes of racial pride, self-awareness, and love as means of resistance and revolution.

In reading Evans's poetry, one cannot escape being affected by her passion for and love of black people, her pride in black culture and history, and her commitment to politicizing black life. Her poetry both chronicles personal and communal experience as well as challenges and inspires black people to have joy in their heritage. Hoyt W. Fuller Jr. best captured the most important aspects of Mari Evans's work when he stated that "[her] poetry is like fine architecture—solid bast, elegant of line, delightful to contemplate and most important of all, designed to fulfill a vital human need" (quoted in Joyce, p. 2358).

POETRY COLLECTIONS

Where Is All the Music? London: Paul Breman, 1968.
I Am a Black Woman. New York: William Morrow, 1970.
Nightstar: 1973–1978. Los Angeles: University of California Press, 1981.
A Dark and Splendid Mass. New York: Harlem River Press, 1992.

SELECTED ANTHOLOGIES AND WEB SITES WHERE POETRY APPEARS

African American Registry. Online. www.aaregistry.com.
Chapman, Emmanuel, ed. *Black Voices: An Anthology of Afro-American Literature.* New York: New American Library, 1970.
Emmanuel, James A., and Theodore L. Gross, eds. *Dark Symphony: Negro Literature in America.* New York: Free Press, 1968.
Harper, Michael S., and Anthony Walton, eds. *Every Shut Eye Ain't Asleep: An Anthology of Poetry by African Americans Since 1945.* New York: Little, Brown, 1994.

Long, Richard A., and Eugenia Collier, eds. *Afro-American Writing: An Anthology of Prose and Poetry*. New York: New York University Press, 1972.

Miller, E. Ethelbert, ed. *In Search of Color Everywhere: A Collection of African American Poetry*. New York: Stewart, Tabori, and Chang, 1996.

Stetson, Erlene, ed. *Black Sister: Poetry by Black American Women, 1746–1980*. Bloomington: Indiana University Press, 1982.

Worley, Demetrice A., ed. *African-American Literature: An Anthology of Nonfiction, Fiction, Poetry, and Drama*. 2nd ed. Columbus, OH: McGraw-Hill, 1998.

SELECTED ADDITIONAL WORKS

I Look at Me. Chicago, IL: Third World Press, 1973.

Jd. Garden City, NY: Doubleday, 1973.

Singing Black: Alternative Nursery Rhymes for Children. East Orange, NJ: Just Us Books, 1976.

River of My Song. Produced in 1977.

Boochie. 1979. (one-woman piece)

Eyes. 1979. (musical)

Jim Flying High. Garden City, NY: Doubleday, 1979.

Black Women Writers, 1950–1980: A Critical Evaluation. Garden City, NY: Anchor Press/Doubleday, 1984.

Dear Corrine, Tell Somebody! Love, Annie: A Book about Secrets. East Orange, NJ: Just Us Books, 1999.

"Clifford's Blues." *Crisis* 108.2 (2001): 41.

SELECTED RESOURCES FOR FURTHER REFERENCE.

Dorsey, David. "The Art of Mari Evans." In *Black Women Writers, 1950–1980: A Critical Evaluation*. Editor. Garden City, NY: Anchor Press/Doubleday, 1984.

Ehlert, Alice. Review of "I Look at Me." *School Library Journal* 21.4 (1974): 49.

Furious Flower: Conversations with African American Poets. San Francisco: California Newsreel, 1998.

Henderson, Stephen. *Understanding the New Black Poetry: Black Speech and Music as Poetic References*. New York: Morrow, 1973.

Joyce, Joyce Ann. "Mari Evans." In *The Heath Anthology of American Literature,* vol. 2. Ed. Paul Lauter. Lexington, KY: Heath, 1990, 2358–2359.

Augustina Edem Dzregah

Dana Gioia

(1950–)

Italian American, Mexican American

Photo by Star Black, courtesy of Graywolf Press.

BIOGRAPHY

Born in 1950, Dana Gioia spent his childhood in a predominately Italian and Mexican working-class neighborhood outside of Los Angeles, California. Raised by immigrant parents and the first member of his family to attend college, Gioia is now recognized as a seminal poetic and critical voice in American literary culture.

Gioia publishes prolifically as a poet, essayist, critic, and anthologist and serves as the chairman of the National Endowment for the Arts. His professional aspiration, however, was not always to be a writer; his declared major at Stanford University was music. But in his second year there, he participated in a study-abroad program in Vienna and discovered his passion for literature and a desire to become a writer himself. When he returned to Stanford, he turned his attention to the formal study of literature and upon graduation earned a master's degree and began pursuing a Ph.D. in comparative literature at Harvard. Gioia's formal academic training ended partway through his Ph.D. program in 1977. Claiming a depleted financial status and a sense that graduate school was hurting rather than helping his writing, Gioia moved to New York to enter the business world.

While working his way through the ranks of General Foods Corporation, eventually earning an M.B.A. and becoming a vice president of marketing, Gioia remained fiercely committed to his writing. Every night after work, Gioia would write for two hours. Every weekend, he devoted himself to his craft as well. During this time, he slowly defined his personal poetic style and established his critical framework, resisting the advice from editors and former teachers to emulate his poetic predecessors rather than find his own unique voice. After years of work, he finally succeeded: his first book of poetry, *Daily Horoscope,* was published in 1991 while he was still employed with General Foods and met with critical praise.

His critical writing career also took flight in April 1991 when his essay "Can Poetry Matter" was published in *The Atlantic* and ignited a firestorm of debate within the literary community. In this piece, Gioia decried the state of American poetry, claiming that it had lost its public appeal and instead was read only by a small, isolated group of academic intellectuals. He encouraged poets to write for the "common" reader, who, he claimed, should be regarded as capable of responding to intellectually demanding poetry. The essay received the largest response of any ever published in the magazine, as critics from around the globe responded passionately to Gioia's argument. As they did so, Gioia juggled the responsibilities of his corporate career with the growing attention he was receiving as writer. Finally, in 1992, Gioia gave up his position at General Foods to devote himself totally to his writing career.

Since that time, Gioia's career has been prolific and critically acclaimed. In 1992 he published *Can Poetry Matter: Essays on Poetry and American Culture,* which was a finalist for the 1992 National Book Critics Award in Criticism and named one of the best books of 1992 by *Publishers Weekly.* The volume was reissued in a special tenth-anniversary edition in 2002. Gioia's poetic voice is a powerful one as well; for example, his poetry collection *The Gods of Winter* (1991) was the cowinner of the esteemed Poet's Prize and had the honor of being chosen as the main selection of London's Poetry Society Book Club. *Interrogations at Noon* (2001) won the 2002 American Book Award. Gioia has also written countless reviews and critical essays on dozens of authors, believing that such critical attention will facilitate the return of poetry to mainstream culture. He has edited and coedited bestselling poetry and fiction anthologies, translated several volumes of poetry, served as a music critic for *San Francisco* magazine and as a commentator on American culture and literature for BBC radio, and even written an opera libretto, *Nosferatu,* with composer Alva Henderson.

Although he has spent time as a visiting writer at several universities and served many arts organizations, Gioia continues to identify himself not in relation to any one organization but simply as an independent critic and writer. This organizational independence allows him to turn a objective critical eye toward the poetic and literary communities he reviews as well as to maintain the distinct poetic voice he took so long to discover.

THEMES AND CONCERNS

Gioia believes that "poetry is an art from that demands heightened attention and . . . invites more intense involvement than we normally give to other kinds of speech" (quoted in Brame, p. 40). To encourage the audience to participate in his poems most fully, Gioia relies heavily on form. For him, the form of the poem helps to place the audience in the frame of mind necessary for total immersion in the poem's content. Form and message, then, are intimately connected.

This reliance on form has placed Gioia in league with a school of poets called the New Formalists, who seek to make poetry accessible by relying on traditional forms of meter and rhyme, while at the same time straying from those forms when they become too constraining. Furthermore, New Formalists incorporate novelistic elements such as monologue and narrative, as well as elements of familiar popular culture, into their work. Gioia's identification with New Formalism means that his work is diverse and broad-ranging: sometimes he writes in intricate meter and rhyme, sometimes in free verse; sometimes he narrates the poem, telling his own story, sometimes he creates narrators, or borrows them from other authors' works, to tell stories quite different from his.

Whatever story he tells, however, regardless of the formal choices he makes, Gioia is deeply concerned with issues relevant to his readers. His poems probe beneath the surface of everyday life using the accessible, human language of everyday life. Confronting mortality, valuing and questioning familial ties, connecting with the past, living with nature, struggling with dissatisfaction, facing fears, expressing love, working through grief, revealing or hiding the interior workings of the psyche and the heart—these concerns permeate Gioia's poetry. If at times the poems feel dark, as if Gioia's narrators are struggling to come to terms with a world that is not all that they hoped it might be, they are at other times gentle and breathtakingly beautiful. The worlds created by Gioia's poems, it seems, greatly resemble the worlds of his readers. Thus he eagerly invites them to grapple with life's inherent contradictions: dark and light, violent and tender, a challenge and a reward in one.

POETRY COLLECTIONS

Daily Horoscope. St. Paul, MN: Graywolf Press, 1986.
The Gods of Winter. St. Paul, MN: Graywolf Press, 1991.
Interrogations at Noon. St. Paul, MN: Graywolf Press, 2001.

FINE PRESS POETRY CHAPBOOKS

Daily Horoscope. Iowa City, IA: Windhover Press, 1982.
Two Poems. New York: Bowery Press, 1982.
Letter to the Bahamas. Lincoln, NE: Abattoir Editions, 1983.
Summer. West Chester, PA: Aralia Press, 1983.
Journeys in Sunlight. Seattle, WA: Ex Ophidia, 1986.
Two Poems/Due Poesie. Valeggio, Italy: Stamperia Ampersand, 1987.
Words for Music. City: Parallel Editions, 1987.
Planting a Sequoia. West Chester, PA: Aralia Press, 1991.
The Litany. West Chester, PA: Aralia Press, 1999.

SELECTED ANTHOLOGIES AND WEB SITES WHERE POETRY APPEARS

Collins, Billy, ed. *Poetry 180: A Turning Back to Poetry*. New York: Random House, 2003.

Dana Gioia Online. www.danagioia.net.

Guth, Hans, and Gabriele Rico, eds. *Discovering Literature.* Compact ed. New York, Prentice Hall, 1999.

SELECTED RECENT ADDITIONAL WORKS

Can Poetry Matter: Essays on Poetry and American Culture. St. Paul, MN: Graywolf Press, 1992; tenth-anniversary ed., 2002.

Formal Introductions: An Investigative Anthology. West Chester, PA: Aralia Press, 1994.

Seneca. *The Madness of Hercules.* Baltimore, MD: Johns Hopkins University Press, 1995. (translation)

Certain Solitudes: Essays on the Poetry of Donald Justice. Coedited with William Logan. Fayetteville: University of Arkansas Press, 1997.

"What Is Italian American Poetry?" In *Beyond the Godfather: Italian American Writers on the Real Italian American Experience.* Hanover, NH: University Press of New England, 1997, 167–174.

"Business and Poetry." In *Poetry after Modernism.* Ed. Robert McDowell. Brownsville, OR: Story Line Press, 1998, 222–254.

"James Tate and American Surrealism." *Denver Quarterly* 33.3 (Fall 1998): 70–80.

"Notes on the New Formalism." In *New Expansive Poetry: Theory, Criticism, History.* Ed. R. S. Gwynn. Ashland, OR: Story Line Press, 1999, 15–27.

Nosferatu. St. Paul, MN: Graywolf Press, 2001. (libretto)

"Studying with Miss Bishop." In *Passing the Word: Writers on Their Mentors.* Ed. Jeffrey Skinner and Lee Martin. Louisville, KY: Sarabande, 2001, 203–224.

Twentieth Century American Poetics. Coedited with David Mason and Meg Schoerke. Columbus, OH: McGraw-Hill, 2003.

The Barrier of a Common Language: Essays on Contemporary British Poetry. Ann Arbor: University of Michigan Press, 2004.

SELECTED RESOURCES FOR FURTHER REFERENCE

Abbs, Peter. "Dana Gioia: Poet of a Common World." *Resurgence* 204. Online. http://resurgence.gn.apc.org.

Brame, Gloria. "Paradigms Lost: An Interview with Dana Gioia." *ELF: Electic Literary Forum* 5.1–2 (Spring–Summer 1995): 34–48.

Gwynn, R. S., ed. *New Expansive Poetry: Theory, Criticism, History.* Ashland, OR: Story Line Press, 1999.

Lindner, April. *Dana Gioia.* Boise, ID: Boise State University, 2000.

———. *New Formalist Poets of the American West.* Boise, ID: Boise State University, 2001.

Mason, David. *The Poetry of Life and the Life of Poetry.* Ashland, OR: Story Line Press, 2000.

Peich, Michael. *Dana Gioia & Fine Press Printing.* New York: Kelly/Winterton Press, 2000.

Truesdale, C. W. "Dana Gioia on American Poetry." *North Dakota Quarterly* 61.3 (Summer 1993): 180–191.

Walzer, Kevin. "Dana Gioia and Expansive Poetry." *Italian Americana* 16.1 (Winter 1998): 24–40.

———. *The Ghost of Tradition: Expansive Poetry and Postmodernism*. Ashland, OR: Story Line Press, 2000.

Anne M. Dickson

Courtesy of Nikki Giovanni.

Nikki Giovanni

(1943–)

African American

BIOGRAPHY

Teacher, poet, lecturer, and cancer survivor, Nikki Giovanni was born Yolande Cornelia Giovanni Jr. on June 7, 1943, in Knoxville, Tennessee. She and her sister were raised in Cincinnati, Ohio, by her parents, Jones "Gus" Giovanni and Yolande Cornelia Watson. In 1960 she graduated from high school early to enroll at Nashville's Fisk University. She was dismissed from Fisk in 1961, but returned in 1964 with a renewed interest in writing. She now excelled in her classes, became editor of the university's literary magazine, and reestablished the Fisk chapter of the Student Nonviolent Coordinating Committee (SNCC). She also met several important figures in the Black Arts Movement, including LeRoi Jones (now Amiri Baraka). In 1967, after graduating with a B.A. in history and moving back to Cincinnati, Giovanni began to write the poetry that would later make up her first published volume. That year, she also organized the first Black Arts Festival in Cincinnati, became a managing editor of *Conversation,* a local revolutionary magazine, and received a Ford Foundation fellowship to begin graduate school in social work at the University of Pennsylvania.

In 1968, Giovanni left the University of Pennsylvania to enter Columbia University's School of Fine Arts with the assistance of a grant from the National Foundation of the Arts. Although she left Columbia without having received her M.F.A., by the end of 1968 she had borrowed enough money to publish her first collection of poetry, *Black Feeling, Black Talk.* In order to generate publicity for the collection, Giovanni organized a party at Birdland, a local club; the line to get into the party was so long that reporters from the nearby offices of the *New York Times* featured the event on the front page of the metro section. *Black Feeling, Black Talk* sold 10,000 copies over the next eight months. She published her second collection of poetry, *Black Judgement* (1969), with a grant from the Harlem Council of the Arts. In August 1969, Giovanni gave birth to her only child, Thomas Watson Giovanni.

The 1970s were a busy and fruitful time for Giovanni. In 1970, her first two volumes of poetry were reissued under the title *Black Feeling, Black Talk/ Black Judgement,* reflecting a growing interest in Giovanni's work. She established NikTom Ltd. and edited and published one of the first anthologies of poetry by black women, *Night Comes Softly.* After the birth of her son, Giovanni also began to write for children, publishing the first of four collections of poetry for children in 1971. Also in 1971 she produced an album, *Truth Is on Its Way,* which features Giovanni reading her poetry against the backdrop of gospel music; the album became an overnight success. By 1972, Giovanni had achieved literary stardom and mainstream public acceptance, and in 1973 she was one of eight women to receive a Woman of the Year Award from the *Ladies' Home Journal.*

Giovanni has been a professor of English at Virginia Polytechnic Institute in Blacksburg, Virginia, since 1987. That year, PBS produced a film about her life, *Spirit to Spirit: The Poetry of Nikki Giovanni,* and she received an honorary doctorate of humanities degree from Fisk University, one of ten honorary doctoral degrees she has been awarded. Among her many other accolades, Giovanni has been named Outstanding Woman of Tennessee (1985) and has received the Langston Hughes award for Distinguished Contributions to Arts and Letters (1996) and the NAACP Image Award for Literature for two collections of poetry, *Love Poems* (1998) and *Blues: For All the Changes* (2000).

THEMES AND CONCERNS

Giovanni was once known as the "Princess of Black Poetry" because of the militant and revolutionary nature of some of the poetry from her first two collections, such as "Nigger, can you kill?" "Of Liberation," and "The True Import of Present Dialogue." Early reviewers tended to gravitate toward her radical poems, in part because they represented a strong female voice within the Black Arts and Black Power Movements of the 1960s. Not all of her early poems can be described as militant, however, and these serve as precursors to the kind of intimate poetry about family, love, and the difficulties of living in contemporary America that characterize most of Giovanni's career as a writer and public figure.

Critics did not react kindly to her nonmilitant poems, and many accused Giovanni of repudiating her black heritage and previous political commitments. But Giovanni has said that the reason for this shift is that the militant stance became less useful to her: "What are we going to do with a stance? Literature is only useful as it reflects reality" (quoted in Tate, p. 63). Also, Giovanni felt that the political climate was no longer militant by the 1970s. Interestingly, as critical response to Giovanni's writing became more negative in the early to middle 1970s, public response became positive and sales of her writing steadily increased, especially after the success of her spoken-word albums and the popularity of her public appearances.

Politics did not disappear from Giovanni's poetry altogether, however, for her poems and essays demand engagement in and with the political and social world. Many of her poems recognize acts of courage of common African American people living their lives; they celebrate icons of black culture, from Martin Luther King Jr. to Tupac Shakur, and they commemorate contemporary events, such as the terrorist attacks of September 11, 2001. But most of Giovanni's poetry is introspective, lyrical, and emotional, often focusing on the struggles she faced as a single mother, a black woman, and a poet. In "My House," for example, she expresses frustration about not being able to vocalize love for herself or for her lover due to the limits of the English language. Other poems capture moments such as the experience of standing on a street corner or of experiencing lightning on a summer evening. In these instances, Giovanni's poetry reaches toward the universality of human experience, using personal references to evoke similar sensations within our own lives.

Giovanni's work outside poetry has received generally good reviews, especially her spoken-word albums. Her essays, such as those in *Sacred Cows,* tend to examine poetry and its value to writers and readers, often explaining her poetry in the process. For example, she writes that poetry is much like the slave experience of surviving by finding a "human voice to guide us and a human voice to answer the call" (p. 58). For Giovanni, poetry makes that connection, and through her complex and still-evolving voice, she demonstrates the necessity for poetry to know who we are and how we connect to other people. "Art is a connection. I liked being a link. I hope the chain will hold" (p. 58).

POETRY COLLECTIONS

Black Feeling, Black Talk. Detroit, MI: Broadside Press, 1968.
Black Judgement. Detroit, MI: Broadside Press, 1969.
Black Feeling, Black Talk/Black Judgement. Detroit, MI: Broadside Press, 1970; New York: William Morrow, 1989.
Poems of Angela Yvonne Davis. Detroit, MI: Broadside Press, 1970.
Re: Creation. Detroit, MI: Broadside Press, 1970.
Spin a Soft Black Song: Poems for Children. New York: Hill and Wang, 1971, 1987.
My House. New York: William Morrow, 1972.
Ego-Tripping and Other Poems for Young People. Chicago, IL: Lawrence Hill, 1973, 1993.
The Women and the Men. New York: Quill, 1975.
Cotton Candy on a Rainy Day. New York: William Morrow, 1978.
Vacation Time: Poems for Children. New York: William Morrow, 1980.
Those Who Ride the Night Winds. New York: William Morrow, 1983.
The Genie in the Jar. New York: Henry Holt, 1996.

The Selected Poems of Nikki Giovanni. New York: William Morrow, 1996.
The Sun Is So Quiet: Poems. New York: Henry Holt, 1996.
Love Poems. New York: William Morrow, 1997.
Blues: For All the Changes: New Poems. New York: William Morrow, 1999.
The Nikki Giovanni Poetry Collection. New York: HarperAudio, 2002. (CD)
Quilting the Black-Eyed Pea: Poems and Not Quite Poems. New York: William Morrow, 2003.

SELECTED ANTHOLOGIES WHERE POETRY APPEARS

Adoff, Arnold, ed. *I Am the Darker Brother: An Anthology of Modern Poems by African Americans.* New York: Simon & Schuster, 1968, 1997.
Dance, Daryl Cumber, ed. *Honey, Hush! An Anthology of African American Humor.* New York: W. W. Norton, 1997.
Gilbert, Derrick I. M., ed. *Catch the Fire!!! A Cross-Generational Anthology of Contemporary African-American Poetry.* New York: Riverhead Books, 1998.
Hill, Patricia Liggins, ed. *Call & Response: The Riverside Anthology of the African American Literary Tradition.* Boston, MA: Houghton Mifflin, 1998.
Linthwaite, Illona, ed. *Ain't I a Woman: A Book of Women's Poetry from Around the World.* New York: Wings Books, 1993.
Quashie, Kevin, R. Joyce Lausch, Keith D. Miller. *New Bones: Contemporary Black Writers in America.* Upper Saddle River, NJ: Prentice-Hall, 2001.

SELECTED ADDITIONAL WORKS

Gemini: An Extended Autobiographical Statement on My First Twenty-five Years of Being a Black Poet. New York: Viking Press, 1971, 1976.
A Dialogue: James Baldwin and Nikki Giovanni. New York: J. B. Lippincott, 1973.
A Poetic Equation: Conversations Between Nikki Giovanni and Margaret Walker. Washington, DC: Howard University Press, 1983.
Sacred Cows . . . And Other Edibles. New York: William Morrow, 1988.
Grand Mothers: Poems, Reminiscences, and Short Stories about the Keepers of Our Traditions. Editor. New York: Henry Holt, 1994.
Racism 101. New York: William Morrow, 1994.
Shimmy, Shimmy Like My Sister Katie: Looking at the Harlem Renaissance Through Poetry. New York: Henry Holt, 1996.
Grand Fathers: Reminiscences, Poems, Recipes, and Photos of the Keepers of Our Traditions. Editor. New York: Henry Holt, 1999.
Paint Me Like I Am: Teen Poems from WritersCorps. New York: Harper Tempest, 2003.

SELECTED RESOURCES FOR FURTHER REFERENCE

Bloom, Harold. *Contemporary Black American Poets and Dramatists.* New York: Chelsea House, 1995.
Fowler, Virginia C. *Conversations with Nikki Giovanni.* Jackson: University Press of Mississippi, 1992.

———. *Nikki Giovanni*. New York: Twayne, 1992.

Skog, Susan, ed. *Embracing Our Essence: Spiritual Conversations with Prominent Women*. New York: Health Communications, 1995.

Tate, Claudia. *Black Women Writers at Work*. New York: Continuum, 1983.

Rachael Groner

Diane Glancy

(1941–)

American Indian (Cherokee)

Photo by Dave Scheele, courtesy of Diane Glancy.

BIOGRAPHY

Helen Diane Hall (now Diane Glancy) was born on March 18, 1941, in Kansas City, Missouri. Her mother, Edith Wood Hall, was of English and German descent while her father, Lewis Hall, was part Cherokee Indian. Through her childhood, she lived in Kansas City, Missouri, Indianapolis, Indiana, and St. Louis, Missouri, and graduated from Normandie High School in St. Louis in 1959. Continuing on to college, Diane received a B.A. in English in 1964 from the University of Missouri. In 1964 she also married Dwane Glancy and they had two children, David and Jennifer. The Glancys were divorced in 1983. In the same year, Diane received an M.A. in creative writing from Central State University in Edmond, Oklahoma. She was awarded an M.F.A. from the University of Iowa in 1988. Her master's thesis later became the book *Lone Dog's Winter Count* (1992).

Professionally, Glancy was a part-time artist-in-residence for the Oklahoma Arts Council from 1982 to 1992. In this capacity, she traveled across the state visiting schools and classrooms, and used the long hours behind the wheel to develop her poems and prose. In 1992 she left Oklahoma and took her present position as a professor of English at Macalester College in St. Paul, Minnesota. At the college, she teaches courses on creative writing and Native American literature.

In addition to her teaching responsibilities, Diane Glancy continues to write poetry, novels, short stories, and plays. She has received numerous awards for her ten collections of poetry. For example, she won the *Milkweed Chronicle* Lakes and Prairies Prize for *One Age in a Dream* in 1986, followed by the 1992 Minnesota Book Award for Poetry for the book *Long Dog's Winter Count*. In 1998, Diane Glancy was awarded the prestigious Capricorn Prize from *Writer's Voice* for *Iron Woman*. In 2001 she received the National Federation of State Poetry Societies Stevens Manuscript Prize for her poetry collection *Stones for a Pillow* and in the same year was given the Cherokee Medal of Honor from the Cherokee Honor Society in Talhequah, Oklahoma.

Glancy has also published literary collections that contain prose including short stories, novellas, and novels. Two notable awards among the many she has received are the 1993 American Book Award for *Claiming Breath* from the Before Columbus Foundation and the 2003 Oklahoma Book Award for *Mask Maker.* Awards for her dramas include the Wordcraft Circle of Native Writers Playwriting Award in 1997. Glancy has also received a number of grants and fellowships, including a National Endowment for the Humanities Summer Institute Fellowship, a Newberry Library Fellowship, a Sundance Screening Fellowship at UCLA, and a Works in Progress Fellowship at the Red Eye Theatre in Minneapolis.

THEMES AND CONTENTS

Diane Glancy is a poet, novelist, playwright, short story writer, and essayist. In her literary career, she first attracted critical attention as a poet. She is one-eighth Cherokee, and her literary contribution is based on themes relating to this ethnic heritage. Although she has always lived in the world outside the American Indian cultures, she chose early in her career to redefine herself as a Native American. Her struggle with this decision and its consequences is the primary theme that pervades her body of work. As a poet, one of her contributions is the voice she gives to those people who are only part American Indian and have grown up outside a Native American culture. Much of her work in poetry and prose centers on finding a center for oneself when life is split between two very different worlds. Many examples of this theme can be found in her *Iron Woman* collection, in poems such as "Aunt Fannie Fixes Bison Bourguinon" and "Use of the Bed."

Another major theme that infuses her poetry is the juxtaposition of American Indian spirituality and Christianity. Since she herself was raised in Christianity, she struggles in her poetry with the differences and looks for commonalities between the two systems, as in the poem "Well, You Push Your Mind Along the Road." Here, she speaks of her quest for a unified personal spirituality, and the reader can see how Glancy has been spiritually enlightened by her journey. She also addresses themes of history, and the effect of the modern world on American Indian community. Her poetry also touches on secondary themes that deal with issues of ordinary life, including middle age, divorce, death, power, and survival.

Although she debuted as a poet, most of Glancy's critical acclaim is for her novels and short stories. *Pushing the Bear, The Only Piece of Furniture in the House, Claiming Breath,* and *Flutie* are among her most notable prose works.

POETRY COLLECTIONS

Brown Wolf Leaves the Res and Other Poems. Marvin, SD: Blue Cloud Quarterly, 1984. (chapbook)
One Age in a Dream. Minneapolis, MN: Milkweed, 1986.
Offering: Poetry and Prose. Duluth, MN: Holy Cow! Press, 1988.
Iron Woman. Minneapolis, MN: New Rivers Press, 1990.
Long Dog's Winter Count. Albuquerque, NM: West End Press, 1992.
Coyote's Quodlibet. Tucson, AZ: Chax Press, 1995. (chapbook)
Boom Town. Goodhue, MN: Minnesota Humanities Commission and Black Hat Press, 1997.
(Ado)ration. Tucson, AZ: Chax Press, 1999.
Relief of America. Chicago, IL: Tia Chucha Press, 2000.
Shadow's Horse. Tucson: University of Arizona Press, 2003.

SELECTED ANTHOLOGIES WHERE POETRY APPEARS

Glancy, Diane, and Mark Nowak, eds. *Visit Teepee Town: Native Writings after the Detours.* Minneapolis, MN: Coffee House Press, 1999.
Gonzalez, Ray, ed. *With-out Discovery: A Native Response to Columbus.* Broken Moon Press, 1992.
Heyen, William, ed. *September 11, 2001: American Writers Respond.* Silver Spring, MD: Etruscan Press, 2002.
The Pushcart Prize XVIII: Best of the Small Presses, 1993–1994. New York: Pushcart, 1994.
Reed, Ishmael, ed. *From Totems to Hip Hop: A Multicultural Anthology of Poetry across America.* New York: Thunder's Mouth Press, 2003.
Trout, Lawana, ed. *Native American Literature: An Anthology.* New York: McGraw-Hill, 1999.

SELECTED FICTION, NONFICTION, AND EDITED COLLECTIONS

Trigger Dance. Boulder, CO: Fiction Collective Two, 1990.
Braided Lives: An Anthology of Multicultural American Writing. Editor, with others. St. Paul: Minnesota Humanities Commission, 1991.
Claiming Breath. Lincoln: University of Nebraska Press, 1992.
Two Worlds Walking: Short Stories, Essays, & Poetry by Writers with Mixed Heritage. Editor, with C. W. Truesdale. Minneapolis, MN: New Rivers Press, 1994.
Monkey Secret. Evanston, IL: TriQuarterly Books, 1995.
Only Piece of Furniture in the House. Wakefield, RI: Moyer Bell, 1996.
Pushing the Bear: A Novel of the Trail of Tears. New York: Harcourt Brace, 1996.
West Pole. Minneapolis: University of Minnesota Press, 1997.
Flutie. Wakefield, RI: Moyer Bell, 1999.
Voice That Was in Travel: Stories. Norman: University of Oklahoma Press, 1999.

Mask Maker. American Indian Literature and Critical Studies Series vol. 42. Norman: University of Oklahoma Press, 2002.

Stone Heart: A Novel of Sacajawea. Woodstock and New York: The Overlook Press, 2003.

SELECTED DRAMA

Segwohi. Produced in Tulsa, OK, 1987.
Testimony. Produced in Tulsa, OK, 1987.
Wetjob. Produced in Tulsa, OK, 1987.
Stick Horse. Produced in Aspen, CO, 1988.
Lesser Wars. Produced in Minneapolis, MN, 1989.
Halfact. Produced in San Diego, CA, 1994.
War Cries: A Collection of Plays. Duluth, MN: Holy Cow! Press, 1997.

SELECTED RESOURCES FOR FURTHER REFERENCES

Diane Glancy Faculty Homepage. Online. www.macalester.edu/~glancy.
Grossman, Mary Ann. "Writer Treads Softly, a Foot in Each World." *St. Paul Pioneer Dispatch,* November 4, 1990, pp. 7D, 8D.
Stensrud, Karen. "Listening for the Voices: An Interview with Diane Glancy." *Red Weather* no. 19 (Spring 2000): 113–119.
Swann, Brian, and Krupat, Arnold. *I Tell You Now: Autobiographical Essays by Native American Writers.* Lincoln: University of Nebraska Press, 1997.

Sue Czerny

Eamon Grennan

(1941–)

Irish American

BIOGRAPHY

Photo by Diane Zucker, courtesy of Graywolf Press.

Eamon Grennan was born in Dublin, Ireland, in 1941 to Thomas P. Grennan, an educational administrator, and Evelyn Yourell Grennan. He says that he experienced an "apolitical upbringing as a middle-class suburban Dubliner" (*Facing the Music,* p. xv). Grennan's childhood and adolescent years were spent in Dublin, and he credits one of his teachers at his boarding school for introducing him to the wonders of Shakespeare, Wordsworth, and other influential writers. As Grennan studied literature during the early 1960s at University College, Dublin, he was further spellbound by his professors' ability to read critically each subtle nuance of a line of poetry or prose. He was greatly influenced by this New Critical approach to reading texts, and this interest carried through his graduate career and his current work as a writer and scholar.

After obtaining an M.A. in literature from University College, Dublin, in 1964, Grennan continued with his scholarly study and his focus on close, critical readings of texts at Harvard University. He completed a Ph.D. in 1973, writing a dissertation on Shakespeare's history plays. Although trained as a scholar of the Renaissance, today Grennan has shifted some of his critical focus to Irish literature. A prolific scholar, Grennan has published more than twenty critical articles and books on literature, from Irish poets to Chaucer, Shakespeare, and Spenser. Grennan has received the PEN Award for Poetry in Translation for *Selected Poems of Giacomo Leopardi,* as well as awards from the National Endowment for the Arts, the National Endowment for the Humanities, and the John Simon Guggenheim Foundation.

Currently the Dexter M. Ferry Professor of Literature at Vassar College in Poughkeepsie, New York, Grennan divides his time between New York and his cottage in the west of Ireland. Much of his recent poetry and criticism has been written in Ireland during sabbatical leaves from Vassar. Grennan shares his life with partner Rachel Kitzinger and his three children from his marriage to Joan Perkins: Kate, Conor, and Kira.

THEMES AND CONCERNS

Much of Grennan's poetry contains images from the natural world; poems such as "Cows," "Daughter and Dying Fish," and "Sea Dog" (all from *As If It Matters*) require readers to question the distinction between human and nonhuman beings. In "Sea Dog," the observer encounters a decaying animal on a beach and examines, in intricate detail, the physical characteristics that have been frozen through death. Grennan describes this sea dog as "hairless" and "faintly human," and moves our thoughts from the image of death on the beach to questions of mortality, community, and loss. By asking readers to consider the blurred lines between the human and nonhuman, he points out the intimate connection between our lives and the natural world, and he is able to move beyond the distinctions to make moral observations about the world in which we live.

Many of Grennan's poems contain moments or elements of everyday domestic events. Through ordinary scenes, the poet considers such themes as relationships and marriage, sexuality, and death and loss. For example, in Grennan's recent collection *Selected and New Poems* (2000), "Heirloom" describes a small glass saltcellar that he has taken from his mother's home, presumably after her death. The poem moves from describing this saltcellar to recounting the scenes of domestic disharmony of his childhood. This small object, even in later years, seems to contain the tears of a troubled marriage and the residual pain that a young boy, now a grown man, carries with him. Similarly, his poem "Laundromat" describes a scene of drying laundry, but also manages to tell the story of the breakup of a relationship.

Grennan's use of concrete images of everyday life as art connects his poetry to a kind of "still-life" painting of ordinary scenes. He associates his type of poetry with the artistry of Dutch painters. In an interview with Ben Howard done for *The Cortland Review*, Grennan explains:

> I love the degree to which Jan Steen and Vermeer and de Hooch, in particular, offer themselves up as great models of the way art handles the ordinary, and that, to me, is, of course, the sort of ground, the base of most of the stuff I do. . . . [I]n them, I find the most elaborate and the most convincing and the most complete version of that particular activity, namely the taking of the ordinary and the finding something in it.

In addition to writing poetry, Grennan has made significant contributions to literary studies. His critical essays and books on literature include *Facing the Music: Irish Poetry in the Twentieth Century*, a text that celebrates and critiques the work of writers such as James Joyce, W. B. Yeats, Patrick Kavanaugh, and Paul Muldoon. Grennan describes his style of criticism as one that approaches the text "as an independent but not free-floating entity, rooted in the 'presence' of an author and, by implication, the author's context" (p. xv). Grennan approaches each writer as an individual and charts his own critical and personal response to his work. He urges readers of his critical texts to return to the poets' words and experience them for themselves.

POETRY COLLECTIONS

Wildly for Days. Oldcastle, Ireland: Gallery Press, 1983.
What Light There Is. Oldcastle, Ireland: Gallery Press, 1987.
As If It Matters. Oldcastle, Ireland: Gallery Press, 1991.
So It Goes. Oldcastle, Ireland: Gallery Press, 1995.
Relations: New and Selected Poems. St. Paul, MN: Graywolf Press, 1998.
Selected and New Poems. Oldcastle, Ireland: Gallery Press, 2000.
Still Life with Waterfall. Oldcastle, Ireland: Gallery Press, 2001.

SELECTED ANTHOLOGIES AND WEB SITES WHERE POETRY APPEARS

Bookmark. Online. www.startribunme.com/stonline/html/books/bookmark/ podium/html.
Collins, Billy, ed. *Poetry 180: A Turning Back to Poetry.* New York: Random House, 2003.
Fallon, Peter, and Derek Mahon, eds. *The Penguin Book of Contemporary Irish Poetry.* New York: Penguin, 1991.

SELECTED ADDITIONAL WORKS

"Arm and Sleeve: Nature and Custom in The Comedy of Errors." *Philological Quarterly* 59.2 (Spring 1980): 150–164.
"In a Topographical Frame: Ireland in the Poetry of Louis MacNeice." *Studies: An Irish Quarterly Review* 70 (Summer–Autumn 1981): 145–161.
"Pastoral Design in the Poetry of Patrick Kavanagh." *Renascence: Essays on Values in Literature* 34.1 (Autumn 1981): 3–16.
"'To the Point of Speech': The Poetry of Derek Mahon." In *Contemporary Irish Writing.* Ed. James Brophy and Raymond Porter. Boston, MA: Twayne, 1983, 15–31.
"A Piecemeal Meditation on Kavanagh's Poetry." In *Patrick Kavanagh: Man and Poet.* Ed. Peter Kavanagh. Orono: University of Maine, 1986, 339–350.
"The Women's Voices in Othello: Speech, Song, Silence." *Shakespeare Quarterly* 38.3 (Autumn 1987): 275–292.
"The Poet Joyce." In *James Joyce: The Artist and the Labyrinth.* Ed. Augustine Martin. London: Ryan, 1990, 121–145.
"Contemporary Irish Poetry: Introduction." *Colby-Quarterly* 28.4 (December 1992): 181–189.
Selected Poems of Giacomo Leopardi. Trans. Eamon Grennan. Princeton, NJ: Princeton University Press, 1997.

Facing the Music: Irish Poetry in the Twentieth Century. Omaha, NE: Creighton University Press, 1998.

"Fantasy Echo: Oracles, Enigmas." *Parnassus: Poetry in Review* 24.2 (2000): 333–349.

SELECTED RESOURCES FOR FURTHER REFERENCE

Cahill, Tim. "Things Both Ways: An Interview with Eamon Grennan." *Writers Online.* New York State Writers' Institute. www.albany.edu/writers.

Fitzgerald-Hoyt, Mary. "Vermeer in Verse: Eamon Grennan's Domestic Interiors." *New Hibernia Review: A Quarterly Record of Irish Studies* 2.1 (Spring 1998): 121–131.

Fleming, Deborah. "The 'Common Ground' of Eamon Grennan." *Eire: A Journal of Irish Studies* 28.4 (Winter 1993): 133–149.

Howard, Ben. "Interview with Eamon Grennan." *Cortland Review* 12 (February 20 2003). Online. www.cortlandreview.com/issue/12/grennan12.html.

———. "Secular and Sacred." *Poetry* 176.1 (April 2000): 29–32.

Jennifer McNamara Dressler

Jessica Hagedorn

(1949–)

Filipino American

BIOGRAPHY

Jessica Hagedorn, poet and fiction writer, dramatist, multimedia artist, performance artist, and singer, was born in Manila in 1949. From an early age, Hagedorn loved movies (both locally made and Hollywood made) and Tagalog radio serials. After her parents divorced, she moved first to San Diego and then to San Francisco in the 1960s, where she was influenced in her teens by Beat and post-Beat literary culture and where she studied theater arts at the American Conservatory Theater after high school. She participated in the Kearny Street Writers' Workshop, bringing her into contact with Asian American culture, which tempered her education in the Western cultural tradition.

Her poetry earned her early notice from Kenneth Rexroth, who included her work in a 1973 anthology, *Four Young Women: Poems.* Subsequent volumes include both fiction and poetry: *Dangerous Music* (1975), *Pet Food and Tropical Apparitions* (1981), which won the American Book Award in 1983, and *Danger and Beauty* (1993).

Hagedorn has always been a multimedia artist as well as a writer. For example, in 1975, Hagedorn formed a band called West Coast Gangster Choir; when she moved to New York in 1978, the band reformed under the name Gangster Choir, a "poet's band" (Uba, p. 102) that mixed poetry and drama with its music. She also performed in a trio called Thought Music between 1988 and 1992. Multimedia theater productions include *Mango Tango, Airport Music,* and *Teenytown,* which has been described as a combination of "music, acting, poetry, theatrical performances, and television parody within a historically resonant context of the nineteenth-century minstrel show" that comments on racism (Uba, pp. 102–103). She has also written plays for television and radio and has been a commentator on National Public Radio's *Crossroads.* Her continuing commitment to the visual arts is seen in her contribution to a book of photographs by Marissa Roth, *Burning Heart: A Portrait of the Philippines.*

Hagedorn is also an acclaimed fiction writer. Her first novel, *Dogeaters,* appeared in 1990; it was nominated for the National Book Award and won a Before Columbus Award. A theatrical version of the novel was performed in

La Jolla and New York. She has written two more novels, *The Gangster of Love* (1996) and *Dream Jungle* (2003). Ishmael Reed has called her novels "the kinds of novels that will be written in the next century" (quoted in Sengupta). There are close links between her poetry and novels, with phrases from the poems sparking paragraph-long images in the prose. She is also the editor of *Charlie Chan Is Dead* (1993), an exciting and influential collection of contemporary Asian American fiction.

Jessica Hagedorn's recent grants and awards have included the Lila Wallace–*Reader's Digest* Fund Writer's Award, the National Endowment for the Arts Creative Writing Fellowship, the Sundance Theater Lab Fellowship, and the NEA-TCG Theatre Residency Fellowship. She lives in New York City with her husband and daughter.

THEMES AND CONCERNS

Hagedorn's wide-ranging experience in the performing arts, as well as the early influence of the Beat poets, allow her to integrate her poetic sensibility with music and drama. She sees poetry as something to be performed, and the image of dancing is a recurrent one in her poems. For instance, in "Sorcery," she comments on the rhythm of words as so powerful that one can't help dancing; "Canto Negro" begins with the word *dancing;* and "The Woman Who Thought She Was More Than a Samba" reflects on the speaker's relationships in terms of the dances they evoked. The speaker in "Yolanda Meets the Wild Boys" describes performer Yolanda's egging on the audience to orgiastic sexual dancing.

Some of Hagedorn's poems center on allusions to popular singers and songs, such as "I Went All the Way Out Here Looking for You, Bob Marley" and "Motown/Smokey Robinson." "All Shook Up" incorporates lines from song lyrics with French, Tagalog, and Spanish phrases in a diatribe against racism in Paris and Manila that focuses on Elvis Presley's appropriation of black rhythm and blues. Form, as well as content, embody her preoccupation with performance: repetition of rhythmic lines works as it does in song lyrics.

The world that Hagedorn dramatizes is a disenchanted postcolonial world, often featuring people who live on the streets and struggle to survive drug abuse, prostitution, and madness, as well as racial stereotyping, denigration of women, and political corruption, whether the streets are Manila's or New York's. Anger pervades her poems. The title of her first group of poems, "The Death of Anna May Wong," refers to the Asian American actress who portrayed stereotypical Asian women in Hollywood films of the 1930s and 1940s. In "Ming the Merciless," Hagedorn rebels against media clichés of "the yellow peril." "Solea" mentions rapists who seek out Asian women and the locks necessary for securing New York apartment doors against them. "The Song of Bullets," which has been included in several recent anthologies, contains a vow to remember the victims of violence in the Philippines and to "stay angry," not allowing her "rage" to diminish as her daughter grows, aware that the child "may never see" her mother's country, now being torn apart by conflict.

Hagedorn names a multicultural mix of influences on her writing: Victor Hernández Cruz, Ntozake Shange, Frederico Garcia Lorca, Serafin Syquia, several French surrealist poets, and the American Beat poets (Tabios, p. 272). Exhilarating and disturbing, Hagedorn's poetry and fiction reflect a unique sensibility forged in an exciting mixture of media influences.

POETRY COLLECTIONS

Dangerous Music. San Francisco, CA: Momo's Press, 1975.
The Woman Who Thought She Was More Than a Samba. San Francisco, CA: Momo's Press, 1978. (broadside)
Pet Food and Tropical Apparitions. San Francisco, CA: Momo's Press, 1981.
Danger and Beauty. New York: Penguin, 1993.
Visions of a Daughter Foretold, with Paloma Hagedorn Woo. Milwaukee, WI: Woodland Pattern Book Center, 1994. (chapbook)

SELECTED ANTHOLOGIES WHERE POETRY APPEARS

Bruchac, Joseph, ed. *Breaking Silence: An Anthology of Contemporary Asian American Poets.* Greenfield Center, NY: Greenfield Review Press, 1983.
Donnelly, Margarita, Beverly McFarland, and Micki Reaman, eds. *A Fierce Brightness: Twenty-five Years of Women's Poetry.* Corvallis, OR: Calyx Books, 2002.
Hongo, Garrett, ed. *The Open Boat: Poems from Asian America.* New York: Doubleday/Anchor, 1993.
Hoover, Paul. *Postmodern American Poetry.* New York: W. W. Norton, 1994.
Lew, Walter K., ed. *Premonitions: The Kaya Anthology of New Asian North American Poetry.* New York: Kaya, 1995.
Lim, Shirley Geok-lin, Mayumi Tsutakawa, and Margarita Donnelly, eds. *The Forbidden Stitch: An Asian American Women's Anthology.* Corvallis, OR: Calyx Books, 1989.
Mirikitani, Janice, et al., eds. *Time to Greez! Incantations from the Third World.* San Francisco, CA: Glide/Third World Communications, 1975.
Rexroth, Kenneth, ed. *Four Young Women: Poems by Jessica Tarahata Hagedorn, Alice Karle, Barbara Szerlip, and Carol Tinker.* New York: McGraw-Hill, 1973.

SELECTED ADDITIONAL WORKS

Chiquita Banana. Third World Women. San Francisco, CA: Third World Communications, 1972, 118–127.
Where the Mississippi Meets the Amazon. With Thulani Nkabinda and Ntozake Shange. Staged in New York, 1977. (play)
Mango Tango. Staged in New York, 1978. (play)
A Nun's Story. Broadcast on *Alive from Off Center* (public television), 1988. (teleplay)

Holy Food. Broadcast on *The Radio Stage,* WNYC, 1989. (radio play)
"On Theater and Performance." *MELUS: The Journal of the Society for the Study of the Multi-Ethnic Literature of the United States* 16.3 (Fall 1989–1990): 13–15.
Dogeaters. New York: Pantheon, 1990. Play staged in La Jolla, CA, 1998.
Teenytown. With Laurie Carlos and Robbie McCauley. In *Out from Under: Texts by Women Performance Artists.* Ed. Lenora Champagne. New York: Theatre Communications Group, 1990, 89–117.
Tenement Lover. In *Between Worlds: Contemporary Asian-American Plays.* Ed. Misha Berson. New York: Theatre Communications Group, 1990, 75–90.
Two Stories: Carnal and Los Gabrieles. Minneapolis, MN: Coffee House Press, 1992.
Airport Music. With Han Ong. Staged in New York and Berkeley, CA, 1993. (play)
Charlie Chan Is Dead: An Anthology of Contemporary Asian American Fiction. Editor. New York: Penguin, 1993.
Fresh Kill. Airwaves Project in Association with Independent Television Service, Channel Four Television, UK, 1994.
The Gangster of Love. Boston: Houghton, 1996. (novel)
Burning Heart: A Portrait of the Philippines. Photos by Marissa Roth. New York: Rizzoli, 1999.
Dream Jungle. New York: Viking, 2003.

SELECTED RESOURCES FOR FURTHER REFERENCE

Bloom, Harold, ed. *Asian American Women Writers.* Philadelphia, PA: Chelsea House, 1997.
Bonetti, Kay. "An Interview with Jessica Hagedorn." *Missouri Review.* Online. www.english.uiuc.edu/maps/poets/g_l/hagedorn/about.htm.
Cheung, King-Kok. *Words Matter: Conversations with Asian American Writers.* Honolulu: University of Hawaii Press, 2000.
Foo, Josephine. "Poetry Chooses Her Listener." *Amerasia Journal* 20.3 (1994): 11–17.
Gonzalez, N.V.M., and Oscar V. Campomanes. "Filipino American Literature." In *An Interethnic Companion to Asian American Literature.* Ed. King-Kok Cheung. New York: Cambridge University Press, 1997, 62–124.
Huot, Nikolas. "Jessica Tarahata Hagedorn (1949–)." In *Contemporary American Women Poets: An A-to-Z Guide.* Ed. Catherine Cucinella. Westport, CT: Greenwood Press, 2002, 163–167.
Pearlman, Mickey. "Jessica Hagedorn." In *Listen to Their Voices: Twenty Interviews with Women Who Write.* Ed. Mickey Pearlman. New York: W. W. Norton, 1993, 134–142.
San Juan, Epifanio, Jr. "Mapping the Boundaries: The Filipino Writer in the U.S.A." *Journal of Ethnic Studies* 19.1 (1991): 117–132.
Sengupta, Somini. "Jessica Hagedorn: Cultivating the Art of the Melange." *Modern American Poetry Project.* Online. www.english.uiuc.edu/maps/poets/g_l/hagedorn/about.htm.
Tabios, Eileen. *Black Lightning: Poetry-in-Progress.* New York: Asian American Writers' Workshop, 1998.

Trudeau, Lawrence J. "Jessica Hagedorn." In *Asian American Literature: Reviews and Criticism of Works by American Writers of Asian Descent.* Ed. Lawrence Trudeau. Detroit, MI: Gale Research, 1999, 114–125.

Uba, George. "Jessica Hagedorn (1949–)." In *Asian American Poets: A Bio-Bibliographical Critical Sourcebook.* Ed. Guiyou Huang. Westport, CT: Greenwood Press, 2002, 101–111.

Wong, Sau-ling Cynthia, and Stephen H. Sumida, eds. *A Resource Guide to Asian American Literature.* New York: Modern Language Association Press, 2001.

Alice Trupe

Suheir Hammad

(1973–)

Palestinian American

BIOGRAPHY

Suheir Hammad was born in 1973 in a Palestinian refugee camp in Jordan. As a young child, she briefly resided in Beirut, living in the shadow of the Lebanese civil war. She emigrated to the United States at the age of five and grew up in Sunset Park, Brooklyn. The oldest of five children, she was raised by a homemaker and a grocer. Hammad found little connection between the work of other Arab American writers and her life in Brooklyn, so she began writing to narrate her own struggles. Her early writing was manifested in graffiti and inspired by hip-hop. After high school, Hammad enrolled in Hunter College, majoring in cross-cultural literature and women's studies, and immediately began writing a series of poems about her life. Hammad's literary break came in 1995, when she read some of her autobiographical work at a benefit for the Congo. Glenn Thompson, publisher of the independent Harlem River Press, approached her to ask if she had any material to publish. Thompson received much criticism for publishing Hammad, because the mission of the Harlem River Press was ostensibly to publish only black writers. Others in the writing community felt that Hammad, at twenty-three, had not yet paid her dues.

Hammad has published a book of poems, *Born Palestinian, Born Black,* and a memoir, *Drops of This Story,* and is featured in *Listen Up! An Anthology of Spoken Word Poetry.* She is the recipient of the Audre Lorde Writing Award from Hunter College, the Morris Center for Healing Poetry Award, and a New York Mills Artist Residency in Minnesota. Hammad has performed with The All That Band and Rhythms of Aqua.

She has produced a documentary film, *Half a Lifetime,* and is writing a film titled *From Beirut to Brooklyn,* based on her memoir. She made her debut as a playwright with *Blood Trinity* at the 2002 NYC Hip-Hop Theater Festival. She speaks at colleges around the country and writes a literary column for *Stress* magazine. She has completed a children's book on the different ways people pray, and a New Jersey theater has staged her play *Trinity,* about a sixteen-year-old Palestinian American girl, Tina Isa, who was murdered by her parents in 1989 after they found out she was dating a black man. "The story lived and breathed within me. . . . I really felt that this girl was a part of me," Hammad said. "We were the same age when she died. She was a Scorpio and she was bad. I always thought, why was she killed and not me?" ("Brooklyn, Palestine . . .").

Hammad has read her work internationally at bookstores, galleries, museums, and universities. She conducts writing workshops with young people and teaches writing to adults in schools and community centers. Throughout her burgeoning career, Hammad has lent her support to campaigns to free political prisoners (most notably Mumia Abu Jamal, imprisoned for the murder of a Philadelphia policeman), and to end domestic violence, sexual abuse, homophobia, homelessness, police brutality, and global governmental imperialism, and for the promotion of human and students' rights. Hammad is a regular on the NY hip-hop scene and her work has been broadcast on the BBC World Service and Pacifica Radio, where she can be heard voicing her support for such causes as the Palestinian struggle for self-determination. She has raised funds to aid Afghan children and volunteers to work in juvenile detention centers and prisons.

Recently, Hammad was honored by New York University's Asian Pacific American Institute as their "Emerging Artist of 2001." She awaits contracts for her latest collections, *Pariah* and *Zataar Diva*.

THEMES AND CONCERNS

Hammad's writing addresses the concerns of multiculturalism and its effects on peace making, the plights of immigrants in America, critiques of both her native and her American cultures, and displays of her love for both of her homelands. Hammad also attempts to confront the harshness of modern urban life. Hammad's writing and she herself are symbols of the bridging of two worlds and cultures. Hammad attempts to expose racism and sexism, both in her essays and poetry, rallying against media portrayed stereotypes and for self-acceptance, especially for women of color.

Haitian author Edwidge Danticant has described Hammad's memoir as a "brave, poetic . . . book to read and share" ("Brooklyn, Palestine . . ."). Poet Naomi Shihab Nye, also a Palestinian American, describes Hammad's work as "a brave flag over the dispossessed" ("Brooklyn, Palestine . . .").

Hammad's work has taken on further significance in light of the terrorist attacks of 2001, as she is both Muslim and American, Middle Eastern and a New Yorker. Hammad, of course, responded to the tragedy with the written word, penning the poem "First Writing Since," which quickly made its way across the Internet and to an eventual reading on HBO's *Def Poetry Jam*. Hammad and eight other poets spent the summer touring the country in a live version of the television program and made their Broadway debut in late 2002.

POETRY COLLECTIONS

Born Palestinian, Born Black. New York, Harlem Rivers Press, 1996.

SELECTED ANTHOLOGIES AND WEB SITES WHERE POETRY APPEARS

Anglesey, Zoe, ed. *Listen Up! An Anthology of Spoken Word Poetry.* New York: One World, 1999.

Ariga. Online. www.ariga.com/visions/poetry.

Café Arabica. Online. www.cafearabica.com/culture.

The Poetry of Suheir Hammad. The Scream Online Internet Magazine of Art, Photography, Literature 2.1 (January 2002). Online. www.thescreamonline.com/poetry.

ADDITIONAL WORK

Drops of This Story. New York: Harlem River Press, 1996.

SELECTED RESOURCES FOR FURTHER REFERENCE

"Brooklyn, Palestine Flow in Poet Hammad's Veins." March 13, 2001. Online. www.arabia.com/life/article/english.

Hopkinson, Natalie. "The Poetic Success of Suheir Hammad." *Washington Post,* October 13, 2002, p. F1.

Joel Werley

Joy Harjo

(1951–)

American Indian (Muscogee)

BIOGRAPHY

Joy Harjo was born Joy Foster (Harjo is a family name that she later adopted) on May 9, 1951, in Tulsa, Oklahoma. A registered member of the Muscogee (Creek) tribe since birth, she is the daughter of Allen W. Foster, a full-blooded Muscogee, and Wynema Baker Foster, who is part French and part Cherokee. Harjo lived in urban Tulsa—the Oklahoma Muscogee don't have a reservation—until she was fourteen, when her parents sent her to Santa Fe, New Mexico, to attend boarding school at the Institute of American Indian Arts. After graduation, Harjo joined a Native American dance troupe and worked a series of odd jobs before going to college at the University of New Mexico. Coming from a long line of Muscogee painters, Harjo entering the university as an art major, but made what she calls the "painful choice" to switch to poetry after hearing readings by such poets as Galway Kinnell and Simon Ortiz. As she explained to Joseph Bruchac in *Survival This Way:* "maybe that's why I write poetry... because it's one way I can speak. Writing poetry enables me to speak of things that are more difficult to speak of in 'normal' conversation" (p. 94).

Harjo produced her first volume of poetry in 1975—a chapbook titled *The Last Song*—while she was still an undergraduate, signaling the start of a rich and much-lauded poetic career. She graduated in 1976, and that same year received an Academy of American Poetry Award. In 1978, while she was a National Endowment for the Arts fellow (a fellowship she was awarded again in 1992), she completed an M.F.A. at the prestigious University of Iowa Writers' Workshop, and in 1980 she published *What Moon Drove Me to This?* which contains all of the poems in *The Last Song* plus forty-eight new pieces.

Harjo's third volume of poetry, *She Had Some Horses* (1983), secured her reputation as a major contemporary poetic voice, and she has continued to affirm that evaluation with every subsequent poetry collection. These include *Secrets from the Center of the Earth* (1989), a series of prose poems each accompanied by photographs of the Southwest landscape; *In Mad Love and War* (1990), which won, among other laurels, the Delmore Schwartz Memorial Award and the William Carlos Williams Award; *The Woman Who Fell from the*

Sky (1994), an Oklahoma Book Arts Award winner that features Harjo's own reflections on her poems; *A Map to the Next World: Poetry and Tales* (2000); and most recently, *How We Became Human: New and Selected Poems, 1975–2001* (2002). Too numerous to list in their entirety, her awards and honors include the American Indian Distinguished Achievement Award (1990), the American Book Award from the Before Columbus Foundation (1991), the Lifetime Achievement Award from the Native Writers Circle of America (1995), the New Mexico Governor's Award for Excellence in the Arts (1997), a presidential appointment to the National Council on the Arts, and honorary doctorates from various colleges.

Although Joy Harjo is best known as a poet, she has made her mark in many areas, including fiction, nonfiction, painting, and music. Her musical gifts are on display with her band Joy Harjo and The Real Revolution (formerly Joy Harjo and Poetic Justice), for whom she reads musical versions of her poems and plays the saxophone. Music also greatly informs her poetry, many of which are filled with jazzlike rhythms. Harjo has also written a variety of scripts for film and television that highlight Indian concerns. Her short stories and autobiographical pieces appear in a variety of journals, and in 2000 she wrote her first children's book, *The Good Luck Cat*.

Harjo is also a dedicated educator with a strong social consciousness. She has been a writer-in-residence at a number of sites and has held a variety of teaching positions, including professorships at the University of Arizona, the University of New Mexico, and most recently, the University of California at Los Angeles. She has also made many contributions to the field of American Indian and women's studies. For example, in 1989, in order to popularize the works of other Native women writers, she and Gloria Bird edited the anthology *Reinventing the Enemy's Language: North American Native Women's Writing*. Always willing to serve her various communities, she has also been a writer and consultant for Native American Public Broadcasting Consortium and has served on the National Indian Youth Council, the National Endowment for the Arts, the Steering Committee for the En'owkin Centre International School of Writing, and the advisory boards of PEN and PEN New Mexico. She has also worked for the National Association for Third World Writers and has served on the editorial boards of various literary journals.

A mother of two (Phil Dayn and Rainy Dawn) and a grandmother, Joy Harjo currently lives in Hawaii when she is not teaching, giving readings, or performing.

THEMES AND CONCERNS

Harjo's poetry has enormous breadth. Many are narrative poems that tell stories about contemporary men and women—including her poetic counterpart Noni Daylight—who have become silenced or otherwise victimized by racial and social injustices. Some of the most memorable of these are "For

Anna Mae Pictou Aquash," written about a murdered young Indian activist (in *The Woman Who Fell from the Sky*); "Strange Fruit," dedicated to civil rights worker Jacqueline Peters, who was lynched by the Ku Klux Klan (also in *The Woman Who Fell from the Sky*); and "The Woman Hanging from the Thirteenth Floor Window," a moving "everywoman" tale from *She Had Some Horses* (1983).

She also writes creation stories as well as lyrical and prose poems and finds her inspiration both in landscapes and cityscapes. At once mythic in their depth and yet highly personal, her poems resonate with certain central themes. As with so many Indian writers, one is that of survival—the survival of memory, of hope, and of the Native people—as reflected, for example, in "Night Out" and "Autobiography" (*In Mad Love and War*). "Anchorage" (*She Had Some Horses*) and "Deer Dancer" (*In Mad Love and War*) are two additional poems that reflect both this thematic strand as well as the equally familiar theme of alcohol abuse.

Although there is anger in many of Harjo's poems, there is also the strong belief in love and the resurrection of the spirit, a belief that seems to get stronger with each collection. In such poems as "Transformations," "The Real Revolution Is Love" (both from *In Mad Love and War*), and "Letter from the End of the Twentieth Century" (from *The Woman Who Fell from the Sky*), where the spirit of a murdered man returns to find and forgive his killer, Harjo's belief in the future and the transforming power of language and of love are evident. It also appears as a beacon of hope in her very recent poem "When the World as We Knew It Ended," written in the aftermath of September 11, 2001.

Harjo's poetry is often highly imagistic, featuring animals—often the horse, as in the much-anthologized "She Had Some Horses"—rain, the Moon, and other images from the natural world to summon the complexity of the Earth, humanity, and the spirit as well as the interdependence of all living things. But with equal regularly, one finds human-made images such as telephones, busy city streets, and airports, all of which signal her awareness of how distanced people can be from one another, both physically and metaphorically.

POETRY COLLECTIONS

The Last Song. Las Cruces, NM: Puerto del Sol Press, 1975. (chapbook)
What Moon Drove Me to This? New York: I. Reed Books, 1980.
She Had Some Horses. New York: Thunder's Mouth Press, 1983.
Secrets from the Center of the World. Illustrated by Steven Strom. Tucson: University of Arizona Press, 1989.
In Mad Love and War. Middletown, CT: Wesleyan University Press, 1990.
Fishing. Oxhead Press, 1992. (chapbook)
The Woman Who Fell from the Sky. New York: W. W. Norton, 1994.
A Map to the Next World: Poetry and Tales. New York: W. W. Norton, 2000.
How We Became Human: New and Selected Poems, 1975–2001. New York: W. W. Norton, 2002.

SELECTED RECENT NONFICTION, CHILDREN'S FICTION, AND MUSIC

Joy Harjo and Poetic Justice. *Furious Light*. Bethesda, MD: Watershed, 1986.
———. *The Woman Who Fell from the Sky*. New York: W. W. Norton, 1994.
Spiral of Memory: Interviews. Editor, with Laura Coltelli. Ann Arbor: University of Michigan Press, 1995.
Joy Harjo and Poetic Justice. *Letter from the End of the Twentieth Century*. Boulder, CO: Silver Wave Records, 1996.
Reinventing the Enemy's Language: North American Native Women's Writing. Editor, with Gloria Bird. New York: W. W. Norton, 1997.
The Good Luck Cat. San Diego, CA: Harcourt Brace, 2000.
Joy Harjo and Poetic Justice. *Native Joy*. Mekko Records, 2003.

SELECTED ANTHOLOGIES WHERE POETRY APPEARS

Harris, Marie, and Kathleen Aguero, eds. *An Ear to the Ground: An Anthology of Contemporary American Poetry*. Athens: University of Georgia Press, 1989.
Heyen, William, ed. *September 11, 2001: American Writers Respond*. Silver Spring, MD: Etruscan Press, 2002.
Hobson, Geary, ed. *The Remembered Earth: An Anthology of Contemporary Native American Literature*. Albuquerque: University of New Mexico Press, 1981.
Moyers, Bill, ed. *The Language of Life: A Festival of Poets*. New York: Doubleday, 1996.
Piercy, Marge, ed. *Early Ripening: American Women's Poetry Now*. New York: Pandora, 1987.

SELECTED RECENT SOURCES FOR FURTHER REFERENCE

Amrani, Nora Harwit. *American Indian Women Poets: Women Between the Worlds*. New York: Vantage Press, 1993.
Bell, Dan. "Ode to Joy." *Village Voice Literary Supplement*, April 2, 1991.
Bruchac, Joseph. *Survival This Way: Interviews with American Indian Poets*. Tucson: University of Arizona Press, 1987, 87–103.
Coltelli, Laura, ed. *Winged Words: American Indian Writers Speak*. Lincoln: University of Nebraska Press, 1990.
Crawford, John, and Patricia Clark Smith. *This Is about Vision: Interviews with Southwestern Writers*. Albuquerque: University of New Mexico Press, 1990.
Pettit, Rhonda. *Joy Harjo*. Boise, ID: Boise State University Press, 1998.
The Power of the Word. With Bill Moyers. PBS, 1989.

Linda Cullum

Linda Hogan

(1947–)

American Indian (Chickasaw)

BIOGRAPHY

In her poem "Heritage," Linda Hogan writes of the homelessness of her people. Indeed, Hogan's ancestral family, displaced from its riverbank lands on the lower Mississippi, was forced into "Indian Territory" in Oklahoma by the end of the nineteenth century. Hogan, born on July 17, 1947, to a Chickasaw father and non-Native mother in Denver, Colorado, was ultimately affected by this ancestral displacement for the entirety of her life. Throughout her youth, her own sense of dislocation mimicked that of her people's past. She spent part of her childhood in Colorado and the remainder in Germany, where her father was stationed as a sergeant in the U.S. Army; summers were spent with relatives in Oklahoma. In her late teens, she moved to California, taking a position as a nurse's aide. After her marriage, she worked as a teacher's aide in Maryland while her husband went to school, before returning to Colorado to earn a bachelor's degree from the University of Colorado–Colorado Springs and a master's degree in English and creative writing at the University of Colorado–Boulder in 1978.

Her endeavors led to an avid career in writing plays, novels, and poems, many of which reflect her multiple roles as a feminist, an avid environmentalist, and a political ideologist. She is currently an associate professor at University of Colorado and has received a Guggenheim grant as well as grants from the National Endowment for the Arts and the Minnesota Arts Board. Her work has been celebrated in literary circles of western America; in July 1998 she received the Lifetime Achievement Award from Native Writers Circle of the Americas, while *The Book of Medicines* won the National Book Critics' Circle Award and the Colorado Book Award in 1993. Her earlier collection, *Seeing Through the Sun,* won the American Book Award from the Before Columbus Foundation. Her novels have also won awards, including *Mean Spirit,* which won the Oklahoma Book Award and was one of three finalists for a Pulitzer Prize. Hogan's recent work with Brenda Peterson, a writer as passionate about the environmental preservation as herself, celebrates the human connection with the "green world" and draws on writers such as Zora Neale Hurston and Kathleen Norris to draw attention to a diminishing resource.

THEMES AND CONCERNS

Reflecting her fractured heritage, Hogan's poetry is filled with her attempt at restoration, from transitory images of the sloping land and resilient, hard-shelled herps of Oklahoma in *Calling Myself Home* (1979), to the haunted rooms and branded floorboards of urban Minnesota in *Savings* (1988). Simultaneously, many of her poems focus on the cultural displacement of her people and the sense of loss generated by their compulsory transition from their homeland to the reservation.

In *Other Words: American Indian Literature, Law, and Culture,* Jace Weaver reflects on the necessity of cultural healing in the displaced community, noting that "in communities that have too often been fractured and rendered dysfunctional by the effects of more than five hundred years of colonialism, to promote communalist values means to participate in the healing of the grief and sense of exile felt by Native communities and the pained individuals in them. . . . Linda Hogan testifies to this healing when she titles a volume of her poetry *The Book of Medicines*" (p. 49).

Indeed, much of Hogan's poetry in this recent collection revolves around the need for cultural healing. For example, in "The History of Red" she describes an infant Chickasaw, born from the womb of her displaced ancestors, as an innately wounded individual. She ponders the precolonial existence of her people by creating a metaphor for the indentured dogs leading men to food in "Bear Fat." Drawing the metaphor to define the plight of her oppressed people, she wonders if the domesticated animals recall when they were feral. Simultaneously, she seems to see the salve to centuries of sorrow and loss as an ancestral womblike state in "Harvesters of Night and Water," where refuge is unattainable. Neither man nor woman can return to the unconscious security of the womb; the horrific, inhumane deeds that led to the Trail of Tears and other tragedies remain irreparable.

Hogan's work as a whole reflects the overwhelming oppression and bittersweet joys her people have endured. Her melodic language and reflection on myth serve her goal of restoration of identity, or at least remembrance. In her haunting, chanting language, she manages to resurrect the lost dialect of her ancestors as well as the wonder of her own childhood, while simultaneously creating a map of the Chickasaw past for generations to come.

POETRY COLLECTIONS

Calling Myself Home. Greenfield Center, NY: Greenfield Review Press, 1979.
Daughters, I Love You. Loretto Heights Monograph Series. Denver, CO: Loretto Heights, 1981.
Eclipse. Los Angeles: American Indian Studies Center, University of California, 1983.
Seeing Through the Sun. Amherst: University of Massachusetts Press, 1985.
Savings. Minneapolis, MN: Coffee House Press, 1988.
Red Clay: Poems and Stories. Greenfield Center, NY: Greenfield Review Press, 1991.

The Book of Medicines: Poems. Minneapolis, MN: Coffee House Press, 1993.

SELECTED ANTHOLOGIES WHERE POETRY APPEARS

Daniels, Jim, ed. *Letters to America: Contemporary American Poetry on Race.* Detroit, MI: Wayne State University Press, 1995.

Evers, Larry, and Ofelia Zepeda, eds. *Home Places: Contemporary Native American Writing from SunTracks.* Tucson: University of Arizona Press, 1995.

Gilbert Sandra M., and Susan Gubar, eds. *The Norton Anthology of Literature by Women.* New York: W. W. Norton, 1996.

Gillan, Maria M., and Jennifer Gillan, eds. *Unsettling America: An Anthology of Contemporary Multicultural Poetry.* New York: Penguin, 1994.

Glancy, Diane, and Mark Nowak, eds. *Visit Teepee Town.* St. Paul, MN: Consortium, 1999.

Harjo, Joy, and Gloria Bird, eds. *Reinventing the Enemy's Language: Contemporary Native American Women's Writings of North America.* New York: W. W. Norton, 1998.

Niatum, Duane, ed. *Harper's Anthology of 20th Century Native American Poetry.* San Francisco, CA: Harper, 1988.

Sewell, Marilyn, ed. *Claiming the Spirit Within: A Sourcebook of Women's Poetry.* Boston, MA: Beacon Press, 1996.

Smelcer, John E., D. L. Birchfield, and Duane Niatum, eds. *Durable Breath: Contemporary Native American Poetry.* Chugiak, AK: Salmon Run, 1994.

SELECTED ADDITIONAL WORKS

That Horse. With Charles Colbert Henderson. Acomita, NM: Pueblo of Acoma Press, 1985.

The Stories We Hold Secret: Tales of Women's Spiritual Development. Editor, with Carol Buechal and Judith McDaniel. Greenfield Center, NY: Greenfield Review Press, 1986.

The Big Woman. Ithaca, NY: Firebrand Press, 1987.

Mean Spirit. New York: Ivy Books, 1992.

From Women's Experience to Feminist Theology. Sheffield: Sheffield Academic Press, 1995.

Dwellings: A Spiritual History of the Living World. New York: Touchstone Books, 1996.

Intimate Nature: The Bond Between Women and Animals. Editor, with Brenda Peterson and Deena Metzger. New York: Fawcett Columbine, 1997.

Solar Storms. New York: Scribner, 1997.

Power. New York: W. W. Norton, 1999.

The Sweet Breathing of Plants. Editor, with Brenda Peterson. New York: North Point Press, 2001.

"What Holds the Water, What Holds the Light." In *Getting over the Color Green: Contemporary Literature of the Southwest.* Ed. Scott Slovic. Tucson: University of Arizona Press, 2001, pp. 310–313.

The Woman Who Watches Over the World: A Native Memoir. New York: W. W. Norton, 2001.

Sightings: The Gray Whales' Mysterious Journey. With Brenda Peterson. Washington, DC: National Geographic Society, 2002.

The Failure of Love. Unpublished manuscript.

Face to Face: Women Writers on Faith, Mysticism, and Awakening. New York: North Point Press, 2004.

SELECTED RESOURCES FOR FURTHER REFERENCE

Berner, Robert L. "Review of *The Book of Medicines.*" *World Literature Today* 68.2 (Spring 1994): 407–408.

Bruchac, Joseph, ed. *Survival This Way: Interviews with American Indian Poets.* Tucson: University of Arizona Press, 1987, 119–134.

Clark Smith, Patricia, ed. *This Is About Vision: Interviews with Southwestern Writers.* Albuquerque: University of New Mexico Press, 1990, 141–156.

Coltelli, Laura, editor. *Winged Words: American Indian Writers Speak.* Lincoln: University of Nebraska Press, 1990, 71–88.

St. Clair, Janet. "Uneasy Ethnocentrism: Recent Works of Allen, Silko, and Hogan." *Studies in American Indian Literatures* 6.1 (1994): 82–98.

Weaver, Jace. *Other Words: American Indian Literature, Law, and Culture.* Norman: University of Oklahoma Press, 2001.

Wilson, Norma C. *The Nature of Native American Poetry.* Tucson: University of Arizona Press, 2000.

———. "Nesting in the Ruins." In *English Postcoloniality: Literatures from Around the World.* Ed. Radhika Mohanram and Gita Rajan. Westport, CT: Greenwood Press, 1996, 179–188.

Womack, Craig. "Book Reviews." *American Indian Quarterly* 17.1 (Winter 1993): 102–110.

Alice D'Amore

Garrett Kaoru Hongo

(1951–)

Japanese American

Photo © Shuzo Uemoto.

BIOGRAPHY

Influential poet and editor Garrett Hongo was born in Volcano, Hawaii, in 1951. His father, an electrical technician, and his mother, a personnel analyst, were natives of Hawaii descended from Japanese immigrant plantation laborers. When Hongo was a child, his parents moved to the Mainland and the family settled in a working-class neighborhood in South Los Angeles, an urban, ethnically diverse community. His family's move was later viewed by Hongo as an uprooting that resulted in feelings of alienation. This alienation, as well as the racial/cultural diversity of his Los Angeles neighborhood and school, exercised great influence over Hongo's later literary life.

Hongo's grandfather, who was American-born but educated in Japan, was a leader in the Hawaiian Japanese community and was questioned and imprisoned by the FBI the day after the attack on Pearl Harbor. Such tragic and humiliating experiences of his family and of other Japanese Americans had a great impact on Hongo, as did his schooling, which ignored the Japanese American experience and place in American society and history. Hongo grew up feeling the tension of opposing traditions: that of attesting to what one has seen and experienced (exemplified in Western classical literature) and that of forbidding discussion of certain subjects (such as the Japanese American relocation during World War II), evident in both his family and the history he studied in high school.

Unlike the rest of his family, Hongo's grandfather encouraged him not to be silent about the Japanese American experience during World War II; he was an important influence in Hongo's development. A second influential figure was Wakako Yamauchi. In her teens during the relocation, her writing was crucial to Hongo's understanding of the Japanese American experience, not only during the relocation, but before and after it as well. Hongo has credited Yamauchi with being his emotional inspiration and has edited a significant volume of her works. Hongo has said that above all, he writes for his father, who taught him by example to embrace difference and to eschew hatred.

Hongo earned a B.A. from Pomona College and an M.F.A. at the University of California, Irvine. In the M.F.A. program, he studied under C. K. Williams, the teacher Hongo credits with inspiring him to take himself seriously as a writer. Hongo pursued graduate studies in Far Eastern Languages at the University of Michigan and in critical theory at the University of California, Irvine. Currently the director of graduate studies in creative writing at the University of Oregon, Hongo is married and lives with his wife, Cynthia, a violinist and musicologist, and their two sons.

Hongo's first publication was a play, *Nisei Bar and Grill* (1976). In 1978, Hongo, Lawson Fusao Inada, and Alan Chong Lau published their joint poetic work *The Buddha Bandits Down Highway 99.* His first poetry collection, *Yellow Light,* was published in 1982 and won the Wesleyan Poetry Prize. Hongo's second collection of poetry, *River of Heaven,* was the Lamont Poetry Selection of the Academy of American Poets in 1987 and a finalist for the 1989 Pulitzer Prize. Hongo's prose work *Volcano* (1995), the recipient of the Oregon Book Award for Literary Nonfiction, is a memoir of his return to his birthplace that blends natural history, cultural/family heritage, and personal alienation and belonging. Over the years, his poetry has appeared in *American Poetry Review, Parnassus, Ploughshares,* and *The New Yorker,* among others.

As an editor, Garrett Hongo has produced a number of important anthologies. His 1993 work *The Open Boat: Poems from Asian America* was followed in 1994 by *Songs My Mother Taught Me: Stories, Plays, and Memoir by Wakako Yamauchi.* He also served as editor for *Under Western Eyes: Personal Essays from Asian America* (1995). Hongo was profiled in Bill Moyers's PBS series *The Power of the Word* and is one of fourteen writers and poets who appear in the video *Art of the Wild* to discuss their philosophies of and love for the natural world.

In addition, Hongo was the founder of the Seattle theater group Asian Exclusion Act and its artistic director from 1975 to 1977. From 1976 to 1977 he served as executive director of the Asian Multi Media Center in Seattle and was the Seattle Arts Commission Poet-in-Residence in 1978. Before joining the faculty at the University of Oregon, Hongo taught at the University of Missouri, where he was poetry editor of the *Missouri Review,* and at the University of California–Los Angeles, the University of Houston, and the University of California–Irvine. Throughout his career as an academic and writer, Garrett Hongo has garnered a number of awards and commendations. For example, he won a National Book Award in 1994 and the Kingsley Tufts Poetry Award in 1995; he has also been awarded a Thomas J. Watson fellowship, a Guggenheim fellowship, an NEA fellowship, and a Rockefeller Foundation fellowship. Most recently, he was awarded the 2000–2001 University of Oregon College of Arts & Sciences Distinguished Professorship.

THEMES AND CONCERNS

Garrett Hongo did not forget the humiliation of his grandparents during World War II, his own alienation growing up "between cultures" in Los Angeles, or his realization that the history he and his family had witnessed—the history of the Japanese in America—was ignored or suppressed by the official version of history and even within Japanese American culture itself. These memories and experiences are the primary concerns of his poetry. Hongo's poetry has often been called "expansive" because it comprises the personal and the universal (Arakawa). His poetry blends lyrical description and narrative, often with humor. Many of his poems are character studies and first-person narrations, focusing on individual people and their lives. His style is dramatic and powerful, his language both earthy and elegant.

Hongo's feeling of responsibility to his ancestors and his belief in the importance of honoring a cultural past that has been dishonored have shaped his work. *Yellow Light,* his first collection, is about the forgotten people—forgotten by the culture and by literature. In poems such as "Off from Swing-Shift," a portrait of his father, a factory worker, and "Kubota," a narrative about a plantation worker, Hongo portrays working-class laborers with respect and love. "Stepchild," another poem in *Yellow Light,* focuses on how the speaker in the poem has been affected by the fact that the Japanese American experience has been excluded from the "official" version of history in U.S. history books.

The need for dignity, specific to the Japanese American experience but also universal, is a theme in Hongo's second collection, *The River of Heaven.* The poems in this volume express a whole range of viewpoints through which Hongo reconstructs the past. "O-Bon: Dance for the Dead" meditates on memory and the past; the first-person narratives "Pinoy at the Coming World" and "Jigoku: On the Glamour of Self-Hate" illustrate Hongo's self-professed "desire to contact . . . those places and peoples from which I've been separated by either history or personality" ("Garrett Kaoru Hongo," p. 4). The poem "96 Tears" revisits Hongo's own past as a high school advanced-placement student, separated in yet another way from his fellows.

Hongo also has a keen sense of place, whether in Hawaii or the streets of Los Angeles. In poems so different in subject as "Eruption: Pu'u O'o," about a Hawaiian volcano, "Four Chinatown Figures," a stark description of a meeting of cultures in an urban alley, and "The Cadence of Silk," a lyrical tribute to basketball, Hongo combines elegance and realism.

POETRY COLLECTIONS

The Buddha Bandits Down Highway 99. With Lawson Fusao Inada and Alan Chong Lau. Mountain View, CA: Buddhahead, 1978.
Yellow Light. Middletown, CT: Wesleyan University Press, 1982.
The River of Heaven. New York: Knopf, 1988.

SELECTED ADDITIONAL WORKS

The Nisei Bar and Grill. 1976. (play).
The Open Boat: Poems from Asian America. Editor. New York: Anchor Books Doubleday, 1993.
Songs My Mother Taught Me: Stories, Plays, and Memoir by Wakako Yamauchi. Editor. New York: Feminist Press, 1994.
Under Western Eyes: Personal Essays from Asian America. Editor. New York: Anchor Books, 1995.
Volcano: A Memoir of Hawai'i. New York: Knopf, 1995.
Introduction to *Hot Spots: America's Volcanic Landscapes,* by Len Jenshel. New York: Little, Brown, 2001.

SELECTED ANTHOLOGIES WHERE POETRY APPEARS

Asian American Literature: An Anthology. New York: McGraw-Hill, 1999.
Buckley, Christopher, and Gary Young, eds. *The Geography of Home: California's Poetry of Place.* Berkeley, CA: Heydey Books, 2001.
Gach, Gary, ed. *What Book?! Buddha Poems from Beat to Hiphop.* Berkeley, CA: Parallax Press, 1998.
Hong, Maria, ed. *Growing Up Asian American.* New York: Avon Books, 1995.
Srikanth, Rajini, and Esther Y. Iwanaga, eds. *Bold Words: A Century of Asian American Writing.* Piscataway, NJ: Rutgers University Press, 2001.
Tabios, Eileen, ed. *Black Lightning: Poetry in Progress.* Philadelphia, PA: Temple University Press, 1998.

SELECTED RESOURCES FOR FURTHER REFERENCE

Arakawa, Suzanne K. "Garrett Hongo." *Encyclopedia of American Literature.* Online. www.english.uiuc.edu/maps/poets/g_l/hongo/about.htm.
"Garrett Kaoru Hongo." *Gale Literary Databases: Contemporary Authors.* Gale Group, 2001. Online. www.galegroup.com.
Huang, Guiyou, ed. *Asian American Autobiographers: A Bio-Bibliographical Critical Sourcebook.* Westport, CT: Greenwood, 2001.
Slowik, Mary. "Beyond Lot's Wife: The Immigration Poems of Marilyn Chin, Garrett Hongo, Li-Young Lee, and David Mura." *MELUS: The Journal of the Society for the Study of the Multi-Ethnic Literature of the United States* 25.3–4 (Fall–Winter 2000): 221–231.

Stacy Pauley

Lawson Fusao Inada

(1938–)

Japanese American

Photo by Chris Briscoe, courtesy of Coffee House Press.

BIOGRAPHY

Lawson Fusao Inada was born in Fresno, California, in 1938, a third-generation Japanese American (Sansei). Inada's father was a dentist by profession, but his paternal roots were shared with a sharecropper people. He is proud to say that his maternal grandfather owned the Fresno Fish Store. In May 1942, Inada's family joined over 100,000 other Japanese Americans relocating to internment camps. The Inadas' incarceration began at the Fresno County Fairgrounds, but they were later moved to a camp in Arkansas and then to one in Colorado. By the time the war was over in 1945, Inada's boyhood memories were of being confined in barracks-type housing and seeing the world through barbed-wire fences.

Inada recounts that his youth in Fresno was shaped by a multiracial culture and music. "A non-Buddhist, I joined the Black and Chicano set. The main thing then was music: Johnny Ace, The Clovers, Little Walter, etc., and on into Pres and Bird. They made me want to 'say' something" ("About Lawson Inada"). Deeply influenced by the emerging musical genre, he hung out with jazz artists at the local clubs, often mistaken by bartenders as being over eighteen. He studied at Fresno State University (now California State University at Fresno), where he took up the bass.

Inada's meeting with poet Philip Levine became a career turning point, setting him in pursuit of the written word. After graduating from Fresno in 1959, he studied writing on a fellowship at the University of Iowa. A teaching appointment took him to the University of New Hampshire at Durham from 1962 to 1965. He returned to the West Coast to attend graduate school at the University of Oregon, earning his M.F.A. in 1966. He has taught at Southern Oregon State College (now Southern Oregon University) since, except for leaves to fill occasional visiting lecturer positions. He received a teaching excellence award from Southern Oregon in 1984.

Inada has published three collections of poems. *Before the War: Poems as They Happened* (1971) was one of the first Asian American single-author volumes of poetry from a major New York publishing house. *Legends from Camp* appeared in 1992 and won an American Book Award. *Drawing the Line* (1997) won an Oregon Book Award. Other awards have included National Endowment for the Arts creative writing fellowships in 1972 and 1985, a Pioneer Writers Award from Asian-American Writers Conference in 1975, and an Arizona Commission for the Arts research fellowship in 1990. In 1991, Inada was named Oregon State Poet of the Year.

Inada was one of four editors of the influential anthologies *Aiiieeeee! An Anthology of Asian American Writers* (1974) and *The Big Aiiieeeee! An Anthology of Chinese American and Japanese American Literature* (1991). He has also coedited or edited collections of Japanese American experience: *In This Great Land of Freedom: The Japanese Pioneers of Oregon* (1993) and *Only What We Could Carry: The Japanese American Internment Experience* (2000). He has been involved in a wide range of creative writing workshops and literary organizations, including the Third World Writers Festival at Central Washington State College, the Society for the Study of Multi-Ethnic Literature of the United States, and the Asian-American Writers Conference.

Other projects have included recording "Mother Goose Rap-Along" tapes to accompany children's books, performing in a 1974 documentary that links images of Fresno's downtown with his poems, and hosting a radio program, *Talk Story: The Written Word*. Inada is married and has two sons, Miles Fusao (named for Miles Davis) and Lowell Masao (named for Robert Lowell). The latter is a multimedia artist who also teaches at Southern Oregon University.

THEMES AND CONCERNS

The years of internment in the desert camps form the content of much of Inada's poetry. He is known as one of the earliest voices—and a key one at that—in Asian American literature on the Japanese American experience during the war years. Inada became a leading spokesperson about this experience, shocked that a people, by virtue of their ancestral origins, could undergo the government's racial profiling equivalent to exile. His essay review "Ghostly Camp, Alien Nation," on the relocation and evacuation during the war years, details and recreates vignettes of life at camp.

Jazz is another important influence in Inada's poetry, contributing to his rhythms, forms, diction, and use of repetition as well as subject matter. Much of his poetry is communicated more effectively through performance than reading. Noted by critics and often cited in this regard is his poem "Two Variations on a Theme by Thelonius Monk as Inspired by Mal Waldron." He has written paeans to jazz artists and singers such as Louis Armstrong, Charlie Parker, and Billie Holiday; and penned poetry for Miles Davis and Charles Mingus. Unlike other institutional entities in American mainstream culture and politics, the genre of jazz neither excluded nor isolated but instead provided an inclusive home to most racially subordinated youth.

Immersing himself in the emerging art of performance poetry or spoken-word gatherings, Inada considers performing his poetry live as the best mode of publishing and disseminating his work. He has combined his readings with musicians' performances and has also livened rap performances with other contemporary rap poets such as Al Robles. It has been said that "his poetics of performance posits his art not as an object that transcends time but as a process that shapes time. Inada appropriates the value that is ascribed to a finalized, written text for a mode that is oral and dynamic" (*Heath*).

POETRY COLLECTIONS

3 Northwest Poets. With Albert Drake and Douglas Lawder. Madison, WI: Quixote Press, 1970.
Before the War: Poems as They Happened. New York: Morrow, 1971.
The Buddha Bandits Down Highway 99. With Garrett Hong and Alan Chong Lau. Mountain View, CA: Buddhahead Press, 1978.
Legends from Camp. Minneapolis, MN: Coffee House Press, 1992.
Drawing the Line. Minneapolis, MN: Coffee House Press, 1997.

SELECTED ADDITIONAL WORKS

Aiiieeeee! An Anthology of Asian American Writers. Editor, with Frank Chin, Jeffery Paul Chan, and Shawn Hsu Wong. 1974. Washington, DC: Howard University Press, 1983.
Kondo, Alan, dir. *I Told You So.* Performed by Lawson Inada. Videocassette. Visual Communications, 1974.
Hey Diddle Rock. With Patti Moran McCoy (composer) and Kathleen Bullock (illustrator). Ashland, OR: Kids Matter, 1986.
Hickory Dickory Rock. With Patti Moran McCoy (composer) and Kathleen Bullock (illustrator). Ashland, OR: Kids Matter, 1986.
Humpty Dumpty Rock. With Patti Moran McCoy (composer) and Kathleen Bullock (illustrator). Ashland, OR: Kids Matter, 1986.
Rock-a-Doodle Doo. With Patti Moran McCoy (composer) and Kathleen Bullock (illustrator). Ashland, OR: Kids Matter, 1986.
Dong, Arthur, dir. *Claiming a Voice: The Visual Communications Story.* Videocassette. DeepFocus Productions and Visual Communications, 1990. (interview)
The Big Aiiieeeee! An Anthology of Chinese American and Japanese American Literature. Editor, with Jeffery Paul Chan, Frank Chin, and Shawn Wong. New York: Meridian, 1991.
In This Great Land of Freedom: The Japanese Pioneers of Oregon. Editor, with Akemi Kikumura, Mary Worthington, and Eiichiro Azuma. Los Angeles: Japanese American National Museum, 1993.
Only What We Could Carry: The Japanese American Interment Experience. Editor. Berkeley, CA: Heyday Press, 2000.

SELECTED ANTHOLOGIES WHERE POETRY APPEARS

Chang, Juliana, ed. *Quiet Fire: A Historical Anthology of Asian American Poetry, 1892–1970.* New York: Asian American Writers' Workshop, 1996.

Chin, Frank, and Shawn Wong, eds. *Yardbird Reader.* Vol. 3. Berkeley, CA: Yardbird, 1974.

Gaess, Roger, ed. *Leaving the Bough: 50 American Poets of the 80s.* New York: International Publishers, 1982.

Gee, Emma, ed. *Counterpoint: Perspectives on Asian America.* Los Angeles: UCLA Asian American Studies Center, 1976.

Hongo, Garrett. *The Open Boat: Poems from Asian America.* New York: Doubleday/Anchor, 1993.

Hsu, Kai-yu, and Helen Palubinskas, eds. *Asian-American Authors.* Boston: Houghton Mifflin, 1972.

Kherdian, David, ed. *Settling America: The Ethnic Expression of 14 Contemporary Poets.* New York: Macmillan, 1974.

Mirikitani, Janice, ed. *Time to Greez! Incantations from the Third World.* San Francisco: Glide/Third World Communications, 1975.

Sherman, Mark, and George Katagiri, eds. *Touching the Stones: Tracing One Hundred Years of Japanese American History.* Portland, OR: Oregon Nikkei Endowment, 1994.

SELECTED RESOURCES FOR FURTHER REFERENCE

"About Lawson Inada." *Modern American Poetry.* Online. www.english.uiuc.edu/maps/poets/g_l/inada/about.htm.

Chang, Julia. "Reading Asian American Poetry." *MELUS: The Journal of the Society for the Study of the Multi-Ethnic Literature of the United States* 21.1 (Spring 1996): 81–98.

Grotjohn, Bob. "Centering Our Legends: Lawson Fusao Inada's *Legends from Camp.*" *Poetry and the Public Sphere.* Online. www.english.rutgers.edu/grotjon.htm.

The Heath Anthology of American Literature. 4th ed. Ed. Paul Lauter. Textbook Site. Online. www.college.hmco.com/english/lauter/heath.

Wong, Sau-ling Cynthia. *Reading Asian American Literature: From Necessity to Extravagance.* Princeton, NJ: Princeton University Press, 1993.

Yogi, Stan. "Yearning for the Past: The Dynamics of Memory in Sansei Internment Poetry." In *Memory and Cultural Politics: New Approaches to American Ethnic Literatures.* Ed. Amritjit Singh, Joseph T. Skerrett Jr., and Robert E. Hogan. Boston, MA: Northeastern University Press, 1996, 245–265.

Zhang, Benzi. "Mapping Carnivalistic Discourse in Japanese-American Writing." *MELUS: The Journal of the Society for the Study of the Multi-Ethnic Literature of the United States* 24.4 (Winter 1999): 19–40.

Reme A. Grefalda

June Jordan

(1936–2002)

African American

Photo © Jill Posener.

BIOGRAPHY

June Jordan was born July 9, 1936, in Harlem, New York. She was the only child of Granville Jordan, a postal clerk and Panamanian immigrant, and Mildred (Fisher) Jordan, a nurse and Jamaican immigrant. Her childhood was quite tumultuous, and she suffered regular abuse at the hands of her father. Yet her father also passed on to Jordan his love of literature, and her mother nurtured Jordan's desire to write even though she had to abandon her own dreams of becoming an artist. In the mid-1960s her mother committed suicide, which had a profound effect on Jordan.

Jordan attended the local public schools of New York as well as a preparatory school and began writing poetry as a child. She enrolled at Barnard College after graduating from high school in 1953, and there she met Michael Meyer, a white Columbia University student whom she later married in 1955. When Meyer was accepted at the University of Chicago to pursue graduate study in anthropology, Jordan went with him and subsequently enrolled at the university herself in 1955. But she returned to Barnard in 1956, before leaving the university for the last time in 1957. In 1958, Jordan gave birth to Christopher David Meyer, whom she supported by holding a variety of jobs, including freelance writer, research writer, and urban planner, among others. She and Meyer divorced in 1965.

Jordan enjoyed a varied career as poet, essayist, novelist, editor, educator, and author of children's books. She started her writing career by publishing in a number of magazines and newspapers, under the name June Meyer. But she achieved widespread attention with the publication of her first book of poetry, *Who Look at Me* (1969). Since then, her work has garnered many grants and awards. She received a Rockefeller Foundation fellowship for creative writing in 1969, a Creative Artists Public Service Program poetry grant in 1978, a National Endowment for the Arts fellowship in 1982, and a New York Foundation for the Arts fellowship in poetry in 1985, among others. Her book

His Own Where was a National Book Award finalist and won the *New York Times* Outstanding Young Adult Novels selection in 1971. She also won the Nancy Bloch Award for *The Voices of the Children* that same year. In 1997 she received the President's Certificate of Service and Contribution to the Arts, and in 1998 she was awarded the Lifetime Achievement Award by the National Black Writers' Conference.

Jordan also had a significant impact in the literary world due to her academic career. She held teaching positions at a number of schools, including the City College of the City University of New York, Sarah Lawrence College, the State University of New York at Stony Brook, and Yale University. She joined the faculty of the University of California at Berkeley in 1989 and remained there until 2001; she was professor of Afro-American studies and women's studies. While at Berkeley, she also directed the program Poetry for the People, "a forum for developing student and community poets" (Gates and McKay, p. 2228). In 1998, Jordan was honored by Berkeley students when they awarded her the Students' Choice Louise Patterson African American Award for outstanding African American faculty.

June Jordan died of breast cancer on June 14, 2002, in Berkeley, California.

THEMES AND CONCERNS

In addition to poetry, June Jordan wrote in several different genres, including novels, plays, essays, and children's works. Her work is at once both highly political and highly personal. She has a direct, emphatic style and communicates strong opinions on social and political issues. Using her own experiences in creating an identity as an African American woman, Jordan uses her writing to give a voice to those she feels are underrepresented and overlooked in society. One of her most prominent stylistic techniques is the use of Black English, in the use of both vocabulary and pattern, which gives her poetry a casual, conversational tone that contrasts her often serious, grave subject matter. Jordan is specifically concerned with addressing issues affecting young African Americans, as well as other audiences of color. In an interview, Jordan says of her work, "I have tried to hinge everything I write to the truth of my personal experience, to give my writing a kind of anecdotal quality, because then people can see how I got there" (quoted in Nelson, p. 51).

Jordan's many poetry collections reflect her passion about political and societal issues, as well as her desire to improve conditions for humanity. In her first book of poetry, *Who Look at Me* (1969), she focuses on her personal journey of maturation, as well as her experiences with white people in the 1960s. The title poem of this collection examines the way Jordan thinks white people view minorities and also shows her growing concern with getting beyond victimization and moving toward resistance. *Things That I Do in the Dark* (1977), edited by Toni Morrison, continues the themes of self-actualization. Her collection *Passion: New Poems, 1977–1980* focuses on violence in society, as well as both racial and gender discrimination. The collection *Living Room* deals with her views on the Palestinian people, and her growing identification with them. Although Jordan's work focuses primarily on African American concerns, it represents her involvement and awareness of many different issues and groups of people. In fact, the multiple causes she championed drew some negative criticism from reviewers who felt she was taking on too many causes, especially in her compilation of poetry *Naming Our Destiny* (1989), which spans thirty years of her work. However, most criticism of her work has been favorable.

POETRY COLLECTIONS

Who Look at Me. New York: Crowell, 1969.
Some Changes. New York: Dutton, 1971.
New Days: Poems of Exile and Return. New York: Emerson Hall, 1973.
Okay Now. New York: Simon and Schuster, 1977.
Things That I Do in the Dark: Selected Poetry. New York: Random House, 1977.
Passion: New Poems, 1977–1980. Boston, MA: Beacon Press, 1982.
Living Room: New Poems. New York: Thunder's Mouth Press, 1985.
High Tide—Marea Alta. Willimantic, CT: Curbstone Press, 1987.
Campaigns: Selected Poems. London: Virago Press, 1989.
Naming Our Destiny: New and Selected Poems. New York: Thunder's Mouth Press, 1989.
Haruko/Love Poetry: New and Selected Love Poems. London: Serpent's Tail, 1993.
Kissing God Goodbye: New Poems. New York: Doubleday, 1997.

SELECTED ANTHOLOGIES WHERE POETRY APPEARS

Gates, Henry Louis, Jr., and Nellie McKay, eds. *The Norton Anthology of African American Literature*. New York: W. W. Norton, 1997.
Gilbert, Derrick I. M., ed. *Catch the Fire!!! A Cross-Generational Anthology of Contemporary African-American Poetry*. New York: Riverhead Books, 1998.
Miller, E. Ethelbert, ed. *In Search of Color Everywhere: A Collection of African American Poetry*. New York: Stewart, Tabori, and Chang, 1996.
Stetson, Erlene, ed. *Black Sister: Poetry by Black American Women, 1746–1980*. Bloomington: Indiana University Press, 1981.

SELECTED ADDITIONAL WORKS

The Voice of the Children. Editor. New York: Holt, 1970.
His Own Where. New York: Crowell, 1971.
Dry Victories. New York: Holt, 1972.
Fannie Lou Hamer. New York: Crowell, 1972.
New Life: New Room. New York: Crowell, 1975.
In the Spirit of Sojourner Truth. Produced at Public Theater, New York, May 1979.
Civil Wars. Boston, MA: Beacon Press, 1981.

For the Arrow That Flies by Day. Produced at the Shakespeare Festival, New York, April 1981.

The Break. Produced in New York, 1984.

Freedom Now Suite. Produced in New York, 1984.

The Music of Poetry and the Poetry of Music. Produced in New York and Washington, DC, 1984.

Bobo Goetz a Gun. Willimantic, CT: Curbstone Press, 1985.

I Was Looking at the Ceiling and Then I Saw the Sky. Produced at Lincoln Center, New York, 1985.

On Call: Political Essays, 1981–1985. Boston, MA: South End Press, 1985.

Bang Bang Uber Alles. Produced in Atlanta, GA, 1986.

Moving Towards Home: Political Essays. London: Virago Press, 1989.

Affirmative Acts: Political Essays. New York: Anchor Books, 1998.

Technical Difficulties: African American Notes on the State of the Union. New York: Pantheon Books, 1998.

Soldier: A Poet's Childhood. New York: Basic Books, 2000.

Some of Us Did Not Die: New and Selected Essays of June Jordan. New York: Basic/ Civitas Books, 2002.

SELECTED RESOURCES FOR FURTHER REFERENCE

Andrews, William, Frances Smith Foster, and Trudier Harris, eds. *The Oxford Companion to African American Literature.* New York: Oxford University Press, 1997.

Brogan, Jacqueline Vaught. "From Warrior to Womanist: The Development of June Jordan's Poetry." In *Speaking the Other Self: American Women Writers.* Ed. Jeanne Campbell Reesman. Athens: University of Georgia Press, 1997, 198–209.

Erickson, Peter. "After Identity: A Conversation with June Jordan." *Transition: An International Review* No. 63 (1993): 132–149.

———. "Putting Her Life on the Line—The Poetry of June Jordan." *Hurricane Alice: A Feminist Quarterly* 7.1 (Winter–Spring 1990): 4–5.

Freccero, Carla. "June Jordan." In *African American Writers.* Ed. Valerie Smith. New York: Scribner's, 1991, 443–460.

Harjo, Joy. "An Interview with June Jordan." *High Plains Literary Review* 3.2 (Fall 1988): 60–76.

MacPhail, Scott. "June Jordan and the New Black Intellectuals." *African American Review* 33.1 (Spring 1999): 57–71.

Nelson, Jill. "A Conversation with June Jordan." *Quarterly Black Review of Books* 1 (May 1994): 50–53.

Kyla Heflin

Maurice Kenny

(1929–)

American Indian (Mohawk)

Photo by Julian Block, courtesy of Maurice Kenny.

BIOGRAPHY

A poet, editor, publisher, and professor, Maurice Kenney was born on August 16, 1929, in Watertown, New York. His father, Andrew Anthony Kenny, was a Mohawk, and his mother, Doris Marie Parker Herrick Kenny Welch, is of Seneca descent. He spent his early life in the foothills of the Adirondack Mountains with his parents and three sisters. When he was thirteen his parents separated, and in 1942 Kenny, his mother, and one of his sisters moved to Bayonne, New Jersey. After one year in New Jersey, however, he moved back to be with his father in Watertown.

In 1952, Kenny enrolled at Butler College in Indianapolis. While there, poets Werner Beyer, Roy Marz, and John Crowe Ransom encouraged Kenny to take up prose, for they did not think he had the natural abilities to be a poet. In 1956, upon graduating from Butler with a B.A. in English, he moved back to New York State and enrolled at St. Lawrence University in Canton. There he met the novelist Douglas Angus, who pushed him to go back to poetry, which he did. Kenny continued on to New York University, where he studied under the poet Louise Bogan, who profoundly influenced his work by showing him how to craft a sharp sense of detail into his poetry. In the 1960s Maurice Kenny lived for short times in Mexico, the Virgin Islands, and Chicago before settling in Brooklyn. He returned to the Saranac Lake area of New York State in the 1990s, where he is now a professor at North Country Community College.

Maurice Kenny has always been involved in the community and in promoting the arts. He has traveled extensively to give readings of his poetry and other works, and has served as an artist-in-residence for colleges, universities, and Native American organizations. He has also served as a member of the board of the New York Foundations for the Arts, the New York State Council of the Arts, and the North Carolina Arts Council.

Superlative accolades for Maurice Kenny are easy to find. Michael Wilson in the *Dictionary of Literary Biography* calls him "one of the most innovative and influential poets to emerge from the renaissance of American Indian literature during the 1970's" (p. 138). Robert Berner in *World Literature Today* describes Kenny as "the most distinguished figure in the renaissance that has occurred in American Indian Poetry over the last three decades" (p. 169). His work has been published in over 100 journals and he has received many awards for his work, including Pulitzer Prize nominations for *Blackrobe* in 1982 and for *Between Two Rivers* in 1987. He was also the recipient of the Best Anthology Award from the *Bloomsbury Review* for *Wounds Beneath the Flesh* in 1983, an American Book Award from the Before the Columbus Foundation for *Mama's Poems* in 1984, and a National Public Radio Award from the Corporation for Public Broadcasting for *Blackrobe* in 1984. In 1996, Kenny received the prestigious Elder Recognition Award from the Wordcraft Circle of Native Writers.

THEMES AND CONCERNS

Maurice Kenny has explored many themes in his varied and prolific poetry. His poetry often shows his respect for the natural world and reflects concerns of Native American cultures. In his collections *North* (1977), *I Am the Sun* (1979), *Kneading the Blood* (1981), and *Is Summer This Bear* (1985), his writing reflects his own Iroquois roots as well as the heritage of other Native American tribes. The dominant theme in much of his poetry is the search for home as a sense of a place where someone belongs. As a child, his family dispersed when his parents separated, and his concept of "home" needed to be less concrete and more open and fluid. He strives in his poetry to have the reader identify with his work by interweaving fine and unique details into his verse. In this way, the reader can identify and feel at home within his poetry.

Another important theme of Kenny's is retelling actual events through poetry. Kenny is renowned for two collections of poems that tell the story of historical figures. The first, *Blackrobe*, tells the story of Isaac Jogues, a Catholic missionary priest who preached among the Mohawks until his death in 1646. The second collection is titled *Tekonwatonti/Molly Brant (1735–1795): Poems of War*. Tekonwatonti, or Molly, was a Mohawk Indian, the wife of a British nobleman, who organized her people to side with the British against the French in the hope the British would allow the Mohawks to keep their native lands. In both collections, poems tell the stories of these main characters not just from their eyes, but often from the perspective of those who are observing or interacting with the title character. For example, in *Blackrobe*, Kenny writes poems that appear to the reader to come from Isaac Jogues, from the Mohawk Indians he encounters, and even from the French cardinal Richelieu.

His most personal collection of poetry is the critically acclaimed *Mama Poems*, which is the poetry of the real people in his own life. He has also published two notable collections: *Between Two Rivers* was nominated for the Pulitzer Prize, and his latest work, *Carved Hawk,* serves as a fine capstone to an illustrious body of work.

POETRY COLLECTIONS

Dead Letters Sent and Other Poems. NY: Troubador Press, 1958.
North: Poems of Home. Marvin, SD: Blue Cloud Quarterly, 1977.
Dancing Back Strong the Nation: Poems. Marvin, SD: Blue Cloud Quarterly Press, 1979.
I Am the Sun. Buffalo, NY: White Pine Press, 1979.
Kneading the Blood. New York: Strawberry Press, 1981.
Smell of Slaughter. Marvin, SD: Blue Cloud Quarterly Press, 1982.
Mama Poems. New York: White Pine Press, 1984.
Is Summer This Bear. Saranac Lake, NY: Chauncy Press, 1985.
Between Two Rivers: Selected Poems, 1956–1984. Fredonia, NY: White Pine Press, 1987.
Wounds Beneath the Flesh. Fredonia, NY: White Pine Press, 1987.
Blackrobe: Isaac Jogues, b. March 11, 1607, d. October 18, 1646—Poems. Saranac Lake, NY: Chauncy Press, 1988.
Greyhounding This America: Poems and Dialog. Chico, CA: Heidelberg Graphics, 1988.
Tekonwatonti/Molly Brant, 1735–1795: Poems of War. Fredonia, NY: White Pine Press, 1992.
In the Time of the Present: Poems. East Lansing: Michigan State University Press, 2000.
Carved Hawk: New and Selected Poems, 1953–2000. Fredonia, NY: White Pine Press, 2002.

SELECTED ANTHOLOGIES WHERE POETRY APPEARS

Bruchac, Joseph, ed. *New Voices from the Longhouse.* Greenfield Center, NY: Greenfield Review, 1989.
———. *Returning the Gift: Poetry and Prose from the First North American Native Writers' Festival.* Tucson: University of Arizona Press, 1994.
Hobson, Geary, ed. *The Remembered Earth: An Anthology of Contemporary Native American Literature.* Albuquerque: University of New Mexico Press, 1981.
Ortiz, Simon, ed. *Earth Power Coming.* Tsaile, AZ: Navajo Community College Press, 1983.
Velie, Alan, ed. *American Indian Literature: An Anthology.* Norman: University of Oklahoma Press, 1999.

SELECTED FICTION

Rain and Other Fictions. Fredonia, NY: White Pine Press, 1990.
On Second Thought: A Compilation. Norman: University of Oklahoma Press, 1995.
Backward to Forward: Prose Pieces. Fredonia, NY: White Pine Press, 1997.
Tortured Skins and Other Fictions. East Lansing: Michigan State University Press, 2000.

SELECTED RESOURCES FOR FURTHER REFERENCE

Barron, Patrick. "Maurice Kenny's Tekonwatonti/Molly Brant: Poetic Memory and History." *MELUS: The Journal of the Society for the Study of the Multi-Ethnic Literature of the United States* 25 (Fall–Winter 2000): 31–64.

Berner, Robert L. "Maurice Kenny." *World Literature Today* 65 (Winter 1991): 169.

Bruchac, Joseph. *Survival This Way.* Tucson: University of Arizona Press, 1987, 145–155.

Fast, Robin Riley. "Resistant History: Revisiting the Captivy [Captivity] Narrative in 'Captivity' and Blackrobe: Isaac Jogues." *American Indian Culture and Research Journal* 23.1 (1999): 69–86.

Kenny, Maurice, and Karen Strom. "Maurice Kenny." Online. www.hanksville.org/storytellers/kenney.

Swann, Brian, and Arnold Krupat, eds. *I Tell You Now: Autobiographical Essays by Native American Writers.* Lincoln: University of Nebraska Press, 1987.

Wilson, Michael D. "Maurice Kenny." *Dictionary of Literary Biography.* Vol. 175. Detroit, MI: Gale, 1997.

Witalec, Janet, ed. *Smoke Rising: A Native North American Companion.* Detroit, MI: Visible Ink Press, 1995.

Sue Czerny

Galway Kinnell

(1927–)

Irish American

BIOGRAPHY

A first-generation American, Galway Kinnell was born on February 1, 1927, in Providence, Rhode Island, to James Cott Kinnell and Elizabeth Mills Kinnell. His father, a carpenter and teacher, had emigrated from Scotland, and his mother, from Ireland. Kinnell attended public schools in Pawtucket, Rhode Island, until his senior year, when he earned a scholarship to Wilbraham Academy in Massachusetts for his final year of high school. While studying at this academy, he began his interest in poetry and creative writing and was inspired to apply for an Ivy League education. Kinnell was accepted to Princeton University in 1944, but left later that year to serve with the U.S. Navy until his return to Princeton in 1946. His interest in creative writing continually growing, he spent the summer of 1947 at Black Mountain College studying with his mentor and fellow poet Charles G. Bell and then graduated from Princeton summa cum laude in 1948. Bell recalls the first time he read Kinnell's poetry: "the last couplet had a romantic fierceness that amazed me. The man who had done that could go beyond any poetic limits to be assigned" (quoted in Nelson, p. 25). Kinnell then went to the University of Rochester, obtaining his M.A. in English in 1949.

Kinnell has spent the majority of his career working as a teacher and prolific writer. From 1955 to 1957 he taught at the University of Grenoble in France on a Fulbright grant, and while there he created a French translation of Rene Hardy's novel *Bitter Victory*. During the next few years, Kinnell provided expertise in creative writing by teaching at universities across the United States, including Juniata College in Pennsylvania, Colorado State University, Reed College in Oregon, the University of California at Irvine, and the University of Iowa. In 1959 he was awarded another Fulbright grant to teach and study in Iran.

Returning to the United States in 1960, Kinnell continued his literary career and began his work in social activism, which continues to shape his writing. He published his first book of poetry, *What a Kingdom It Was,* in 1960. It received favorable critical reviews, and in 1961 Kinnell received a Guggenheim Award, followed by a National Institute of Arts and Letters

Award in 1962. At this time, he also campaigned for civil rights and worked for a voter registration campaign in Louisiana, a job that resulted in Kinnell spending a week in jail. In 1964 he published *Flower Herding on Mount Monadnock.* In 1965 he began a twenty-year marriage to Ines Delgado de Torres. They had two children together, Maud Natasha in 1966, and Finn Fergus in 1968. During the Vietnam era, Kinnell protested the war by writing and reading poetry at many antiwar protests, including the "Poets for Peace" poetry reading in New York City.

During the 1970s and 1980s, Kinnell garnered numerous awards for his poetry and translations. In 1974 he received the Shelley Prize from the Poetry Society of America, and the following year he was awarded the Medal of Merit from the National Institute of Arts and Letters. In 1978 he received a Fulbright professorship at the University of Nice and the Harold L. Landon Translation Prize. In 1983 he was awarded the Pulitzer Prize for *Selected Poems,* and he was the cowinner of the American Book Award. Throughout these years, he continued his social activism by speaking out against nuclear weapons and the nuclear arms race. He organized a reading in New York City, "Poets Against the End of the World," in 1982.

The past fifteen years have yielded much new poetry, including the publication of *Imperfect Thirst* in 1994 and *A New Selected Poems* in 2000. Kinnell is a regular contributor to the *New Yorker Magazine,* and he has held the position of Samuel F. B. Morse Professor of Fine Arts at New York University since 1985.

THEMES AND CONCERNS

Despite Kinnell's social activism, he has been characterized as a "nature poet" by many scholars and critics, a term that he asserts does not suggest the full range of his poetry. His poems are largely set in natural rather than urban scenes, and some of his most recognized and acclaimed poems are titled "The Bear," "The Porcupine," and "Saint Francis and the Sow." For Kinnell, though, the natural world does not simply include animals; his treatment of death in the animal kingdom calls for us to consider our intimate connection with other beings and our common fate as inhabitants of the same planet. In *Walking Down the Stairs,* he claims, "The best poems are those in which you are not this or that person, but anyone, just a person. If you could go farther, you would no longer be a person but an animal. If you went farther still you would be the grass, eventually a stone. If a stone could speak your poem would be its words" (p. 23).

Kinnell asks readers to move beyond this distinction between the natural world and humankind and also asks them to probe the boundaries that separate each individual from another. His poetry, therefore, calls humans to see each other as inextricably linked with the natural world and intimately connected to each other. He objects to the tendency of poetry to create a persona, an "I," that closes off the inner self and fails to dig deeply into the soul of the poet. For Kinnell, any attempt to live without connection to other individuals and the natural world is a misguided and undesirable goal.

Many critics and scholars also note Kinnell's concern with mortality and his vivid descriptions of death and dying. For Kinnell, though, it is not the details of death that should be focused on; his intense and vivid descriptions of death serve to reveal a central conflict that he wants readers to consider. He explains in *Walking Down the Stairs*, "Yes, as death has two aspects—the extinction which we fear, and the flowing away into the universe which we desire—there is a conflict within us that I want to deal with" (p. 23). He asks readers to imagine death with all of the reality and pain of individual death, but also to consider how death might return us to some sort of identity that is more alive and open than the consciousness we now possess. He demonstrates this perspective in his poem "Freedom, New Hampshire," written about his brother's death.

Stylistically, Kinnell has moved from formal concerns with form, meter, and verse to a free verse that captures the rhythms of contemporary speech. Critic Richard Calhoun claims that Kinnell is an "important, if still unacknowledged, postmodernist—personal but still universal, more direct than ambiguously indirect, more narrative than symbolist, characteristically more surrealistic than realistic, and freer in verse and looser in structure than he had been while attempting, in his earliest verse, to write the well-made poem according to the strictures of the New Criticism" (p. x).

POETRY COLLECTIONS

What a Kingdom It Was. Boston, MA: Houghton Mifflin, 1960.
Flower Herding on Mount Monadnock. Boston, MA: Houghton Mifflin, 1964.
Body Rags. Boston, MA: Houghton Mifflin, 1968.
First Poems 1946–1954. Mt. Horeb, WI: Perishable Press, 1970.
The Shoes of Wandering. Mt. Horeb, WI: Perishable Press, 1970.
The Book of Nightmares. Boston, MA: Houghton Mifflin. 1971.
The Avenue Bearing the Initial of Christ into the New World: Poems 1946–1964. Boston, MA: Houghton Mifflin, 1974.
Three Poems. New York: Phoenix Book Shop, 1976.
Mortal Acts, Mortal Words. Boston, MA: Houghton Mifflin, 1980.
Selected Poems. Boston, MA: Houghton Mifflin, 1982.
The Past. Boston, MA: Houghton Mifflin, 1985.
When One Has Lived a Long Time Alone. New York: Knopf, 1990.
Imperfect Thirst. Boston, MA: Houghton Mifflin, 1994.
A New Selected Poems. Boston, MA: Houghton Mifflin, 2000.

SELECTED ANTHOLOGIES WHERE POETRY APPEARS

Hill, Helen, ed. *New Coasts and Strange Harbors: Discovering Poems.* New York: Crowell, 1974.

Moyers, Bill, ed. *The Language of Life: A Festival of Poets.* New York: Doubleday, 1996.

Rosenberg, Liz, ed. *The Invisible Ladder: An Anthology of Contemporary American Poems for Young Readers.* New York: Henry Holt, 1996.

Strand, Mark, ed. *The Contemporary American Poets: American Poetry Since 1940.* New York: Penguin, 1969.

SELECTED ADDITIONAL WORKS

The Poems of Francois Villon. Translator. New York: Signet Books, 1965.

Black Light. Boston: Houghton Mifflin, 1966.

"The Poetics of the Physical World." *Iowa Review* 2 (Summer 1971): 113–126.

Walking Down the Stairs: Selections from Interviews. Ann Arbor: University of Michigan Press, 1978.

How the Alligator Missed Breakfast. Boston: Houghton Mifflin, 1982.

The Essential Whitman. Editor. Hopewell, NJ: Ecco Press, 1987.

"Poetry, Personality, and Death." In *A Field Guide to Contemporary Poetry and Poetics.* Ed. Stuart Friebert, David Walker, and David Young. Oberlin, OH: Oberlin College Press, 1997, 255–271.

The Essential Rilke. Translator, with Hannah Liebmann. Hopewell, NJ: Ecco Press, 1999.

SELECTED RESOURCES FOR FURTHER REFERENCE

Calhoun, Richard J. *Galway Kinnell.* New York: Twayne, 1992.

Marranca, Richard. "An Interview with Galway Kinnell." *Indiana Review* 18.2 (1995): 188–195.

Nelson, Howard, ed. *On the Poetry of Galway Kinnell: The Wages of Dying.* Ann Arbor: University of Michigan Press, 1987.

Tuten, Nancy Lewis. *Critical Essays on Galway Kinnell.* Ed. Nancy Lewis. New York: G. K. Hall, 1996.

———. "The Language of Sexuality: Walt Whitman and Galway Kinnell." *Walt Whitman Quarterly* 9.3 (1992): 134–141.

Weston, Susan B. "To Take Hold of the Song: The Poetics of Galway Kinnell." *Literary Review: An International Journal of Contemporary Writing* 31.1 (1987): 73–85.

Zimmerman, Lee. *Intricate and Simple Things: The Poetry of Galway Kinnell.* Chicago: University of Illinois Press, 1987.

Jennifer McNamara Dressler

Irena Klepfisz

(1941–)

Polish American, Jewish American

BIOGRAPHY

A child survivor of the Holocaust, Irena Klepfisz was born in occupied Poland in 1941. After her father was murdered in the Warsaw Ghetto uprising in 1943, she and her mother fled first to the Polish countryside and then to Sweden in 1946. In 1949, when Klepfisz was eight, she and her mother reached the United States and settled in a Jewish working-class neighborhood in the Bronx, New York.

Throughout her childhood and early adulthood, Klepfisz struggled with her Jewish identity. In one sense, her community instilled in her a deep sense of her Jewishness. Yiddish language (the language spoken by millions of Jews from Eastern and Central Europe) and Jewish culture surrounded her, and she shared with her community a reverence for the Jewish past. At the same time, however, this identification with her community alienated her in some respects from her American surroundings. She found that her culture and heritage were not valued in mainstream American culture; American school rarely covered Jewish subjects. What's more, her language background made school difficult for her: her first languages were Polish and Swedish, and at home she was surrounded by Yiddish. English was difficult for her, and she struggled with it throughout her grade school and high school years.

Despite her problems with English throughout her early schooling, Klepfisz was determined to major in English at the City College of New York (CCNY), where she earned her B.A. She then went on to earn her M.A. and Ph.D. in English from the University of Chicago. During her secondary and post-secondary education, she began to make sense of her identity and to define the poetic voice that would help her express it. Although there was no formal course on Yiddish literature at CCNY, she and a small group of her colleagues worked privately with CCNY professor and prominent Jewish scholar Max Weinreich (who was teaching in the German-language department) to create one. Upon completing it, Klepfisz went on to do more work on her own, and this work solidified her love of Yiddish literature and prompted her desire to work more closely with her Jewish past. At the University of Chicago, furthermore, Klepfisz came to understand the importance of language

163

in preserving a link to that past. It was during this period that Klepfisz began writing poetry. She had long struggled with expressing her thoughts in essay form, which she found too limiting, but poetry allowed her the freedom to confront relevant subjects with the emotions and in the form she found most appropriate.

Klepfisz's poetic voice became even stronger in the 1970s and 1980s as her context for writing expanded. While she initially wrote poetry only about issues surrounding the Holocaust, in the 1970s Klepfisz became intimately concerned with feminist and gay issues as well. Her first poetry appeared in *periods of stress*, a self-published collection of poetry that Klepfisz produced cooperatively with four other lesbian writers in 1977. At the same time, she cofounded *Conditions*, a magazine devoted to publishing work by and about women, especially women who are normally marginalized by society. In 1982, Klepfisz merged her concerns—the Jewish culture and women's/gay issues— thanks in large part to the publication of Evelyn T. Beck's anthology *Nice Jewish Girls: A Lesbian Anthology*. After contributing to this work, which sought to challenge anti-Semitism and focus on the cultural and historical contributions of Jewish women and lesbians, Klepfisz became committed to honoring the diversity that exists with the Jewish culture and to centralizing the place of Jewish women in history. In 1983, following a trip to Poland to commemorate the fortieth anniversary of the Warsaw Ghetto uprising, Klepfisz's commitment to memorializing the Jewish past and maintaining Jewish culture in the present became even more profound. To these ends, she published several collections of poetry that highlight her concerns: *Keeper of Accounts* (1982), *Different Enclosures* (1985), and *A Few Words in the Mother Tongue: Poems Selected and New (1971–1990)* (1990). Additionally, she coedited *Found Treasures: Stories by Yiddish Women Writers* in 1984 and *The Tribe of Dina: A Jewish Women's Anthology* in 1989 to bring Jewish women's voices and experiences into the spotlight.

Today, Klepfisz is politically active and vocal. She has published essays on topics ranging from the Middle East peace process, to reproductive rights for women, to the commercialization of the Holocaust, to homophobia (some of these essays are collected in *Dreams of an Insomniac: Jewish Feminist Essays, Speeches, and Diatribes*). She has also visited Israel in an attempt to bridge the culture gap between American and Middle Eastern Jews, and she has spoken at political conventions and rallies worldwide.

THEMES AND CONCERNS

Throughout her work, Klepfisz experiments with form and style, sometimes merging prose and poetic forms, sometimes arranging words in patterns on a page, and sometimes leaving large white spaces around words or stanzas. And just as the forms she chooses to express her poetry are wide ranging, so is the subject matter of the poems themselves.

The central concerns of Klepfisz's poetry have changed over time. In the 1960s, Klepfisz wrote almost exclusively about the Holocaust and the suicide of her friend and Holocaust survivor Elva. In the 1970s this intensely personal poetry turned outward. While attention the Holocaust was still present, so was her interest in women's rights, lesbianism, gay issues, and the world of work (especially as it concerns women). The 1980s witnessed a merging of Klepfisz's interests, as she began writing poetry about past and present Jewish issues from a contemporary feminist perspective. At this time, a central motif is also the recovery of silenced Jewish women's voices from history.

Her most recent work continues this simultaneous concentration on the past and present. The preservation of the Yiddish language is a recurring motif, and several poems include both English and Yiddish words. Similarly, maintaining a Jewish cultural identify and respecting the diversity that exists within that identity are central concerns as well. The importance of memory, of a secure link to the past, and of resisting total assimilation into a foreign culture—whether that culture is American or a particular branch of Judaism—are recurring themes throughout. Embedded in all of Klepfisz's work is the assumption that writing poetry is a form of political action, a method of making one's solitary voice, a community's voice, or a subculture's voice heard.

POETRY COLLECTIONS

periods of stress. Brooklyn: Out & Out Books, 1977.
Keeper of Accounts. Watertown, MA: Persephone Press, 1982.
Different Enclosures. London: Onlywomen Press, 1985.
A Few Words in the Mother Tongue: Poems Selected and New (1971–1990). Portland, OR: Eighth Mountain Press, 1990.

SELECTED ANTHOLOGIES WHERE POETRY APPEARS

Beck, Evelyn T., ed. *Nice Jewish Girls: A Lesbian Anthology.* Watertown, MA: Persephone Press, 1982.
Forche, Carolyn, ed. *Against Forgetting: Twentieth-Century Poets of Witness.* New York: W. W. Norton, 1993.
Howe, Florence, ed. *No More Masks: An Anthology of Twentieth-Century American Women Poets.* New York: HarperCollins, 1993.

ANTHOLOGIES EDITED

Found Treasures: Stories by Yiddish Women Writers. Editor, with Frieda Forman et al. Toronto: University of Toronto Press, 1984.
The Tribe of Dina: A Jewish Women's Anthology. Editor, with Melanie Kay Kantrowitz. Montpelier, VT: Sinister Wisdom Books, 1986. Rev. and expanded ed., Boston, MA: Beacon Press, 1989.
Jewish Women's Call for Peace: A Handbook for Jewish Women on the Israeli/Palestinian

Conflict. Editor, with Rita Falbel and Donna Nevel. Ithaca, NY: Firebrand Books, 1990.

SELECTED FICTION AND NONFICTION

Dreams of an Insomniac: Jewish Feminist Essays, Speeches, and Diatribes. Portland, OR: Eighth Mountain Press, 1990.

"Forging a Woman's Link in Di Goldene Keyt: Some Possibilities for Jewish American Poetry." In *Conversant Essays: Contemporary Poets on Poetry.* Ed. James McCorkle. Detroit: Wayne State University Press, 1990, 370–375.

Introduction to *Found Treasures: Stories by Yiddish Women Writers.* Ed. Frieda Forman et al. Toronto: Second Story Press, 1994.

"Di yerushe/The Legacy: A Parable about History and Bobe-mayses, Barszcz and Borsht, and the Future of the Jewish Past." *Prairie Schooner* 71.1 (Spring 1997): 7–12.

"It Is Not a Child I Wish to Mother, It Is Myself." *Reproductive Health Matters* 7.13 (May 1999): 96–102.

SELECTED RESOURCES FOR FURTHER REFERENCE

Burstein, Janet. *Writing Mothers, Writing Daughters: Tracing the Maternal in Stories by American Jewish Women.* Urbana: University of Illinois Press, 1996.

Hedley, Jane. "Nepantilist Poetics: Narrative and Cultural Identity in the Mixed Language Writings of Irena Klepfisz and Gloria Anzaldúa." *Narrative* 4.1 (January 1996): 36–54.

Kwintner, Michelle. "Irena Klepfisz." In *Contemporary Lesbian Writers of the United States.* Ed. Sandra Pollack and Denise Knight. Westport, CT: Greenwood, 1993, 287–291.

Levitt, Laura. "Feminist Spirituality." In *Spirituality and the Secular Quest.* Ed. Peter Van Ness. New York: Crossroad, 1996, 305–334.

McCorkle, James. "Contemporary Poetics and History: Pinsky, Klepfisz and Rothenberg." *Kenyon Review* 14.2 (Winter 1992): 171–188.

Pacernick, Gary. *Meaning and Memory: Interviews with Fourteen Jewish Poets.* Columbus: Ohio State University Press, 2001.

Peterson, Nancy J. *Against Amnesia: Contemporary Women Writers and the Crisis of Historical Memory.* Philadelphia: University of Pennsylvania Press, 2001.

Roth, Laurence. "Pedagogy and the Mother Tongue: Irena Klepfisz's 'Di rayze aheym/The Journey Home.'" *Symposium: A Quarterly Journal in Modern Literatures* 52.4 (Winter 1999): 269–278.

Rothschild, Matthew. "Israel Isn't David . . . It's Goliath." *Progressive* 65.7 (July 2001): 27–29.

Shreiber, Maeera Y. "The End of Exile: Jewish Identity and Its Diasporic Poetics." *PMLA: Publications of the Modern Language Association of America* 113.2 (March 1998): 273–287.

Anne M. Dickson

Etheridge Knight

(1931–1991)

African American

Photo from *The Essential Etheridge Knight*, by Etheridge Knight, © 1986. Reprinted by permission of the University of Pittsburgh Press.

BIOGRAPHY

Etheridge Knight was born in Corinth, Mississippi, on April 19, 1931. His parents, Etheridge "Bushie" and Belzora (Cozart) Knight, raised him with his two brothers and four sisters in the poor, rural community of Paducah, Kentucky. His childhood was difficult and he left school at the age of fourteen, shortly after eighth grade. Knight spent his time in pool halls and bars until he joined the U.S. Army at the age of sixteen.

Serving as a medical technician, he stayed in the service from 1947 to 1951, until he was wounded by shrapnel in Korea and discharged. During the war he became addicted to drugs, and his addiction was increased as a result of the treatment for his injury after he returned to the United States. To support his habit he committed crimes, and in 1960 was convicted of armed robbery and was incarcerated at Indiana State Prison from 1960 to 1968.

It was during his time in prison that he began to write poetry. However, before he began to write, he practiced his poetic talents by reciting "toasts," a traditional African art form consisting of long, narrative poems with rhymed couplets that are memorized and recited orally. Toasts allowed Knight to compose and articulate his thoughts on drugs, racial conflicts, sex, and violence using street slang, prison vocabulary, obscenities, and African American vernacular. While in prison, Knight developed contacts with other African American poets such as Sonia Sanchez, Gwendolyn Brooks, and Dudley Randall. His first book, *Poems from Prison* (1968), with a preface written by Brooks, was published by Randall's Broadside Press while he was still incarcerated.

After his release, Knight married several times, first to poet Sonia Sanchez in 1968, then to Mary Ann McAnally and to Charlene Blackburn. He fathered three children, Mary Tandiwe, Etheridge Bambata, Isaac Bushie, and adopted three others, Morani Sanchez, Mongou Sanchez, and Anita Sanchez. He earned his B.A. in American poetry and criminal justice from Martin Center University in Indianapolis, Indiana, in 1990.

Etheridge Knight enjoyed a varied career. In addition to writing poetry, he served as writer-in-residence at several universities, including the University of Pittsburgh, (1968–1969), Hartford University (1969–1970), and Lincoln University (1972). He also contributed numerous poems and articles to magazines and journals such as *Black Digest, Essence, Motive,* and *American Report.* He was the poetry editor for *Motive* in 1972 and a contributing editor for *New Letters* in 1974. He gave poetry readings quite widely during this time, but by 1974 his marriage to Sanchez had ended and Knight sought treatment for his continuing narcotics addiction.

Knight received several awards for his poetry, most notably a Pulitzer Prize nomination in 1973 and a National Book Award nomination in the same year for *Belly Song and Other Poems.* He was the recipient of two National Endowment for the Arts grants (1972 and 1980) as well as a Self-Development Through the Arts grant (1974) and a Guggenheim fellowship (1974). His final collection of poems, *The Essential Etheridge Knight* (1986), was awarded the American Book Award in 1987.

Etheridge Knight died in 1991 of lung cancer. However, his legacy continues in many ways. In 1992 he was posthumously awarded the Indiana Governor's Award for Literature and in 1998 he was posthumously inducted into the literary Hall of Fame. Most notably, since the late 1990s, an Etheridge Knight Festival of the Arts has been held to pay tribute to the poet. It is sponsored by Etheridge Knight Inc., an organization "designed to promote the arts and the appreciation of the arts for youths, youths at risk, adults, seniors, incarcerated individuals and those underserved in the arts programming in the city [of Indianapolis]" (*Etheridge Knight Festival*).

THEMES AND CONCERNS

Most of Knight's poetry was critically well received, and he has been compared to African American poets Langston Hughes, Gwendolyn Brooks, and Sonia Sanchez. He became one of the most popular poets of the Black Arts Movement. His poetry, which deals with his personal issues with drugs, prison, war, and prejudice, was considered very important in portraying the African American experience in the 1960s and 1970s.

Knight's poetry focuses on the African American experience in the United States. As he began to write while still in prison, confinement, constriction, and freedom are major themes in his poems, as are manhood and racial oppression. Knight also often wrote about his personal struggles with drugs and his relationships with women. Related to these themes, time and space become important elements in his works. His signature style, as first seen in the poem "The Idea of Ancestry," includes the use of slashes, colons, commas, exaggerated spacing, and unusual spellings to portray the way the lines would sound in an oral reading. Another important stylistic element of his poetry is the use of "street" language, drug culture vocabulary, and black slang.

Although critics at times criticized his use of unpoetic language and strident politics, most of his work was highly commended.

Written while Knight was still serving his prison sentence, *Poems from Prison* is a collection of riveting poems about prison life. Knight often examines the theme of imprisonment, both within the context of the prison and within the context of society, focusing particularly on the African American experience. Howard Nelson says of *Poems from Prison,* "Within the bleakness of steel bars and concrete walls, the frustration, immobility, rage, fear, and loneliness of prison life, and the long stretches of prison time, Knight twisted the space and created poems of remarkable force and clarity."

Born of a Woman is Knight's most critically acclaimed collection. It has three sections: "Inside-Out," "Outside-In," and "All About—And Back Again." In an interesting combination, the first section deals with poems about prison life, the second section is focused on the theme of love, and third section includes poems on a variety of subjects and themes. One of the most notable poems is "The Stretching of the Belly," about the pregnancy of his wife.

Belly Song and Other Poems was also a critical success and was nominated for a Pulitzer Prize and a National Book Award. Knight believed that human feeling begins in the belly, and that this is where emotions such as love, fear, pain, and happiness have their genesis. This collection has poems that deal with many of these conflicting emotions, love poems celebrating nature and sexuality, as well as political poems about freedom, racism, and prison. He also writes of his own ancestors and uses some autobiographical material in his work. In this collection, Knight includes a poem that is actually a written version of a toast, "Dark Prophecy, I Sing of Shine." The poem is about a black coal stoker aboard the *Titanic* who saves himself as the ship is going down, challenging the fate of his class, race, and gender.

POETRY COLLECTIONS

Poems from Prison. Detroit, MI: Broadside Press, 1968.
2 Poems for Black Relocation Centers. Detroit, MI: Broadside Press, 1968.
For Black Poets Who Think of Suicide. Detroit, MI: Broadside Press, 1972.
A Poem for Brother/Man. Detroit, MI: Broadside Press, 1972.
Belly Song and Other Poems. Detroit, MI: Broadside Press, 1973.
Born of a Woman: New and Selected Poems. Boston, MA: Houghton Mifflin, 1980.
The Essential Etheridge Knight. Pittsburgh: University of Pittsburgh Press, 1986.

SELECTED ANTHOLOGIES WHERE POETRY APPEARS

Brooks, Gwendolyn, ed. *A Broadside Treasury.* Detroit: Broadside Press, 1971.
Harper, Michael S., and Anthony Walton, eds. *Every Shut Eye Ain't Asleep: An Anthology of Poetry by African Americans Since 1945.* New York: Little, Brown, 1994.
Hill, Patricia Liggins, ed. *Call & Response: The Riverside Anthology of the African American Literary Tradition.* Boston, MA: Houghton Mifflin, 1998.

Miller, Adam, ed. *Dices and Black Bones: Black Voices of the Seventies*. Boston, MA: Houghton Mifflin, 1970.

Quashie, Kevin, R. Joyce Lausch, and Keith D. Miller, eds. *New Bones: Contemporary Black Writers in America*. Upper Saddle River, NJ: Prentice-Hall, 2001.

Randall, Dudley, ed. *Black Poets*. New York: Bantam Books, 1971.

SELECTED ADDITIONAL WORKS

For Malcolm. Contributor. Detroit, MI: Broadside Press, 1967.

Voce Negre dal Carcere. 1968, original ed. English ed. published as *Black Voices from Prison*. New York: Pathfinder Press, 1970.

So My Soul Can Sing. Guilford, CT: Jeffrey Norton, 1986.

SELECTED RESOURCES FOR FURTHER REFERENCE

Anaporte, Jean Easton. "Etheridge Knight: Poet and Prisoner: An Introduction." *Callaloo* 19.4 (Fall 1996): 941–946.

Etheridge Knight Festival. Online. www.aalbc.com/events/ekfestival.htm.

Hill, Patricia Liggins. "'Blues for a Mississippi Black Boy': Etheridge Knight's Craft in the Black Oral Tradition." *Mississippi Quarterly* 36.1 (Winter 1982–1983): 21–33.

Hurd, Myles Raymond. "The Corinth Connection in Etheridge Knight's 'The Idea of Ancestry.'" *Notes on Mississippi Writers* 1 (January 25, 1993): 1–9.

Johnson, Thomas. "Excerpts from Notes of an Oral Rhapsodist: An Introduction to the Poetry and Aesthetic of Etheridge Knight." *Worcester Review* 19.1–2 (1998): 79–83.

Joyce, Ann. "The Poetry of Etheridge Knight: A Reflection of an African Philosophic/Aesthetic." *Worcester Review* 19.1–2 (1998): 105–118.

Madhubuti, Haki R. "Etheridge Knight: Making Up Poems." *Worcester Review* 19.1–2 (1998): 90–104.

McKim, Elizabeth Gordan. "Etheridge Knight in Conversation." *Worcester Review* 19.1–2 (1998): 132–139.

Nelson, Howard. "Belly Songs: The Poetry of Etheridge Knight." *The Hollins Critic* XVIII.5 (December 1981): 1–11.

Premo, Cassie. "On Etheridge Knight's Life and Career." *Modern American Poetry Project*. Online. www.english.uiuc.edu/maps/poets/g_l/knight/life.htm.

Rowell, Charles H. "An Interview with Etheridge Knight." *Callaloo* 19.4 (Fall 1996): 967–980.

Tracy, Steven C. "A MELUS Interview: Etheridge Knight." *MELUS: The Journal of the Society for the Study of the Multi-Ethnic Literature of the United States* 12.2 (Summer 1985): 7–23.

Werner, Craig. "The Poet, the Poem, the People: Etheridge Knight's Aesthetic." *Obsidian* 7.2–3 (Summer–Winter 1981): 7–17.

Kyla Heflin

Yusef Komunyakaa

(1947–)

African American

BIOGRAPHY

Yusef Komunyakaa, a Pulitzer Prize–winning poet, was born in Bogalusa, Louisiana, in 1947. He is the oldest of five children. His father was a carpenter who strained the family greatly through his abuse and extramarital affairs. Komunyakaa portrays his complex and complicated relationship with his father in various poems.

In 1968, Komunyakaa worked as an information specialist during his military deployment to Vietnam; he served as a correspondent and managing editor of the *Southern Cross* and as a reporter for the *Stars and Stripes,* both military newspapers. His service in Vietnam earned him the Bronze Star. After Vietnam, he entered the University of Colorado and earned his B.A. He did graduate work at Colorado State University, where he earned an M.A., and the University of California, Irvine, where he received an M.F.A. in 1980. He then moved to New Orleans and began to teach at the University of New Orleans. In 1985 he married Mandy Sayer, an Australian novelist and short fiction writer.

Komunyakaa was inspired to write as a teenager when he read James Baldwin's collection of essays *Nobody Knows My Name.* He wrote his first poem in high school, but it was over a decade after his tour of duty in Vietnam that Komunyakaa established his own writing career by composing poems about that experience. These were published in his collection *Dien Cai Dau* (1988), which won the Dark Room Poetry Prize. Other notable volumes of poetry include *I Apologize for the Eyes in My Head* (1986), winner of the San Francisco Poetry Center Award; *Neon Vernacular: New and Selected Poems 1977–1989* (1994), which won the Pulitzer Prize and the Kingsley Tufts Poetry Award; and most recently, *Thieves of Paradise* (1998), a finalist for the National Book Critics Circle Award.

Critics have responded favorably to Yusef Komunyakaa's work. In a book review of *Pleasure Dome* and *Talking Dirty to the Gods in Poetry,* David Wojahn calls Komunyakaa one of our period's most significant and individual voices (p. 168). Another critic, Robert Haas, states that Komunyakaa's poetry collection *Dien Cai Dau* is probably the best book of poems by an American about the Vietnam War (www.washingtonpost.com). Honors that Yusef Komunyakaa has won include the Thomas Forcade Award (1991), the William Faulkner Prize from the Universite de Rennes (1994), the Hanes Poetry Prize (1997), and fellowships from the Fine Arts Work Center in Provincetown and the Louisiana Arts Council. In 1999 he became a chancellor of the Academy of American Poets. Komunyakaa currently teaches at Princeton University, where he is professor in the Council of Humanities and Creative Writing.

THEMES AND CONCERNS

In all his poetry, from the earliest collections in 1984 to *Pleasure Dome* in 2001, Komunyakaa displays a passionate concern for sociopolitical and cultural issues that include the themes of war, racism, the condition of black men and women, human relationships, the environment, a strong critique of capitalism, and the misuse of science and technology. For instance, in "Autobiography of My Alter Ego," Komunyakaa writes about the war experiences that American soldiers encountered in Vietnam and critiques the negative results of this conflict. Here, one pictures the strong human resolve under the most stressful conditions possible. Fear and the awareness of impending death permeate the soldiers' consciousness. Even as they huddle between the hills around Cam Rahn Bay, the men, and by extension the readers, are made aware of the terrible paradox of the beauty of nature in the midst of the ongoing destruction. The persona of the poem is angry about the conflict and is especially galled at the forces that create such desperate situations for ordinary men. These themes and concerns run through the *Dien Cai Dau* collection and go beyond the war to describe the confused, painful, and lost psychological states in which most Vietnam veterans find themselves.

Komunyakaa's interest in popular culture and his ability to weave that interest into larger cultural critiques is evidenced by poems like "Woebegone." Here he gives a picture of tattooed and pierced youth who have taken subculture mainstream. Irony and a tongue-in-cheek attitude/tone are evident in the persona's remark that this fashion trend is a painful one that measures love by the number of scars one has. The persona then critiques the tendency of capitalist-oriented business to co-opt genuine protests and social concerns into mainstream business opportunities and pleasure, while ignoring pressing social issues of poverty, crime, and drug abuse, especially among the working and minority groups.

Science and technology receive Komunyakaa's harsh critique in the poem "The Devil's Workshop." Here, Komunyakaa condemns Western scientists' and industrialists' experimentations that have no moral or humane basis and that only serve as tools to promote and ensure global dominance of particular countries. The poem touches on ecological concerns and the slowly unfolding potential for ecological disaster on a huge scale due to the West's selfish use of science and technology. Despite the critique inherent in the poem, hope is introduced in the picture of children demonstrating against these scientific and technological pollutions, and Nature itself is also described as fighting against the machinations of the demon master scientist by throwing a wrench in his carefully orchestrated plans and experiments.

Other poems such as "I Apologize for the Eyes in My Head" portray the vulnerable position of black men in a racist world and the circumstances that seek to deny them the right to claim the full benefits of their American citizenship. This poem, like some of his others, is marked by dark humor, sarcasm, and irony implicit in the fact that black men are forced to explain their presence and literally apologize for their human attributes.

Explaining his concern with so many varied themes and issues in his poetry, Komunyakaa has argued that it is crucial that a poet be able to empathize with different people and to place him- or herself in different situations and times. His work is a testament to that vision.

POETRY COLLECTIONS

Lost in the Bonewheel Factory. Amherst, MA: Lynx House Press, 1979.
Copacetic. Middletown, CT: Wesleyan University Press, 1984.
I Apologize for the Eyes in My Head. Middletown, CT: Wesleyan University Press, 1986.
Toys in a Field. Black River Press, 1986. (chapbook)
Dien Cai Dau. Middletown, CT: Wesleyan University Press, 1988.
February in Sydney. Unionville, IN: Matchbooks, 1989. (chapbook)
Magic City. Middletown, CT: Wesleyan University Press, 1992.
Neon Vernacular: New and Selected Poems, 1977–1989. Middletown, CT: Wesleyan University Press, 1993.
Thieves of Paradise. Middletown, CT: Wesleyan University Press, 1998.
Talking Dirty to the Gods. New York: Farrar, Straus, & Giroux, 2000.
Pleasure Dome: New & Collected Poems, 1975–1999. Middletown, CT: Wesleyan University Press, 2001.

SELECTED ANTHOLOGIES AND WEB SITES WHERE POETRY APPEARS

Andrews, William L., et al., eds. *The Literature of the American South: A Norton Anthology.* New York: W. W. Norton, 1998.
Bly, Robert, ed. *The Best American Poetry.* New York: Simon and Schuster, 1999.
Christopher, Nicolas, ed. *Walk on the Wild Side: Urban American Poetry Since 1975.* New York: Scribner's, 1994.
Daniels, Jim, ed. *Letters to America: Contemporary American Poetry on Race.* Detroit, MI: Wayne State University Press, 1995.
Gates, Henry Louis, Jr., and Nellie McKay, eds. *The Norton Anthology of African American Literature.* New York: W. W. Norton, 1997.
Howard, Richard, ed. *The Best American Poetry.* New York: Simon and Schuster, 1995.

Kitchen, Judith, and Mary Paumier Jones, eds. *In Brief: Short Takes on the Personal.* New York: W. W. Norton, 1999.
Pinsky, Robert, ed. The *Handbook of Heartbreak.* New York: Rob Weisbach Books, 1998.
Reed, Ishmael, ed. *From Totems to Hip Hop: A Multicultural Anthology of Poetry Across America.* New York: Thunder's Mouth Press, 2003.
Rich, Adrienne, ed. *The Best American Poetry.* New York: Simon and Schuster, 1996.
Tate, James, ed. *The Best American Poetry.* New York: Simon and Schuster, 1997.
Yusef Komunyakaa Homepage. Online. www.ibiblio.org/ipa/kom.

SELECTED ADDITIONAL WORKS

The Jazz Poetry Anthology. Editor, with J. A. Sascha Feinstein. Bloomington: Indiana University Press, 1991.
The Second Set: The Jazz Poetry Anthology. Editor, with J. A. Sascha Feinstein. Bloomington: Indiana University Press, 1996.
Love Notes from the Madhouse. Live recordings at Chopin Theatre, Chicago, September 12, 1997, with jazz ensemble led by John Tchicai (poems from Neon Vernacular and Thieves of Paradise), 8th Harmonic Breakdown, 1998.
Blue Notes: Essays, Interviews, and Commentaries. Ed. Radiclani Clytus. Ann Arbor: University of Michigan Press, 2000.
"More Than a State of Mind." *Studies in the Literary Imagination* 35.1 (2002): 163–164.
The Best American Poetry 2003. Editor. New York: Scribner's, 2003.

SELECTED RESOURCES FOR FURTHER REFERENCE

Aubert, Alvin. "Rare Instances of Reconciliation." Review of *Dien Cai Dau,* by Yusef Komunyakaa. *Epoch* 38.1 (1989): 67–72.
Gilyard, Keith. Review of *Blue Notes,* by Yusef Komunyakaa. *African American Review* 35.4 (2001): 677–679.
Gotera, Vincente F. "Lines of Tempered Steel: An Interview with Yusef Komunyakaa." *Callaloo* 13.2 (1991): 215–228.
Panel on the Poetry of Yusef Komunyakaa. Online. www.ibiblio.org/ipa/kom.
Ploughshares: The Literary Journal at Emerson College. www.pshares.org/authordetails.

Augustina Edem Dzregah

Tato Laviera

(1951–)

Puerto Rican (Nuyorican)

Photo by Georgia McInnis, © Arte Público Press.

BIOGRAPHY

Afro–Puerto Rican poet and playwright Tato Laviera was born in Santurce, Puerto Rico in 1951 but moved with his mother and sisters to the Lower East Side of New York City in 1960. As such, he often identifies himself as a Nuyorican, a term that refers to an individual of Puerto Rican descent who is born and reared in New York City, thereby claiming both islands as his or her cultural legacies.

One of the bestselling Puerto Rican poets in the United States, Laviera is a spoken-word poet and a performer of his poetry. His early youth was spent in Catholic schools and after graduating from high school, he briefly attended Cornell University and Brooklyn College. He went to work as director of the "University of the Streets," an educational alternative established in the Lower East Side that offered classes to adults at community centers and helped them get into college. He taught basic writing skills at Rutgers University's Livingston College from 1970 to 1973 and taught in the Department of Puerto Rican Studies from 1979 to 1981. During that time he also directed the Association of Community Service. He has published four books of poetry with Arte Público Press, the major distributor of Latino/Latina literature in the United States. His first book, *La Carreta Made a U-Turn* (1979), was followed by *Enclave* (1981), *AmeRícan* (1989), and *Mainstream Ethics* (1989). Laviera is currently performing his work throughout the country and promoting his plays as well as doing community service in New York City.

THEMES AND CONCERNS

Major themes in Laviera's poetry include the tension between Puerto Rican and Nuyorican societies and identity; language and bilingualism as ethnic identity markers; life in *el barrio;* music and popular culture; the denouncement of social institutions such as schools, Puerto Rican and U.S. governments, and the Catholic church; and the history of Puerto Rican immigration to the United States and Operation Bootstrap in the 1940s and 1950s. There is also the pervasive presence of African Caribbean and African American cultures.

Although Laviera's poetry was originally addressed to the Puerto Rican community in New York and presented in the Nuyorican Café, it is poetry for the masses; as Laviera has noted, the displacement experienced by Puerto Ricans in New York that he describes is not a Puerto Rican problem exclusively. In an interview with Juan Flores, Laviera explains:

> It's a universal problem. The Dominicans have it; the Latin Americans have it; the Africans who go to France and England have it. They have to adapt. The Nuyorican is a displacement. It has to do with people from native countries having to come to mother countries and adapt to them. So the Nuyorican is not a phenomenon of the Puerto Ricans in New York and the Puerto Ricans on the island. It's a worldwide phenomenon. (p. 82)

Laviera's poetry has the value of bilingualism within, and the fact that some of it is untranslatable (street language and slang) may make its reading difficult for non-Spanish speakers. Yet the use of both languages expresses what Laviera refers to as the needs of "the bilingual moment," in which neither Spanish nor English is sufficient for helping the audience to understand the situation and challenge of the Nuyorican experience. As a colloquial poet Laviera relates his poetry to the tradition of rapping in New York City. His poetry responds to issues of bilingual education, social criticism, and language (Spanish in the United States). He celebrates "AmeRícan," or "I-am-a-Rican," meaning someone who comes from two cultures to make one, especially people of Latin American heritage who are now struggling with Anglo culture. He loves to bring to life his poems with expression and attitude as only an "AmeRícan" can do.

Laviera defines himself as an "AmeRícan" because he is both a member of that vast part of the Western Hemisphere that speaks Spanish and a member of the smaller part that speaks English. Therefore, he uses the term "AmeRícan" to define not just the Puerto Rican part of his heritage, but also his Anglo culture. Laviera uses this term to define everyone with a dual culture. The force that propels this poetry is a sense of social injustice encircled by a feeling of outrage at the conditions in which the Puerto Rican immigrants find themselves in most large urban centers like New York. It is bearing witness to the endless cycle of poverty and discrimination that drives the denunciation of this poetry. There is also anger at what the poet perceives to be the submissiveness of a people who come to the big city in search the "American dream." Laviera's poetry best exemplifies the new genre of bilingual poetry in the United States.

POETRY COLLECTIONS

La Carreta Made a U-Turn. Houston, TX: Arte Público Press, 1976.
Enclave. Houston, TX: Arte Público Press, 1981.
AmeRícan. Houston, TX: Arte Público Press, 1985.
Mainstream Ethics (Ética Corriente). Houston, TX: Arte Público Press, 1988.

SELECTED ANTHOLOGIES WHERE POETRY APPEARS

Algarín, Miguel, and Bob Holman, eds. *Aloud: Voices from the Nuyorican Poets Cafe.* New York: Henry Holt, 1994.

Algarín, Miguel, and Miguel Piñero, eds. *Nuyorican Poetry: An Anthology of Puerto Rican Words and Feelings.* New York: William Morrow, 1975.

Kanellos, Nicolas, ed. *Hispanic-American Literature: A Brief Introduction and Anthology.* New York: HarperCollins, 1995.

Olivares, Julián, and Evangelina Vigil Piñon, eds. *Decade II: A Twentieth Anniversary Anthology.* Houston, TX: Arte Público Press, 1993.

Reed, Ishmael, et al., eds. *The Before Columbus Foundation Poetry Anthology: Selections from the American Book Awards, 1980–1990.* New York: W. W. Norton, 1992.

ADDITIONAL WORK

"Olú Clemente." Cowritten with Miguel Algarín. *Nuevos Pasos: Chicano and Puerto Rican Drama.* Houston, TX: Arte Público Press, 1989. (play)

SELECTED RESOURCES FOR FURTHER REFERENCE

Aparicio, Frances. "La Vida es un Spanglish Disparatero: Bilingualism in Nuyorican Poetry." In *European Perspectives on Hispanic Literature of the United States.* Ed. Genvieve Faber. Houston, TX: Arte Público Press, 1988, 147–160.

Binder, Wolfgang. "Celebrating Life: The AmeRícan Poet Tato Laviera." Introduction to *AmeRícan,* by Tato Laviera. Houston, TX: Arte Público Press, 1985, 5–10.

Birthwrite: Growing Up Hispanic. Dir. Luis R. Torres. KAET Channel 8 in association with the Hispanic Research Center. Phoenix, AZ: Arizona State University, 1988. (video)

Flores, Juan, et al., eds. "La Carreta Made a U-Turn: Puerto Rican Language and Culture in the United States." *Daedalus* 110.2 (Spring 1981): 193–217.

Hernández, Carmen Dolores. *Puerto Rican Voices in English: Interviews with Writers.* Westport, CT: Praeger, 1997.

Luis, William. *Dance Between Two Cultures: Latino Caribbean Literature Written in the U.S.* Nashville, TN: Vanderbilt University Press, 1997.

Zimmerman, Marc. *U.S. Latino Literature: An Essay and Annotated Bibliography.* Chicago, IL: MARCH/Abrazo Press, 1992.

José Irizarry

Li-Young Lee

(1957–)

Chinese American

BIOGRAPHY

Li-Young Lee was born on August 19, 1957, in Jakarta, Indonesia, where his parents had settled after their exile from China. Shortly after Lee's birth, his father, who had been a physician to Mao before the family's flight from China, was imprisoned for political reasons by the Sukarno regime. In 1959 the senior Lee escaped, and the family left Indonesia to spend five years moving through Asia and living in Hong Kong, Macau, and Japan. Finally, in 1964 the family arrived in the United States, where Li-Young Lee's father served as a Presbyterian minister until his death. These apparently disparate strains of experience, place, and especially literature—the classic Chinese poets and the King James Bible—come together in Lee's poetry.

Lee earned a B.A. from the University of Pittsburgh and studied at both the University of Arizona and the State University of New York. In 1998 he was awarded an honorary Doctor of Humane Letters by the State University of New York–Brockport. Now living in Chicago near his extended family, Lee is married and he and his wife, Donna, have two children. In addition to being a writer and a popular speaker on college campuses, Lee is an artist for a fashion accessories company.

At the age of twenty-nine, Lee published his first collection, *Rose* (1986), which won the New York University Delmore Schwartz Memorial Poetry Award, the first of many awards and achievements for Lee, the youngest contemporary American poet to be anthologized in the *Norton Anthology of American Literature*. *Rose* was followed in 1990 by *The City in Which I Love You*. This collection was the 1990 Lamont Poetry Selection of the Academy of American Poetry. In 1995 Lee published a prose memoir, *The Winged Seed: A Remembrance*, winner of the American Book Award from the Before Columbus Foundation. Eleven years after the publication of *The City in Which I Love You*, Lee's much-anticipated third poetry collection, *Book of My Nights* (2001), was published. In 2001, poetry from *Rose* was adapted for the stage by Mary Ashley as *The Weight of Memory* and performed in New York in 2001. His poetry has appeared in many journals and anthologies, including three volumes of the *Pushcart Prize: Best of the Small Presses* anthologies, and Lee was featured on *The Power of the Word*, a PBS series with Bill Moyers.

Lee is a consistently busy and popularly invited participant in poetry festivals, including the Woodstock Poetry Festival, the Brunders Creative Arts Festival, the Folger Poetry Festival, and the Geraldine R. Dodge Poetry Festival. He is equally in demand at colleges and universities and has taught at the Iowa Writers' Workshop, the University of Oregon, the University of Texas Austin, the Writers' Center of Bethesda, and Northwestern University. In 1999 he was named to the American Voices Residency; he was the Mackey Chair at Beloit College in 1998–1999, the 2001 Millet Writing Fellow at Wesleyan University, and the Iolani Keables Chair (Hawaii) in 2002.

Other awards include National Endowment of the Arts fellowships in 1986 and 1995, the I. B. Lavan Award in 1986, and a Guggenheim fellowship in 1987. In 1988 Lee received the Writer's Award from the Mrs. Giles Whiting Foundation. The Illinois Arts Council, the Commonwealth of Pennsylvania, and the Pennsylvania Council on the Arts have all also awarded grants to Lee.

THEMES AND CONCERNS

One reason that Li-Young Lee's poetry has received such acclaim is its language, which is notable for its simplicity. In the foreword to *Rose*, Lee's first collection, Gerald Stern comments on the power of Lee's language when he observes that it "releases—even awakens—feelings" (p. 10). In addition, Lee's fine and striking descriptions of details of the senses make reading his poetry a vibrant sensory experience for readers. Lee cites both classical Chinese poetry (specifically of the T'ang and Sung dynasties) and the King James Bible (The Songs of Solomon) as important influences on his sense of language and poetry. His writing is intimate, fluid, and lyrical.

Lee has said that his drawing, by revealing to him a depth in the world not normally perceived, is responsible for his careful observation of the natural world. It has been suggested that Lee uses his descriptions of nature to express his emotional and mental state, a device used in classical Chinese poetry. However, more likely is Stern's explanation that as a poet, Lee has "a willingness to let the sublime enter his field of concentration and take over" (p. 9). Lee reveals and meditates on the sacred in the ordinary. In fact, in an interview Lee described poetry as "the practice of the sacred" (Marshall, *Range of the Possible*, p. 6). Many have compared him to Walt Whitman, Theodore Roethke, and Rainer Maria Rilke.

Li-Young Lee's consistent themes are family, love, and memory. In *Rose*, he writes about his father and the loss of his father, even writing his father's memories in some poems. Stern calls the father the "critical myth" of this book (p. 9). It is through these memories—his father's and those he has shared with his father—that Lee connects with his ethnic heritage rather than by making his ethnicity an overt or prominent theme. In both "The Gift" and "Persimmons," for example, Lee meditates on the beloved qualities of his father, which are, in fact, his heritage. The poems in *Rose* (1986) ("Eating Together," for example) also develop another important theme in Lee's work—that of life's progression toward death.

In Lee's second collection, *City in Which I Love You* (1990), the thematic emphasis moves to Lee himself and his own identity, reflecting on both his greater history as an exile and a Chinese American and on the meaning of his individual life. Propelled by his desire to connect with his fellow humans, the poet searches sometimes nightmarish cityscapes in the central and title poem, while "The Cleaving," which ends the collection, deals with assimilation, with the individual identity created by personal, individual experience rather than by ethnic and cultural memory.

Lee has addressed this seeming progression or transformation of the place of his cultural/ethnic identity in his poetry. He has explained that he does not wish to be defined as an "Asian American writer" because, although as a child he certainly did experience life in exile, the ethnic memories about which he writes are his parents' memories, ordered and remembered by the poet. So although the exile's feelings of disconnection and dislocation find expression in Lee's work, these themes are not narrowly "cultural" in *City in Which I Love You*. And they are even less so in Lee's third collection, *Book of My Nights.*

In *Book of My Nights,* Lee's primary theme is, in his own words, that it is "OK to die" (Jordan, p. 1). Sleep and death are linked in this volume, and Lee has described the poems in it as "lullabies" (p. 1). Although memory and family continue to be thematically significant in this collection, this poetry is also highly introspective; during his sleepless nights, Lee meditates, contemplates, and achieves revelations about the self. Lee's sharp sense of mortality is a common thread running through his three books of poetry but finds its fullest expression in *Book of My Nights.* The poems in this collection combine sensory immediacy and metaphysical reflection.

POETRY COLLECTIONS

Rose. Rochester, NY: BOA Editions, 1986.
The City in Which I Love You. Rochester, NY: BOA Editions, 1990.
Book of My Nights. Rochester, NY: BOA Editions, 2001.

ADDITIONAL WORKS

The Winged Seed: A Remembrance. New York: Simon and Schuster, 1995.

SELECTED ANTHOLOGIES WHERE POETRY APPEARS

Anderson, Maggie, and David Hassler, eds. *Learning by Heart: Contemporary American Poetry about School.* Iowa City: University of Iowa Press, 1999.
Collier, Michael, and Stanley Plumly, eds. *The New Bread Loaf Anthology of Contemporary American Poetry.* Lebanon, NH: University Press of New England, 1999.

Diaz, Junot, ed. *The Beacon Best of 2001: Great Writing by Women and Men of All Colors and Cultures.* Boston, MA: Beacon Press, 2001.

Garrison, David Lee, and Terry Hermsen, eds. *Food Poems.* Huron, OH: Bottom Dog Press, 1998.

Gillan, Maria M., and Jennifer Gillan, eds. *Unsettling America: An Anthology of Contemporary Multicultural Poetry.* New York: Penguin, 1994.

Hongo, Garrett, ed. *The Open Boat: Poems from Asian America.* New York: Anchor Press, 1993.

Milosz, Czeslaw, ed. *A Book of Luminous Things: International Anthology of Poetry.* Fort Worth, TX: Harcourt, 1998.

Murray, G. E., and Kevin Stein, eds. *Illinois Voices: An Anthology of Twentieth-Century Poetry.* Champaign: University of Illinois Press, 2001.

Srikanth, Rajini, and Esther Y. Iwanaga, eds. *Bold Words: A Century of Asian American Writing.* Piscataway, NJ: Rutgers University Press, 2001.

SELECTED RESOURCES FOR FURTHER REFERENCE

Cheung, King-Kok, ed. *Words Matter: Conversations with Asian American Writers.* Honolulu: University of Hawaii Press, 2000.

Huang, Guiyou, ed. *Asian American Autobiographers: A Bio-Bibliographical Critical Sourcebook.* Westport, CT: Greenwood, 2001.

Jordan, Marie. "An Interview with Li-Young Lee." *Writer's Chronicle.* Online. www.awpwriter.org/magazine/writers/mjohnson.htm.

Logan, William. "The Real Language of Men." *New Criterion* 21.4 (December 2002): 73–80.

Marshall, Tod, ed. *Range of the Possible: Conversations with Contemporary Poets.* Spokane: Eastern Washington University Press, 2002.

———. "To Witness the Invisible: A Talk with Li-Young Lee." *Kenyon Review* 22.1 (Winter 2000): 129–148.

Stern, Gerald. Foreword to *Rose,* by Li-Young Lee. Rochester, NY: BOA Editions, 1986.

Tabios, Eileen. "Li Young Lee's *Universe-Mind*—A Search for the Soul." In *Black Lightning.* Ed. Eileen Tabios. Philadelphia, PA: Temple University Press, 1998, 109–132.

Xiaojing, Zhou. "Inheritance and Invention in Li-Young Lee's Poetry." *MELUS: The Journal of the Society for the Study of the Multi-Ethnic Literature of the United States* 21.1 (Spring 1996): 113–133.

Yu, Timothy. "Form and Identity in Language Poetry and Asian American Poetry." *Contemporary American Literature* 41 (Fall 2000): 422–462.

Stacy Pauley

Photo by Dan Gray, courtesy of Shirley Geok-lin Lim.

Shirley Geok-lin Lim
(1944–)
Chinese American, Malaysian American

BIOGRAPHY

Born in Malacca, Malaysia, Shirley Geok-lin Lim seems to have been destined for a dual identity from her naming, in honor of American child-star Shirley Temple. Living in poverty with her father and five brothers after her mother abandoned the family, literally going hungry, Lim consumed words voraciously at the British Roman Catholic convent school she attended. Her postsecondary career began at the University of Malaya, which she attended on scholarship from 1964 to 1969, earning a B.A. with first-class honors in English. She then traveled to the United States to study English and American literature at Brandeis University, completing her Ph.D. in 1973.

Lim published her first poem in the *Malacca Times* at the age of ten. She has published five books of poetry: *Crossing the Peninsula and Other Poems* (1980), which won the Commonwealth Poetry Prize for Best First Book; *No Man's Grove and Other Poems* (1985); *Modern Secrets: New and Selected Poems* (1989); *Monsoon History: Selected Poems* (1994); and *What the Fortune Teller Didn't Say* (1998).

A prolific writer in both creative and scholarly genres, Lim is also known as a writer of fiction and memoirist, and she has won awards in several venues. She won an Asiaweek Short Story Award for "Mr. Tang's Uncles" in 1982. *Among the White Moon Faces*, her 1996 memoir, won the American Book Award. Her scholarly reputation is well established through her editing of anthologies and critical writing. Her 1989 anthology *The Forbidden Stitch: Asian American Women's Writing*, coedited with Mayumi Tsutakawa and Margarita Donnelly, won an American Book Award.

Her stories and poems have been included in more than sixty anthologies, and over one hundred of her articles, short stories, poems, and reviews have been published in periodicals that include *Journal of American Studies, American Studies International, River Styx, Asia, Perspective: Women's Studies, New Literary History, Journal of Commonwealth Literature, Commentary,* and *In-*

sight. She has served on the editorial board of *Feminist Studies* and coedited a special issue in 1993; she founded and served as editor for *Asian America: Journal of Culture and the Arts* (1992–1993); she founded and served as advisory editor to *Yuan Yang: Journal of Hong Kong and International Writing* (2000); she coedited a special issue of *Ariel* (2001); and she has served on the editorial board of *MELUS, Women's Studies Quarterly, New Literatures Review,* and *Short Story Journal.* She maintains an advisory position on several other journals.

Lim has taught at colleges and universities in the United States and Asia, has chaired the women's studies program at the University of California, Santa Barbara, and currently teaches courses in world and minority literatures and creative writing at the same institution. Scholarly awards have included National Endowment for the Humanities grants, the Mellon Fellowship, and a Fulbright Distinguished Lecturer Award. Shirley Geok-lin Lim is also widely known as a speaker and reader from her works. Current writing projects include a second novel and a critical study of gender and nation in representations of Asian American life and culture.

THEMES AND CONCERNS

Shirley Lim began writing at age nine, and poetry has played a vital role throughout her life. From childhood, she says that she has

> loved the idea of going into space where there is language which is yours, which is completely private, and which you can do anything with—you can curse someone you cannot curse otherwise, you can create a space of beauty when all around you there is poverty and deprivation. The act of writing poems is the act that has centered me all my life. (quoted in Moyers)

Lim's Westernized parents brought her a biculturalism that was further nourished in school, and her poems make reference to poets Samuel Taylor Coleridge, Pablo Neruda, and Marianne Moore and painters Paul Cezanne and Edvard Munch, among others. Yet she bridges cultures through both form and content. Her powerful poem "Pantoun for Chinese Women" addresses the killing of female babies, using a Malayan verse form to foreground Chinese culture's devaluing of girls and women.

A number of poems deal with language. For instance, "Learning English," which begins the volume *Monsoon History,* portrays the ways in which forsaking the languages of childhood for the common tongue of the Commonwealth distance the child from family and home. "Walking Around in a Different Language" describes listening to spoken German on the street, and "The Shape of Words" describes the feel of words in the mouth.

Themes of loss and separation give an elegiac feel to many of her poems about family. She chronicles early memories of her mother's presence in her life and strives to make sense of her leaving, and she remembers the hunger and dreams of food that characterized her impoverished childhood. Reaching back through the years and across an ocean, she addresses her father at a younger age, after he has died in China without a visit from her. These poems of loss are counterbalanced by later poems that explore her deep love for her American husband and son.

Family themes are closely allied to the strong sense of place that permeates Lim's poetry. She sees Malaysia more sharply as an exile and shares her vision in clear images of its people. Her poems about "Learning to Love America" form the last section of *What the Fortune Teller Didn't Say*. She claims the ability to act as her own ancestor in California, where no one will sit beside a Chinese immigrant on the train. The poem titled "Learning to Love America" is one of her most memorable ones, linking American culture with the Pacific pounding California's shoreline, with fresh vegetables and flowers, and with the strongest family tie: giving birth to an American son.

Reading Lim's poems is a powerfully moving experience, furnishing intimate insight into the transitions from childhood through stages of womanhood and cumulatively presenting a remarkable portrait of a woman who has grown into a complex and multifaceted identity as an American.

POETRY COLLECTIONS

Crossing the Peninsula & Other Poems. Kuala Lumpur: Heinemann Educational Books (Asia), 1980.
No Man's Grove and Other Poems. Singapore: National University of Singapore, 1985.
Modern Secrets: New and Selected Poems. London: Dangaroo Press, 1989.
Monsoon History: Selected Poems. London: Skoob Pacifica, 1994.
What the Fortune Teller Didn't Say. Minneapolis, MN: West End Press, 1998.

SELECTED ANTHOLOGIES WHERE POETRY APPEARS

Bartlett, Elizabeth, ed. *Literary Olympians, 1992: An International Anthology*. Boston, MA: Ford-Brown, 1992.
Blanchard, Margaret, ed. *From the Listening Place: Languages of Intuition*. Portland, ME: Astarte Shell Press, 1997.
Ford, Marjorie, and Jon Ford, eds. *Imagining Worlds*. New York: McGraw-Hill, 1994.
Gillan, Maria M., and Jennifer Gillan, eds. *Unsettling America: An Anthology of Contemporary Multicultural Poetry*. New York: Penguin, 1994.
Gioseffi, Daniela, ed. *On Prejudice: A Global Perspective*. New York: Anchor, 1993.
Lew, Walter K., ed. *Premonitions: The Kaya Anthology of New Asian North American Poetry*. New York: Kaya, 1995.
Loh, C. Y., and I. K. Ong, eds. *The Pen Is Mightier Than the Sword*. 2nd ed. London: Skoob Pacifica, 1994.

Maier, Mary Anne, and Joan Shaddox Isom, eds. *The Leap Years: Women Reflect on Change, Loss, and Love*. Boston, MA: Beacon Press, 1999.

Muller, Gilbert H., and John A. Williams, eds. *Bridges: Literature Across Cultures*. New York: McGraw-Hill, 1994.

Wang, L. Ling-chi, and Henry Yiheng Zhao, eds. *Chinese American Poetry: An Anthology*. Seattle: University of Washington Press, 1992.

SELECTED ADDITIONAL WORKS

Another Country and Other Stories. Singapore: Times Books International, 1982.

The Forbidden Stitch: An Asian American Women's Anthology. Editor, with Mayumi Tsutakawa and Margarita Donnelly. Corvallis, OR: Calyx Books, 1989.

Approaches to Teaching Kingston's The Woman Warrior. New York: Modern Language Association of America Press, 1991.

One World of Literature: An Anthology of Contemporary Global Literature. Editor, with Norman Spencer. Boston, MA: Houghton Mifflin, 1992.

Reading the Literatures of Asian America. Editor, with Amy Ling. Philadelphia, PA: Temple University Press, 1992.

Writing Southeast/Asia in English: Against the Grain. London: Skoob Pacifica, 1994.

Life's Mysteries: The Best of Shirley Lim. Singapore: Times Books International, 1995.

Among the White Moon Faces: An Asian-American Memoir of Homelands. New York: Feminist Press, 1996.

Two Dreams: Short Stories. New York: Feminist Press, 1997.

Asian American Literature: An Anthology. Editor. Chicago, IL: NTC/Contemporary Press, 1999.

Power, Race, and Gender in Academe: Strangers in the Tower? Editor, with Maria Herrera-Sobek. New York: Modern Language Association of America Press, 2000.

Tilting the Continent: An Anthology of Southeast Asian American Writing. Editor. St. Paul, MN: New Rivers Press, 2000.

Joss and Gold. New York: Feminist Press, 2001.

SELECTED RESOURCES FOR FURTHER REFERENCE

Buck, Claire, ed. *The Bloomsbury Guide to Women's Literature*. New York: Macmillan, 1992.

Karamcheti, Indira. "In the City of Lionesses." *Women's Review of Books* 19.10–11 (July 2002): 22–23.

Means, Laurel. Introduction to *Monsoon History*, by Shirley Geok-lin Lim. London: Skoob, 1994.

———. "The 'Orient-ation' of Eden: Christian/Buddhist Dialogics in the Poetry of Shirley Geok-lin Lim." *Christianity and Literature* 43.2 (Winter 1994): 189–203.

Moyers, Bill. *Fooling with Words*. PBS Online. www.pbs.org/wnet/foolingwithwords/main_biolim.html.

Shelton, Pamela L. *Contemporary Women Poets*. Detroit, MI: St. James Press, 1998.

Singh, Kirpal. "An Interview with Shirley Geok-lin Lim." *Ariel: A Review of International English Literature* 30.4 (October 1999): 135–141.

Wisker, Gina. *Post-Colonial and African American Women's Writing: A Critical Introduction.* New York: Macmillan, 2000.

Alice Trupe

Czeslaw Milosz

(1911–)

Polish American

Photo © Jerry Bauer.

BIOGRAPHY

World-renowned writer of both poetry and prose Czeslaw Milosz was born into a Polish-speaking family in Szetejnie, Lithuania, in 1911. Milosz counts himself among the last of the Polish Lithuanians, recalling, "We were something else, Lithuanians, but not in the accepted twentieth-century sense, which says that to be a Lithuanian you have to speak Lithuanian" (Czarnecka and Fuit, p. 4). Milosz's father, Alexander, was a highway engineer for the tsar's army from 1914 to 1918, and Milosz and his family, including his mother, Weronika, and younger brother, Andrzej, traveled throughout Russia and Siberia when Milosz was a child. History collided with Milosz for the first time when the family was in the Russian town of Rzhev at the outbreak of the October Revolution in 1917. After the revolution, Milosz returned to Szetejnie to live with his grandparents.

Milosz received a degree in law in 1934 from Stefan Batory University in Vilnius. It was during his time as a student that he had his first poems published in the university's literary journal in 1930. Also during this period, in 1933, Milosz published his first volume of poetry, *Poem in Frozen Time*.

Milosz fled to Warsaw during World War II, where he married Janina Dluska, with whom he had two sons: Antoni, born in 1947, and Piotr, born in 1951. Milosz worked for the new government of the People's Republic of Poland and was stationed in New York and Washington during the early postwar years. In 1950 he was transferred to Paris, but his family remained in the United States, as it was clear that Milosz was slowly being drawn into a trap by Polish leaders who were becoming less indulgent of his public ambivalence toward Communism. While on a holiday in Warsaw, the Polish authorities took away his passport, effectively imprisoning him in Communist Poland. In January 1951, however, Milosz was inexplicably allowed to return to work in Paris, where he sought political asylum, thus beginning his official life in exile.

Milosz's time in France was very unhappy, as he was separated from his family, nearly poor, and faced with a small audience for his Polish-language poems. In 1960 he emigrated to America, becoming a professor of Slavic languages and literature at the University of California at Berkeley. In the United States, Milosz eventually became resigned to—and even accepting of—his new life. In 1973, *Selected Poems,* the first volume of Milosz's poetry in English, was published. Up to that point, Milosz had been seen as more of a political essayist in English-speaking circles, and from this publication he would finally begin to gain recognition as a poet.

In 1980 Milosz's writings were rewarded with the Nobel Prize for literature, and the following year he visited Poland for the first time since his exile thirty years previous. Receiving the Nobel Prize finally gave Milosz recognition within his homeland, and many of his writings began to be published there.

In 1991, upon the collapse of the Soviet regime, Milosz was welcomed back to Poland with fully opened arms. Milosz's acceptance was also eased by the fact that his condemnation of the Soviet system was now the predominant mode of thought across Europe. Throughout the decades, various governments, and countries, Milosz has never stopped being a writer. He currently resides in both Berkeley and Krakow with his second wife, Carol.

THEMES AND CONCERNS

Now in his tenth decade, Milosz, like most poets, has faced the specter of death through the written word. Facing truths, serving as confession, dealing with desire: these universal themes find themselves strongly embodied in Milosz's poetry. Milosz is a survivor, whether faced with revolution in Russia, or the horror of war—as in the battle of Warsaw under the Nazis—or under the oppression of the subsequent Communist regime. The hardness gleaned from such experiences manifests itself in his writings. Admittedly, some of that hardness might be lost in translation, and critics often note that the explosive force of his native tongue reminds one of that which defies translation. Even Milosz himself acknowledges that some of the tones and ironies of his earlier, more formal writings are not captured when translated into English, further proof that Milosz is at heart and mind a Polish poet.

Milosz was one of the first writers to face the horrific realities of mass slaughter and genocide. In his 1945 work *Rescue,* he "took on the task of responding to the war, asking how its events had changed our conceptions of ourselves and of history" (Vendler, p. 72). He writes of the massacre of ordinary civilians and the extermination of Jews in the Warsaw ghetto. Poems such as "sky-carousel," "Campo dei Fiori," and "A Poor Christian Looks at the Ghetto" all show Milosz trying to cope with such atrocities while they were still before his eyes. The war scarred all those it touched, and Milosz was one of the first to articulate the pain. Throughout his writing career, Milosz has faced the concept that human institutions do little to restrain human barbarity. Finding some ethical foundation in his Roman Catholicism, Milosz's writings frequently deal with religion, both in its darkness and in its light, one of the many contradictions of human nature Milosz has faced in his life experience, and subsequently in his poetry.

POETRY COLLECTIONS

Trzy Zimy (Three Winters). Warsaw: Wladyslaw Mortkowicz, 1936.
Ocalenie (Rescue). Warsaw: Czytelnik, 1945.
Swiatlo Dzienne (The Light of Day). Paris: Instytut Literacki, 1954.
Traktat Poetycki (A Poetical Treatise). Paris: Instytut Literacki, 1957.
Krol Popiel i Inne Wiersze (King Popiel and Other Poems). Paris: Instytut Literacki, 1962.
Gucio Zaczarowany (Gucio Enchanted). Paris: Instytut Literacki, 1965.
Miasto bez Imienia (City Without a Name). Paris: Instytut Literacki, 1969.
Gdzie Slonce Wschodzi i Kedy Zapada (Where the Sun Rises and Where It Sets). Paris: Instytut Literacki, 1974.
Hymn o Perle (The Poem of the Pearl). Paris: Instytut Literacki, 1982.
Nieobjeta Ziemia (The Unencompassed Earth). Paris: Instytut Literacki, 1984.
Kroniki (Chronicles). Paris: Instytut Literacki, 1987.
The Collected Poems, 1931–1987. New York: Ecco Press, 1988.
Dalsze Okolice (Farther Surroundings). Cracow: Znak, 1991.
Na Brzegu Rzeki (Facing the River). Cracow: Znak, 1994.
Facing the River: New Poems. New York: Ecco, 1996.
To (It). Cracow: Znak, 2000.
Milosz's ABC's. New York: Farrar, Straus, & Giroux, 2001.
New and Collected Poems, 1931–2001. New York: Ecco, 2001.
Druga Przestrzen (The Second Space). Cracow: Znak, 2002.

SELECTED ANTHOLOGIES AND WEB SITES WHERE POETRY APPEARS

Berg, Stephen, David Bonanno, and Arthur Vogelsang. *The Body Electric: America's Best Poetry from the American Poetry Review.* New York: W. W. Norton, 2000.
Forche, Carolyn, ed. *Against Forgetting: Twentieth-Century Poets of Witness.* New York: Norton, 1993.
Hamill, Susan, ed. *The Gift of Tongues: Twenty-five Years of Poetry from Copper Canyon Press.* Port Townsend, WA: Copper Canyon Press, 1996.
Internet Poetry Archive. Online. www.ibiblio.org.
The Nobel Prize Internet Archive. Online. www.almaz.com.

SELECTED ADDITIONAL WORKS

Zniewolony Umysl (The Captive Mind). Paris: Instytut Literacki, 1953.
Dolina Issy (The Issa Valley). Paris: Instytut Literacki, 1955.
Zdobycie Wladzy (The Seizure of Power). Paris: Instytut Literacki, 1955.

Rodzinna Europa (Native Realm). Paris: Instytut Literacki, 1959.
The History of Polish Literature. New York: Macmillan, 1969.
Widzenia nad Zatokq San Francisco (A View of San Francisco Bay). Paris: Instytut Literacki, 1969.
Prywatne Obowiazki (Private Obligations). Paris: Instytut Literacki, 1974.
Emperor of the Earth. Berkeley: University of California Press, 1976.
Ziemia Ulro (The Land of Ulro). Paris: Instytut Literacki, 1977.
Bells in Winter. New York: Ecco Press, 1978.
Ogrod Nauk (The Garden of Science). Paris: Instytut Literacki, 1979.
Nobel Lecture. New York: Farrar, Strauss, Giroux, 1981.
Postwar Polish Poetry: An Anthology. Editor. Berkeley: University of California Press, 1983.
The Witness of Poetry. Cambridge, MA: Harvard University Press, 1983.
Zaczynajac od Moich Ulic (Beginning with My Streets). Paris: Instytut Literacki, 1985.
Beginning with My Streets: Essays and Recollections. New York: Farrar, Straus, & Giroux, 1991.
Szukanie Ojczyzny (In Search of a Homeland). Cracow: Znak, 1992.
A Year of the Hunter. New York: Farrar, Straus, and Giroux, 1994.
Metafizyczna Pauza (The Metaphysical Pause). Cracow: Znak, 1995.
Book of Luminous Things: An International Anthology of Poetry. Editor. New York: Harcourt Brace, 1996.
Legendy Nowoczesnosci (Modern Legends: War Essays). Cracow: WL, 1996.
Abecadlo Milosza (Milosz's Alphabet). Cracow: WL, 1997.
Piesek Przydrozny (Roadside Dog). Cracow: Znak, 1997.
Zycie na Wyspach (Life on Islands). Cracow: Znak, 1997.
Inne Abecadlo (A Further Alphabet). Cracow: WL, 1998.
Wyprawa w Dwudziestolecie (An Excursion Through the Twenties and Thirties). Cracow: WL, 1999.
A Treatise on Poetry. New York: Ecco Press, 2001.

SELECTED RESOURCES FOR FURTHER REFERENCE

Czarnecka, Ewa, and Aleksander Fiut. *Conversations with Czeslaw Milosz*. Trans. Richard Lourie. New York: Harcourt Brace Jovanovich, 1987.
Faggen, Robert, ed. *Striving Towards Being: The Letters of Thomas Merton and Czeslaw Milosz*. New York: Farrar, Straus, & Giroux, 1997.
Fiut, Aleksander. *The Eternal Moment: The Poetry of Czeslaw Milosz*. Berkeley: University of California Press, 1987.
Mozejko, Edward. *Between Anxiety and Hope: The Poetry and Writing of Czeslaw Milosz*. University of Alberta Press, 1988.
Vendler, Helen. "Ashes of Centuries: Czeslaw Milosz's Epic Realism." *Harper's Magazine*, April, 2002, pp. 72–76.

Joel Werley

Janice Mirikitani

(1941–)

Japanese American

BIOGRAPHY

Poet and activist Janice Mirikitani was born a "Sansei," or third-generation Japanese American, in Stockton, California. Her grandparents had immigrated from Japan to Hawaii in the early twentieth century, working on plantations until they saved enough to move on to California. Like many other Japanese Americans of her generation, she spent her early childhood in an internment camp in Rohwer, Arkansas.

Mirikitani's parents moved to Chicago at the end of World War II, hoping to escape some of the racism of the West Coast, but their arranged marriage ended in divorce shortly after the move. As a single parent, Mirikitani's mother worked at two to three jobs before remarrying. The family moved to California, where Mirikitani's grandparents had returned after the war, establishing their own small chicken and vegetable farm north of San Francisco. Then Mirikitani's unhappy childhood became nightmarish, as she was abused sexually almost daily (Nimura, pp. 233–234).

She attended the University of California at Los Angeles (UCLA), earning a B.A., and received a teaching certificate from the University of California at Berkeley in 1963. She taught for a year, but, as Mirikitani was openly expressive about controversial topics, she was asked not to return. She then took a job as an administrative assistant at Glide Memorial United Methodist Church, an institution that would shape much of her later career. After a brief marriage in 1966 and the birth of a daughter in 1967, Mirikitani took graduate courses in creative writing at San Francisco State University.

There she joined the Asian American Political Alliance. Amid the campus ferment of the 1960s, this organization, with others, was campaigning for the formation of an ethnic studies department, and an artists' collective, Third World Communications, was formed. Mirikitani became the editor of the first Asian American literary magazine, *Aion,* and she began editing anthologies of women's and Asian American writing.

Mirikitani's writing, editing, and activism fuel one other, and her work at Glide Memorial Church, in the impoverished Tenderloin district of San Francisco, has fused the three. She has taken a leadership role in directing its many outreach programs for the homeless, incest survivors, battered women, and other victims of violence, poverty, and prejudice. Many of her own poems deal with incest and violence against women, and she has edited anthologies of abuse victims' accounts.

In 1982, Mirikitani married the Reverend Cecil Williams, pastor of Glide Memorial. She has spoken frankly of the challenges of their biracial marriage—Reverend Williams is African American—and the prejudices of both Asian American and African American family and community members.

Mirikitani's four volumes of her poetry and prose are *Awake in the River* (1978), *Shedding Silence: Poetry and Prose* (1987), *We, the Dangerous: New and Selected Poems* (1995), and *Love Works* (2001). Her poems have appeared in *Bamboo Ridge, Feminist Studies,* and *Amerasia Journal,* and both poetry and prose have been included in several collections of Asian American or Japanese American writing, as well in a 2002 volume published by UCLA's Asian American Studies Center, *Asian Americans on War & Peace,* a response to September 11, 2001.

In 2000, Mirikitani was named the second Poet Laureate of San Francisco, following the path blazed by Lawrence Ferlinghetti. The program for Mirikitani's inaugural speech read in part: "[H]er work with the Glide Memorial Foundation has been one of [our] best marriages of art and social consciousness and is the type of image San Francisco has always fostered. Because of that social consciousness she is one of the best known San Francisco poets in the world" (quoted in "Breaking Silence").

THEMES AND CONCERNS

"Breaking silence" is an overarching theme in Janice Mirikitani's work. Her poem by this name celebrated her mother's 1981 testimony before the Commission on Wartime Relocation and Internment of Japanese American Civilians. The years of silence maintained by many Japanese Americans who had suffered the privations of the camps and the confiscation of their property kept them complicit in the fiction that concentration camps were for other World War II civilians, not Americans. The significance and power of Mirikitani's and other Japanese Americans' poetry was acknowledged by Joseph Bruchac when he titled an anthology of Asian American poetry *Breaking Silence* (1983).

Mirikitani's title for her second volume of poetry and prose, *Shedding Silence,* applies this central theme to poems about the incest and abuse she experienced as well as to racist violence and soul-destroying stereotyping. Her poetry is often not easy to read, containing vivid images of pain and hatred. The frightening poems "Healthy Choices" and "Zipper," for example, are dramatic accounts of violent sexual assault from its victim's perspective. Such poems are angry poems, but it is clear that telling the stories of violent acts is the first step toward assuming new strength as survivor, not victim. Her highly personal poems, expressing anger against her father for leaving her and against her mother for averting her eyes from the constant abuse, and deep compassion for other women who have gathered to tell their stories and work together toward healing, point the way for other victims of abuse.

Mirikitani's rage extends to racist intolerance in many contexts: the violence of soldiers and ex-soldiers against women, white supremacists' threats against nonviolent demonstrations by people of color, the horrendous violence wrought by atomic bombs on Japanese cities. But the passion her poems embody is not only rage—healing emotions of love and compassion and her championing of the oppressed are present too. Her appreciation of her mother's "breaking silence" is accompanied by respect for the barrier through which Japanese Americans have courageously broken to claim justice. Mirikitani writes poems of deep love for her second husband and daughter, such as "Soul Food" and "For a Daughter Who Leaves."

Janice Mirikitani's accomplishment is truly remarkable. Not only has she overcome abuse and injustice for herself, but she helps others find the courage to speak.

POETRY COLLECTIONS

Awake in the River. San Francisco, CA: Isthmus Press, 1978.
Shedding Silence: Poetry and Prose. Berkeley, CA: Celestial Arts, 1987.
We, the Dangerous: New and Selected Poems. Berkeley, CA: Celestial Arts, 1995.
Love Works. San Francisco Poet Laureate Series no. 2. San Francisco, CA: City Lights Foundation, 2001.

SELECTED ADDITIONAL WORKS

Third World Women. Editor. San Francisco, CA: Third World Communications, 1972.
Time to Greez! Incantations from the Third World. Editor. San Francisco, CA: Glide/ Third World Communications, 1975.
Ayumi: A Japanese American Anthology. Editor, with the Japanese American Anthology Committee. San Francisco: Japanese American Anthology Committee, 1980.
Breaking Free: A Glide Songbook. With Cecil Williams. San Francisco: Glide Word Press, 1989.
I Have Something to Say about This Big Trouble: Children of the Tenderloin Speak Out. Editor, with Cecil Williams. San Francisco, CA: Glide Word Press, 1989.
"Rebirth: Janice's Story" (autobiographical narrative). In *No Hiding Place: Empowerment and Recovery for Our Troubled Communities.* Ed. Cecil Williams with Rebecca Laird. San Francisco, CA: HarperSanFrancisco, 1992, 64–76.
Watch Out! We're Talking. Editor. San Francisco, CA: Glide Word Press, 1993.
A Celebration with Maya Angelou, Guy Johnson, and Janice Mirikitani on the Occasion of Guy Johnson's 50th Birthday (sound recording). San Francisco: Don't Quit Your Day Job Records, 1996.
"Spoils of War" (short story). *Shedding Silence: Poetry and Prose.* Reprinted in *Asian American Literature: A Brief Introduction and Anthology.* Ed. Shawn Wong. New York: HarperCollins, 1996, 186–201.

SELECTED ANTHOLOGIES WHERE POETRY APPEARS

Anzaldúa, Gloria, ed. *Making Face, Making Soul/Haciendo Caras.* San Francisco, CA: Aunt Lute, 1990.

Asian Women United of California, ed. *Making Waves: An Anthology of Writing by and about Asian American Women.* Boston, MA: Beacon Press, 1989.

Bruchac, Joseph, ed. *Breaking Silence: An Anthology of Contemporary Asian American Poets.* Greenfield Center, NY: Greenfield Review Press, 1983.

Fisher, Dexter, ed. *The Third Woman: Minority Women Writers of the United States.* Boston, MA: Houghton Mifflin, 1980.

Hiura, Jerrold Asao, ed. *The Hawk's Well: A Collection of Japanese American Art and Literature.* Vol. 1. San Jose, CA: Asian American Art Projects, 1986.

Hongo, Garrett, ed. *The Open Boat: Poems from Asian America.* New York: Anchor/Doubleday, 1993.

Madison, D. Soyini, ed. *The Woman That I Am: The Literature and Culture of Contemporary Women of Color.* New York: St. Martin's, 1994.

SELECTED RESOURCES FOR FURTHER REFERENCE

"Breaking Silence: Janice Mirikitani, San Francisco's New Poet Laureate." *Poetry Flash: A Poetry Review and Literary Calendar for the West* no. 285 (May–June 2000). Online. www.poetryflash.org/archive.285.mirikitani.html.

Crawford, John F. "Notes Toward a New Multicultural Criticism: Three Works by Women of Color." In *A Gift of Tongues: Critical Challenges in Contemporary American Poetry.* Ed. Marie Harris and Kathleen Aguero. Athens: University of Georgia Press, 1987, 155–195.

"Janice Mirikitani." Interview with Angels Carabi, 1994. In *Truth-Tellers of the Times: Interviews with Contemporary Women Poets.* Ed. Janet Palmer Mullaney. Ann Arbor: University of Michigan Press, 1998, 66–74.

"Janice Mirikitani." Interview with Grace Kyungwon Hong. In *Words Matter: Conversations with Asian American Writers.* Ed. King-Kok Cheung. Honolulu: University of Hawaii Press, 2000, 123–139.

Lashgari, Deirdre, ed. *Violence, Silence, and Anger: Women's Writing as Transgression.* Charlottesville: University Press of Virginia, 1995.

Leitner-Rudolph, Miryam. *Janice Mirikitani and Her Work.* Vienna, Austria: Braumueller, 2001.

Nimura, Tamiko. "Janice Mirikitani." In *Asian American Poets: A Bio-Bibliographical Critical Sourcebook.* Ed. Guiyou Huang. Westport, CT: Greenwood Press, 2002, 233–242.

Oktenberg, Adrian. "No More Madame Butterfly." *Women's Review of Books* 5.5 (February 1988): 13.

Usui, Masami. "'No Hiding Place, New Speaking Space': Janice Mirikitani's Poetry of Incest and Abuse." *South Asian Literature* 32 (1996): 56–65.

Yamamoto, Traise. *Masking Selves, Making Subjects: Japanese American Women, Identity, and the Body.* Berkeley: University of California Press, 1999.

Alice Trupe

James Matseo Mitsui

(1940–)

Japanese American

Photo by Fran Martiny, courtesy of University of Washington Press.

BIOGRAPHY

Poet and teacher James Matseo Mitsui is a Nisei (a second-generation Japanese American) born to Japanese immigrants in Skykomish, Washington, in 1940. A year later, the family was interned in Tule Lake Relocation Camp in California, where they remained for a year and a half before receiving permission to return to eastern Washington, where his father worked on the railroad. The early experience of internment left a lasting impression on Mitsui, and many of his poems dramatize the relocation experience.

Mitsui attended school in Odessa, Washington, which he calls "wheat country" (quoted in O'Connell, p. 131) before earning a B.A. in education from Eastern Washington University (1963) and a B.A. and M.A. (1974) in English from the University of Washington. Among his teachers were poets and fiction writers Richard Blessing, Nelson Bentley, Richard Hugo, William Stafford, and David Wagoner.

Mitsui began writing poetry at the age of twenty-eight, when, as he said, "Poetry found me" (quoted in Bruchac, p. 193). He published his first volume, *Journal of the Sun*, in 1974; it received the Pacific Northwest Booksellers' Award for 1974, and he was awarded a National Endowment for the Arts fellowship in 1976. His second volume, *Crossing the Phantom River* (1978), brought Mitsui a *Choice* Outstanding Academic Book Award in 1980. *After the Long Train: Poems* was published in 1986. In the same year fifteen of his poems were included with poems by Janice Mirikitani, Jerrold Asao Hiura, and Zukin Hirasu in *The Hawk's Well: A Collection of Japanese American Art and Literature,* published by Asian American Art Projects. *From a Three-Cornered World: New and Selected Poems* appeared in 1997.

For over thirty years, Mitsui lived in Seattle, Washington, teaching high school English and creative writing. He retired in 1999 and now resides in Cocolalla, Idaho.

THEMES AND CONCERNS

Mitsui's poetry is very personal, a window into his family life as well as into Japanese American experiences that include the degradation of internment during World War II. He researched the camp experience, since he did not remember it himself, and wrote about it because he was "outraged" by both the treatment and the fact that it "wasn't getting in the history books" and was even "suppressed" (quoted in O'Connell, p. 130). Mitsui's poetry is frequently included on lists of sources on the internment camp experience. However, while this acknowledgment is a testimony to internment's importance and his vivid rendering of it, it is important not to lose sight of the *literary* value of Mitsui's poetry.

Many of Mitsui's poems are inspired by visual images. A photograph sparked the early poem "Photograph of a Child, Japanese-American Evacuation, Bainbridge Island, Washington, March 30, 1942." The details of place and date included in the title, as in titles of other poems, give the poem a strong sense of veracity and, moreover, impel the reader to understand the poignancy of the visual image of the boy clutching his model U.S. military plane, interested in the journey he is making, in contrast with the adults who are going with him.

Photographs inspire, or are included as details in, personal poems as well; see, for instance, "Skykomish, 1913. A Photograph," which is Part II of a long poem about Mitsui's father titled "Section Hand, Great Northern Railway." Mitsui describes two family pictures in "Minoru Mitsui." He begins his poem "Visiting My Mother at Kawabe House" with brief descriptions of the family pictures in his mother's apartment. The photographs anchor the family in intergenerational connections and link Mitsui with relatives in Japan whom he has never known.

Artistic images suggest other poems. Mitsui names Edward Hopper, Andrew Wyeth, and Asian artists as visual influences ("*Poets*West Directory"). His poem "Shrike on Dead Tree" describes a painting by the seventeenth-century artist Miyamoto Musashi, using lines of one to three syllables to convey a vertical visual text as well as a simply rendered concrete verbal image. Another poem, "Exhibition," vividly portrays a bronze horse in a museum display case. Mitsui briefly describes Hopper's rendering of light in his "Spring Poem for the Sake of Breathing, Written after a Walk to Foster Island." Yet it is not only famous artists whose paintings are cherished in Mitsui's poems, for he also describes a "Painting by a Mental Patient, Weaverville City Jail, California, 1922." The vase his father crafted from a stump at Tule Lake sits on his desk, where it continues to symbolize the complex simplicity of his father's life ("Wooden Flower Vase").

Many of Mitsui's poems about his father, deeply personal, attest to the mixture of fear, joy, pride, and embarrassment our parents inspire in us, as he recalls his father's blue-collar job, his drinking, and his strength. As Mitsui, in later poems, anticipates his children's marriages and his becoming a grand-parent, he conjures memories of his mother's juggling bean bags at age seventy-two and, years earlier, her stocking up on Golden Delicious apples for the winter. "Christmas Poem, 1987" recalls the snowy Christmases of his childhood. His love for his wife, his children, and his home life are rendered concrete, and through these poems, the reader comes to know the important people in Mitsui's life.

"Places, locations, are . . . important to me," Mitsui has said (*"Poets*West Directory"). The images of places in his poems frame experiences—for instance, "Cape Alava," which describes a three-mile winter hike to the ocean's edge with a friend. Place and a photographic image come together in the vivid images of ten couplets in "Paris Windows: Some Linked Bantu." The immediacy of place, as well as warm friendship, permeates "Fishing in Eagle Harbor with Garrett Hongo," in which Mitsui blends details of a concrete, particular fishing trip, the friends' mutual interests in sports and poetry, and the sometimes jarring but, in this poem, humorous experience of sharing their poetry with white Americans. Mitsui confronts this experience realistically, although he has said, "I've always wanted my poems to be published and accepted and printed because they were good poems" rather than as the work of "the token Asian poet" (quoted in O'Connell, p. 132).

Mitsui names James Wright and Pablo Neruda as favorite and influential poets (Bruchac, p. 193) and also cites William Carlos Williams's imagery as an influence (*"Poets*West Directory"). Garrett Hongo has described Mitsui's poems as "memorable, finely honed—combining imagistically startling vignettes, witty and melancholy ars poetica, and moving personal reminiscence" (*From a Three-Cornered World*). Understated and subtle, highly visual, rhythmic, and insightful, James Masao Mitsui's poems deserve to be more widely known.

POETRY COLLECTIONS

Journal of the Sun. Port Townsend, WA: Copper Canyon Press, 1974.
Crossing the Phantom River. St. Paul, MN: Graywolf Press, 1978.
After the Long Train: Poems. Minneapolis, MN: Bieler Press, 1986.
From a Three-Cornered World: New and Selected Poems. Seattle: University of Washington Press, 1997.

SELECTED ANTHOLOGIES WHERE POETRY APPEARS

Bruchac, Joseph, ed. *Breaking Silence: An Anthology of Contemporary Asian American Poets.* Greenfield Center, NY: Greenfield Review Press, 1983.
Gillan, Maria, and Jennifer Gillan, eds. *Unsettling America: Race and Ethnicity in Contemporary American Poetry.* New York: Viking/Penguin, 1994.
Gordon, Ruth, ed. *Pierced by a Ray of Sun: Poems about the Times We Feel Alone.* New York: HarperCollins, 1995.

Hamill, Sam, ed. *The Gift of Tongues: Twenty-five Years of Poetry from Copper Canyon Press.* Port Townsend, WA: Copper Canyon Press, 1996.

Harris, Marie, and Kathleen Aguero, eds. *An Ear to the Ground: An Anthology of Contemporary American Poetry.* Athens: University of Georgia Press, 1989.

Hongo, Garrett, ed. *The Open Boat.* New York: Doubleday/Anchor, 1993.

Ives, Rich, ed. *Rain in the Forest, Light in the Trees: Contemporary Poetry from the Northwest.* Missoula, MT: Owl Creek Press, 1983.

Tsutakawa, Mayumi, and Alan Lau, eds. *Turning Shadows into Light.* Seattle, WA: Young Pine Press, 1982.

SELECTED RESOURCES FOR FURTHER REFERENCE

Hongo, Garrett. *From a Three-Cornered World.* Online. www.washington.edu/uwpress/asian.amer.studies.html.

O'Connell, Nicholas. "James Mitsui." In *At the Field's End: Interviews with 22 Pacific Northwest Writers.* Ed. Nicholas O'Connell. Seattle: University of Washington Press, 1998, 128–144.

"*Poets*West Directory: Who's Who in Northwest Poetry." Online. www.poetswest.com/directory3.htm.

Alice Trupe

N. (Navarre) Scott Momaday

(1934–)

American Indian (Kiowa)

BIOGRAPHY

Momaday was born Navarre Scott Mammedaty on February 27, 1934, in Lawton, Oklahoma, but the family name was later changed to Momaday by Scott's father, a full-blooded Kiowa Indian named Alfred Morris Mammedaty. His mother, the former Mayme Natachee Scott, was of Scottish, French, and Cherokee descent. The first two years of Scott Momaday's life were spent on a Kiowa reservation, but his parents, who were teachers, held a series of jobs. Momaday grew up as a Kiowa on Navajo and Pueblo reservations, all the while being raised by his parents to be part of the larger American culture. This complex mix of cultures served him well and became an important part of his poetry.

For his basic education, he attended the Franciscan Mission School in Jemez, New Mexico, the Indian School in Santa Fe, and a high school in Bernalili, New Mexico. After then attending the Augusta Military School in Virginia, he earned a degree in political science from University of New Mexico in Albuquerque. In 1956 he attended the University of Virginia Law School. While there, he had the opportunity to meet the novelist William Faulkner, who profoundly influenced him. He graduated in 1958 and went to his first teaching job on the Jicarilla Apache reservation.

The year 1959 was a momentous year for Scott Momaday. While teaching at the Apache reservation, he met his wife, Gaye Mangold, whom he married in 1959; they have three daughters. Also in 1959 he received the Wallace Stegner creative writing fellowship to attend Stanford University. That year he met his mentor, the postsymbolist poet Yvor Winters, who guided Momaday through the doctorate program. His thesis was an edition of the works of Frederick Goddard Tuckerman, a nineteenth-century postsymbolist poet. That same year, Momaday published his first poetry.

In addition to writing and speaking, Dr. Momaday has taught at Stanford University, the University of Arizona at Tucson, and the University of California at Berkeley. At Berkeley he designed the graduate program in Indian studies. In 1962 he received the Academy of American Poets Prize for "The Bear." He received a Guggenheim fellowship in 1996 and 1967. In 1969 he received the Pulitzer Prize for fiction for his book *House Made of Dawn.* In 1974 he began taking art lessons from Leonard Baskin and has since become an accomplished artist. In his collection *In the Presence of the Sun,* he drew the sixteen shields that accompany the sixteen stories in the book.

THEMES AND CONCERNS

Scott Momaday is a novelist, poet, autobiographer, nonfiction writer, artist, and editor. Momaday is not only prolific in his own right, but volumes have been written on this author. He is perhaps the most famous of the Indian writers to emerge from the Native American Renaissance of the last half of the twentieth century. Indeed, this renaissance began with the publication of Momaday's novel *House Made of Dawn* in 1968. Native authors agree that it would be difficult to overestimate the impact of Scott Momaday on Native American literature; they feel that by winning the Pulitzer Prize in 1969, Momaday opened the door for other American Indian writers to be recognized by both publishers and critics. Further, Momaday's essay "The Man Made of Words" has been described by Joseph Bruchac, himself a noted poet, critic, and publisher, as "one of the most important contemporary statements about the American Indian writer" (p. 174).

One influence on Momaday's work was his mother, Mayme Natachee Scott Momaday, a poet in her own right. She believed in "self-imagining" as a way of identifying with one's lost Native American heritage. Scott Momaday follows this practice in his work, as he states in his 1970 essay "The Man Made of Words." Another influential source was Yvor Winters, Momaday's adviser during his graduate studies at Stanford. He was a profound influence on the poetic techniques and devices Momaday would master. Under the tutelage of Winters, Momaday began to play with syllables. This became the foundation of his poetry. His two most famous poems, "The Bear" and "Angle of Geese" (both in *Angle of Geese and Other Poems*), use syllabic verse and vivid description in the postsymbolist tradition. In each four-line stanza, the first and third lines have five syllables, the second and fourth have seven syllables.

His poetry is sophisticated in structure and somber in tone. He often writes of death. In "Old Bear," which is based on William Faulkner's Old Ben in his short story "The Bear," Momaday writes of the death of an old bear that was maimed long ago by a hunter's trap. In "Angle of Geese" he compares the death of a friend's young child with the death of a goose shot and killed while in flight. Another major theme in Momaday's work is that of Kiowa traditions, culture, and belief. Other concerns include humanity's relationship to the earth and the nature of reality.

Although Momaday's first book, *Angle of Geese and Other Poems* (1974), contains only eighteen poems, "Angle of Geese" and "The Bear" are still considered masterpieces. These eighteen, plus two new poems, make up the first of three parts of his second volume of poetry, *The Gourd Dancer* (1976). Each part is dedicated to one of his daughters. The predominant theme in the first part is death: the death of individual creatures and his fear that his culture may be dying. In the second part, titled "The Dream," we see Momaday's search for his identity framed in the oral and storytelling traditions of his people. This section is written in poetry and prose stanzas and recounts the Kiowa tradition of the Gourd Dance. Poems such as "The Carriers of the Dream Wheel" and "The Colors of Night" remind us how ancient these sacred traditions are and how long American Indians have lived in harmony with their world. The themes in the third part are eclectic, going from the beauty of the earth to the destruction of the Indian culture. *The Gourd Dancer* supports the assertion that Momaday is very much a "multicultural" writer, in the truest sense of the term. Because of his background, he moves easily from one culture to another.

Although he is possibly the most famous of current American Indian writers, N. Scott Momaday has refused to position himself as the voice of his generation of writers. He modestly protests that if he were to do this, it would not leave room for all the other voices that need to be heard.

POETRY COLLECTIONS

Angle of Geese and Other Poems. Boston, MA: Godine, 1974.
The Gourd Dancer. New York: Harper & Row, 1976.
In the Presence of the Sun: Stories and Poems, 1961–1991. New York: St. Martin's Press, 1992.

SELECTED ANTHOLOGIES WHERE POETRY APPEARS

Bruchac, Joseph. *Songs from This Earth on Turtle's Back.* Greenfield Center, NY: Greenfield Review Press, 1989.
LaGuardia, Dolores, and Hans Guth, eds. *American Visions: Multicultural Literature for Writers.* New York: McGraw-Hill, 1994.
Niatum, Duane, ed. *Carriers of the Dream Wheel.* New York: Harper & Row, 1975.
———. *Harper's Anthology of 20th Century Native American Poetry.* San Francisco, CA: Harper & Row, 1987.

SELECTED ADDITIONAL WORKS

The Journey of Tai-Me. Santa Barbara: University of California, 1967.
House Made of Dawn. New York: Harper & Row, 1968.
The Way to Rainy Mountain. Albuquerque: University of New Mexico Press, 1969.
The Names: A Memoir. New York: Harper & Row, 1976.
The Ancient Child. New York: Doubleday, 1989.
Circle of Wonder: A Native American Christmas Story. Santa Fe, NM: Clear Light, 1994.
The Man Made of Words: Essays, Stories, Passages. New York: St. Martin's Press, 1997.
In the Bear's House. New York: St. Martin's Press, 1999.

SELECTED RESOURCES FOR FURTHER REFERENCE

Bruchac, Joseph. *Survival This Way: Interviews with American Indian Poets*. Tucson: University of Arizona Press, 1987, 173–191.

Buffalo Trust. N. Scott Momaday, founder and chairman. Online. www.sidecanyon.com/buffalotrust.htm.

Dickinson-Brown, Roger. "The Art and Importance of N. Scott Momaday." *Southern Review* 14.1 (January 1978): 30–45.

Mason, Kenneth C. "Beautyway: The Poetry of N. Scott Momaday." *South Dakota Review* 18.2 (1980): 61–83.

Schubnell, Matthias. *N. Scott Momaday: The Cultural and Literary Background*. Norman: University of Oklahoma Press, 1985.

Wiget, Andrew, ed. *Dictionary of Native American Literature*. New York: Garland, 1994.

Woodard, Charles L. *Ancestral Voice: Conversations with N. Scott Momaday*. Lincoln: University of Nebraska Press, 1989.

Sue Czerny

Pat Mora

(1942–)

Chicana/Mexican American

Photo © Arte Público Press.

BIOGRAPHY

Patricia Estella Mora was born in El Paso, Texas, on January 19, 1942, the daughter of an optician, Raúl Antonio Mora, and Estella Delgado Mora. Her parents' home was mostly Spanish-speaking, with the influence of her four grandparents who had come to Texas from Mexico to escape revolution in the early twentieth century. She attended Catholic schools in El Paso and went on to graduate with a B.A. from Texas Western College in 1963 and an M.A. in English from the University of Texas at El Paso in 1967. After obtaining her B.A., Mora taught English in the El Paso Independent School District and El Paso Community College and eventually returned to the University of Texas at El Paso as an instructor. From 1981 to 1989 she served as a university administrator and museum director.

Pat Mora has developed one of the broadest audiences of any Hispanic poet in the United States, encompassing both children and adults. Her narrative style and the healing messages of her poems have made her work accessible to a wide age range, and as a result, her poems have been made into children's books and have been reprinted in many elementary, middle, and high school textbooks. Many of these characters and plots are based on family members as well as personal and family experiences. Her poem "1910," for example, is based on a true story told to her by her maternal aunt Ignacia, who is also the star of her children's book *A Birthday Basket for Tía*. As a result of her universal voice, Mora has become a popular speaker and guest presenter at gatherings of teachers and education professionals around the country.

Mora began publishing poetry in the late 1970s in small magazines such as the *Americas Review* and was a part of the first wave of the Chicano literary movement. Her first volume of poetry appeared in 1984, with four others following over the next thirteen years. In 1992 her first children's book was published, and this has proved to be her most prolific genre, totaling eighteen books of poetry and prose in all. As an acclaimed author of adult and children's books, Pat Mora is a tireless activist working to bring literacy to Latino/Latina children everywhere. Since 1997, when she launched her project Día de los Niños/Día de los Libros, Mora has reached a wide audience and received an enthusiastic response from educators, particularly in the National Council of Teachers of English, to whose members she has addressed on numerous occasions.

She has received many literary honors and awards, including a National Endowment for the Arts fellowship in 1994, the prestigious Premio Aztlan Literature Award in 1997, and three Southwest Book Awards. Her publishing in children's literature has also garnered her numerous awards; these include the 2001 Parent's Guide Children's Media Award for *Love to Mamá,* the 1999 Book Publishers of Texas Award for Best Book for Children or Young People for *This Big Sky,* and the Choices Award—Cooperative Children's Books Centers and the Stepping Stones Award for *The Desert Is My Mother.* Most recently, Pat Mora received a Civitella Ranieri fellowship to write in Umbria, Italy, in 2003.

Mora is the mother of three children, William, Elizabeth, and Cecilia, all from her first marriage to William Burnside. In 1984 she married archaeologist Vernon Lee Scarborough, with whom she has traveled extensively. When Scarborough accepted a position at the University of Cincinnati, Mora began dividing her time between Cincinnati and Santa Fe, New Mexico.

THEMES AND CONCERNS

The titles of Mora's volumes of poetry are strongly indicative of her most prevailing themes. Her first book, *Chants,* reveals her interest in shamanism and biculturalism, while her second book, *Borders,* indicates her most prominent theme in the years that followed. Mora explores themes of borders in the literal sense, having grown up in a border state with Mexico, and in cultural, socioeconomic, gender, and global senses as well. This theme is interwoven with her heavy feminist perspective as well as with her promotion of reading, or "bookjoy," in children.

Mora addresses borders of all types in her writing. While borders can serve to provide perspective from which to observe and understand two cultures, such a vantage point tends to make one feel like an outsider, so alienation also becomes a central condition of border life. She approaches borders as a position of power, a place in which to bridge divisions, heal wounds, and facilitate mutual understanding. In her poem "Malinché's Tips: Pique from Mexico's Mother," Mora addresses both her border status and the alienation that this thrusts upon her. The poem describes how she pulls from her past as a descendant of Mexicans to function in her life as a American. Mora also sees the border in terms of social class and racism. Skin color is featured prominently as a border in "Mexican Maid," and class differences are highlighted in "Illegal Aliens." Borders serve to both divide people and to give power to them. In her poems "Legal Aliens," "Abuelita Magic," and "Curandera," Mora addresses borderlands as centers of power in themselves.

Other strong themes include identification with the desert, nature, and the influence of her ancestors. Mora's poems draw strength from her family members as well as other poets and intellectuals. She incorporates their messages coupled with their traditional ways to create poetry that speaks both a universal message of familial influence and a distinctly Mexican worldview. The emphasis on her female ancestors fits with her feminist beliefs, which also appear in writing featuring the women of other Third World and oppresses countries. She addresses issues of gender and relationships from this feminist perspective, but also ties in the theme of the borders that separate men and women.

POETRY COLLECTIONS

Chants. Houston, TX: Arte Público Press, 1984.
Borders. Houston, TX: Arte Público Press, 1986.
Communion. Houston, TX: Arte Público Press, 1991.
Agua Santa: Holy Water. Boston, MA: Beacon Press, 1995.
Confetti: Poems for Children. New York: Lee & Low Books, 1996.
Aunt Carmen's Book of Practical Saints. Boston, MA: Beacon Press, 1997.
My Own True Name: New and Selected Poems for Young Adults. Houston, TX: Piñata Books/Arte Público Press, 2000.

SELECTED ANTHOLOGIES WHERE POETRY APPEARS

Carlson, Lori M., ed. *Cool Salsa: Bilingual Poems on Growing Up Latino in the United States.* New York: Fawcett Juniper, 1995.
Gillan, Maria M., and Jennifer Gillan, eds. *Unsettling America: An Anthology of Contemporary Multicultural Poetry.* New York: Penguin/Putnam, 1994.
Hernández Cruz, Victor, Leroy V. Quintana, and Virgil Suárez, eds. *Paper Dance: 55 Latino Poets.* New York: Persea Books, 1995.
Milligan, Bryce, et al., eds. *Daughters of the Fifth Sun: A Collection of Latina Fiction and Poetry.* New York: Riverhead Books, 1995.
———. *¡Floricanto Sí! A Collection of Latina Poetry.* New York: Penguin/Putnam, 1998.
Rich, Adrienne, and David Lehman, eds. *The Best American Poetry 1996.* New York: Scribner, 1996.

SELECTED FICTION, NONFICTION, AND CHILDREN'S LITERATURE

A Birthday Basket for Tía. New York: Simon & Schuster, 1992.
Nepantla: Essays form the Land in the Middle. Albuquerque: University of New Mexico Press, 1993.

Delicious Hullabaloo: Pachanga Deliciosa. Houston, TX: Piñata Books/Arte Público Press, 1994.

The Desert Is My Mother: El Desierto Es Mi Madre. Houston, TX: Piñata Books/Arte Público Press, 1994.

Listen to the Desert: Oye al Desierto. New York: Clarion Books, 1994.

Pablo's Tree. New York: Simon & Schuster, 1994.

The Gift of the Poinsettia: El Regalo de la Flor de Nochebuena. Houston, TX: Piñata Books/Arte Público Press, 1995.

House of Houses. Boston, MA: Beacon Press, 1997.

This Big Sky. New York: Scholastic Press, 1998.

Love to Mamá: A Tribute to Mothers. New York: Lee & Low Books, 2001.

A Library for Juana. New York: Knopf, 2002.

SELECTED RESOURCES FOR FURTHER REFERENCE

Alarcón, Norma. "Interview with Pat Mora." In *Third Woman: Texas and More*. Ed. Norma Alarcón et al. Berkeley, CA: Third Woman Press, 1986, 121–126.

Barrera, Rosalinda B. "Profile: Pat Mora, Fiction/Nonfiction Writer and Poet." *Language Arts* 75.3 (March 1998): 221–227.

Henderson, Darwin. "Listening to the Desert: A Conversation with Pat Mora." *Ohio Journal of English Language Arts* 41.1 (Fall 2000): 12–17.

Hurtado, Aída. "Sitos y Lenguas: Chicanas Theorize Feminisms." *Hypatia: A Journal of Feminist Philosophy* 13.2 (Spring 1998): 134–160.

Ikas, Karin Rosa. "Pat Mora: Poet, Writer, and Educator." In *Chicana Ways: Conversations with Ten Chicana Writers*. Ed. Karin Rosa Ikas. Reno: University of Nevada Press, 2002, 126–149.

Murphy, Patrick D. "Conserving Natural and Cultural Diversity: The Prose and Poetry of Pat Mora." *MELUS: The Journal of the Society for the Study of the Multi-Ethnic Literature of the United States* 21.1 (Spring 1996): 59–69.

———. "Ecofeminism and Postmodernism-Agency, Transformation, and Future Possibilities." *NWSA Journal* 9.3 (Fall 1997): 41–59.

Rebolledo, Tey Diana. "Pat Mora." In *This Is about Vision: Interviews with Southwestern Writers*. Ed. John F. Crawford, William Balassi, and Annie O. Eysturoy. Albuquerque: University of New Mexico Press, 1990, 129–139.

Rosenmeier, Rosamond. "Three Poets: Three Feminist Worlds." *Sojourner: The Women's Forum* 17 (1992): 39–41.

Telgen, Diane, and Jim Kamp, eds. *Notable Hispanic American Women*. Detroit, MI: Gale Research, 1993.

Torres, Lourdes. "Chicana Writers Explore the Land in the Middle." *Sojourner: The Women's Forum* 19 (1994): 10–12.

Bronwen West

Paul Muldoon

(1951–)

Irish American

Photo © Jerry Bauer.

BIOGRAPHY

Poet and professor Paul Muldoon was born in County Armagh, Northern Ireland, in June 1951. His father, Patrick Muldoon, helped to support his family by working a variety of jobs that kept him tied closely to the land, including mushroom and vegetable farming. His mother, Brigid Regan Muldoon, worked as a schoolteacher, and the family eventually settled near the small town of the Moy in Armagh so his mother could be near her primary school in Collegelands. This town of the Moy is featured in the landscape of many of Muldoon's poems.

Although Muldoon has lived in the United States for more than fifteen years, his years in Belfast continue to shape him as a writer. In 1969, Muldoon went to study English at Queen's University in Belfast, and here he met the poet Seamus Heaney, who was teaching at Queen's and would have a profound impact on Muldoon's poetry. Heaney introduced Muldoon to other poets in Belfast and helped him to publish his first collection of poetry, *New Weather,* at the age of twenty-one. In 1973, prior to graduation from Queen's University, Muldoon also met his first wife, Anne-Marie Conway. Muldoon spent the next thirteen years working for the BBC as a producer for radio and television programs. During this time, his marriage ended, and he spent some time in a serious relationship with the artist Mary Earl Powers. His other poetry collections published during the 1970s and early 1980s, *Mules, Why Brownlee Left,* and *Quoof,* frequently address the political situation in Northern Ireland, with its constant violence and conflict.

In 1986, after Muldoon's father died, he left Northern Ireland and spent some time writing and teaching in the Republic of Ireland and England. In 1987 he moved permanently to the United States, where he currently resides with his wife, the novelist Jean Hanff Korelitz, and their two children. He published *Madoc—A Mystery: The Annals of Chile* and *Hay* after immigrating to America. In addition to poetry, Muldoon has also written a libretto, *Shining Brow,* two plays, *Monkeys* and *Six Honest Serving Men,* and several children's books. He also has published numerous critical articles and edited or translated several books of Irish poetry.

Paul Muldoon has received many honors and awards for his poetry. For example, in 1991 he was awarded the Sir Geoffrey Faber Memorial Award, and in 1994 he received the T. S. Eliot Award for *Annals of Chile*. In 1996 he was awarded both the American Academy of Arts and Letters Award in Literature and the Irish Times Irish Literature Prize for *New Selected Poems*. Currently, Muldoon directs the Creative Writing Program and holds the position of Howard G. B. Clark Professor of Humanities and Creative Writing at Princeton University. He also holds the honorary position of Professor of Poetry at Oxford.

THEMES AND CONCERNS

Muldoon's poetry appears, at first glance, to be intensely personal and, indeed, his poems are often concerned with individual human relationships, the family, and one's homeland and community. However, readers may find themselves asking broader questions about the influence of one's home and family on personal identity or subjectivity, or wondering about the relationship between sex and violence, or between our inner lives and our cultural experiences.

Muldoon spent his childhood in Northern Ireland, in a society that was being torn apart by religious and political struggles and violence. His family was part of the Catholic minority, and the question of loyalty was never far from the consciousness of Northern Ireland's citizens. Clair Wills points out that Muldoon's style of Irish lyric poetry may be especially well suited to address these kinds of tensions because lyric poetry has always told the story of Irish history through a kind of meditation on one's inner life. She writes, "Certainly the concept of an inner life is not an easy one, particularly in the current philosophical climate, and arguably it has never really been possible to abstract it from social and historical forces. Indeed, one way of understanding the concept of an inner life is as something social—people by the past (through mourning) and the future" (*Reading Paul Muldoon*, p. 20). Readers cannot separate the inner life of the speakers in Muldoon's poems from the political climate that shaped Muldoon's own experience.

Many critics view the violence and pain in Muldoon's poetry as his way of addressing the violence he observed while living in both rural Northern Ireland and Belfast. Poems such as "Christo's" (*Meeting the British*) directly address the history of the "Troubles" and specific events such as hunger strikes. Others, such as "The Wishbone," use a common event—here a father and son watching television and planning their evening meal—to introduce questions of national or political loyalty. Other poems, such as "Blemish," "The Merman," "Cheesecake," and "At Martha's Deli" (all from *Mules*) link sexual contact with violence.

Muldoon's poetry has been greatly influenced by his mentor, Seamus Heaney, and also by the diction and imagery of Robert Frost. Muldoon's first collection of poetry, *New Weather,* seems to echo the landscape and descriptions of typical Frost poems. Tim Kendall points out in *Paul Muldoon* the direct influence of Robert Frost in the poem "Wind and Tree" (*New Weather*), claiming that "Frost is the pervasive presence in Muldoon's early work" (p. 29).

Eamon Grennan provides a careful analysis of Muldoon's grammar, syntax, and tone of voice in "A World of Difference: Reading into Muldoon" and "Works & Days: Wordsmith Muldoon," both of which appear in Grennan's essay collection *Facing the Music: Irish Poetry in the Twentieth Century.* In this essay, Grennan explains that Muldoon continually plays with our grammatical expectations and our experience of how words and language usually behave. Grennan writes, "A result of this bewildering, almost indecently kinetic nature of subject and verb is a speedy unsettling of any firm sense of identity, and an equally rapid undermining of any sure sense of time or of the status of action" (p. 338). As readers, we are faced with a slippery sense of time and of subjectivity, and we are asked to question the certainty of our worldview. As the subject of a poem slips and changes, we are challenged to experience the world from multiple perspectives at once. In the midst of these slippages and uncertainties, however, Muldoon's voice remains "reserved and intimate" and provides a centered, calming effect that serves to reassure readers that we can know the world and trust our perspective (Grennan, p. 342).

POETRY COLLECTIONS

New Weather. London: Faber, 1973.
Mules. Winston-Salem, NC: Wake Forest University, 1977.
Why Brownlee Left. Winston-Salem, NC: Wake Forest University, 1980.
Quoof. Winston-Salem, NC: Wake Forest University, 1983.
The Wishbone. Oldcastle: Gallery Press, 1984.
Mules and Early Poems. Winston-Salem, NC: Wake Forest University, 1985.
Meeting the British. Winston-Salem, NC: Wake Forest University, 1987.
Selected Poems 1968–1986. New York: Ecco Press, 1987.
Madoc—A Mystery. London: Faber, 1990.
Annals of Chile. New York: Farrar, Straus, & Giroux, 1994.
The Prince of the Quotidian. Winston-Salem, NC: Wake Forest University, 1994.
New Selected Poems 1968–1993. London: Faber, 1996.
Hopewell Haiku. Easthampton: Warwick Press, 1997.
Hay. London: Faber, 1998.
Poems 1968–1998. London: Faber, 2001.
Moy Sand and Gravel. London: Faber, 2002.
Unapproved Road. Hopewell, NJ: Pied Oxen Printers, 2002.

SELECTED ANTHOLOGIES AND WEB SITES WHERE POETRY APPEARS

Collins, Billy, ed. *Poetry 180: A Turning Back to Poetry*. New York: Random House, 2003.

Fallon, Peter, and Derek Mahon, eds. *The Penguin Book of Contemporary Irish Poetry*. New York: Penguin, 1991.

Official Paul Muldoon Homepage. Online. www.paulmuldoon.net.

Ramazani, Shahah, ed. *The Norton Anthology of Modern and Contemporary Poetry*. New York: W. W. Norton, 2003.

SELECTED ADDITIONAL WORKS

The Scrake of Dawn: Poems by Young People from Northern Ireland. Editor. Belfast: Blackstaff Press, 1979.

The Faber Book of Contemporary Irish Poetry. Editor. London: Faber, 1986.

The Essential Byron. Editor. New York: Ecco Press, 1989.

Shining Brow. London: Faber, 1993.

"Paul Muldoon Writes. . . ." *Poetry Book Society Bulletin* 162 (Autumn 1994): 1–2.

Six Honest Serving Men. London: Faber, 1995.

Paul Muldoon Unplugged. New York: Faber/Penguin Audiobooks, 1997.

"Getting Round: Notes Towards an *Ars Poetica*." *Essays in Criticism* 48.2 (April 1998): 107–128.

"The Point of Poetry." *Princeton University Library Chronicle* 59.3 (Spring 1998): 503–516.

To Ireland, I. Oxford: Oxford University Press, 2000.

SELECTED RESOURCES FOR FURTHER REFERENCE

Buchanan, Barbara. "Paul Muldoon: 'Who's to Know What's Knowable?'" In *Contemporary Irish Poetry*. Ed. E. Andrews. London: Macmillan, 1992, 310–327.

Burt, Paul. "Paul Muldoon's Binocular Vision." *Harvard Review* 7 (Fall 1994): 95–107.

Grennan, Eamon. *Facing the Music: Irish Poetry in the Twentieth Century*. Omaha, NE: Creighton University Press, 1999.

Kendall, Tim. *Paul Muldoon*. Bridgend, Wales: Seren, 1996.

Stabler, J. "'Alive in the Midst of Questions': A Survey of the Poetry of Paul Muldoon." *Verse* 8.2 (Summer 1991): 52–61.

Stanfield, P. "Another Side of Paul Muldoon." *North Dakota Quarterly* 57.1 (Winter 1993): 129–143.

Wills, Clair. "Paul Muldoon: Dubious Origins." In *Improprieties: Politics and Sexuality in Northern Ireland*. Oxford: Oxford University Press, 1993, 194–235.

———. *Reading Paul Muldoon*. Newcastle upon Tyne: Bloodaxe Books, 1998.

Wilson, W. "Paul Muldoon and the Poetics of Sexual Difference." *Contemporary Literature* 28.3 (Fall 1987): 317–331.

Jennifer McNamara Dressler

David Mura

(1952–)

Japanese American

BIOGRAPHY

David Mura, a poet, creative nonfiction writer, and performance artist, is a third-generation Japanese American (Sansei), born on June 17, 1952, in Chicago, Illinois. Painfully aware of his parents' life in internment camps during World War II, he grew up ambivalent about his Japanese ancestry to the point of denial, subconsciously considering himself white. Consequently, he learned nothing of the culture or language of his parents and grandparents. Of his childhood and adolescence in a Chicago suburb, he says:

> I think I grew up in some way shameful about my Japanese background. . . . In the camps, my father's high school teacher told him, "When you get out, you have to be not 100 percent American, but 200 percent American." And one of the things American culture is designed to do is give us the picture that white middle-class reality is the only reality. I grew up, in a way, thinking that, desiring that. My whole life as a writer has been in stripping away that desire in myself. (quoted in Solovitch)

In 1974, Mura graduated with a B.A. in English literature from Grinnell College, Iowa. He followed this with graduate studies at the University of Minnesota until 1979. In 1984 he received a U.S.–Japan Creative Artist Fellowship, which allowed Mura "to reclaim and know that side of my family which my parents hadn't talked about. I could see how long a distance my parents had had to travel from their culture to American streets" (quoted in Solovitch). At the same time, this experience reconfirmed his sense of American identity.

Mura broke into the literary scene with his collection of poems *After We Lost Our Way,* which won the 1989 National Poetry Series Contest. His second volume of poetry, *The Colors of Desire* (1995), won the Carl Sandburg Literary Award from the Friends of the Chicago Public Library. In between the publication of these two collections, in 1991, he completed an M.F.A. at Vermont College.

Mura's nonfiction includes *A Male Grief: Notes on Pornography & Addiction* (1987) and two award-winning memoirs. *Turning Japanese: Memoirs of a Sansei* (1991) garnered the Josephine Miles Book Award from the Oakland PEN and a Minnesota Book Award for Biography and was listed among *New York Times* Notable Books of the Year. *Where the Body Meets Memory: An Odyssey of Race, Sexuality, and Identity* (1995) won a Minnesota Book Award for Memoir. Eileen Tabios recalls Mura as saying that he wrote memoirs "partly to lay out a context for his poems—that otherwise no one else might do so, or perhaps do so in a manner that Mura would appreciate" (quoted in Ikeda). Also in 1995, Mura was awarded a Lila Wallace–Reader's Digest Writer's Award.

Mura's openness to all creative forms brought him from poetry and memoir to performing arts. His performance piece *Relocations: Images from a Sansei,* which premiered in 1990 at Intermedia Arts, Minneapolis, addresses many of the same issues of cultural identity as his literary texts. With African American writer Alexs Pate, Mura created and performed a multimedia piece, *Secret Colors,* which premiered in 1984 at the Walker Art Center, Minneapolis; the film version, *Slowly, This,* was broadcast in the PBS series *Alive TV.* Another performance piece, *The Winged Seed,* is an adaptation of poet Li-Young Lee's memoir. Other collaborative partners in various performance pieces have included Ester Suzuki, Maria Cheng, Tom Rose, Kim Hines, pianist Jon Jang, and actor Kelvin Han Yee.

Mura has served as artistic director of the Asian American Renaissance, a Minnesota arts organization, and has taught and conducted workshops at the University of Minnesota, St. Olaf College, the Loft Literary Center in Minneapolis, the University of Oregon, and the University of San Francisco. He lives in Minneapolis with his wife and three children. Mura's most recent publication, *Song for Uncle Tom, Tonto, and Mr. Moto* (2002), is a collection of essays and interviews in which he discusses his poetic sensibility and his views of the complexity of the field of Asian American poetry.

THEMES AND CONCERNS

Mura has challenged those critical approaches that look at Asian American literary texts solely in terms of their faithful rendering of racial experience. Like Garrett Hongo and others, he asserts that the Asian American experience is complex and varies widely. He also argues for valuing formal experimentation and works in a variety of genres. Nonetheless, confronting and embracing one's racial identity has been an ongoing theme in Mura's works. He has made extensive use of the dramatic monologue, and in juxtaposing poems representing different individual perspectives and experiences, he has placed such monologues in dialogue with each other. In his first volume of poetry, *After We Lost Our Way,* Mura juxtaposes monologues by Issei, Nisei, and Sansei (first-, second-, and third-generation Japanese American speakers), whose varying responses to the disruptive and humiliating experience of the internment camps ironically dramatize, and thus challenge, racist stereotypes that underpinned the discrimination. Mura links racial discrimination with sexual discrimination in his series of monologues centering on Italian writer and film director Pier Paolo Pasolini, whose homosexuality brought him notoriety and condemnation.

The importance of a creative work going through revisions and changes is reflected in the step-by-step draft stages of his poem "Colors of Desire," featured in *Black Lightning: Poetry-in-Progress,* edited by Eileen Tabios. In an interview, Mura has cautioned students against being satisfied with their initial efforts and arriving at the "perfect poem":

> There are sometimes things that you want to write about where you know you're going to write badly at first. You're going to write badly because it's coming out of a part of your unconscious that you have not understood yet, or because it's related to experiences which your culture has not given you a language to express yet. Part of the impetus for poetry is to find a language for experience, and feelings, and thoughts, that haven't yet been expressed. When you're breaking that new ground, you can't expect perfection or excellence right off the bat. (Teachers & Writers Collaborative)

David Mura is a poet and multigenre artist of distinction who has wrestled with racial issues and other past ghosts, confronted them, articulated them, and discovered his true affection for the world and his place in it.

POETRY COLLECTIONS

After We Lost Our Way. New York: Dutton, 1989.
The Colors of Desire: Poems. New York: Anchor Books, 1995.

SELECTED ANTHOLOGIES AND WEB SITES WHERE POETRY APPEARS

Bold Type. Online. www.randomhouse.com.
Hongo, Garrett, ed. *The Open Boat: Poems from Asian America.* New York: Anchor Books Doubleday, 1993.
Moramarco, Fred, and Al Zolynas, eds. *Men of Our Time: An Anthology of Male Poetry in Contemporary America.* Athens: University of Georgia Press, 1992.
Moyers, Bill, ed. *The Language of Life: A Festival of Poets.* New York: Doubleday, 1995.

SELECTED NONFICTION

A Male Grief: Notes on Pornography & Addiction: An Essay. Minneapolis: Milkweed Editions, 1987.

Turning Japanese: Memoirs of a Sansei. New York: Atlantic Monthly Press, 1991.

Where the Body Meets Memory: An Odyssey of Race, Sexuality, and Identity. New York: Anchor Books, 1996.

"How History Stains the Colors of Desire." In *Black Lightning: Poetry in Progress.* Ed. Eileen Tabios. Philadelphia: Temple University Press, 1998, 333–378.

"In the Realm of the Sansei." *Nerve.* 2000. Online. www.nerve.com/personalessays/mura/sansei.

Song for Uncle Tom, Tonto, and Mr. Moto. Poets on Poetry Series. Ann Arbor: University of Michigan Press, 2002.

"On *The Winged Seed* & The Process of Adaptation." *Artists' Journal.* Pangea World Theater. Online. www.pangeaworldtheater.org.

SELECTED PERFORMANCES, PLAYS, AND FILMS

Relocations: Images from a Japanese American. 1990. (multimedia performance)

Invasion. 1994. (play)

Secret Colors. With Alexs Pate. 1995. (multimedia performance)

Silence and Desire. With Tom Rose, Kim Hines, and Maria Cheng. 1994. (play)

Slowly This. With Alexs Pate. Produced by *Alive TV. Silent Children.* 1997. (film)

The Winged Seed. 1997.

Internment Voices. With Esther Suzuki. 1998. (play)

SELECTED RESOURCES FOR FURTHER REFERENCE

Barron, Ronald. *A Guide to Minnesota Writers.* Edina, MN: Burgess International Group, 1993.

Ikeda, Stewart David. *AAV Q&A: Eileen Tabios. Asian American Village.* Online. www.imdiversity.com/villages/asian.

Minnesota Historical Society. "David Mura." *Minnesota Author Biographies Project.* Online. http://people.mnhs.org/authors.

Slowik, Mary. "Beyond Lot's Wife: The Immigration Poems of Marilyn Chin, Garrett Hongo, Li-Young Lee, and David Mura." *MELUS: The Journal of the Society for the Study of the Multi-Ethnic Literature of the United States* 25.3–4 (Fall–Winter 2000): 221–231.

Solovitch, Sara. "Finding a Voice." *Mercury News,* June 30, 1991. Online. www.sarasolo.com/mn2b.html.

Teachers & Writers Collaborative. *Poets Chat,* November 1999. *Poets on Poetry.* Online. www.twc.org/forums/poetschat.

Reme A. Grefalda

Marilyn Nelson

(1946–)

African American

Photo © Doug Anderson.

BIOGRAPHY

Marilyn Nelson, who dropped her married name "Waniek" in 1995, was born April 26, 1946, in Cleveland, Ohio. Her father, Melvin, was in the U.S. Air Force, and her mother, Johnnie (Mitchell), was a teacher. Nelson has been married twice. She and her first husband, Erdmann F. Waniek, married in 1970 and were divorced in 1979. She married Roger R. Wilkenfeld in 1979; they divorced in 1998. She has two children, Jacob and Dora.

Nelson received her B.A. from the University of California, Davis, in 1968. She went on to earn her M.A. from the University of Pennsylvania in 1970, and her Ph.D. from the University of Minnesota in 1978. She began her teaching career at Lane Community College in Eugene, Oregon, as an assistant professor of English (1970–1972). From 1972 to 1973, she taught English at Norre Nissum Seminariam, Norre Nissum, Denmark, before returning to the United States to teach at St. Olaf College, Northfield, Minnesota, as an instructor in English from 1973 to 1978. Nelson has been a professor of English at the University of Connecticut, Storrs, since 1978. She teaches a variety of courses, including creative writing, African American literature, and American ethnic literatures. She maintains a Homepage, which she calls "Marilyn Nelson's Labrinyth," that contains a wealth of information about her and her poetry.

Marilyn Nelson's poetry has been widely recognized, and she has received numerous awards and honors for her work. She was a Kent fellow in 1976, a National Endowment for the Arts fellow in 1981 and 1990, a Fulbright teaching fellow (France) in 1995, and a J. S. Guggenheim Memorial Foundation fellow in 2001. She has won two Pushcart Prizes, the 1990 Connecticut Arts Award, and an ACLS Contemplative Practices fellowship. *The Homeplace* was a finalist for the 1991 National Book Award and won the 1992 Annisfield-Wolf Award. *The Fields of Praise: New and Selected Poems* was a finalist for the 1997 National Book Award, the PEN Winship Award, and the Lenore

Marshall Prize. This collection won the 1998 Poets' Prize. More accolades for her writing followed in 2001 with her sixth book of poetry, *Carver: A Life in Poems*. It won the 2001 Boston Globe/Hornbook Award for Excellence in Children's Literature and the Flora Stieglitz Straus Award, was named a Newberry Honor Book and a Coretta Scott King Honor Book, and was a finalist for the 2001 National Book Award. She was also named Poet Laureate for the State of Connecticut in 2001; she will serve a five-year term.

THEMES AND CONCERNS

Marilyn Nelson employs a variety of styles and addresses a variety of subjects in her work. Each collection of her poetry has a unique theme, including relationships, society, family issues, and lighter themes in her children's collection. Her poems are somewhat autobiographical, often inspired by her own memories and experiences.

Nelson's most critically acclaimed work to date is her latest collection, *Carver: A Life in Poems*, published in 2001. This collection tells the story of George Washington Carver, a highly respected African American inventor, botanist, and scholar who is best known for his research of crops, especially peanuts. The collection consists of forty-four poems that describe Carver's life in an unusual use of poetry as biography. The book also contains photographs and prose sections that give further explanation of events in Carver's life.

Nelson's first collection, *For the Body* (1978), is mainly focused on interpersonal relationships between individuals, but also addresses group relations in family and society. While not entirely biographical, Nelson does draw inspiration from settings and events from her childhood.

Mama's Promises (1985) is a collection that deals mainly with examining the role of women in society. Her poems focus especially on women and marriage. Nelson uses spiritual and biblical allusions and themes in her other works, but these are more prevalent in this collection, as "Mama" is revealed to be God. The collection *Magnificat* (1994) also has a spiritual focus, since it describes Nelson's religious discovery and deepening faith. The poems deal with the many facets of Nelson's spirituality and the process of examining her faith. For example, the poem "Plain Songs" describes the struggle between holiness and worldliness, with the speaker finally coming to an appreciation of ordinary things.

Nelson also has a collection of poetry for children, *The Cat Walked Through the Casserole and Other Poems for Children* (1984). Written with Pamela Espeland, it is a collection of humorous poems focused primarily on family life. The title poem is about the antics of the family pets. She shifts gears back to the familiar terrain of her own life stories with the collection *The Homeplace* (1990). This volume tells the stories of her family history, such as her great-

great-grandmother's experiences as a slave in the South, and her father's service during World War II as one of the Tuskegee Airmen. The stories that serve as the inspiration for these poems were told to Nelson orally, and she retains the oral style by utilizing dialect, quotations, and first-person narration. In *The Fields of Praise: New and Selected Poems* (1997), Nelson continues to examine the themes of domestic concerns, relationships, family, motherhood, marriage, racism, and society.

Monica Rowe writes in *American Visions* that Nelson "is a powerful writer, able to evoke images of stirring and lasting impressions. Her poems know no boundaries and are as eclectic as they are universal" (p. 30). Marilyn Nelson's poetry has only just begun to receive the critical attention it deserves.

POETRY COLLECTIONS

For the Body. Baton Rouge: Louisiana University Press, 1978. (as Marilyn Nelson Waniek)

The Cat Walked Through the Casserole and Other Poems for Children. Minneapolis, MN: Carolhoda, 1984. (as Marilyn Nelson Waniek, with Pamela Espeland)

Mama's Promises. Baton Rouge: Louisiana State University Press, 1985. (as Marilyn Nelson Waniek)

The Homeplace. Baton Rouge: Louisiana State University Press, 1990. (as Marilyn Nelson Waniek)

Magnificat. Baton Rouge: Louisiana State University Press, 1994. (as Marilyn Nelson Waniek)

The Fields of Praise: New and Selected Poems. Baton Rouge: Louisiana University Press, 1997.

Carver: A Life in Poems. Asheville, NC: Front Street, 2001.

SELECTED ANTHOLOGIES AND WEB SITES WHERE POETRY APPEARS

The Atlantic Online. Poetry Pages. www.theatlantic.com/unbound/poetry.

Feinstein, Sascha, and Yusef Komunyakaa, eds. *The Jazz Poetry Anthology*. Bloomington: Indiana University Press, 1991.

Harper, Michael S., and Anthony Walton, eds. *The Vintage Book of African American Poetry*. New York: Vintage, 2000.

Marilyn Nelson Homepage. Online. www.ucc.uconn.edu/~waniek.

SELECTED ADDITIONAL WORKS

Dahlerup, Pil. *Literary Sex Roles*. Translator. Minneapolis: Minnesota Women in Higher Education, 1975.

"The Gender of Grief." *Southern Review* 29.2 (Spring 1993): 405–419.

Rasmussen, Halfdan. *Hundreds of Hens and Other Poems for Children*. Translator, with Pamela Espeland. Minneapolis, MN: Carolhoda, 1984.

SELECTED RESOURCES FOR FURTHER REFERENCE

Gardiner, Suzanne. "Bootleg, Jackleg Medicine: Curing as Only Generations Can." *Parnassus: Poetry in Review* 17.1 (1992): 65–78.

Gwynn, R. S. "Review of *The Fields of Praise: New and Selected Poems.*" *Hudson Review* 51.1 (Spring 1998): 257.

Hacker, Marilyn. "Review of *The Fields of Praise: New and Selected Poems.*" *Women's Review of Books* 33.1 (May 1998): 179.

Kitchen, Judith. "Review of *The Fields of Praise: New and Selected Poems.*" *Georgia Review* 51.4 (Winter 1997): 756.

Rowe, Monica Dyer. "Recent & Relevant Collections of Poetry." *American Visions* 13.1 (February–March 1998): 30–32.

Ullmann, L. "Solitaries and Storytellers, Magicians and Pagans: Five Poets in the World." *Kenyon Review* 13.2 (Spring 1991): 179–193.

Kyla Heflin

Duane Niatum (aka Duane McGinness, Crow's Son, Little Crow)

(1938–)

American Indian (Klallam)

BIOGRAPHY

Poet, short story writer, essayist, and editor, Duane Niatum was born in 1938 in Seattle, Washington, where he has spent most of his life. He was born Duane McGinness, but took on his great-grandfather's Indian name, Niatum. He was raised by his maternal grandfather, "Old Patsy," who called Niatum "Little Crow." During his childhood with his grandfather, he learned the ways and traditions of the Klallam, a Salishan tribe of salmon fishermen whose name means "strong people." At the age of seventeen, Niatum joined the U.S. Navy and spent two of his four years of service in Japan. He went on to receive his undergraduate degree in English from the University of Washington, under the direction of such teachers as Theodore Roethke and Elizabeth Bishop. He later received an M.A. from Johns Hopkins University in 1972, where, as a graduate student, he taught American and European literature writing seminars.

After his schooling, he served as the editor of Harper and Row's Native American Author Series, for which he is probably most well known. He also taught high school English and literature and eventually served again as an editor for the *Carriers of the Dream Wheel* anthology (1975). In addition to recognition for these editorial works, Niatum has also published volumes of his own award-winning poetry. He received the First Prize in Poetry from the Pacific Northwest Writer's Conference in 1966 and 1970 and the Governor's Award from the State of Washington in 1971. He also received the Mary K. Dearborn Literature Award from the Seattle Music and Art Foundation in 1968, as well as numerous other literary grants and awards. His book *Songs for the Harvester of Dreams* was awarded the American Book Award in 1982 by the Before Columbus Foundation.

Niatum also worked with the elderly through the Artist in the City program of the Seattle Arts Commission. Most recently he received a Ph.D. from the University of Michigan in the American Culture program, writing his dissertation on the life and art of Aleut sculptor John Hoover. He has served as a visiting instructor for many institutions, including the University of

Washington, Eastern Washington University, and the University of Michigan. He has also been a visiting instructor at the Foundation Scholaire et Culturelle Internationale Complexe de Valbonne in Valbonne, France, a teaching curriculum developer in the College of Education at the University of Washington, and an assistant librarian in libraries at the University of Washington and the New York Historical Society. He was also involved with the Poets in the Schools programs in Arizona, New Mexico, Oregon, and Washington.

In addition to publishing his own poetry volumes and editorial works, Niatum has performed at numerous poetry readings, from the Phoenix Indian High School to the International Poetry Festival to the Library of Congress. His poetry is included in over one hundred magazines and newspapers and over forty anthologies and has also been translated into over thirteen languages.

THEMES AND CONCERNS

Duane Niatum's works are concerned with Nature's importance in life and art as well as the individual's personal relationship with the elements of Nature. This central belief can be seen, for example, in Niatum's poetry collection *Ascending Red Cedar Moon* (1974); the title alludes to the fact that the cedar was the sacred tree of the Northwest Coast. He also draws heavily from personal experience in his work. For example, his first book, *After the Death of an Elder Klallam* (1970), can be seen as an elegy to his grandfather. In this work, Niatum confirms his Klallam teachings, survival strategies, and all the elements of his environment. In *Digging Out the Roots* (1977), Niatum again uses personal experiences—this time of incarcerations as a youth—to inspire his poetry. His Klallam roots, relationship with his environment, and personal experiences seem to influence most of Niatum's writings. His poetical form tends toward free verse that often models natural speech patterns. Particularly in *Drawings of the Song Animals,* "dreaming is a central theme, and Niatum juxtaposes dream-like images against natural reality" (Womack). Despite the highly personal nature of Niatum's poetry, however, it is infused with more universal themes as well, including relationships, death, and the continuity of the Indian people.

POETRY COLLECTIONS

Breathless. First produced at University of Washington, 1968. (experimental verse drama)

Ascending Red Cedar Moon. New York: Harper and Row, 1969.

After the Death of an Elder Klallam. Santa Fe, NM: Baleen, 1970.

A Cycle for the Woman in the Field. Baltimore, MD: Laughing Man Press, 1973. (chapbook)

Taos Pueblo: Poems. Greenfield Center, NY: Greenfield Review, 1973.

Digging Out the Roots. New York: Harper and Row, 1977.

Turning to the Rhythms of Her Song. City: Seattle, WA: Jawbone Press, 1977.
(chapbook)
To Bridge the Dream. Laguna, NM: A Press, 1978. (chapbook)
Pieces. New York: Strawberry Press, 1981. (chapbook)
Songs for the Harvester of Dreams. Seattle: University of Washington Press, 1981.
Raven and the Fear of Growing White. New York: Bridge Press, 1983. (chapbook)
Stories of the Moons. Marvin, SD: Blue Cloud Quarterly Press, 1987.
Drawings of the Song Animals: New and Selected Poems. Duluth, MN: Holy Cow!
Press, 1990.
Songs from the Storyteller's Stone. Self-published, 1994; reprinted 1997. (chapbook)
The Green Kite. South Seattle, WA: Wessel & Lieberman, 1995.
Learning to Live with Darkness Like the Crows. Self-published (edition of 100), 1997.
(chapbook)
Stories from the Land of Red Cedar. Self-published, 1999. (chapbook)

SELECTED ANTHOLOGIES WHERE POETRY APPEARS

The Before Columbus Foundation Poetry Anthology, 1980–1990. New York: W. W.
Norton, 1992.
Dodge, Robert K., and Joseph B. McCullough, eds. *New and Old Voices of Wah'Kon-Tah.* New York: International Publishers, 1985.
Highwater, Jamake, ed. *Words in the Blood: Contemporary Indian Writers of North
and South America.* New York: New American Library, 1984.
Hobson, Geary, ed. *The Remembered Earth: An Anthology of Contemporary Native
American Literature.* Santa Fe: University of New Mexico Press, 1981.
Kenny, Maurice, ed. *Wounds Beneath the Flesh.* Fredonia, NY: White Pine Press, 1991.
Lerner, Andrea, ed. *Dancing on the Rim of the World: An Anthology of Contempo-
rary Northwest Native American Poetry.* Tucson: University of Arizona Press,
1990.
*Returning the Gift: Poetry and Prose from the First North American Native Writers'
Festival.* Tucson: University of Arizona Press, 1994.
Smelcer, John E., and D. L. Birchfield, eds. *Durable Breath: Contemporary Native
American Poetry.* Chugiak, AK: Salmon Run Press, 1994.
Trafzer, Clifford E., ed. *Blue Dawn, Red Earth: New Native American Storytellers.*
New York: Anchor Books, 1996.
White, James L., ed. *First Skin Around Me: Contemporary American Tribal Poetry.*
City: Moorhead, MN: Territorial Press, 1976.

SELECTED FICTION, NONFICTION, AND EDITED
COLLECTIONS

Carriers of the Dream Wheel. Editor. New York: Harper & Row, 1975.
"Niatum on Niatum." *Niagara Magazine* 5 (Summer 1976): 5–6.
"My Aim as a Writer." *Greenfield Review* 11 (Winter–Spring 1984): 1–4.
"The Mistress of the House." *North Dakota Quarterly* 53 (Spring 1985): 110–118.
I Tell You Now: Autobiographical Essays by Native American Writers. Ed. Brian Swann
and Arnold Krupat. Lincoln: University of Nebraska Press, 1987.

"On Stereotypes." In *Recovering the Word: Essays on Native American Literature.* Ed. Brian Swann and Arnold Krupat. Berkeley: University of California Press, 1987, 552–562.

Harper's Anthology of Twentieth Century Native American Poetry. Editor. New York: Harper & Row, 1988.

"History Is the Palette, What Colors Inform Their Poems." *Wooster Review* 8 (Spring 1988): 115–125.

"Crow's Bun." In *Talking Leaves: Contemporary Native American Short Stories.* Ed. Craig Lesley. New York: Dell, 1991, 208–216.

"Traveling the Road That Once Was You." *North Dakota Review* 59.4 (1991): 55–60.

"The Transformational Tracks of a Marginalized Life." *Paradoxa* 6.15 (2001): 75–85.

SELECTED RESOURCES FOR FURTHER REFERENCE

Bromley, Anne. "The Reality of Dreamtime in Some Contemporary Native American Poetry." *Greenfield Review* 11 (Winter–Spring 1984): 18–28.

Bruchac, Joseph. *Survival This Way: Interviews with American Indian Poets.* Tucson: University of Arizona Press, 1987, 193–210.

Prampolini, Gaetano. "The Heart's the Actor: A Conversation with Duane Niatum." *Native American Literatures: A Forum* 4–5 (1992–1993): 81–103.

Ramsey, Jarold. "On Niatum's Songs for the Harvester of Dreams." *Studies in American Indian Literature* 6 (Fall 1982): 6–13.

———. *Reading the Fire: The Traditional Indian Literatures of America.* Seattle: University of Washington Press, 1999.

———. "Word-Magic." *Parnassus* 5 (Fall/Winter 1975): 165–175.

Smith, Eugene. "A Spinner of Dreams." *Greenfield Review* 11 (Winter–Spring 1984): 14–17.

Wiget, Andrew, ed. *Handbook of American Indian Literature.* New York: Garland Press, 1994.

Witalec, Janet, ed. *Smoke Rising: The Native North American Literary Companion.* Detroit, MI: Visible Ink Press, 1995.

Womack, Craig. "Book Reviews." *American Indian Quarterly* 17.1 (Winter 1993): 102–111.

Heather Draper

Naomi Shihab Nye

(1952–)

Palestinian American

BIOGRAPHY

Naomi Shihab Nye was born in St. Louis, Missouri, on March 12, 1952, the daughter of a Palestinian father and an American mother. Nye began writing poetry as soon as she learned how to write, finding a comfort in the manipulation of words and the tranquility of the process. Her childhood poetry at first focused on her Germanic heritage, and she had her first poem published at the age of seven. At the age of fourteen, Nye's family moved to Jerusalem, where she attended a year of high school and met her Palestinian grandmother, putting Nye in touch with her second heritage, a connection that would deeply influence her writing.

Nye's family then moved to San Antonio, Texas, where as a teenager she was published in children's and teen magazines such as *Seventeen*. She received her B.A. from Trinity University in San Antonio, Texas, in 1974, and while a student there her works began to appear in various literary journals. Nye's book publications followed, although she has never worked with an agent, instead using her own resources and drive to get her works to publishers. She has worked as a freelance writer, editor, speaker, and educator. Like most writers, Nye has always been a reader, and she names William Stafford as her favorite poet.

Nye is the author of ten collections of poems, including *Red Suitcase* (1994), *Come with Me: Poems for a Journey* (2000), and *19 Varieties of Gazelle: Poems of the Middle East* (2002). She has received awards from the Texas Institute of Letters and the International Poetry Forum, and her work has been rewarded with a Guggenheim fellowship, two Jane Addams Children's Books Awards, the Lavan Award from the Academy of American Poets, and the Carity Randall Prize. Other awards include four Pushcart Prizes, the Patterson Poetry Prize, and many notable book and best book citations from the American Library Association. She has been featured on two PBS documentaries, *The Language of Life* with Bill Moyers and *The United States of Poetry*, and has twice traveled to the Middle East and Asia for the U.S. Information Agency, promoting international goodwill through the arts.

Nye's poems and short stories have appeared in various journals and reviews throughout North America, Europe, and the Middle and Far East. Besides her collections of poetry, Nye has also written children's books, made music and poetry recordings, translated poetry, and served as editor on several anthologies of children's poetry, including *This Same Sky: A Collection of Poems from Around the World* (1992), which contains translations of over one hundred poets from sixty-eight different countries. She has also written a book of essays titled *Never in a Hurry*. In 1997, Nye published her first young adult novel, the multiple award-winning *Habibi,* which is a semiautobiographical account of Nye's experiences as an Arab American teenager living in Jerusalem during the 1970s.

She still resides in San Antonio, where she lives with her husband and son. Most recently she has contributed to an anthology titled *911: The Book of Help,* which is a collection of stories and poems by children's writers that was inspired by the events of September 11, 2001.

THEMES AND CONCERNS

Nye's multiethnic heritage and the places she has lived play a central role in her writing. The distinctiveness of her various homes, such as St. Louis, Jerusalem, and San Antonio, leads to a varied body of work, as her writing attempts to reconcile her diverse worlds and experiences. In addition to her many homes, Nye is a traveler, adding more experiences for source material. In addition to her own heritage, Nye draws on the voices of the Mexican Americans who live near her home in San Antonio, as well as the perspectives of Arab Americans like herself and the ideas and practices of the different local subcultures of America.

Nye credits teaching as part of her creative process. Although she sees teaching and writing as separate processes, she also believes that they are reciprocal. Helping students with their writing is a delight for Nye, and it also feeds her own creativity. While Nye seeks to broaden the minds of her students, showing them that the world of the written world is populated by more than just American writers, she has also attempted to broaden the range of traditional poetry anthologies. In fact, her first anthology, *This Same Sky,* came about after teachers told her that they wanted more international poetry for their students but were without access to such material.

Nye has gained a reputation for poetry that shows ordinary events, people, and objects from a new perspective. She says, "For me the primary source of poetry has always been local life, random characters met on the streets, our own ancestry sifting down to us through small essential daily tasks" (*Contemporary Authors*). In the book *Seeing the Blue Between,* which is an inspirational work for young writers, Nye shows how she embraces the process of revising the written word, commenting, "Now I see revision as a beautiful word of hope." This is evidenced in her poem "How do I know when a poem is finished?" (Janeczko, p. 172).

Nye has pursued a variety of themes throughout her writing career. In her first collection of poetry, *Different Ways to Pray* (1980), she explores the shared experiences and differences between cultures, a predominant theme in her body of work. Nye's poetry flows from everyday scenes, while celebrating the similarities between us all, as well as our diversity, a timely concern that seeks to bridge the divide between Nye's two disparate heritages. The collection *Yellow Glove,* published in 1986, reflects a new, more mature perspective that was influenced by the continuing unrest in the Middle East and Nye's confrontation with the tragedy and sorrow found there.

Nye's writing has never been more timely than in the post–September 11, 2001, world. She has contributed to the anthology *911: The Book of Help* and released a collection of her own Middle Eastern poems, *19 Varieties of Gazelle.* The latter opens with a poem about a young man released from prison on the day of the September 11 attacks and is followed by Nye's reflections on that fateful day. The subsequent poems in the collection detail her Palestinian heritage in its similarities and differences, beauties and turmoils. Nye's work continues to demonstrate themes of peace, cultural understanding, and acceptance of one other's diversity.

POETRY COLLECTIONS

Different Ways to Pray. Portland, OR: Breitenbush, 1980.
Hugging the Jukebox. New York: Dutton, 1982.
Yellow Glove. Portland, OR: Breitenbush Books, 1986.
Invisible. Denton, TX: Trilobite Press, 1987.
Mint. Brockport, NY: State Street Press Chapbooks, 1991.
Red Suitcase. Brockport, NY: Boa Editions, 1994.
Words Under the Words. Portland, OR: Eighth Mountain Press, 1995.
Fuel. Rochester, NY: Boa Editions, 1998.
Come with Me: Poems for a Journey. New York: Greenwillow Books, 2000.
19 Varieties of Gazelle: Poems of the Middle East. New York: Greenwillow Books, 2002.

SELECTED ANTHOLOGIES AND WEB SITES WHERE POETRY APPEARS

The Atlantic Online. www.theatlantic.com.
Cart, Michael, Marianne Carus, and Marc Aronson, eds. *911: The Book of Help.* Chicago, IL: Cricket Books, 2002.
Gwynn, R. S., ed. *American Poets Since World War II.* Detroit, MI: Gale, 1992.
Janeczko, Paul B. *Seeing the Blue Between: Advice and Inspiration for Young Poets.* Cambridge, MA: Candlewick, 2002.
Sale, Richard B., ed. *Texas Poets in Concert: A Quartet.* Denton: University of North Texas Press, 1990.
Sewell, Marilyn, ed. *Claiming the Spirit Within: A Sourcebook of Women's Poetry.* Boston, MA: Beacon Press, 2001.
Shelton, Pamela L., ed. *Contemporary Women Poets.* Detroit, MI: St. James Press, 1998.

SELECTED FICTION, NONFICTION, CHILDREN'S FICTION, AND EDITED COLLECTIONS

This Same Sky: A Collection of Poems from Around the World. Editor. New York: Four Winds Press, 1992.
Sitta's Secrets. New York: Four Winds Press, 1994.
Benito's Dream Bottle. New York: Simon & Schuster, 1995.
That Tree Is Older Than You Are: Poems and Stories form Mexico. Editor. New York: Simon & Schuster, 1995.
I Feel a Little Jumpy Around You: A Book of Her and His Poems Collected in Pairs. Editor, with Paul Janeczko. New York: Simon & Schuster, 1996.
Never in a Hurry: Essays on People and Places. Columbia: University of South Carolina Press, 1996.
Habibi. New York: Simon & Schuster, 1997.
Lullaby Raft. New York: Simon & Schuster, 1997.
The Space Between Our Footsteps: Poems and Paintings from the Middle East. New York: Simon & Schuster, 1998.
What Have You Lost? New York: Greenwillow Books, 1999.
Salting the Ocean: 100 Poems by Young Poets. Editor. New York: Greenwillow Books, 2000.
Mint Snowball. Tallahassee, FL: Anhinga Press, 2001.
The Flag of Childhood: Poems from the Middle East. Editor. New York: Aladdin, 2002.

SELECTED RESOURCES FOR FURTHER REFERENCE

Barenblat, Rachel. "Interview with Naomi Shihab Nye." *Pif Magazine,* 2000. Online. www.pifmagaxine.com.
Contemporary Authors. 2002. Online. www.galegroup.com.
Contemporary Women Poets. Detroit: St. James Press, 1997.
"Naomi Shihab Nye: In Her Own Words." Online. www.harperchildrens.com.
West, Phil. "Many Voices." *Austin Chronicle*. Online. www.auschron.com/issues/vol15/issue50.

Joel Werley

Simon J. Ortiz

(1941–)

*American Indian, Acoma Pueblo
(Aaquumeh hano)*

Photo © David Burckhalter.

BIOGRAPHY

Poet, short-story writer, essayist, and children's author, Simon Ortiz was born on May 27, 1941, in Albuquerque, New Mexico. One of eight children, he was raised in the Acoma Indian Pueblo of McCarty's, called Deetiziyamah in the Acoma language. In his early childhood, Simon Ortiz spoke only the Acoma language, which is often present in his poetry. His father, Joseph, was a railroad worker and was often away from home for long periods of time. Simon Ortiz recounts that both his parents were good storytellers and singers; both of these qualities have had their effects on him. He often says that his first writings were songs, and his simple and direct poetic style is similar to storytelling. In fact, Ortiz claims to view himself more as a storyteller than a poet; his poetry is narrative in style, because he feels each work *must* tell a story.

Ortiz received his elementary education in Indian schools and published his first poem—for his mother, Mamie—in the school newspaper while he was in the fifth grade. In the 1950s it was traditional for Indian children to be sent away to boarding schools, so for grades seven through twelve Ortiz lived at St. Catherine's School, an American Indian boarding school in Albuquerque. In 1962, at the age of twenty-one, Simon Ortiz committed himself to becoming a writer. He attended Fort Lewis College for two years, but left to serve in the U.S. Army from 1963 to 1966. He returned to his studies first at the University of New Mexico (1966–1968) and then at the prestigious Writers' Workshop at the University of Iowa, where he earned an M.F.A. in 1969.

Simon Ortiz taught at San Diego State University and the Institute of the American Indian Arts in 1974, at Navajo Community College from 1975 to 1977, and at the College of Marin from 1976 to 1979. In 1979 he joined the faculty of the University of New Mexico; in May 2002 that institution awarded Ortiz an honorary Doctor of Letters. Currently, Simon Ortiz is a professor at the University of Toronto. He also remains politically active, and lectures extensively.

Ortiz has been married four times, but all of the marriages have ended in divorce. He has a son and two daughters and often dedicates his poetry to his children.

THEMES AND CONCERNS

Through his poetry, Ortiz strives to preserve and continue American Indian traditions and culture, confident that they will survive due to the efforts of those who, like himself, will continue to document and celebrate their culture. For example, in the poem "A Story of How a Wall Stands" (*A Good Journey*), Ortiz tells the story of his father taking him to repair the wall of their 400-year-old church in Acoma. His father uses the situation to remind his son to look deep inside for the true nature of things, just as the wall still stands only because the inner structure is strong enough to support the outer layer. He turns a simple day's work into an elegant story of community history on the outside and cultural tradition passing from a father to a son on the inside.

Another theme in Ortiz's work is the effect of cross-cultural encounters. He frequently addresses how Western and Native cultures share a cruel past and still often have opposing views over philosophical and environmental issues. He also questions whether true progress is being made as he observes political and social ills such as alcoholism and what he calls society's "war on animals." However, Ortiz may be best known for writing about the land and a sense of place, which he ties together with a sense of what it means to be a Native American. When Ortiz started to write in the 1960s, he strove to impress upon his readers that the stereotypes of the American Indian in feathers and animal hides was not the true experience of the Native American today. Another concern often expressed is that Western civilization must recognize that survival depends on humankind's respect for the earth and environment; he urges his readers to an awareness of the drastic and wasteful impact that the Western desire to subdue and exploit the earth has had on the planet. However, his sense of urgency is often tempered by an underlying and subtle confidence that change will come soon and that the general culture will move in a positive earth-sustaining direction.

Simon Ortiz has published five major works: *Going for the Rain, A Good Journey, Fight Back, From Sand Creek,* and *After and Before the Lightning. Going for the Rain,* published in 1976, is divided into four sections that center on his own experiences: "The Preparation," "Leaving," "Returning," and "The Rain Falls." Together, these sections give us a picture of what it is like for a Native American to be raised in his own traditions, to go out to the larger American culture, and return to his Place, where he feels roots and knows he belongs. Ortiz writes about Indian life and everyday rituals. He writes about belonging to the land and how this certain place where he was born give him a sense of security and a feeling that this is where he was destined to be. His narrative style comes alive in poems that feature Coyote, a trickster and transformer whom Ortiz uses as both narrator and subject.

A Good Journey (1977) is the journey of the generations through life, from grandparents to parents to children, while *Fight Back* (1980) was published to commemorate the 300th anniversary of the 1680 Pueblo Revolt against the Spanish colonialists. Ortiz compares the revolt to the exploitative treatment of Native Americans by the U.S. government where large uranium deposits are on Indian land. Ortiz himself worked for a very short time for a uranium mining company before continuing with his college education. With his poetry he hopes to inspire fellow American Indians to demand respect and claim what is rightfully theirs.

In 1974 and 1975, Simon Ortiz spent time at the Veterans Administration Hospital in Colorado; *From the Sand Creek* is the result of that experience. Published in 1981, shortly after the Vietnam War ended, this book contains forty-five poems, each with a short explanation on the opposite page. Of all his books, this contains poetry that is bleak, despairing, and profoundly sad. Fort Lyons Colorado Veterans Hospital coincidentally is built on the site where, in the winter of 1864, U.S. troops massacred one-fifth of the Cheyenne and Arapaho tribes after promising them peace and safety. Simon Ortiz parallels the same sadness and hopelessness between the sick veterans he sees in the hospital and the Native Americans who were in the same place 110 years before. In 1982 this collection won the prestigious Pushcart Prize for Poetry Published by a Small Press.

In *After and Before the Lightning,* Simon Ortiz recounts in poetry another of his life experiences, this time as an assistant professor at Sinte Gleska College on the Lakota Sioux Reservation in South Dakota. This collection is a journal in poetic form that starts in autumn 1985 and ends on the first day of spring in 1986. It chronicles the stark reality of the hard winters in South Dakota and its effect on the people there. The poet writes not only of his physical place, but of humankind's place in the universe and how quickly life can be taken away. Today, Simon Ortiz continues to be an important voice in American Indian poetry and a major influence on younger poets.

POETRY COLLECTIONS

Going for the Rain. New York: Harper & Row, 1976.
A Good Journey. Berkeley, CA: Turtle Island, 1977.
Fight Back: For the Sake of the People, for the Sake of the Land. Albuquerque: Institute for Native American Development, University of New Mexico, 1980.
From the Sand Creek: Rising in This Heart Which Is Our America. New York: Thunder's Mouth Press, 1981.

A Poem Is a Journey. Bourbonnas, IL: Patricia Lieb and Carol Schott, 1981. (chapbook)

Woven Stone: A 3-in-1 Volume of Poetry and Prose. Tucson: University of Arizona Press, 1991.

After and Before the Lightning. Tucson: University of Arizona Press, 1994.

SELECTED ANTHOLOGIES AND WEB SITES WHERE POETRY APPEARS

Bruchac, Joseph. *Songs from This Earth on Turtle's Back.* Greenfield Center, NY: Greenfield Review Press, 1983.

Counterbalance Poetry. Online. www.counterbalancepoetry.org.

Harris, Marie, and Kathleen Aguero, eds. *An Ear to the Ground: An Anthology of Contemporary American Poetry.* Athens: University of Georgia Press, 1989.

Hobson, Geary, ed. *The Remembered Earth: An Anthology of Contemporary Native American Literature.* Albuquerque: University of New Mexico Press, 1981.

Niatum, Duane, ed. *Carriers of the Dream Wheel: Contemporary Native American Poetry.* New York: Harper & Row, 1975.

———. *Harper's Anthology of 20th Century Native American Poetry.* San Francisco, CA: Harper & Row, 1987.

SELECTED ADDITIONAL WORKS

Song, Poetry, and Language: Expression and Perception. Tsaile, AZ: Navajo Community College Press, 1977.

Howbah Indians Stories. Tucson, AZ: Blue Moon Press, 1978.

Fightin': New and Collected Stories. New York: Thunder's Mouth Press, 1983.

Speaking for the Generations: Native Writers on Writing. Editor. Tucson: University of Arizona Press, 1998.

SELECTED RESOURCES FOR FURTHER REFERENCE

Bruchac, Joseph, ed. *Survival this Way: Interviews with American Indian Poets.* Tucson: University of Arizona Press, 1987, 211–229.

Gould, Janice, and Dean Rader. *Speak to Me in Words.* Tucson: University of Arizona Press, 2001.

Jaffee, Harold. "Speaking Memory." *The Nation,* April 3, 1982, pp. 406–408.

Lincoln, Kenneth. *Native American Renaissance.* Los Angeles: University of California Press, 1983, 183–221.

Swann, Brian, and Arnold Krupat. *I Tell You Now: Autobiographical Essays by Native American Writers.* Lincoln: University of Nebraska Press, 1987.

Wiget, Andrew. *Simon Ortiz.* Boise, ID: Boise State University, 1986.

———, ed. *Dictionary of Native American Literature.* New York: Garland, 1994.

Sue Czerny

Linda Pastan

(1932–)

Jewish American

BIOGRAPHY

Born Linda Olenik in New York City in 1932, Linda Pastan is a Jewish, urban, feminist poet. She describes herself as a lonely child who struggled to fit in: "By the time I was five or six, I had a series of facial tics so virulent that I still can't do the mouth exercises my dentist recommends for fear I won't be able to stop doing them" ("Yesterday's Noise," p. 15).

Pastan received a B.A. from Radcliffe College in 1954, an M.L.S. from Simmons College in 1955, and an M.A. in 1957 from Brandeis University. It wasn't until 1971, however, at the age of thirty-nine, that she first published her poetry. Her early themes include domestic matters and family relationships, and while she continues to write about these subjects, she has turned an eye toward the many concerns that contemporary women face, as well as issues of mortality.

Pastan served on the staff of the Bread Loaf Writers' Conference for twenty years and has received many awards. In 1954, for example, she won first place in the *Mademoiselle* poetry contest. (Sylvia Plath placed second.) Her other awards include a Pushcart Prize, a Dylan Thomas Award (1958), the Di Castagnola Award (1978), and the Maurice English Award (1986). She has also received fellowships from the National Endowment for the Arts (1972) and the Maryland Arts Council (1978). Two collections of poetry, *PM/AM* (1982) and *Carnival Evening: New and Selected Poems, 1968–1998* (1998), were finalists for the National Book Award. She also served as Poet Laureate of Maryland from 1991 to 1995. Linda Pastan is married to Ira Pastan and currently lives in Potomac, Maryland.

THEMES AND CONCERNS

Aspects of domestic life pervade nearly all of Linda Pastan's poems. Loaves of warm bread, bottles of cold milk, and eight-year-old daughters riding bicycles help bring the reader into the poems by stimulating all five of the reader's senses. Pastan possesses the unique ability to locate broad concepts in well-crafted still-life scenes. Life's rhythms and responsibilities are reflected in these images of domesticity: a heap of laundry, a stack of dirty dishes, a sagging mattress. Liz Rosenberg comments that "Pastan understands understatement, juxtaposition, and contraction. Her poems can come like gasps, or move beautifully among open spaces" (p. F1).

The relationship between lovers is another subject related to domestic life that Pastan explores. For instance, in "Wildflowers," a poem that beautifully captures Pastan's wit, the speaker cleverly compares her partner/husband to the dandelions that invade her lawn; both the partner and the weeds are unruly, and both have been picked for precisely that reason. Intimacy is never a constant for Pastan, whose lovers alternately come together and separate both emotionally and physically. Life and its relationships are cyclic, and Pastan incorporates this concept movingly in her works.

To fully understand Pastan's belief in the cyclic nature of relationships and existence, one would have to turn to the collection of poems that compose *The Five Stages of Grief*. These poems are organized in five sections that correspond to the theoretical stages of grief: denial, anger, bargaining, depression, and acceptance. They unmistakably, as one would expect, take up the question of aging and mortality. Yet these are not the only Pastan poems to do so. "Grief" is about a friend's dying son, while "Death's Blue-Eyed Girl" (both in *Aspects of Eve*) describes Death as a magician who made "Elaine" suddenly disappear, and each beautifully presents Pastan's skill at personification.

One of Pastan's more moving poems is "Funerary Tower" (*The Five Stages of Grief*), wherein the speaker remembers a visit to her father's grave. The speaker's restrained emotion moves quickly past the sentimentalism of remembering her lost parent and focuses instead on observing her mother, who is busy tending to the landscape of the gravesite. The impatient speaker turns her attention to hurrying her mother home, causing the reader to grow unsettled by the speaker's focus on her mother's behavior rather than addressing her own emotional reaction to her father's absence.

Closely related to Pastan's treatment of domesticity and mortality is her focus on nature. Poems like "A Symposium: Apples," "Eclipse," and "Hurricane Watch" explore the speaker's relationship to elements of nature, frequently personifying them. Pastan also has written several poems about the act of writing. "Voices" presents the speaker-poet who, in contemplating the task of writing, runs through a stop sign and gets pulled over by a police officer. "Soundings" expresses the speaker's contentious relationship with the books that line her rooms as she imagines them taking her life and threatening to drown her in a sea of language. Never far from political issues either, Pastan has also written several poems about the plight of Jews in contemporary society. In these ("On Watching the Israeli War on TV" is one good example), the speaker identifies with the Israelis, despite the geographical distance between them.

POETRY COLLECTIONS

A Perfect Circle of Sun. Chicago, IL: Swallow Press, 1971.
Aspects of Eve: Poems. New York: Liveright, 1975.
On the Way to the Zoo: Poems. Washington, DC: Dryad Press, 1975.
The Five Stages of Grief: Poems. New York: Norton, 1978.
Selected Poems of Linda Pastan. London: J. Murray, 1979.
Even as We Sleep. Athens, OH: Croissant, 1980.
Setting the Table: Poems. Washington, DC: Dryad Press, 1980.
Waiting for My Life: Poems. New York: Norton, 1981.
PM/AM: New and Selected Poems. New York: Norton, 1982.
A Fraction of Darkness: Poems. New York: Norton, 1985.
The Imperfect Paradise: Poems. New York: Norton, 1988.
Heroes in Disguise: Poems. New York: Norton, 1991.
An Early Afterlife: Poems. New York: Norton, 1995.
Carnival Evening: New and Selected Poems, 1968–1998. New York: Norton, 1998.
The Last Uncle. New York: Norton, 2002.

SELECTED ANTHOLOGIES AND WEB SITES WHERE POETRY APPEARS

The Cortland Review, no. 7. Online. www.courtlandreview.com.
Howe, Florence, ed. *No More Masks: An Anthology of Twentieth-Century American Women Poets.* New York: HarperCollins, 1993.
Knudson, R. R., and May Swenson, eds. *American Sports Poems.* New York: Orchard Books, 1988.
Lifshin, Lyn, ed. *Tangled Vines: A Collection of Mother and Daughter Poems.* San Diego, CA: Harcourt Brace, 1992.
Linda Pastan. Online. www.alittlepoetry.com/pastan.html.
Norton Poets Online. www.nortonpoets.com.

SELECTED ADDITIONAL WORK

"Yesterday's Noise: The Poetry of Childhood Memory." *Writer* 105.10 (1992): 15–18.

SELECTED RESOURCES FOR FURTHER REFERENCE

Chadwyck-Healey Inc. "Biography: Linda Pastan." 1999. Online. www.dlxs.org/products.
Chappell, Fred. "Brief Cases: Naked Enterprises." *Southern Review* 28.1 (1992): 174–183.
Rosenberg, Liz. "A Poet of Wholeness." *Boston Globe,* August 30, 1998, p. F1.

Amy C. O'Brien

Photo by Ira Wood, © Leapfrog Press.

Marge Piercy
(1936–)
Jewish American

BIOGRAPHY

Novelist, poet, essayist, and reviewer Marge Piercy was born and grew up in Detroit, Michigan. She was raised Jewish by her mother and maternal grandmother, the Lithuanian daughter of a rabbi to whom Piercy was extremely close. Her father, a Welsh immigrant and nonpracticing Presbyterian, had much less of an influence on her life. Piercy credits her mother, who was a voracious reader and compelling storyteller, with inspiring her to be a poet, although Piercy left home at the age of seventeen because she and her mother constantly fought. The two women did not become close until late in her mother's life.

While in grade school, Piercy contracted German measles and then rheumatic fever and nearly died. Weak and confined to bed, she found comfort in reading. In *Early Grrrl* (1999), Piercy explains that she began writing poetry at fifteen, after her family moved to a larger house where she had a room of her own in which she could write and enjoy privacy.

Piercy excelled in the public schools she attended in Detroit and earned a full scholarship to the University of Michigan, where she received a B.A. in 1957. In 1958 she earned an M.A. from Northwestern University, which she attended on a fellowship. Although Piercy struggled in college with the expectations of women's roles both in the academy and in society, she excelled academically, earning several awards for her fiction and poetry.

Actively involved in the Civil Rights Movement, Piercy demonstrated against the war in Vietnam, helped found the NACLA (North American Congress on Latin America), was an active participant in SDS (Students for a Democratic Society), and started an MDS (Movement for a Democratic Society) chapter in Brooklyn. Acutely aware of women's rights, Piercy noticed discrepancies in the treatment of women within the SDS and eventually left the organization to work on the women's liberation movement.

Piercy began teaching at Indiana University in 1960 but left two years later to pursue a career as a full-time professional writer. She has made her living as a writer ever since. She has led writing workshops, given readings, and lectured at more than 350 institutions around the world and has served as writer-in-residence at several, including the University of Kansas (1971), Holy Cross University (1976), and the University of Cincinnati (1986). The Writers' Conference in Rochester and the Aspen Writers' Conference are among the professional organizations that have benefited from the poetry workshops she has led.

Piercy has received numerous awards, including the Arthur C. Clarke Award for Best Science Fiction Novel published in the United Kingdom, the Patterson Poetry Prize for Best Book of the Year, the May Sarton Award of the New England Poetry Club, and the Sheaffer-PEN/New England Award for Literary Excellence. She has been honored by the National Endowment for the Arts and earned membership to Phi Kappa Phi and Phi Beta Kappa.

Piercy has served as a consultant to numerous organizations, including the New York State Council on the Arts, the Massachusetts Council on the Arts and Humanities, the Massachusetts Cultural Council, the Coordinating Council of Literary Magazines, and the American Poetry Center. She was poetry editor of *Tikkun* and currently edits *Lilith*. Her work has been anthologized in over 200 collections and translated into sixteen languages. She married her third husband, publisher Ira Wood, in 1982. Together they have authored a play, *The Last White Class*, and a novel titled *Storm Tide*. The couple lives in Cape Cod, Massachusetts.

THEMES AND CONCERNS

Piercy's poetry is both pointed and powerful and frequently draws a connection between the individual—specifically the speaker—and nature. This thematic emphasis evolved shortly after Piercy and her second husband moved from Detroit to Cape Cod in the 1960s. This move was occasioned by Piercy's chronic bronchitis and subsequent need to leave the city for cleaner air. The collection *Twelve-Spoked Wheel Flashing* (1978) beautifully links the speaker to nature, using the twelve-spoked wheel as a metaphor for the twelve months of the year. The collection's eponymous first poem depicts the speaker tumbling head over heels through the months of the year as if she were tied to the twelve-spoked wheel.

This collection and others focus heavily on the winter months, which bring cold, snow, and long nights marked by loneliness, desolation, and hopelessness. Nature's forces bring nor'easters and drought, and these conditions, coupled with the cold gray of Greater Grand Rapids and Lake Michigan, serve as poignant metaphors against which Piercy juxtaposes portraits of the warmth and security of home and the comfort of the lovers' intimate relationship. As the winter wears on, the poet longs for the sun and warmth that the spring and summer months will bring.

Other themes that pervade Piercy's poetry include war, writing, and gardening. For example, in "The New Novel," the text of her latest creation is personified as it pushes forth from her; the theme of gardening emerges in "The first salad of March" and "The love of lettuce," both of which celebrate nature's abundance and a plentiful summer harvest. The notion of gender inequality also creeps steadily into Piercy's poetry. In "The meaningful exchange," she describes the differences between men and women in terms of their perceptions and communication, and both "Women of letters" and "For shelter and beyond" call for a coming together of women everywhere for validation, community, friendship, and companionship. "For shelter and beyond" catalogues the many ways women may be battered—by rape, poverty, divorce, and medical practices surrounding childbirth—before it speaks to a need for sisterhood.

In her novels, Piercy also addresses political and gender issues. *Vida* centers on the decline of the antiwar movement, and *Three Women* is about a grandmother, mother, and daughter who live together. Her science fiction novels include *Dance the Eagle to Sleep,* which sheds light on the problem of gender inequality and the social problems that cause oppression, *Woman on the Edge of Time,* and *He, She, and It.* Piercy remains committed to issues of gender equality, not only in her fiction and poetry but also in her political activism.

POETRY COLLECTIONS

Breaking Camp. Middletown, CT: Wesleyan University Press, 1968.
Hard Loving. Middletown, CT: Wesleyan University Press, 1969.
4-Telling. Trumansburg, NY: TI Crossing Press, 1971.
To Be of Use. New York: Doubleday, 1973.
Living in the Open. New York: Knopf, 1976.
Twelve-Spoked Wheel Flashing Poems. New York: Random House, 1978.
The Moon Is Always Female. New York: Knopf, 1980.
Circles on the Water: Selected Poems of Marge Piercy. New York: Knopf, 1982.
Stone, Paper, Knife. New York: Knopf, 1983.
My Mother's Body. New York: Knopf, 1985.
Available Light. New York: Knopf, 1988.
Mars and Her Children. New York: Knopf, 1992.
The Eight Chambers of the Heart. London: Penguin, 1995.
What Are Big Girls Made Of? New York: Knopf, 1997.
Written in Bone: The Early Poems of Marge Piercy. Nottingham, UK: Five Leaves, 1998.
The Art of Blessing the Day: Poems with a Jewish Theme. New York: Knopf, 1999.
Early Grrrl. Wellfleet, MA: Leapfrog Press, 1999.

SELECTED ANTHOLOGIES WHERE POETRY APPEARS

Gillan, Maria M., and Jennifer Gillan, eds. *Unsettling America: An Anthology of Contemporary Multicultural Poetry.* New York: Penguin, 1994.

Lifshin, Lyn, ed. *Tangled Vines: A Collection of Mother and Daughter Poems*. San Diego, CA: Harcourt Brace, 1992.

Morgan, Robin, ed. *Sisterhood Is Powerful: An Anthology of Writings from the Women's Liberation Movement*. New York: Random House, 1970.

Shields, Mike, ed. *Century: 100 Major Modern Poets*. Wirral, UK: Orbis International Literary Journal, 1996.

SELECTED ADDITIONAL WORKS

Going Down Fast. New York: Trident, 1969.

Dance the Eagle to Sleep. Garden City, NY: Doubleday, 1970.

Small Changes. New York: Doubleday, 1973.

The High Cost of Living. New York: Harper and Row, 1978; Fawcett, 1980.

The Last White Class. With Ira Wood. Trumansburg, NY: Crossing Press, 1979.

Vida. New York: Summit, 1980; Fawcett, 1981.

Parti-Colored Blocks for a Quilt. Ann Arbor: University of Michigan Press, 1982.

Fly Away Home. New York: Summit, 1984; Fawcett/Ballantine, 1985.

Early Ripening: American Women's Poetry Now. Editor. New York: Pandora, 1987.

Gone to Soldiers. New York: Summit, 1987; Fawcett/Ballantine, 1988.

Summer People. New York: Summit, 1989, Fawcett/Ballantine, 1990.

The Earth Shines Secretly: A Book of Days. Cambridge, MA: Zoland Books, 1990.

He, She, and It. New York: Knopf, 1991; Fawcett/Ballantine, 1993.

The Longings of Women. New York: Fawcett, 1994.

Storm Tide. With Ira Wood. New York: Fawcett/Ballantine, 1998.

Three Women. New York: William Morrow, 1999.

SELECTED RESOURCES FOR FURTHER REFERENCE

Altman, Meryl. "Lives on the Line." *Women's Review of Books* 19.7 (2002): 6–7.

Decter, Ann. "The Craft of Writing." *Herizons* 14.3 (2001): 40–41.

Doherty, Patricia. *Marge Piercy: An Annotated Bibliography*. Westport, CT: Greenwood Press, 1997.

Farr, Marie T. "Revisiting a Classic Feminist Technotopia." *WE International* 42–43 (1998): 16–17.

Marge Piercy Homepage. Online. www.archer-books.com/piercy.

Neverow, Vara. "The Repair of the World: The Novels of Marge Piercy." *Utopian Studies* 8.1 (1997): 227–230.

Rodden, John. "A Harsh Day's Light: An Interview with Marge Piercy." *Kenyon Review* 20.2 (1998): 132–143.

Rodríguez, Johnette. "Fighting Words: Marge Piercy's Powerful Poetry and Prose." *Providence Phoenix*, September 27, 2002.

Shands, Kerstin W. *The Repair of the World: The Novels of Marge Piercy*. Westport, CT: Greenwood Press, 1994.

Amy C. O'Brien

Photo courtesy of Gabrielle Motta-Passajou.

Leroy V. Quintana

(1944–)

Chicano/Mexican American

BIOGRAPHY

Born June 10, 1944, in Albuquerque, Leroy Quintana spent his formative years with his grandparents in Raton, New Mexico, although he moved back and forth between them and his parents throughout his childhood. Quintana is known as *"hijo del pueblo,"* which is also the title of his first published book of poetry, because this native son's writing is so distinctly New Mexican, marked by stories about the close-knit community of Mexican Americans and the dazzling landscape. James White has said that "Quintana writes simply of growing up around the silent and powerful people of the Southwest . . . of the little Spanish-American towns, the people, their struggles, and the larger energy of that great foreign landscape here in America" (pp. 31–32). Quintana credits his grandparents' storytelling as a major influence in his writing. Like other important Chicano writers from New Mexico, his work has been described as "deeply rooted in the oral tradition of New Mexico and inspired by a sense of place" (Marquez, p. 7).

Quintana attended parochial schools and graduated from Albuquerque High School, the city's oldest and most racially mixed school. He then began his collegiate studies at the University of New Mexico, where he majored in anthropology. However, in 1967 he began a two-year stint with the 101st Airborne Division of the U.S. Army and with Long Range Reconaissance Patrol (LRRPs), serving in the Vietnam War. This experience became the focus of his "angry" poems and served as the foundation of his book *Interrogations* (1990). In 1971, Quintana returned to school and earned a B.A. in English. During Quintana's return to the University of New Mexico, he began writing poetry and served as editor for the school's literary journal. For a short period after graduation, Quintana worked as an alcoholism counselor before returning to school, another experience that made its way into his writing. In 1974, Quintana received his M.A. in English from New Mexico State

University. Upon graduation he began teaching at the university and in 1976 published his first collection of poetry, *Hijo del Pueblo*.

Quintana's success and achievement have brought him great honors. In 1981, Quintana received both the important American Book Award and the Southwest Book Award for *Sangre*. He was also named the first winner of the Premio Tomás Rivera, a prize cosponsored by *World Literature Today* and the University of Oklahoma Press and offered biennially for a book that contributes substantially to the understanding of Chicano/Chicana culture. He has often been called his generation's foremost spokesman on Chicano/Chicana literature, culture, and education. Quintana went on to publish *The History of Home* (1993), for which he won another American Book Award, *My Hair Turning Gray Among Strangers* (1996), and *The Great Whirl of Exile* (1999). He lives and works in California, where he teaches English at San Diego Mesa College.

THEMES AND CONCERNS

Quintana's works are marked by traditional Mexican folklore, storytelling devices, and modern methods of composition. Throughout his works, the themes of self-discovery, war, and the impact of modern society upon Chicano culture are prevalent. His poems use direct and often unadorned language to relay snapshots of life. In *The History of Home,* for example, many of the poems' titles are names of characters, Mitch, Stevie, Freida, Evelyn, Manuel, Mrs. Walsh, who let the school-age Quintana talk with his friend Richard in study hall, and Georgy, who was so thin that you would have to say "*flaco*" at least twice to describe him. The poems in this volume provide images and stories to attach to the people he introduces us to, including himself. In "Imagining Myself," he speaks of the ironic humiliation he felt when his mother purchased him a brand new bicycle when all he wanted was an old one like the ones his friends' fathers got at the police auction.

Quintana occasionally uses a Spanish word in a poem but rarely translates it; in "Las Piojocitas," for example, he describes the Sánchez sisters as being full of *piojos* and goes on to list their other offenses: they smoked, drank, knew a lot of men, and wore tight skirts, bright sweaters, junk jewelry, and ruby red lipstick. The non-Spanish speaker cannot exactly guess what the word *piojos* might mean except that it must be unsavory, and indeed it is, for it means "lice." The reader who knows the word may commence to scratching at the sight of it, and so Quintana makes the most of his small use of this potent word. In *My Hair Turning Gray Among Strangers,* he includes a poem titled "Soyla," which is not a Spanish word or name. However, Quintana quickly draws a portrait of why it should be a formal name for the character of Sofía, who complains that she is (*soy la*), the one who does all of the chores, and more.

Quintana often plays with his words and, as Jerry Bradley has stated, "Though uncommonly simple, the poems are frequently powerful and haunting . . . he has learned well the value of silence and understatement in poetry. In fact he achieves a kind of profundity by trying to avoid it, a talent too few writers can master" (p. 90). Leroy Quintana's work is at times bittersweet, occasionally sadly nostalgic, simply poignant, and always compassionate.

POETRY COLLECTIONS

Hijo del Pueblo: New Mexico Poems. Las Cruces, NM: Puerto Del Sol Press, 1976.
Sangre. Las Cruces, NM: Prima Agua, 1981.
Interrogations. Silver Spring, MD: Burning Cities Press, 1990.
The History of Home. Tempe, AZ: Bilingual Press, 1993.
My Hair Turning Gray Among Strangers. Tempe, AZ: Bilingual Press, 1996.
The Great Whirl of Exile. Willimantic, CT: Curbstone Press, 1999.

SELECTED ANTHOLOGIES WHERE POETRY APPEARS

Collins, Billy, ed. *Poetry 180: A Turning Back to Poetry.* New York: Random House, 2003.
Daydi-Tolson, Santiago, ed. *Five Poets of Aztlan.* Tempe, AZ: Bilingual Review Press, 1985.
Espada, Martín, ed. *El Coro: A Chorus of Latino and Latina Poetry.* Amherst: University of Massachusetts Press, 1997.
Keller, Gary D., and Francisco Jimenez, eds. *Hispanics in the United States: An Anthology of Creative Literature.* Tempe, AZ: Bilingual Press, 1980.
Neiderman, Sharon, and Miriam Sagan, eds. *New Mexico Poetry Renaissance.* Santa Fe, NM: Red Crane Books, 1994.
Ortiz, Simon J., and Consuelo Pacheco, eds. *A Ceremony of Brotherhood.* Albuquerque, NM: Academia Press, 1980.

SELECTED ADDITIONAL WORKS

Paper Dance: 55 Latino Poets. Editor, with Victor Hernández Cruz and Virgil Suarez. New York: Persea, 1995.
La Promesa and Other Stories: Chicana and Chicano Visions of the Americas. Vol. 1. Norman: University of Oklahoma Press, 2002.

SELECTED RESOURCES FOR FURTHER REFERENCE

Benson, Douglas K. "A Conversation with Leroy V. Quintana." *Bilingual Review/ La Revista Bilingüe* 12.3 (1987): 218–229.
———. "Inner and Outer Realities of Chicano Life: The New Mexican Perspective of Leroy V. Quintana." *Perspectives on Contemporary Literature* 12 (1986): 20–28.
———. "Intuitions of a World in Transition: The New Mexico Poetry of Leroy V. Quintana." *Bilingual Review/La Revista Bilingüe* 12.1–2 (1987): 62–80.

Bradley, Jerry. "Review of Hijo del Pueblo." *New Mexico Humanities Review* 5.1 (1982): 90.

Foss, Phillip, Jr. "Familial Portraits." *Contact II* 6 (Winter–Spring 1984–1985): 33.

Glade, Jon Forrest. "War and Injustice." *American Book Review* 16.1 (April–May 1994): 21.

González, Ray. "A Chicano Verano." *The Nation* 256.22 (June 7, 1993): 772–774.

Jones, Tayari. "Memories, Boiled and Strained." *The Progressive* 63.11 (November 1999): 43–44.

Kopp, Karl. "Hijo del Pueblo: Leroy V. Quintana." *American Book Review* 1 (December 1977): 19–20.

Lomeli, Francisco A., and Donaldo W. Urioste. *Chicano Perspectives in Literature: A Critical and Annotated Bibliography.* Albuquerque, NM: Pajarito, 1976.

Márquez, Antonio C. Introduction to *The History of Home,* by Leroy Quintana. Tempe, AZ: Bilingual Press/Editorial Bilingüe, 1993, 3–14.

Martinez, Demetria. "The Other Side of the Tracks." *The Progressive* 60.9 (September 1996): 43.

White, James L. "Review of Hijo del Pueblo." *Dakotah Territory* (1977–1978): 15, 91–92.

Cecilia Rodríguez Milanés

Ishmael Reed (aka Emmett Coleman)
(1938–)

African American

BIOGRAPHY

Poet, novelist, essayist, and playwright, Ishmael Reed was born on February 22, 1938, in Chattanooga, Tennessee. He is the son of Henry Lenoir and Thelma Coleman, though he received his surname from his stepfather, autoworker Bennie Reed. Reed's family moved to Buffalo, New York, when he was four. He attended Millard Filmore College and the University of Buffalo, though financial difficulties forced him to withdraw from the latter before earning a degree. Reed is married to dancer and choreographer Carla Blank and has two children.

In Buffalo, Reed wrote for the *Empire Star Weekly,* a local black newspaper, and cohosted a radio show that was canceled after Reed interviewed Malcolm X. Reed moved to New York City in 1962, where he worked in a hospital, at an unemployment office, and as an editor of the *Newark Advance,* a weekly newspaper. While in New York, he helped found *East Village Other,* a well-known and acclaimed underground newspaper. He was also active in the Umbra Writers Workshop, a black poetry collective that contributed substantially to the development of the Black Arts Movement.

In 1967, Reed moved to Oakland, California, where he still lives. That same year he published his first novel, *Free-Lance Pallbearers,* a satire of Newark politics that included critiques of black Muslim politics, African Americans who had assimilated, Western society, novels of black self-discovery, and both white and black liberals. This novel also established Reed's use of African American narrative structures as a way to establish a black aesthetic. In 1969, Reed's second novel, *Yellow Back Radio Broke Down,* introduced his concept of Neohoodooism, an aesthetic that permeates most of his work. Hoodoo is the African American form of Voodoo, which is generally misunderstood and sensationalized but is actually just a New World form of traditional African religious practices. For Reed, the New World mixing of race and culture creates a positive, hybrid, multicultural America. Thus, understanding black America, as well as other cultural groups, is essential to understanding America overall.

Reed is a prolific writer and committed teacher. He has published five books of poetry, nine novels, and four collections of essays. Further writing includes television productions, plays, operas, and songs. He is also active as an editor and publisher, and most notably, cofounded in 1976 the Before Columbus Foundation to produce and distribute the work of unknown writers. He also has an active Internet presence and two of his magazines, *KONCH* and *VINES*, have been available at his Web site (www.ishmaelreedpub.com) since the late 1990s. Reed has been a visiting professor at Harvard, Yale, Dartmouth, the State University of New York at Buffalo, and many other schools and has taught at the University of California at Berkeley for more than thirty years.

Reed has been honored with numerous awards and nominations. In 1973 he was a finalist for the National Book Award for both *Conjure* and *Mumbo Jumbo,* and in 1974 he was nominated for the Pulitzer Prize and won the John Simon Guggenheim Memorial Foundation Award. He also received the Richard and Hilda Rosenthal Foundation Award in 1975, the American Civil Liberties Award in 1978, and the Pushcart Prize in 1979.

THEMES AND CONCERNS

Reed's work is known for its mixing of disparate elements and for its wide-ranging scope, tools he uses to challenge his readers to consider all available versions of truth and of history. His use of broad ranging materials also mirrors the eclectic nature of Hoodoo and Neohoodooism, both multifaceted concepts of reality that are born from the varied experiences of African-descended people in the Americas. His Neohoodoo depictions of society are primarily satirical and often sharply criticize Western religion, politics, and technology. Poems like "Neo-HooDoo Manifesto" and "The Neo-HooDoo Aesthetic," as well the novel *Mumbo Jumbo* (1972), illustrate Reed's concept of Neohoodooism and his use of satire.

Reed is, however, just as quick to turn his satirical gaze to African American culture and tradition, as he does in the novels *The Free-Lance Pallbearers* (1967) and *Flight to Canada* (1976). Yet his commitment to a black aesthetic remains clear, and he often alludes to African American literature and folktales and ancient African histories (consider the poem "I am a cowboy in the boat of Ra") and uses black language patterns and rhythms in his work. Indeed, another way to understand Reed's multifaceted conception of reality is to consider neohoodooism as part of the trickster tradition. Trickster characters are complex and ephemeral, changing in form and meaning, but always illuminating—or at least hinting—of the larger, hidden patterns of existence. The poem "Railroad Bill, a Conjure Man" features the character Railroad Bill, who changes physical form to stay alive and elude capture from various police and other authority figures. At the same time, Railroad Bill is a real person, Morris Slater, who uses his wits to survive. The multiple possibilities here establish a connection between the patterns of existence as understood in the religious thought of Hoodoo and also in the real life of the individual.

Reed's use of original forms adds depth and meaning in his work. His understanding of Neohoodooism allows and encourages this type of critical attention to all cultures and traditions because it values hybridity and acknowledges the effect that centuries of interaction—not all of it positive—have had on shaping views of the world. Like the trickster, Reed distorts the traditional forms of Western poetry and prose, sometimes reversing them, sometimes fusing them with African structures. His work is highly eclectic, blending forms and symbols from a wide variety of cultures and times.

POETRY COLLECTIONS

Catechism of d Neoamerican Hoodoo Church. London: Paul Breman, 1970.
Conjure: Selected Poems, 1963–1970. Amherst: University of Massachusetts Press, 1972.
Chattanooga: Poem. New York: Random House, 1973.
A Secretary to the Spirits. New York: NOK, 1978.
New and Collected Poetry. New York: Atheneum, 1988.

SELECTED ANTHOLOGIES WHERE POETRY APPEARS

Feinstein, Sascha, and Yusef Komunyakaa, eds. *The Jazz Poetry Anthology*. Bloomington: Indiana University Press, 1991.
Harper, Michael S., and Anthony Walton, eds. *Every Shut Eye Ain't Asleep: An Anthology of Poetry by African Americans Since 1945*. New York: Little, Brown, 1994.
Kaufman, Alan, ed. *The Outlaw Bible of American Poetry*. New York: Thunder's Mouth Press, 1999.
Long, Richard, and Eugenia Collier, eds. *Afro-American Writing: An Anthology of Prose and Poetry*. New York: New York University Press, 1972.

SELECTED ADDITIONAL WORKS

The Free-Lance Pallbearers. Garden City, NY: Doubleday, 1967.
Yellow Back Radio Broke Down. Garden City, NY: Doubleday, 1969.
19 Necromancers from Now. Garden City, NY: Doubleday, 1970.
Mumbo Jumbo. Garden City, NY: Doubleday, 1972.
The Last Days of Louisiana Red. New York: Random House, 1974.
Flight to Canada. New York: Random House, 1976.
Shrovetide in Old New Orleans. Garden City, NY: Doubleday, 1978.
The Ace Boons. 1980. (play)
Personal Problems. 1981. (video)
God Made Alaska for the Indians: Selected Essays. New York: Garland, 1982.
The Terrible Twos. New York: St. Martin's/Marek, 1982.
Reckless Eyeballing. New York: St. Martin's, 1986.
Savage Wilds. 1988. (film)
Writin' Is Fightin': Thirty-seven Years of Boxing on Paper. New York: Atheneum, 1988.
The Terrible Threes. New York: Atheneum, 1989.

Savage Wilds II. 1990. (film)
The Before Columbus Foundation Fiction Anthology. Editor. New York: W. W. Norton, 1992.
Airing Dirty Laundry. Reading, MA: Addison-Wesley, 1993.
Japanese by Spring. New York: Atheneum, 1993.
Multi-America: Essays on Cultural War and Cultural Peace. New York: Viking, 1997.
Another Day at the Front: Dispatches from the Race War. New York: Basic Books, 2003.
From Totems to Hip Hop: A Multicultural Anthology of Poetry Across America. Editor. New York: Thunder's Mouth Press, 2003.

SELECTED RESOURCES FOR FURTHER REFERENCE

Boyer, Jay. *Ishmael Reed.* Boise, ID: Boise State University Press, 1993.
Bush, Glen. "Ishmael Reed: Post-Modern and Narrative Architecture in Mumbo Jumbo." *MAWA Review* 5.1 (June 1990): 20–23.
Dick, Bruce A., ed. *The Critical Response to Ishmael Reed.* Westport, CT: Greenwood, 1999.
Hume, Kathryn. "Ishmael Reed and the Problematics of Control." *PMLA* 108.3 (May 1993): 506–518.
Lindroth, James. "Images of Subversion: Ishmael Reed and the Hoodoo Trickster." *African-American Review* 30.2 (Summer 1996): 185–196.
Martin, Reginald. *Ishmael Reed and the New Black Aesthetic Critics.* London: Macmillan, 1986.
McGee, Patrick. *Ishmael Reed and the Ends of Race.* New York: St. Martin's Press, 1997.
Mikics, David. "Ism: Postmodern Ethnicity and Underground Revision in Ishmael Reed." In *Essays in Postmodern Culture.* Ed. Eyal Amiran and John Unworth. New York: Oxford University Press, 1993, 294–324.
Mvuyekere, Pierre D. "The Critical Reception of Ishmael Reed." *MFS: Modern Fiction Studies* 46.4 (Winter 2000): 979–983.
Weixlmann, Joe. "African American Deconstruction of the Novel in the Work of Ishmael Reed and Clarence Major." *MELUS: The Journal of the Society for the Study of the Multi-Ethnic Literature of the United States* 17.4 (Winter 1991–1992): 57–79.
Zamir, Shamoon, ed. "Ishmael Reed." *Callaloo* 17.4 (Fall 1994): 1129–1256.

Joseph Register

Courtesy of Alberto Alvaro Ríos.

Alberto Alvaro Ríos
(1952–)
Chicano/Mexican American

BIOGRAPHY

Alberto Alvaro Ríos was born September 18, 1952, in Nogales, Arizona, on the border with Mexico. He began life in a bicultural home raised by his mother, Agnes, who moved from Warrington, Cheshire, England, to marry his father, Alberto Alvaro, who was born in Tapachula, Chiapas, Mexico. Border life in his home and hometown fills his writing with a rich magical realism as well as a poetic style grounded in convention. Ríos received his B.A. in English literature and creative writing in 1974 from University of Arizona, went on to earn another B.A. in psychology in 1975 and earned an M.F.A. in 1979, both from the same university. He attended law school for one year before deciding to pursue writing as a career.

Ríos's memoir, *Capirotada,* suggests a predominantly joyful childhood. His descriptions of his parents and ancestors on both sides of his family show a foundation of bravery and tolerance that seems to have shaped the author himself. As the memoir reveals, Ríos was raised Catholic; he beautifully describes his childhood understanding of the faith and its rituals. As with many other Hispanic writers, he explores the genre, creating a memoir that includes pictures of his family as well as short stories and poetry. Ríos married Maria Guadalupe Barron, a librarian, on September 8, 1979, and has a single son, Joaquin. They moved to Florence, Arizona, and lived there for a year while Ríos worked for the Arizona Commission on the Arts. In 1980 the couple moved to Globe, Arizona, and in 1982 to Apache Junction.

From 1978 through the present, Ríos has held various academic positions, including associate and then full professor at Arizona State University, the director of the Creative Writing Program, a writer-in-residence, and vice chairman for the Arizona Center for the Book. Throughout these various positions he has written twelve books of poetry, fiction, and memoir and has won numerous awards for his writing ability. These include a National Endowment for the Arts grant (1980), the Walt Whitman Award from the National Academy of American Poets (1981), various Pushcart Prizes for fiction (1986) and poetry (1988 and 1989), the New Times Fiction Award (1983), the Western States Book Award (1984), and first place in the 1997 Academy of American Arts poetry contest for "A Man Then Suddenly Stops Moving." Most recently, in 2002 Ríos was nominated for the prestigious National Book Award in poetry.

THEMES AND CONCERNS

Ríos combines elements of a Latin American imagination, the importance of family, the landscape of the West, and a gift for language to produce striking poetry and prose. His writing captures the "border experience" in a literal and figurative way from his own experiences growing up in a multicultural home on the border with Mexico. Some of his common themes include the influence of ancestors, magical realism, coming of age, the contrast between North (United States) and South (Mexico), as well as European versus American perspectives, and race relations exemplify his multiethnic heritage. In *Capirotada*, he writes about the courage and tolerance of his mother's family in England, as well as her own experiences as an ethnic and linguistic outsider in the Mexican American family into which she married.

Throughout his works, Ríos addresses these themes, many common to Hispanic authors, in a highly accessible writing style. Ríos has a gift for voice that allows him to write memoir from both adult and child perspectives, as well as allow his mother and others to speak through him. This approach is mirrored in his poetry and short stories, which also give voice to both men and women. "The Birthday of Mrs. Pineda," for example, allows an oppressed housewife to speak. The accessibility of his works has caused them to be regularly taught and translated, as well as adapted to dance and both classical and popular music.

As with his memoir, Ríos pulls heavily from his family for inspiration. *The Iguana Killer: Twelve Stories of the Heart* contains a title story derived from his father's own experiences growing up in Mexico. The story centers around a young boy who uses a baseball bat to become his country's leading iguana killer. A similar incident is related in *Capirotada*, involving a baseball bat sent to his father by his grandmother in the United States. Being unfamiliar with baseball, his father used the item to hunt iguanas for his family's nourishment. Stories such as these exhibit, as much as his memoir, the contribution his family and their own stories made upon his life.

Like many ethnic writers of the last three decades, Ríos defies generic boundaries in writing his memoir. Parts are written from the perspective of his mother, poetry is included, as are pictures, and the stories, although they flow well within themselves, lack any real chronology. Much of his poetry, however, adheres to more formal stanzaic conventions. Ríos often uses a familiar first-person persona in his poetry, thereby creating an intimate immediacy with the reader. In his narrative poems we are treated to stories about characters who populate his rich imaginative and personal landscape that is border life.

POETRY COLLECTIONS

Elk Heads on the Wall. San Jose, CA: Mango Press, 1979.
Sleeping in Fists. Story, WY: Dooryard Press, 1981.
Whispering to Fool the Wind. New York: Sheep Meadow Press, 1982.
Five Indiscretions. New York: Sheep Meadow Press, 1985.
The Lime Orchard Woman. New York: Sheep Meadow Press, 1988.
The Warrington Poems. Tempe, AZ: Pyracantha Press, 1989.
Teodoro Luna's Two Kisses. New York: W. W. Norton, 1990.
The Smallest Muscle in the Human Body. Port Townsend, WA: Copper Canyon, 2002.

SELECTED ANTHOLOGIES WHERE POETRY APPEARS

Collins, Billy, ed. *Poetry 180: A Turning Back to Poetry.* New York: Random House, 2003.
Cruz, Victor Hernández, Leroy V. Quintana, and Virgil Suárez, eds. *Paper Dance: 55 Latino Poets.* New York: Persea Books, 1995.
Gillan, Maria M., and Jennifer Gillan, eds. *Unsettling America: An Anthology of Contemporary Multicultural Poetry.* New York: Penguin, 1994.
Keller, Gary D., and Francisco Jimenez, eds. *Hispanics in the United States: An Anthology of Creative Literature.* Tempe, AZ: Bilingual Review Press, 1980.
Kopp, Karl, and Jane Kopp, eds. *Southwest: A Contemporary Anthology.* Albuquerque, NM: Red Earth Press, 1977.

SELECTED ADDITIONAL WORKS

The Iguana Killer. Albuquerque: University of New Mexico Press, 1984.
Pig Cookies. San Francisco, CA: Chronicle Books, 1995.
Capirotada. Albuquerque: University of New Mexico Press, 1999.
The Curtain of Trees. Albuquerque: University of New Mexico Press, 1999.

SELECTED RESOURCES FOR FURTHER REFERENCE

Alberto Ríos: Interviews. Online. www.public.asu.edu/%7eaaRíos/interviews.
Alberto Ríos Homepage. Online. www.public.asu.edu.
Saldívar, José David. "The Real and the Marvelous in Nogales, Arizona." *Denver Quarterly* 17.2 (1982): 141–144.
———. "Towards a Chicano Poetics: The Making of Chicano-Chicano Subject 1969–1982." *Confluencia* 1 (Spring 1985): 10–17.
Ullmann, L. "Solitaries and Storytellers, Magicians and Pagans: Five Poets in the World." *Kenyon Review* 13.2 (Spring 1991): 179–193.

Bronwen West

Wendy Rose (aka Chiron Khanshandel, Bronwen Elizabeth Edwards)

(1948–)

American Indian (Hopi, Miwok)

BIOGRAPHY

A poet, artist, and teacher, Wendy Rose was born on May 7, 1948, in Oakland, California. She was born Bronwen Elizabeth Edwards to parents of mixed descent; her father was Hopi, while her mother was Miwok and European. This mixture caused a great struggle for Rose in discovering her identity and later became a major influence on her poetry. Growing up, she lived in the San Francisco Bay area with her older brother, her mother, and her mother's husband. After dropping out of high school in her teen years, she became involved with the bohemian culture in San Francisco and began writing. However, she did return to school, and her academic career stretched from 1966 until 1980. She matriculated at a few different colleges and eventually received her Ph.D. in anthropology from the University of California, Berkeley. She married magician and judo instructor Arthur Murata in 1976. They lived in the Bay area while Rose completed her education, and the couple now lives in the foothills of the Sierra Nevada Mountains, near Yosemite National Park.

During the time that Rose was completing her degrees, she also succeeded in publishing five volumes of poetry. Her first collection, *Hopi Roadrunner Dancing,* was published in 1973; one focus of this collection is the establishment of the Native American rights movements during the 1960s and 1970s. Other volumes published in the 1970s, including *Academic Squaw: Reports to the World from the Ivory Tower* (1977) and *Long Division: A Tribal History* (1976), also allude to her experience as an anthropologist. These volumes and others include what Helen Jaskoski calls a "characteristic structure" in Rose's poetry, in that she "frequently opens a poem with an explanatory note or fragment of text from a journalistic or scholarly source." Her first major collection, *Lost Copper,* was published in 1980. In addition to her poetical works, Rose has also published reviews, essays, and an autobiographical narrative entitled "Neon Scars." Her retrospective collection *Bone Dance: New and Selected Poems, 1965–1993* (1994) contains poems from her previous books and new poems, as well as poems from her early career not previously published.

Currently, Wendy Rose heads the American Indian Studies program at Fresno City College in Fresno, California. She is a member of a number of anthropological organizations, literary societies, and organizations focusing on Native American concerns and has served as a facilitator for the Association of Non-Federally Recognized California Tribes. In addition to writing and teaching, she also works as a researcher, consultant, editor, panelist, bibliographer, adviser, and artist. Her watercolors and pen-and-ink drawings frequently illustrate her own books, as well as those of other authors.

THEMES AND CONCERNS

Rose utilizes free verse in most of her poetry, allowing thoughts and ideas to flow freely yet coherently. One of the major concerns that Rose deals with is what has been termed "whiteshamanism" or the act of non-Indians taking on a literary "shaman" identity to which they are not entitled. The poet feels that this act is one that exploits Native Americans as well as commodifies them. Her sense of injustice as a result of this issue reveals itself in some of her works from *Lost Copper*. In one piece, she speaks to those non-Indian shamans, who take on the Indian identity for shallow and materialistic reasons only to return to their true identity immediately at the end of their poem or story to sell or make money.

Although this sense of injustice and anger at "whiteshamanism" connects all of her works, Rose displays diversity among themes and concerns, as she does in her career choices as poet, scholar, anthropologist, and artist. She deals with the broad range of human experience, from being a woman, a minority, a Native American, and a Native American woman. Her feminist perspective is prevalent along with her experiences as a woman of color. Also in *Lost Copper,* she delves into her connection with the Earth. In *Academic Squaw* and *Long Division,* her academic leanings present themselves as the poet examines the nature of anthropologist and those whom they study, such as Indians. This, in turn, leads to her own search for tribal and personal identity, as an individual. In a sense, anthropologists, like herself, are studying Rose and her ancestors. As with other Native American poets, Rose also concentrates on her search for ancestry, roots, and family connection.

POETRY COLLECTIONS

Hopi Roadrunner Dancing. Greenfield Center, NY: Greenfield Review Press, 1973.
Long Division: A Tribal History. New York: Strawberry Press, 1976; expanded ed., 1981.
Academic Squaw: Reports to the World from the Ivory Tower. Marvin, SD: Blue Cloud Press, 1977.

Aboriginal Tattooing in California. Berkeley: Archaeological Research Facility, University of California, 1979.

Builder Kachina: A Home-Going Cycle. Marvin, SD: Blue Cloud Press, 1979.

Lost Copper. Banning, CA: Malki Museum Press, Morongo Indian Reservation, 1980.

What Happened When the Hopi Hit New York. New York: Contact II, 1982.

The Halfbreed Chronicles & Other Poems. Los Angeles, CA: West End Press, 1985.

Going to War with All My Relations. Flagstaff, AZ: Northland, 1993.

Bone Dance: New and Selected Poems, 1965–1992. Tucson: University of Arizona Press, 1994.

Now Poof She Is Gone. Ithaca, NY: Firebrand Books, 1994.

Itch Like Crazy. Tucson: University of Arizona Press, 2002.

SELECTED ANTHOLOGIES WHERE POETRY APPEARS

Bruchac, Joseph, ed. *Songs from This Earth on Turtle's Back: An Anthology of Poetry by American Indian Writers.* Greenfield Center, NY: Greenfield Review Press, 1983.

Gillan, Maria, and Jennifer Gillan, eds. *Unsettling America: An Anthology of Contemporary Multicultural Poetry.* New York: Penguin, 1994.

Green, Rayna, ed. *That's What She Said.* Bloomington: Indiana University Press, 1984.

Niatum, Duane, ed. *Harper's Anthology of Twentieth Century Native American Poetry.* New York: Harper & Row, 1988.

Sewell, Marilyn, ed. *Claiming the Spirit Within: A Sourcebook of Women's Poetry.* Boston, MA: Beacon Press, 2001.

Skerritt, Joseph T., ed. *Literature, Race, and Ethnicity.* New York: Longman, 2002.

Vizenor, Gerald, ed. *Native American Literature: A Brief Introduction and Anthology.* New York: Longman, 1995.

SELECTED ADDITIONAL WORKS

"Just What's All This Fuss about Whiteshamanism, Anyway?" *Coyote Was Here: Essays on Contemporary Native American Literary and Political Mobilization.* Ed. Bo Scholer. Aarhus, Denmark: University of Aarhus, 1984.

"Neon Scars." In *I Tell You Now.* Ed. Brian Swann and Arnold Krupat. New York: Brompton Books Corporation, 1989, 251–262.

"For Some It's a Time of Mourning." In *With-out Discovery: A Native Response to Columbus.* Ed. Ray Gonzalez. Broken Moon Press, 1992, 3–8.

"The Great Pretenders: Further Reflections on Whiteshamanism." *The State of Native America: Genocide, Colonization and Resistance.* Ed. M. Annette Jaimes. Cambridge, MA: South End Press, 1992, 403–422.

SELECTED RESOURCES FOR FURTHER REFERENCE

Bruchac, Joseph. *Survival This Way: Interviews with American Indian Poets.* Tucson: University of Arizona Press, 1987, 249–269.

Fast, Robin Riley. *The Heart as a Drum: Continuance and Resistance in American Indian Poetry.* Ann Arbor: University of Michigan Press, 1999.

Jaskoski, Helen. Interview with Wendy Rose, April 30, 1994. *Gale's Biography Resource Center*. Online. www.galegroup.com.

Momaday, N. Scott. Introduction to *Lost Copper*, by Wendy Rose. Banning, CA: Malki Museum Press, Morongo Indian Reservation, 1980.

Ruppert, James. "The Uses of Oral Tradition in Six Contemporary Native American Poets." *American Indian Culture and Research Journal* 4.4 (1980): 87–110.

Saucerman, James R. "Wendy Rose: Searching Through Shards, Creating Life." *Wicazo Sa Review* 5 (Fall 1989): 26–29.

Shelton, Pamela L., ed. *Contemporary Women Poets*. Detroit, MI: St. James Press, 1998.

Wiget, Andrew. "Blue Stones, Bones, and Troubled Silver: The Poetic Craft of Wendy Rose." *Studies in American Indian Literatures* 2 (Summer 1993): 29–33.

Heather Draper

Sonia Sanchez

(1934–)

African American

Photo by Leander Jackson, courtesy of Sonia Sanchez.

BIOGRAPHY

Poet and playwright Sonia Sanchez was born Wilsonia Benita Driver on September 9, 1934, in Birmingham, Alabama. Her mother, Lena, died when Sanchez was one year old, and Sanchez was raised by relatives in the South until she and her sister moved to Harlem to live with their father, Wilson L. Driver. After attending public schools there, Sanchez went to Hunter College, earning a bachelor's degree in political science in 1955. She immediately entered a graduate program at New York University, where she studied with noted poet Louise Bogan, but she withdrew after a year. She married and divorced Albert Sanchez, whose surname she uses as a writer, and in 1968 she married activist and poet Etheridge Knight, with whom she had three children. Her marriage to Knight was fraught with difficulty and ended in divorce.

After she left New York University, Sanchez formed a writers' workshop in Greenwich Village, which was attended by such poets as Amiri Baraka, Haki R. Madhubuti, and Larry Neal. Later she formed the "Broadside Quartet," a group of young poets that included Madhubuti, Nikki Giovanni, and Etheridge Knight. Politically, Sanchez supported the integrationist philosophy of the Congress of Racial Equality (CORE) for a time, but shifted to a separatist philosophy due to Malcolm X. Her early poems demonstrate this commitment to the revolutionary Black Power Movement, especially those in her first two published collections, *Home Coming* (1969) and *We a BaddDDD People* (1970). This radical stance earned Sanchez recognition as one of the most important voices of the Black Arts Movement. By the mid-1970s, however, the focus of her writing had turned toward the tensions between black men and black women, a topic that she addressed in her poetry as well as her play, *Uh Huh: But How Do It Free Us?* (1975).

Sanchez joined the Nation of Islam in 1971 but had left it by 1976 because of its repressive attitudes toward women. *A Blues Book for Blue Black Magical Women* (1974) describes her spiritual evolution and her experiences within Islam. Since then, her commitment to promoting women's rights and feminism has grown and has been a constant theme in her poetry; her most well known collection of poetry, stories, letters, and sketches is *homegirls & handgrenades* (1984), which examines the variety of black women's experiences in contemporary American society. Throughout her writing career, Sanchez has been involved in various facets of education. She was an important pioneer in the development of black studies courses and programs at San Francisco State University in the late 1960s and advocated for these programs to be established at other colleges and universities. She began her teaching career in 1965 at the Downtown Community School in New York and has since taught at a variety of colleges and universities, including Rutgers University, Spelman College, Amherst College, and the University of Pennsylvania. In 1972 her commitment to student expression was exhibited when she published an anthology of student writing done in a creative writing class in Harlem: *Three Hundred and Sixty Degrees of Blackness Comin' at You* (1972).

Sanchez has received many honors and awards during the span of her career. She was the first Presidential Fellow at Temple University in Philadelphia and has held the Laura Carnell Chair in English at that university. She has received a National Endowment for the Arts Award (1977), the Lucretia Mott Award (1984), the Peace and Freedom Award from the Women's International League for Peace and Freedom (1988–1989), the Pennsylvania Governor's Award for Excellence in the Humanities (1988), a Pew Fellowship in the Arts (1992), and a PEN Fellowship in the Arts (1993). She is the recipient of several honorary Ph.D.s and has read internationally and on over 500 campuses in the United States. Her books have also been celebrated among critics and readers. *homegirls & handgrenades* won the American Book Award in 1985, and most recently, her poetry collection *Does Your House Have Lions?* (1998) was a finalist for the National Book Critics Circle Award. Sanchez retired from Temple in 1999.

THEMES AND CONCERNS

Sanchez's writing is innovative in content and in structure. Her first few volumes of poetry and prose featured many staggered-line poems—brief and sharp compositions that demonstrate the vitality and searing pain of racism. For example, in "Homecoming," Sanchez contrasts the words the media and others use to describe blackness with her experiences of those words as a black woman. In doing so, she suggests that the truth of a black woman's reality is far harsher than these individual words suggest, exposing the skewed images of black women in contemporary American culture.

Sanchez is also well known for her use of urban Black English in her writing, and some of her early poems seem to record overheard street conversations in lyrical form. She uses unconventional spelling, abbreviations, and dashes to capture the feeling and movement of the spoken word and to represent the community that this language helps to define and enliven. In addition to her use language, the themes that Sanchez seems most interested in are those of oppressed men and women, particularly people of color. Her most well-known publication is *homegirls & handgrenades* (1984), an autobiographical collection of poetry, drawings, short stories, and essays in which she lays bare the experiences of relationships and racism that she and others have had.

She explores similar themes of urban African American experience in *Wounded in the House of a Friend* (1995); here she writes graphically about rape, the murder of a grandmother by her junkie granddaughter, and a mother trading her daughter for crack. More recent publications continue to deal with important contemporary issues that are both universal and that disproportionately affect the underclass, such as *Does Your House Have Lions?* (1997), which focuses on Sanchez's estranged brother, his struggle with and death from AIDS, and the definition of family in times of illness and severe stress. Although Sanchez's work has become more feminist throughout her career, she continues to focus on race and racism, foregrounding her belief that feminism and antiracism must work together.

POETRY COLLECTIONS

Home Coming. Detroit, MI: Broadside Press, 1969.
Liberation Poem. Detroit, MI: Broadside Press, 1970.
We a BadDDD People. Detroit, MI: Broadside Press, 1970.
Ima Talken bout the Nation of Islam. Astoria, NY: Truth Del, 1971.
It's a New Day: Poems for Young Brothas and Sistuhs. Detroit, MI: Broadside Press, 1971.
Love Poems. New York: Aperture, 1973.
A Blues Book for Blue Black Magical Women. Detroit, MI: Broadside Press, 1974.
I've Been a Woman: New and Selected Poems. Chicago, IL: Third World Press, 1978.
homegirls & handgrenades. New York: Thunder's Mouth Press, 1984, 1997.
Generations: Poetry 1969–1985. Lawrenceville, NJ: Red Sea Press, 1986.
Under a Soprano Sky. Lawrenceville, NJ: Africa World Press, 1987.
Continuous Fire: A Collection of Poetry. Lawrenceville, NJ: Africa World Press, 1991.
Autumn Blues: New Poems. Lawrenceville, NJ: Africa World Press, 1994.
Does Your House Have Lions? Boston, MA: Beacon Press, 1995.
Wounded in the House of a Friend. Boston, MA: Beacon Press, 1995.
Like the Singing Coming Off the Drums: Love Poems. Boston, MA: Beacon Press, 1998.
Shake Loose My Skin: New and Selected Poems. Boston, MA: Beacon Press, 1999.

SELECTED ANTHOLOGIES WHERE POETRY APPEARS

Adoff, Arnold, ed. *I Am the Darker Brother: An Anthology of Modern Poems by African Americans*. New York: Simon & Schuster, 1968, 1997.
Gates, Henry, Jr., and Nellie McKay, eds. *The Norton Anthology of African-American Literature, Best American Poetry*. New York: W. W. Norton, 1997.

Gilbert, Derrick I. M., ed. *Catch the Fire!!! A Cross-Generational Anthology of Contemporary African-American Poetry*. New York: Riverhead Books, 1998. (Includes an interview with Sanchez.)

Harper, Michael S., and Anthony Walton, eds. *Every Shut Eye Ain't Asleep: An Anthology of Poetry by African Americans Since 1945*. New York: Little, Brown, 1994.

Hill, Patricia Liggins. *Call & Response: The Riverside Anthology of the African American Literary Tradition*. Boston, MA: Houghton Mifflin, 1998.

Medina, Tony, ed. *Bum Rush the Page: A Def Poetry Jam*. New York: Three Rivers Press, 2001.

Quashie, Kevin, R. Joyce Lausch, and Keith D. Miller. *New Bones: Contemporary Black Writers in America*. Upper Saddle River, NJ: Prentice Hall, 2001.

SELECTED ADDITIONAL WORKS

Sister Son/Ji. 1969. (play)

The Bronx Is Next. 1970. (play)

The Adventures of Fathead, Smallhead, and Squarehead. With Taiwo Duvall, illustrator. New York: Aperture, 1973.

Dirty Hearts '72. 1973. (play)

Uh Huh: But How Do It Free Us? 1975. (play)

Malcolm Man/Don't Live Here No Mo'. 1979. (play)

A Sound Investment: Short Stories for Young Readers. Editor, with John Henrik Clarke. Chicago, IL: Third World Press, 1980, 1993.

Shake Down Memory: A Collection of Political Essays and Speeches. Editor. Lawrenceville, NJ: Africa World Press, 1991.

Continuous Fire: A Collection of Poetry. Editor. Lawrenceville, NJ: Africa World Press, 1994.

Black Cats Back and Uneasy Landings. 1995. (play)

Living at the Epicenter: The Morse Prize in Poetry. With Alison Funk. Boston, MA: Northeastern University Press, 1995.

SELECTED RESOURCES FOR FURTHER REFERENCE

Davis, Elsa. "Lucille Clifton and Sonia Sanchez: A Conversation." *Callaloo* 25.4 (2002): 1038–1074.

Dorr, John, and Lewis MacAdams, prod. and dir. *Sonia Sanchez*. Los Angeles, CA: The Foundation, 1991. (film)

Gabbin, Joan Veal. "The Southern Imagination of Sonia Sanchez." In *Southern Women Writers: The New Generation*. Ed. Tonette Bond Inge and Doris Betts. Tuscaloosa: University of Alabama Press, 1990, 180–203.

Hodges, John, dir. and ed. *Furious Flower: Conversations with African American Poets*. Vol. 2. San Francisco, CA: California Newsreel, 1998. (film)

Jennings, Regina B. "The Blue/Black Poetics of Sonia Sanchez." In *Language and Literature in the African American Imagination*. Ed. Carol Aisha Blackshire-Belay. Westport, CT: Greenwood, 1992, 109–132.

Joyce, Joyce Ann. *Ijala: Sonia Sanchez and the African Poetic Tradition*. Chicago, IL: Third World Press, 1996.

Saunders, James Robert. "Sonia Sanchez's *homegirls & handgrenades:* Recalling Toomer's Cane." *MELUS: The Journal of the Society for the Study of the Multi-Ethnic Literature of the United States* 15.1 (Spring 1988): 73–82.

Tate, Claudia. *Black Women Writers at Work.* New York: Continuum: 1983.

Rachael Groner

Leslie Marmon Silko

(1948–)

American Indian (Laguna, Pueblo)

BIOGRAPHY

Born in Laguna Pueblo, a village on the outskirts of Albuquerque, New Mexico, on March 5, 1948, Leslie Marmon Silko, acclaimed writer of poetry, short fiction, and novels, experienced isolation and displacement not only in white culture but in her own as well. Silko led a rich but solitary childhood, due in part to her diverse heritage consisting of Laguna, Pueblo, Mexican, and White blood. Although she spent her youth educated in a Catholic school, she experienced her true religion through her great-grandmother's tales of Laguna and Keres myth. Throughout her career, Silko has painted a map of her culture, a direct result of her great-grandmother's influence, and readers can readily find the oft-told myths of yellow woman and ka'tsina (kachina) in a majority of Silko's works. However, because of her mixed heritage, Silko considered herself an outsider in the Pueblo, a conflict that structures much of her work.

Not fully accepted by the Laguna people or the whites because of her mixed heritage, Silko lived in a constant and painful transition between two cultures. However, in her isolation, she reveled in her great-grandmother's folklore and her homeland, and her talent blossomed. She received her bachelor's degree from the University of New Mexico in 1969 and published *Laguna Woman*, her first collection of poems, in 1974. Since her first publication, Silko has won numerous accolades, including a Pushcart Prize for Poetry, a grant from the National Endowment of the Arts, the Native Writers' Circle of the Americas Lifetime Achievement Award, and a MacArthur Foundation "Genius" Fellowship. In addition, the New Mexico Endowment for the Humanities Council named Silko a "Living Cultural Treasure." Aside from writing novels and poetry, Silko has taught in New Mexico and Alaska and currently teaches at the University of Arizona in Tucson. She has two children.

THEMES AND CONCERNS

Silko published her first, and only, collection of poetry, *Laguna Woman*, in 1974. She wrote the poems, for which she earned a poetry award from *The*

Chicago Review while teaching at the Navajo Community College in Tsaile, Arizona, and many of the poems reflect the influence of her great-grandmother's oral renderings. While this is her only collection of poetry, her poems are a part of much of her other, critically acclaimed, work, including *Ceremony* (1977), which weaves extraordinary poetry into the tale of a young American Indian captured by the Japanese in World War II, and *Storyteller* (1989), a collection of poetry and stories.

Much of Silko's poetry embodies the Laguna's inherent reverence of nature, where terra firma is caretaker to all. For example, in her poem "Storyteller," Silko writes a lullaby of nature's protection of her inhabitants. She refers back to a universal mythology in which the landscape acts as nurturer and eternal protector of humanity. Coaxing her reader to rest, she cites the maternal earth, the paternal sky, and the sororal rainbow as resolver of all human quandaries. Similarly, in the much darker poem "Long Time Ago" from *Ceremony,* Silko describes the original landscape of the world as eternal, "complete" even before European colonization. In the poem, she depicts a convention of ancient witches, a collective of members of the Navajo tribes as well as the Pueblo, including the Zuni, Hopi, and Laguna, who vie for recognition of their respective talents. The winner, who is the only witch to display her wares through oral tradition, is the creator of the white man, the evil force that threatens the existence of the people as well as the land. The lone witch predicts the coven's destruction by the white man, a being who fails to appreciate nature except as a possession.

In her essay "Empowerment Through Retroactive Prophecy," Lori Burlingame asserts that Silko creates this myth, one outside of standard Pueblo mythology, to give hope to her protagonist. By claiming ancestral responsibility for the creation of the white man and his realm of colonial destruction, Silko compels *Ceremony*'s protagonist, Tayo, "to move beyond victimization into self-determination" and to reinstate "his belief in Laguna Pueblo ideologies, which has been called into question by what he was taught in the white educational system and his experiences in World War II" (pp. 5–6). By reaffirming his sense of power and heritage, Tayo is able to confront his immersion in the conquering white world and journey toward self-awareness, issues Silko declares vital in many of her works.

Silko's ability to convert a painful separation from identity and culture into art, while simultaneously conveying a message of cultural empowerment, places her as a contemporary to esteemed authors such as Louise Erdrich, Paula Gunn Allen, and Linda Hogan. Equally, as an advocate for the preservation of the earth's landscape, the eternal source of life, Silko campaigns for global awareness of humanity as a function of the environment. Where her great-grandmother's landscape is eternal and will thrive without humankind, humanity cannot survive without the landscape.

POETRY COLLECTIONS

Laguna Woman. Greenfield Center, NY: Greenfield Review Press, 1974.
Storyteller. New York: Arcade, 1989. (poems and stories)

SELECTED ANTHOLOGIES WHERE POETRY APPEARS

Harjo, Joy, and Gloria Bird, eds. *Reinventing the Enemy's Language: Contemporary Native American Women's Writings of North America.* New York: W. W. Norton, 1998.

Niatum, Duane, ed. *Carriers of the Dream Wheel: Contemporary Native American Poetry.* New York: Harper & Row, 1975.

Purdy, John, and James Ruppert, eds. *Nothing but the Truth: An Anthology of Native American Literature.* New York: Prentice-Hall, 2000.

SELECTED FICTION AND NONFICTION

"Language and Literature from a Pueblo Indian Perspective." In *English Literature: Opening Up the Canon.* Ed. Leslie Fiedler. Baltimore: Johns Hopkins University Press, 1981, 54–72.

After a Summer Rain in the Upper Sonoran. Madison, WI: Black Mesa Press for Woodland Pattern, 1984.

"Lullaby." In *The Norton Anthology of Literature by Women.* Ed. Sandra M. Gilbert and Susan Gubar. New York: W. W. Norton, 1985, 2383–2390.

The Delicacy and Strength of Lace: Letters Between Leslie Marmon Silko and James Wright. Ed. Anne Wright. St. Paul, MN: Graywolf Press, 1986.

Ceremony. New York: Penguin USA, 1988.

Almanac of the Dead. New York: Simon & Schuster, 1991.

Sacred Water: Narratives and Pictures. Tucson, AZ: Flood Plain Press, 1994.

"Interior and Exterior Landscapes: The Pueblo Migration Stories." In *Landscape in America.* Ed. George F. Thompson. Austin: University of Texas Press, 1995, 155–169.

"Landscape, History, and the Pueblo Imagination." In *The Ecocriticism Reader: Landmarks in Literary Ecology.* Ed. Cheryll Glotfelty and Harold Fromm. Athens: University of Georgia Press, 1996, 264–275.

Yellow Women and a Beauty of the Spirit: Essays on Native American Life Today. New York: Touchstone Books, 1997.

Gardens in the Dunes. New York: Touchstone Books, 2000.

SELECTED RESOURCES FOR FURTHER REFERENCE

Barnett, Louise K., and James L. Thorson, eds. *Leslie Marmon Silko: A Collection of Critical Essays.* Albuquerque: University of New Mexico Press, 2001.

Burlingame, Lori. "Empowerment Through 'Retroactive Prophecy' in D'Arcy McNickle's *Runner in the Sun: A Story of Indian Maize,* James Welch's *Fools Crow,* and Leslie Marmon Silko's *Ceremony.*" *American Indian Quarterly* 24.1 (2000): 1–18.

Dinome, William. "Laguna Woman: An Annotated Leslie Silko Bibliography." *American Indian Culture and Research Journal* 21.1 (1997): 207–280.

Graulich, Melody, ed. *"Yellow Woman" (Women Writers: Texts and Contexts)*. Piscataway, NJ: Rutgers University Press, 1993.

Leslie Marmon Silko. Film by Matteo Bellinelli. Princeton, NJ: Films for the Humanities, 1995.

Powers, Peter Kerry. *Recalling Religions: Resistance, Memory, and Cultural Revision in Ethnic Women's Literature*. Knoxville: University of Tennessee Press, 2001, 65–88.

Rand, Naomi. *Silko, Morrison, and Roth: Studies in Survival*. New York: Peter Lang, 1999.

Seyersted, Per. *Leslie Marmon Silko*. Boise, ID: Boise State University Press, 1980.

St. Clair, Janet. "Uneasy Ethnocentrism: Recent Works of Allen, Silko, and Hogan." *Studies in American Indian Literatures: The Journal of the Association for the Study of American Indian Literatures* 6.1 (1994): 82–98.

Van Dyke, Annette. "The Journey Back to Female Roots: A Laguna Pueblo Model." In *Lesbian Texts and Contexts: Radical Revisions*. Ed. Karla Jay and Joanne Glasgow. New York: New York University Press, 1990, 339–354.

Velie, Alan R. *Four American Indian Literary Masters: N. Scott Momaday, James Welch, Leslie Marmon Silko, and Gerald Vizenor*. Norman: University of Oklahoma Press, 1982.

Weaver, Jace. *Other Words: American Indian Literature, Law, and Culture*. Norman: University of Oklahoma Press, 2001.

Alice D'Amore

Charles Simic

(1938–)

Slavic American

BIOGRAPHY

Born on May 9, 1938, in Belgrade, Yugoslavia, Charles Simic's early years were spent surviving the horrors of war, as his city became a target for first German, then English and American bombings. His father, an engineer, was captured in Italy by the Germans and jailed as a spy, only to be liberated by the American army. Having American business connections and little desire to return to his wife, the elder Simic emigrated to America. Young Simic was therefore left with his mother, a voice teacher, in the political turmoil of Yugoslavia. In 1953 he emigrated with his mother to Paris and a year later reunited with his father in the United States, settling in Chicago.

Simic attended Oak Park High School, where he developed an interest in jazz and participated on the basketball team. It was not until he became a student at the University of Chicago from 1956 to 1959 that Simic began to write poetry. His next stop was New York University, where he continued his studies and writing until 1961, when military duty called. Drafted into the U.S. Army, Simic served as a military police officer in eastern France until 1963. He returned to New York University and received his degree in 1964; he stayed on as a graduate student into the next year.

Simic's many occupations include serving as a proofreader for the *Chicago Sun-Times*, a payroll clerk, a computer programmer, and an editorial assistant for *Aperture*, a photography magazine. He made the transition from Serbo-Croation speaker to teacher and writer of English and has taught at several institutions, including California State College and the University of New Hampshire, where he is professor of English. He has lived in New Hampshire since 1973.

Simic has an extensive publishing history. His first poems, published in 1959 in the *Chicago Review*, show Simic's self-admitted diversity of influences. From Hart Crane to Walt Whitman to Ezra Pound, Simic would frequently reshape his styles and focus. He considers these early years of his writing career to be his most prolific but least successful, going to such lengths as to destroy most of this early work. His first full-length collection of poems, *What the Grass Says*, was published in 1967. Since then he has published more than sixty books in America and abroad: among the most lauded are *Jackstraws* (1999), which was named a *New York Times* Notable Book of the Year; *Walking the Black Cat* (1996), which was a finalist for the National Book Award in poetry; and *The World Doesn't End: Prose Poems* (1989), for which Simic received the Pulitzer Prize for poetry. His most recent work is a new collection of poems titled *Night Picnic*, published in September 2001.

In addition to writing his own poetry, Simic is noted for translating other European writers; he has published many translations of French, Serbian, Croatian, Russian, Macedonian, and Slovenian poetry. Simic has been instrumental in exposing many foreign poets to English readers, and he considers both Serbian and English to be his two mother tongues. Simic considers the translator's ideal to be languages coming from one mother, speaking from different corners of her mouth, and if achieved, translation then "like poetry itself, it is already in the realm of the miraculous" (*Wonderful Words, Silent Truth*, p. 107). In addition to work in poetry, Simic has written four books of essays and was the guest editor of *The Best American Poetry 1992*.

For his poetry and literary translations, Simic has won awards from the American Academy of Arts and Letters and the Poetry Society of America and has received the Edgar Allan Poe Award as well as the PEN Translation Prize. Elected a chancellor of the Academy of American Poets in 2000, his other honors include fellowships from the Guggenheim Foundation, the MacArthur Foundation, and the National Endowment for the Arts.

THEMES AND CONCERNS

Simic's poems embody a variety of themes, from the spiritual to the bitterly humorous, and are frequently shadowed by the threat of violence, lingering evidence of Simic's war-tainted youth. Simic's early experiences with hunger and poverty also influence many of his poems, which are frequently surreal and often nightmarish. These dark themes abound in Simic's collection *A Wedding in Hell*. For example, "The Secret" depicts a first-person view of Simic awaking in the middle of the night, searching for his mother to find her talking to a soldier on the street. The poem evokes the paranoia of Simic's childhood, where warring nationalities and ideologies forced the Yugoslav people to retreat into shells of secrecy. Many of Simic's poems portray God as a dark figure, such as in "Psalm" (*A Wedding in Hell*), where the poet chastises God for allowing madmen to run the world. "Prayer" expresses Simic's horror of an uncomprehending supreme being. Simic's poems are not all dark or angry, nor even surreal. Many poems are vivid descriptions of a moment or an object, such as "Crazy about Her Shrimp" (*A Wedding in Hell*), which is a humorous and hopeful slice of a romantic culinary relationship.

Simic finds himself struggling with his belief that speech and language cannot do justice in portraying what it is to be truly conscious. Because of this,

Simic embraces what some poets may regard as nonsense, in the spirit of imaginative possibility. He has been influenced by many philosophers, such as Wittgenstein and especially Heidegger, who clarified Simic's ideas about the philosophical ambitions of modern poetry and the concept that it is not the poet who speaks through a poem but the work itself. He mimics Heidegger in believing that some poems "open the largest view of the earth, sky, mortals, and their true and false gods" (*Wonderful Words, Silent Truth,* p. 128).

POETRY COLLECTIONS

What the Grass Says. San Francisco, CA: Kayak, 1967.
Somewhere Among Us a Stone Is Taking Notes. San Francisco, CA: Kayak, 1969.
Dismantling the Silence. New York: George Braziller, 1971.
White. New York: New Rivers Press, 1972.
Return to a Place Lit by a Glass of Milk. New York: G. Braziller, 1974.
Biography and a Lament. Hartford: Bartholomew's Cobble, 1976.
Charon's Cosmology. New York: George Braziller, 1977.
Classic Ballroom Dances. New York: George Braziller, 1980.
Austerities. New York: George Braziller, 1982.
Weather Forecast for Utopia and Vicinity. Barrytown, NY: Station Hill Press, 1983.
Selected Poems 1963–1983. New York: George Braziller, 1985.
Unending Blues. New York: Harcourt, 1986.
The World Doesn't End: Prose Poems. New York: Harcourt, 1989.
The Book of Gods and Devils. New York: Harcourt, 1990.
Selected Poems 1963–1983. Rev. and expanded ed. New York: George Braziller, 1990.
Hotel Insomnia. New York: Harcourt, 1992.
A Wedding in Hell. New York: Harcourt Brace, 1994.
Frightening Toys. New York: Faber and Faber, 1995.
Walking the Black Cat. New York: Harcourt, 1996.
Looking for Trouble. New York: Faber and Faber, 1997.
Charles Simic: Selected Early Poems. New York: George Braziller, 1999.
Jackstraws. New York: Harcourt, 1999.
Night Picnic. New York: Harcourt, 2001.

SELECTED ANTHOLOGIES WHERE POETRY APPEARS

Berg, Stephen, and Robert Mezey, eds. *The New Naked Poetry.* Indianapolis, IN: Bobbs-Merrill, 1976.
Field, Edward, ed. *A Geography of Poets.* New York: Bantam, 1979.
Friebert, Stuart, and David Young, eds. *Contemporary American Poetry 1950–1980.* New York: Longman, 1983.
McCullough, Frances Monson, ed. *Earth, Air, Fire, and Water.* New York: Coward, McCann, & Geoghegan, 1971.
Quasha, George, ed. *America: A Prophecy.* New York: Random House, 1973.
Shepard, Jim, ed. *Writers at the Movies: Twenty-six Contemporary Authors Celebrate Twenty-six Memorable Movies.* New York: Perennial, 2000.

Strand, Mark, ed. *The Contemporary American Poets*. New York: World Publishing, 1969.

SELECTED FICTION AND NONFICTION

The Uncertain Certainty. Ann Arbor: University of Michigan Press, 1985.
Wonderful Words, Silent Truth: Essays on Poetry and a Memoir. Ann Arbor: University of Michigan Press, 1990.
Dimestore Alchemy: The Art of Joseph Cornell. New York: Ecco Press, 1992.
Unemployed Fortune Teller. Ann Arbor: University of Michigan Press, 1994.
Orphan Factory: Essays and Memoirs. Ann Arbor: University of Michigan Press, 1997.
A Fly in the Soup: Memoirs. Ann Arbor: University of Michigan Press, 2000.

SELECTED TRANSLATIONS

Four Yugoslav Poets. Northwood Narrows, NH: Lillabulero Press, 1970.
Lali'c, Ivan V. *Fire Gardens*. New York: New Rivers Press, 1970.
Popa, Vasko. *The Little Box*. Washington, DC: Charioteer Press, 1970.
Another Republic: An Anthology of European and South American Poetry. Editor, with Mark Strand. New York: Ecco Press, 1976.
Atlantis: Poems of Slavko Mihalic. Translator, with Peter Kastmiler. Greenfield Center, NY: Greenfield Review Press, 1987.
Popa, Vasko. *Homage to the Lame Wolf*. Oberlin, OH: Oberlin College Press, 1987.
Selected Poems of Tomaz Salamun. New York: Ecco Press, 1987.
Roll Call of Mirrors: Selected Poems of Ivan V. Lali'c. Middletown, CT: Wesleyan University Press, 1988.
Ristovic, Aleksandar. *Some Other Wine and Light*. Washington: Charioteer Press, 1989.
Janevski, Slavko. *Bandit Wind*. Takoma Park, MD: Dryad Press, 1991.
The Horse Has Six Legs: An Anthology of Serbian Poetry. St. Paul, MN: Graywolf Press, 1992.
Night Mail, Novica Tadic. Oberlin, OH: Oberlin College Press, 1992.

SELECTED RESOURCES FOR FURTHER REFERENCE

Baker, David. *Heresy and the Ideal: On Contemporary Poetry*. Fayetteville: University of Arkansas Press, 2000.
Lee, Alan, ed. *The Major Young Poets*. New York: World Publishing, 1971.
Parini, Jay. "A Thirst for the Divine." *Nation* 274 (2002): 19.
Stitt, Peter. *Uncertainty and Plentitude: Five Contemporary Poets*. Iowa City: University of Iowa Press, 1997.

Joel Werley

Cathy Song

(1955–)

Korean American, Chinese American

BIOGRAPHY

Cathy Song was born in Honolulu, Hawaii, where she has spent all of her life except for seven years in New England and three years in Colorado. She attended Wellesley College, where she earned a B.A. in 1977, and Boston University, from which she received her M.F.A. in 1981. Song published her first book, *Picture Bride,* in 1983, for which she received the Yale Younger Poets Award; it was also nominated for the National Book Critics' Circle Award. She has been the recipient of the Shelley Memorial Award, the Hawai'i Award for Literature, the Frederick Bock Prize, the Elliot Cades Award for Literature, a National Endowment for the Arts fellowship, and the Pushcart Prize. Song's subsequent volumes of poetry are *Frameless Windows, Squares of Light* (1988), *School Figures* (1994), and *The Land of Bliss* (2001). In addition to being widely anthologized, Song's poems have appeared on buses in Atlanta and subway cars in New York.

Song does not like to be thought of as an Asian American or Hawaiian writer, hoping that her work transcends regional and ethnic categorizations. Thus, while her writing certainly deals with her ethnicity, its angle is the family relationships and minutiae of everyday life that are universal, rather than explicit exploration of her Korean American and Chinese American experience. Song has said, however, that "to be a writer you have to be a feminist," noting that a writer looks at things from outside the status quo perspective, particularly a writer who offers a minority perspective (Oi).

Cathy Song has been involved in several ways with Bamboo Ridge Press, a Hawaiian publishing house and journal that was started in the late 1970s, before ethnic literature was widely read, to promote local Hawaiian literature. Bamboo Ridge was a major influence on Song, dating from her reading a book of short stories they published when she was starting out as a writer: *A Small Obligation and Other Stories of Hilo,* by Susan Nunes (1982). In these stories, Song found characters whom she could recognize in her own life, and

Photo from *School Figures*, by Cathy Song, © 1994. Reprinted by permission of the University of Pittsburgh Press.

this helped both her and other Hawaiian writers of her generation to see their own experiences as valid material for literature.

Bamboo Ridge published Song's early work, as well as the anthology she edited with Juliet Kono, *Sister Stew: Fiction and Poetry by Women* (1991). Song worked at the press in many capacities over the years—as mail-room clerk, as guest editor, as silent auction cochair, and as managing editor. She speaks of the love and confidence she found in the community at Bamboo Ridge Press—of the faith people had in her to learn on the job, of the labor of love that the jobs became, and of the dedication to helping the next generation of writers recognize their potential. She has also returned this guidance through teaching both writing workshops and university writing courses. Currently Song is the treasurer of Bamboo Ridge Press in Honolulu.

THEMES AND CONCERNS

Cathy Song's writing uses strong visual imagery of the everyday objects to discuss family relationships, community, and immigration. By examining the seemingly mundane and connecting everyday objects and occurrences to art, she creates a world of evocative symbols where a loaf of bread rising becomes unquestionably sensual, toast crumbling comes to signify age and its effects, and stray cats are associated with an unwanted pregnancy. Daily observations are transformed to a greater significance. The poet and subject of the poems stand apart, the poet primarily an observer rather than an actor.

An overarching theme in Song's work is that of family relationships. She writes of the ties between parent and child, between siblings, between husband and wife. She also writes of memories of grandparents and of ancestral history. This theme necessarily brings Song back to the topics of immigration and her Chinese and Korean ancestry. She describes her grandmother's coming from Korea to Hawaii as a picture bride in the poem and collection of that title. In writing about immigration, Song's focus is on the act of leaving. What were her ancestors thinking when they left? What did they bring with them and what was their experience as they arrived? There is a sense of connection to the old land, the former home, but this connection is ephemeral, as if its very existence is called into question through the act of leaving. The connection, however, lives on in the small details and objects of day-to-day life in an Asian American community—the continuous references to mahjong tiles, to jade, to rice paper. These ruminations also strongly reflect the Hawaiian landscape—her grandfather's working in the sugar cane fields, the ubiquity of flowers as both detail and metaphor, the ginger and cowrie shells—and include a string of names, places, terminology, and plants that are distinctly Hawaiian and thus sometimes defined in a glossary in Song's poetry collections.

In addition to painting her own images, Song writes about the work of artists such as Georgia O'Keeffe and Kitagawa Utamaro, connecting their work to the details of daily life and integrating the experience of art and experience of the world so that neither is elevated above the other. Song also addresses the inherent gaps between representation and reality, as shown in the picture bride concept, where the reality can never live up to the expectations the image foists upon its viewer. Color and landscape are central to her poems. Other recurrent imagery includes food, eggshells, insects, and houses—doors, curtains, kitchens, and windows. Song creates a fragile and light landscape in which her subjects act out daily acts of significance.

POETRY COLLECTIONS

Picture Bride. New Haven, CT: Yale University Press, 1983.
Frameless Windows, Squares of Light. New York: W. W. Norton, 1988.
School Figures. Pittsburgh, PA: University of Pittsburgh Press, 1994.
The Land of Bliss. Pittsburgh, PA: University of Pittsburgh Press, 2001.

SELECTED ANTHOLOGIES WHERE POETRY APPEARS

Bruchac, Joseph, ed. *Breaking Silence: An Anthology of Contemporary Asian American Poets*. Greenfield Center, NY: Greenfield Review Press, 1994.

Dove, Rita, and David Lehman, eds. *The Best American Poetry 2000*. New York: Scribner, 2000.

Gemin, Pamela, and Paula Sergi, eds. *Boomer Girls: Poems by Women from the Baby Boom Generation*. Iowa City: University of Iowa Press, 1999.

Gillan, Maria M., and Jennifer Gillan, eds. *Unsettling America: An Anthology of Contemporary Multicultural Poetry*. New York: Penguin Books, 1994.

Hall, Donald, ed. *To Read a Poem*. Fort Worth, TX: Harcourt Brace Jovanovich, 1992.

Hongo, Garrett, ed. *The Open Boat: Poems from Asian America*. New York: Anchor Books Doubleday, 1993.

Peacock, Molly, ed. *Poetry in Motion: 100 Poems from the Subways and Buses*. New York: W. W. Norton, 1996.

Shinder, Jason, ed. *More Light: Father & Daughter Poems—A Twentieth-Century American Selection*. San Diego, CA: Harcourt Brace, 1993.

Smith, Dave, ed. *The Morrow Anthology of Younger American Poets*. New York: Quill, 1985.

SELECTED ADDITIONAL WORK

Sister Stew: Fiction and Poetry by Women. Editor, with Juliet Kono. Honolulu, HI: Bamboo Ridge Press, 1991.

SELECTED RESOURCES FOR FURTHER REFERENCE

"Cathy Song." In *Asian American Literature: Reviews and Criticism of Works by American Writers of Asian Descent*. Ed. Lawrence J. Trudeau. Detroit, MI: Gale, 1999, 421–437.

Fujita-Sato, Gayle K. "'Third World' as Place and Paradigm in Cathy Song's Picture Bride." *MELUS: The Journal of the Society for the Study of the Multi-Ethnic Literature of the United States* 15 (Spring 1988): 49–72.

Oi, Cynthia. "Chick Chat: A Four-Way Conversation with Hawaii's Foremost Writing Women." *Honolulu Star-Bulletin,* February 5, 2001. Online. www.starbulletin.com/2001/02/05/features/story1.html.

Sumida, Stephen. *And the View from the Shore: Literary Traditions of Hawaii.* Seattle: University of Washington Press, 1991.

Wallace, Patricia. "Divided Loyalties: Literal and Literary in the Poetry of Lorna Dee Cervantes, Cathy Song, and Rita Dove." *MELUS: The Journal of the Society for the Study of the Multi-Ethnic Literature of the United States* 18.3 (Fall 1993): 3–20.

Mary Tasillo

Courtesy of Gary Soto.

Gary Soto

(1952–)

Chicano/Mexican American

BIOGRAPHY

Gary Soto was born in Fresno, California, to Manuel and Angie (Treviño) Soto, American-born parents of Mexican ancestry. Living in Fresno, an industrial city in the heart of the San Joaquin Valley, Soto's family worked in factories and fields, and this setting is present in most of his writings. When Soto was five years old, his father died as a result of a factory accident, and so, while growing up, Soto spent time himself as a farmworker in order to help with family expenses.

After graduating from high school in 1970, Soto enrolled in Fresno City College. He intended to pursue a degree in geography but was attracted to writing after reading the poem "Unwanted," by Edward Field. Soto transferred to California State University, Fresno, where he studied with poet Philip Levine, to whose work Soto's has been compared. In 1974, he earned a B.A. from California State University, Fresno, and in 1976 an M.F.A. from the University of California, Riverside. Over the years he has taught as a visiting instructor at a wide range of colleges and universities, but Soto's main academic home has been the University of California, Berkeley, where he held a full-time appointment in English and Chicano studies from 1979 to 1993. Since 1993 he has taught part-time while devoting himself full-time to writing and traveling to conduct readings, workshops, and other forms of contact with his large and growing audience.

Gary Soto first gained notice when, in 1975, he won the *Discovery/The Nation* prize for unpublished poets. The following year his first volume of poems, *The Elements of San Joaquin,* received the International Poetry Forum award for the United States. Soto continues to publish poetry, and his *New and Selected Poems* (1995) was a finalist for both the National Book Award and the *Los Angeles Times* Book Prize. He has also achieved great success writing fiction and nonfiction for adults, as well as poetry, prose, and picture books for younger readers ranging from kindergarten to high school age.

Soto has won numerous awards for publications in all these genres and has received prestigious fellowships from the Guggenheim Foundation and National Endowment for the Arts. He is also comfortable working in nonprint media. He has completed two short films for younger readers and maintains his own Web site, garysoto.com, which he wisely recommends as the best source of accurate information about his life, career, and emerging projects. Soto is married to Catherine Oda, with whom he has one daughter, Mariko, and lives in Berkeley, California. Soto also proudly lists his membership in the Royal Chicano Navy.

THEMES AND CONCERNS

A full appreciation of Soto's work would include comment on his prose and writing for children and young adults, but the scope of this entry focuses on his poetry for adults. Those interested primarily in this body of work will immediately be struck by Soto's starkly documented images of working-class life in California's Central Valley. He captures the natural environment of dust, fields, factory machines, sweat, and baking sunlight, as well as the people of all ages living, working, and humanizing this setting. Critics have compared Soto's portraits with grim prophets of modernity such as Philip Levine, James Wright, and T. S. Eliot. While grounded in the material circumstances of working-class Chicano life, Soto broadens the scope of his creative expression in several ways. He adds existential depth by relating his imagistic details to large themes of life and death, friendship, romantic love, and systemic and interpersonal violence.

His poetry also achieves universalizing ballast through humor. This aspect, which arguably has increased over time, can be self-deprecating or ironic, as when he compares Mexican factory workers fleeing an immigration raid to health-conscious suburbanites who take up jogging. His first-person poems are confessional and introspective, adding a different kind of spiritual leavening to a bedrock of bleak naturalistic imagery. Finally, his poetry often exhibits an imaginative force in which natural objects take on supernatural qualities. When birds embody premonitions or an uncle's graying hair transforms into butterflies, we may feel ourselves entering the literary universe of magical realism. This effect is significant in suggesting how Soto, in verses that are written for the most part in clear, everyday English, evokes an intensely felt experience of Chicano ethnicity. While touching on universal themes that will interest general audiences, Soto has built his poetic world with landscapes, voices, names, and (in the case of magical realism) literary cultural contexts that are both American and decidedly Latin American.

POETRY COLLECTIONS

Heaven. West Chester, PA: Aralia Press, 1970.
The Elements of San Joaquin. Pittsburgh, PA: University of Pittsburgh Press, 1977.
The Tale of Sunlight. Pittsburgh, PA: University of Pittsburgh Press, 1978.
Where Sparrows Work Hard. Pittsburgh, PA: University of Pittsburgh Press, 1981.
Black Hair. Pittsburgh, PA: University of Pittsburgh Press, 1985.
A Fire in My Hands. New York: Scholastic, 1990.
Who Will Know Us? San Francisco, CA: Chronicle Books, 1990.
Home Course in Religion. San Francisco, CA: Chronicle Books, 1991.
New and Selected Poems. San Francisco, CA: Chronicle Books, 1995.
The Sparrows Move South: Early Poems. Berkeley, CA: Bancroft Library Press, 1995.
Super-Eight Movies: Poems. With John Digby. Tuscaloosa, AL: Lagniappe Press, 1996.
Junior College: Poems. San Francisco, CA: Chronicle Books, 1997.
100 Parades. With Molly Fisk. San Francisco: California Poets in the Schools, 2000.
Shadow of the Plum: Poems. San Diego, CA: Cedar Hill, 2002.

SELECTED ANTHOLOGIES WHERE POETRY APPEARS

Adame, Leonard, ed. *Entrance: 4 Chicano Poets—Leonard Adame, Luis Omar Salinas, Gary Soto, Ernesto Trejo.* Greenfield Center, NY: Greenfield Review Press, 1975.
Carlson, Lori M., ed. *Cool Salsa: Bilingual Poems on Growing Up Latino in the United States.* New York: Fawcett Juniper, 1995.
Collins, Billy, ed. *Poetry 180: A Turning Back to Poetry.* New York: Random House, 2003.
Espada, Martín, ed. *El Coro: A Chorus of Latino and Latina Poetry.* Amherst: University of Massachusetts Press, 1997.
Gillan, Maria, and Jennifer Gillan, eds. *Unsettling America: An Anthology of Contemporary Multicultural Poetry.* New York: Penguin, 1994.
Vecchione, Patrice, ed. *The Body Eclectic: An Anthology of Poems.* New York: Holt, 2002.

SELECTED FICTION, NONFICTION, AND EDITED COLLECTIONS

Living up the Street: Narrative Recollections. San Francisco, CA: Strawberry Hill, 1985.
Small Faces. Houston, TX: Arte Público Press, 1986.
California Childhood: Recollections and Stories of the Golden State. Editor. Berkeley, CA: Creative Arts, 1988.
Lesser Evils: Ten Quartets. Houston, TX: Arte Público Press, 1988.
A Summer Life. Hanover, NH: University Press of New England, 1990.
Pieces of the Heart: New Chicano Fiction. San Francisco, CA: Chronicle Books, 1993.
Boys at Work. New York: Delacourte, 1995.
Chato's Kitchen. New York: Putnam, 1995.
Everyday Seductions. Editor. Sea Bright, NJ: Ploughshare Press, 1995.

The Mustache. With Celina Hinojosa. New York: Putnam, 1995.
Summer on Wheels. New York: Scholastic, 1995.
Off and Running. New York: Delacourte, 1996.
The Old Man and His Door. New York: Putnam, 1996.
Snapshots of the Wedding. New York: Putnam, 1996.
Buried Onions. San Diego, CA: Harcourt, 1997.
Novio Boy. San Diego, CA: Harcourt, 1997.
Big Bushy Mustache. New York: Knopf, 1998.
Petty Crimes. San Diego, CA: Harcourt, 1998.
A Natural Man. San Francisco, CA: Chronicle Books, 1999.
The Effects of Knut Hamsun on a Fresno Boy: Recollections and Short Essays. New York: Persea, 2000.
Nickel and Dime. Albuquerque: University of New Mexico Press, 2000.
Poetry Lover. Albuquerque: University of New Mexico Press, 2001.
Amnesia an a Republican County. Albuquerque: University of New Mexico Press, 2003.

SELECTED POETRY AND PROSE WORKS FOR CHILDREN

Father Is a Pillow Tied to a Broom. Pittsburgh, PA: Slow Loris Press, 1980.
The Cat's Meow. San Francisco, CA: Strawberry Hill, 1987.
Baseball in April and Other Stories. San Diego, CA: Harcourt, 1990.
Taking Sides. San Diego, CA: Harcourt, 1991.
The Skirt. New York: Delacourte, 1992.
Too Many Tamales. New York: Putnam, 1992.
Local News. San Diego, CA: Harcourt, 1993.
The Pool Party. New York: Delacourte, 1993.
Crazy Weekend. New York: Scholastic, 1994.
Chato and the Party Animals. New York: Putnam, 1999.
Nerdlandia: A Play. New York: Putnam, 1999.
Jessie de la Cruz: Profile of a United Farm Worker. New York: Persea, 2000.
My Little Car (Mi Carrito). With Linda Dalal Sawaya. New York: Putnam, 2000.
Fearless Fernie: Hanging Out with Fernie and Me. New York: Putnam, 2002.
If the Shoe Fits. New York: Putnam, 2002.

SELECTED RESOURCES FOR FURTHER REFERENCE

De La Fuentes, Patricia. "Ambiguity in the Poetry of Gary Soto." *Revista Chicano-Riqueña* 11.2 (1983): 34–39.
———. "Entropy in the Poetry of Gary Soto: The Dialectics of Violence." *Revista de Temas Hispánicos* 5.1 (1987): 111–120.
———. "Mutability and Stasis: Images of Time in Gary Soto's *Black Hair*." *Americas Review* 17.1 (1989): 100–107.
D'Evelyn, Tom "Soto's Poetry: Unpretentious Language of the Heart." *Christian Science Monitor* 77 (6 March 1985): 19–20.
Fields, Alicia. "Small but Telling Moments." *Bloomsbury Review* 7 (January/February 1987): 10.

Reid, Alastair "The Lenore Marshall Poetry Prize." *Saturday Review* 6 (27 October 1979): 38.

Weigl, Bruce. "Towards a Fine Scrutiny of Experience: Contemporary Poetry in Review." *Poet Lore* 77 (Spring 1982): 44–47.

Williamson, Alan. "In a Middle Style." *Poetry* 135 (March 1980): 348–354.

Kevin Meehan

Gerald Stern

(1925–)

Jewish American

Photo by AP/Wide World Photos.

BIOGRAPHY

Born in Pittsburgh, Pennsylvania, in 1925, Gerald Stern was New Jersey's first Poet Laureate. He has published twelve books of poetry and won many prestigious awards, including the National Book Award, a Guggenheim fellowship, the Lamont Prize, a PEN Award, and the Ruth Lilly Prize for Lifetime Achievement.

In a 1998 interview with Elizabeth Farnsworth on PBS's *Online Newshour,* Stern said that he was neither encouraged to, nor discouraged from, becoming a poet by his parents, who immigrated to the United States from Eastern Europe. "There were no books in my house. . . . And there was no discussion about literature or writing, or reading. It was just a non-existent subject." In fact, Stern did not publish his first collection of poetry until he was forty-three. This collection, *Rejoicings,* won the Lamont Poetry Prize, as did his second book, *Lucky Life* (1976).

At age nine, Stern was profoundly affected by the death of his eight-year-old sister. As a teenager, Stern was a voracious reader. He specifically enjoyed reading religious and political works, and these themes carry over to his own poetry. While Stern does identify himself as a Jewish poet, he does not always consciously identify himself as such. In a 1998 interview with Gary Pacernick for the *American Poetry Review,* Stern explains why:

> I've written poems about the Holocaust . . . poems that turn into a Jewish subject. Different ethnic groups wear their ethnicity in different ways. I guess the more beleaguered they are, the more they feel that ethnic entity. I myself sometimes feel beleaguered as a Jew. I also feel beleaguered in various other ways: as an older person, as a man, as a poet, as a lifetime subversive at universities. (p. 41)

Gerald Stern earned an undergraduate degree from the University of Pittsburgh and was a graduate student at Columbia University. He also served in the U.S. Army. Stern's teaching career brought him to a number of colleges and universities, including Columbia University, New York University, the University of Pittsburgh, and Sarah Lawrence College. Throughout that time, his poetic reputation grew, something that he attributes largely to his many contributions to the highly regarded *American Poetry Review*. He retired in 1996, after teaching at the Writers' Workshop at the University of Iowa for twelve years.

Stern is divorced and has a daughter and a son. He currently lives in Lambertville, New Jersey.

THEMES AND CONCERNS

In a PBS interview with Elizabeth Farnsworth, Stern explained why he writes poetry: "I suppose as I'm explaining myself to others, I'm quintessentially explaining myself to myself." The poems are not confessional, and they do not aim to tell the poet's life story; rather, they are efforts to connect with the reader "so that my life is the reader's life, that the reader can zero in on those aspects of my life as I reveal them, that he can say, yes, that's it, that's what happens to me, that's true. I've been there."

There is a stream-of-consciousness quality to many of Stern's poems as the language gallops forward, twisting and turning on words or phrases. Reviewer John Taylor notices the effect of Stern's language: "Stern's serpentine, kaleidoscopic verses combine, as in a Cubist collage, unexpected juxtapositions or contradictory viewpoints" (p. 639). This is illustrated in "The Sorrows" (*Last Blue*), a poem that begins with the speaker picking up a plum tomato and develops to a reflection of a trip to Paris, a memory of falling down and being helped up, and an altercation with a Moroccan fruit vendor. In the convolutions of the language, space opens for the speaker's personal revelations: he is a grandson of a Polish rabbi, he had sold American typewriters in Paris. Stern combines the seemingly unrelated pieces of this jigsaw puzzle of memories seamlessly, picking up the reader and sweeping him or her along with the swiftly moving lines of poetry.

"The Sorrows," as do most of Stern's poems, echoes times long past. In crafting these reflections, the poet frequently mentions locations that have been central to his life, including many in Pennsylvania and New Jersey. Several pieces (for example, "An Explanation" and "Visiting My Own House in Iowa City") locate the poet as a resident of various states: Pennsylvania, Massachusetts, Iowa, New York. Stern's descriptions of these cities and their landmarks contain an unmistakable air of nostalgia and longing and connects the roving individual to fixed places along his journey. Further demonstrating Stern's reliance on memory, "Memoir" offers a reflection of childhood games and behaviors, moves to a memory of a girlfriend who played harp, and then evolves to a scene years later when the speaker and his wife are hosting a brunch where the harpist is performing. A mix of sentimental regret, long-ing, and nostalgia close this poem.

Images from nature demonstrate the poet's power of observation as the camera lens offers a broad view of the scene, zooms in, and then pans out again. Stern's gaze focuses on leaves that filter the sunlight, a fallen willow tree, and various types of fruit—including apricots, oranges, tomatoes, and strawberries—many of which are personified and yield a kind of blood as they release juice on the speaker's hands and fingers. A range of creatures, too, make their way into Stern's poetry, such as in "In Kovalchik's Garden" (*This Time*), where the speaker's eye lights on a solitary female cardinal exploring a dead pear tree and ridding the tree of its corpses (p. 19).

POETRY COLLECTIONS

Rejoicings, Poems: 1966–1972. Fredericton, N.B.: Fiddlehead Poetry Books, 1973.
Lucky Life. Pittsburgh, PA: Carnegie-Mellon University Press, 1976.
Two Long Poems. Pittsburgh, PA: Carnegie-Mellon University Press, 1977.
The Red Coal. Boston: Houghton Mifflin, 1981.
Paradise Poems. New York: Vintage Books, 1984.
Lovesick. New York: Harper & Row, 1987.
Death Mazurka: Poems. With Charles M. Fishman. Lubbock: Texas Tech University Press, 1989.
Leaving Another Kingdom: Selected Poems. New York: Harper & Row, 1990.
Bread Without Sugar. New York: W. W. Norton, 1993.
Odd Mercy. New York: W. W. Norton, 1995.
This Time: New and Selected Poems. New York: W. W. Norton, 1998.
Last Blue: Poems. New York: W. W. Norton, 2000.
American Sonnets. New York: W. W. Norton, 2002.

SELECTED ANTHOLOGIES AND WEB SITES WHERE POETRY APPEARS

Berg, Stephen, David Bonanno, and Arthur Vogelsang. *The Body Electric: America's Best Poetry from the American Poetry Review.* New York: W. W. Norton, 2000.
Collins, Billy, ed. *Poetry 180: A Turning Back to Poetry.* New York: Random House, 2003.
The Cortland Review no. 20. Online. www.courtlandreview.com.
Gillan, Maria M., and Jennifer Gillan, eds. *Unsettling America: An Anthology of Contemporary Multicultural Poetry.* New York: Penguin, 1994.
Norton Poets Online. www.nortonpoets.com.

SELECTED ADDITIONAL WORKS

Ploughshares Winter 1990–1991: The Literature of Ecstasy. Editor. Boston, MA: Ploughshares Books, 1990.
"Last Blue." *Poetry* 1177.5 (2001): 396–399.

SELECTED RESOURCES FOR FURTHER REFERENCE

Bedient, Calvin. "American Latitude." *Southern Review* 29.4 (1993): 782–792.

"Elizabeth Farnsworth Interviews Gerald Stern after He Wins the National Book Award." *Online Newshour.* www.pbs.org/newshour.

"Forecasts: Nonfiction." *Publishers Weekly* 247.8 (2000): 83.

Hass, Robert, and Yusef Komunyakaa. "How Poetry Helps People to Live Their Lives." *American Poetry Review* 28.5 (1999): 21–27.

Hillringhouse, Mark. "The Poetry of Gerald Stern." *Literary Review* 40.2 (1997): 346.

Pacernick, Gary. "Gerald Stern." *American Poetry Review* 27.4 (1998): 41–51.

Pinsker, Sanford. *Conversations with Contemporary American Writers.* Netherlands: Rodopi Bv Editions, 1985.

Schulman, Grace. "Dance, Song, and Light." *Nation* 266.17 (1998): 49–50, 57.

Taylor, John. "Last Blue." *Antioch Review* 59.3 (2001): 639–640.

Amy C. O'Brien

Mary TallMountain

(1918–1994)

American Indian (Athabaskan)

Photo by Lance Woodruff, courtesy of M. Catherine Costello, TallMountain Literary Executor.

BIOGRAPHY

Mary TallMountain was born Mary Demoski on June 19, 1918, in the small village of Nulato in Central Alaska, just below the Arctic Circle. Her father, Clem Stroupe, was an American of Scotch-Irish descent. While stationed in Nulato with the U.S. Army, he met her mother, Mary Joe Demoski, who was of Athabaskan and Russian descent. Mary Joe was stricken with tuberculosis even before her daughter was born. Two years later, she had a son, Billy. In 1922, knowing that she was dying, Mary Joe allowed her two children to be adopted by the Randles, the government doctor and his wife who worked in the American Indian village. They had already been caring for the children when Mary Joe was too weak to provide for them. Mary Joe gave her children to the doctor not only to give them experiences they would not have in their village, but also in hopes of preventing them from contracting tuberculosis, which was almost inevitable at the time. When the doctor and his wife made it known that they were moving from Nulato permanently, the tribal council intervened and decided that only Mary would be allowed to go. Her brother would have to stay in the village. Thirteen years later, Billy died of tuberculosis at the age of seventeen.

The life of Mary TallMountain is a journey filled with hardships. At age six, when she moved to Oregon with the Randles, she was taken from her mother and brother, removed from her village, and thrown into a completely different world. In addition, her new family would only let her speak English, and she was mocked by other children in school because she was an American Indian. Most horrible of all, Dr. Randle molested her habitually. Eventually, the Randles moved back to Alaska, to the Aleutian Islands, where they thought Mary TallMountain would be more comfortable. Here, Agnes Randle home schooled her for twelve hours each day. TallMountain began to read and write and published her first story in *Child Life* magazine in 1928 when she was ten.

In 1932 the Randles moved to California. Tragedy would again stalk Mary TallMountain. Her adoptive father lost all his savings in the Great Depression, and the family had to become migrant workers for a while. Eventually there were able to settle in Portland, Oregon. Dr. Randle died of heart failure the same year she graduated from high school. She married Dal Roberts at nineteen, but he died three years later. When Mary TallMountain was twenty-seven, Agnes Randle, plagued by both diabetes and Parkinson's disease, committed suicide.

TallMountain left Portland behind and moved to Reno, Nevada, where she became a legal secretary. In Reno, she rediscovered Catholicism and eventually became a secular Franciscan. In her forties, she moved to San Francisco and while there began to develop her addiction to alcohol, which she viewed as a response to the extraordinary tragedies in her life. Realizing the seriousness of her problem after several disturbing incidents, she gave up drinking "cold turkey." This experience is reflected in her writing and also in her empathy for the homeless, elderly, poor, and others abandoned by society. Now in control of her problem, she was able to start her own secretarial business, until once again tragedy struck. She was diagnosed with cancer at age fifty. Although she conquered the disease, it was the personal and financial toll forced her to give up her business and her apartment. Looking for a place she could afford, she moved to the infamous neighborhood of San Francisco known as the Tenderloin. Eventually, her illnesses allowed her to qualify for disability compensation, and finally she was free to read, write, and publish her poetry and stories. She became a regular contributor to *The Way of St. Francis.*

In 1974, upon a friend's recommendation, she took some of her poems to Paula Gunn Allen for a critique. The session turned into a lifelong friendship. Allen served as a mentor who offered encouragement, vision, and purpose to TallMountain. Most important, she encouraged Mary TallMountain to reconnect with her roots by returning to her village in Alaska, and later by relocating her father. In 1976, TallMountain attended a retreat in Arizona and recalled rumors that her father, who had removed himself from her life before her mother died, had gone to Tucson. She found her father through the phone book and remained with him for two years, until he died of cancer in 1978.

In 1977, at the age of fifty-nine, TallMountain published *Nine Poems,* her first chapbook of poetry. After her father's death, she received a grant to travel and teach in Alaskan schools. In 1987 she became a founding member of the Tenderloin Women Writers Workshop, a support group where local women shared their writing. Under her guidance, it became a close-knit community with its own identity and traditions. She continued to publish her poetry through the 1980s. In 1981 her chapbook *There Is No Word for Goodbye* won a Pushcart Prize, and she quickly gained recognition.

In 1992, Mary TallMountain suffered a stroke, which required her to limit her public engagements. That same year she moved to Petaluma, California, where she remained until her death on August 4, 1994. Today her legacy is carried on by the TallMountain Circle, a group whose mission is to preserve the memory of Mary TallMountain and to champion her favorite causes: mentoring other women writers and encouraging community service.

THEMES AND CONCERNS

Several basic themes recur in Mary TallMountain's poetry. One is the clash between Indian and Western cultures in this country, often a theme of Native poets. TallMountain reflects how this affects the individual in poems such as "Indian Blood," which tells how she was ridiculed by white schoolchildren in elementary school in Oregon. This and many other of her poems can be found in *Light on the Tent Wall* (1990), the definitive collection of Tall-Mountain poetry.

Because Mary TallMountain's life was so difficult, it is no surprise that much of her poetry reflects this sense of life as a continuous struggle, a journey from one hardship to the next. TallMountain expressed her spirituality through her poetry as well. She was intrigued by the contrast between Native American spirituality, with its respect for all living things, and Christianity. In poems like "Bright Shining," we see her efforts to reconcile one to the other through common threads.

Her concern for the loss of the natural world as mankind's destruction of nature continues unabated is another principal theme in Mary TallMountain's poetry. In "The Last Wolf," one of her most famous poems, she draws a parallel between her struggle for survival with cancer and the wolf's struggle for survival as man destroys his environment. As the poem ends, she and the wolf find comfort and healing in each other's company.

Childhood memories also play a central role in TallMountain's poetry. In *There Is No Word for Goodbye,* TallMountain chronicles these painful memories—so painful that she created a childhood alter ego named Lidwynne to comfort her through these difficult years (Moyers)—as well as stories told to her by her father as she nursed him during his final battle with cancer. Besides using her poetry for personal catharsis, she also believed that through her remembrances in her poetry and prose, she could help ensure that her Athabaskan people and their culture would not die.

Despite TallMountain's presence in American Indian anthologies of her time, there are few reviews of her collections and even less academic criticism on TallMountain. It is a tribute to her great work that despite this lack of scholarly attention, Mary TallMountain remains highly acclaimed as one of the most important writers of the Native American Renaissance.

POETRY COLLECTIONS

Nine Poems. San Francisco, CA: Friars Press, 1977.
Good Grease. New York: Strawberry Press, 1978.
Light on the Tent Wall: A Bridging. Los Angeles: American Indian Studies Center, University of California, 1990.
Matrilineal Cycle. Oakland, CA: Red Star Black Rose, 1990.
A Quick Brush of Wings. San Francisco, CA: Freedom Voices, 1991.
Listen to the Night: Poems to the Animal Spirits of Mother Earth. Ed. Ben Clarke. San Francisco, CA: Freedom Voices, 1995. (posthumous collection)

SELECTED ANTHOLOGIES WHERE POETRY APPEARS

Allen, Paula Gunn, ed. *Spider Woman's Granddaughters*. Boston, MA: Beacon, 1989.
Bledsoe, Lucy Jane, ed. *Goddesses We Ain't: Tenderloin Women Writers*. San Francisco, CA: Freedom Voices, 1992.
Clarke, Ben, ed. *Listen to the Night: Poems for the Animal Spirits of Mother Earth*. San Francisco, CA: Freedom Voices, 1995.
Lerner, Andrea, ed. *Dancing on the Rim of the World: An Anthology of Contemporary Northwest Native American Writing*. Tucson: Sun Tracks, University of Arizona, 1990.

ADDITIONAL WORK

Green March Moons. Berkeley, CA: New Seed Press, 1987.

SELECTED RESOURCES FOR FURTHER REFERENCE

Allen, Paula Gunn. *The Sacred Hoop: Recovering the Feminine in American Indian Traditions*. Boston, MA: Beacon Press, 1986.
Moyers, Bill. *The Power of the Word*. PBS, 1989.
Swann, Brian, and Arnold Krupat, eds. *I Tell You Now: Autobiographical Essays by Native American Writers*. Lincoln: University of Nebraska Press, 1987; Detroit, MI: Gale Research, 1988.
Wiget, Andrew, ed. *Dictionary of Native American Literature*. New York: Garland, 1994.

Sue Czerny

Luci Tapahonso

(1953–)

American Indian (Navajo)

Courtesy of the University of Kansas/University Relations.

BIOGRAPHY

Luci Tapahonso was born on November 8, 1953, in the Dine community of the Navajo nation in Shiprock, New Mexico. Her mother, Lucille Deschenne Tapahonso, was a member of the Salt Water Clan, and her father, Eugene Tapahonso, was a member of the Bitter Water Clan. The sixth of eleven children in her family, Luci Tapahonso grew up on Dinetah, the largest reservation in the United States, which straddles the corners of Arizona, New Mexico, Colorado, and Utah. She grew up speaking Dine, her native Navajo language, although her first written language was English. She attended elementary school at the Navajo Methodist Mission Boarding School in Farmington, New Mexico, but went on to graduate from Shiprock High School.

Tapahonso attended college at the University of New Mexico, where she received a bachelor's degree in English in 1980 and a master's degree in English and creative writing in 1983. While there, she met Leslie Marmon Silko, who was already a famous American Indian poet. Tapahonso showed Silko some of her poetry, which she had been writing quietly for years. As Tapahonso tells Joseph Bruchac in *Survival This Way,* Silko not only encouraged her to take her poetry seriously, but convinced her that it was important to publish her work and add her voice to the collective American Indian heritage (p. 279). Tapahonso's first two books, *Seasonal Woman* and *One More Shiprock Night,* were both published in 1981 while she was attending graduate school.

Upon graduation in 1983, Luci Tapahonso became an assistant professor of English, American studies, and American Indian studies at the University of New Mexico; she stayed there until 1989. She married Earl Ortiz, an artist, and they had two daughters together, Misty Dawn and Lori Tazbah. These two daughters are the inspiration for and subjects of many of Tapahonso's poems. She and Ortiz divorced in 1987.

In 1989 she took a job as an assistant professor at the University of Kansas and moved to Lawrence, Kansas. The same year, she married Bob G. Martin,

283

who was the president of the Haskell College of Indian Nations. In the preface of *Saanii Dahataal,* she writes that while the area where she lived in Kansas was beautiful, it was very different from the landscape of her native New Mexico. Her poetry and essays from this period contain the realization that her roots in the Navajo and in New Mexico were very deep, and she would always remain part of that community and feel at home on the farm where she grew up.

During this time she published three additional books containing her poetry. In 1987, *A Breeze Swept Through* was published. The next two collections, *Saanii Dahataal* (1993) and *Blue Horses Rush In* (1999), are generally considered her best works. In these, she experiments with language and blends poetry, prose, and prayer together in such an intricate way that she established herself as an American Indian poet comparable to Leslie Silko and Louise Erdrich.

After ten years in Kansas, Luci Tapahonso returned to the Southwest as a professor in the English department at the University of Arizona in Tucson, where she is now a professor of American Indian studies. No matter where she has lived, she has always been heavily involved in community service. Among her many appointments, she has served on the New Mexico Arts Commission Literature Panel (1984–1986) and the Kansas Arts Commission Literature Panel (1990). She was a commissioner on the Kansas Arts Commission (1992–1996), served on the board of directors of Habitat for Humanity (1990–1994), and is currently on the board of the Smithsonian's National Museum of the American Indian.

In addition, Luci Tapahonso has received many awards for her literary contributions and her leadership. In 1998 she received the Kansas Governor's Art Award, and in the same year she was awarded the Mountain and Plains Booksellers Association Poetry Award for her work *Blue Horses Rush In.* In 1999 she received the prestigious Storyteller of the Year Award from the Wordcraft Circle of Native Writers. She also received a Distinguished Woman Award from both the National Association of Women in Education and the Girl Scouts Council. In 2002 she was honored with the American Indian Leadership Award in recognition of her leadership in education, including the establishment of a master's degree program in Indigenous Nations studies at the University of Kansas.

THEMES AND CONCERNS

Luci Tapahonso has published five collections of her work that include her poetry. Although each has it own individual focus, three central themes infuse her work. First is her strong sense of family and community. She communicates a reverence for the Dine land where she grew up. It is a sense that no matter where she lives, she really belongs to the Indian lands near her childhood home of Shiprock, New Mexico. Second, many of her poems are based on memories of herself or others. These memories convey her profound respect for the Navajo traditions and the humor of her people. Her poetry is a unique blending of poetry, song, and prayer and often contains Navajo phrases amid the English. In interviews, she has explained that she writes her poetry first in Navajo and then translates the poetry to English. Sometimes she even preserves the Navajo phrasing and word order in the English translation, as in the poem "Hills Brothers Coffee." Often, she writes a song to accompany her poetry in Navajo, which she sings when she reads her own poetry. It is unfortunate that the music cannot accompany the poems and translation of her works in her books. The third central theme in her poetry is the strength of the women in her culture. Looking at her body of work, all facets of women's lives from birth to death can be found, and the women portrayed all show inner strength even when faced with death.

Her first two poetry collections were published simultaneously in 1981. *One More Shiprock Night* and *Seasonal Woman* are collections that center on the memories, traditions, and sense of community within the Navajo nation. *One More Shiprock Night* includes poetry about Tapahonso's grandmother, mother, and daughters, emphasizing not only the physical continuity of her family, but also the continuity of the Navajo culture, which is preserved by the stories and memories the women pass on to each other. *Seasonal Woman* presents the tragic character of Leona Gray, who appears in many of Tapahonso's poems, several of which address themes of racism and violence. Tapahonso's third collection of poetry is *A Breeze Swept Through,* and in it she begins to explore the rhythms of speech and the interplay of the Navajo and English patterns.

Saanii Dahataal: The Women Are Singing, a highly acclaimed collection of poetry interspersed with prose, is a major contribution to Native American poetry. Written while she was residing in Kansas, this work reflects her sense that she belongs to the place and people where she grew up. There is an underlying theme that people will always be drawn to return to the place they belong. This collection also shows her mastery of translating into English her Navajo-written and Navajo-sung work. She knows when to translate and when to leave the Navajo words and when to preserve the Navajo speech patterns in the English. Her latest work, *Blue Horses Rush In,* returns to her main themes of community and celebrates the joys and sadness of everyday life and rituals of her family and her Navajo community. Beginning and ending with poems about her granddaughters, *Blue Horses* honors the continuity of life that survives the greatest joys and deepest sorrows of ordinary lives.

POETRY COLLECTIONS

One More Shiprock Night: Poems. San Antonia, TX: Tejas Arts Press, 1981.
Seasonal Woman. Santa Fe, NM: Tooth of Time, 1981.
A Breeze Swept Through It. Albuquerque, NM: West End, 1987.
Saanii Dahataal: The Women Are Singing. Tucson: University of Arizona Press, 1993.
Blue Horses Rush In. Tucson: University of Arizona Press, 1997.

SELECTED ANTHOLOGIES WHERE POETRY APPEARS

Allen, Paula Gunn. *The Sacred Hoop: Recovering the Feminine in American Indian Traditions.* Boston, MA: Beacon Press, 1992.

Gattuso, John, ed. *Circle of Nations: Voices and Visions of American Indians.* Hillsboro, NM: Beyond Words Press, 1993.

Kallet, Marilyn, and Patricia Clark, eds. *Worlds in Our Words: Contemporary American Women Writers.* New York: Prentice Hall, 1997.

Melendez, A. Gabriel, ed. *Multicultural Southwest: A Reader.* Tucson: University of Arizona Press, 2001.

Nolte, Judy, ed. *Open Places, City Spaces: Contemporary Writers on the Changing Southwest.* Tucson: University of Arizona Press, 1994.

Vizenor, Gerald, ed. *Native American Literature: A Brief Introduction and Anthology.* New York: HarperCollins, 1995.

SELECTED ADDITIONAL WORKS

"Singing in Navajo, Writing in English: The Poetics of Four Navajo Writers." *Culturefront* 2.2 (1993): 36–41.

Bah Bah's Baby Brother Is Born. Washington, DC: National Organization on Fetal Alcohol Syndrome, 1994.

Navajo ABC. New York: Macmillan, 1995.

Songs of Shiprock Fair. Walnut, CA: Kiva, 1999.

SELECTED RESOURCES FOR FURTHER REFERENCE

Bruchac, Joseph. "A MELUS Interview: Luci Tapahonso." *MELUS: The Journal of the Society for the Study of the Multi-Ethnic Literature of the United States* 11 (Winter 1984): 85–91.

———. *Survival This Way: Interviews with American Indian Poets.* Tucson: University of Arizona Press, 1987, 271–285.

Farah, Cynthia. *Literature and Landscape: Writers in the Southwest.* El Paso: Texas Western Press, 1988.

Moulin, Sylvie. "Nobody Is an Orphan." *Studies in American Indian Literatures* 3.3 (1991): 14–18.

Owens, Louis. *Mixedblood Messages: Literature, Film, Family, Place.* Norman: University of Oklahoma Press, 1998.

This Is about Vision: Interviews with Southwestern Writers. Ed. William Balassi, John F. Crawford, and Annie O. Eysturoy. Albuquerque: University of New Mexico Press, 1987.

Sue Czerny

Quincy Troupe

(1943–)

African American

BIOGRAPHY

Quincy Troupe, author of fourteen books and numerous articles and founder and editor of several journals, was born in New York City on July 23, 1943, to Quincy and Dorothy Troupe. As a baseball player for the old Negro Leagues, Quincy Troupe Sr. moved his family all over the world. Although the Troupes lived in St. Louis, Missouri, Mexico, Cuba, Puerto Rico, and Venezuela, St. Louis was the most influential residence for Quincy Troupe Jr., who was greatly affected by the language and culture of African Americans in this neighborhood home.

Originally, Troupe was a basketball player, playing in high school, college, and the U.S. Army. While stationed in France, Troupe suffered an injury that ended his career, which is when Troupe started to focus on his writing. His first work was a poorly written novel, and as a result he began writing poetry. At first, Troupe studied different forms of poetry in an effort to imitate them. These same forms—tankas, haikus, villanelles, sonnets, and sestinas, among others—are still employed by the poet today. However, the forms are no longer mere imitations. As Troupe has said, "If I do work in another form, I'm about putting my own stamp on the form" (Turner, p. 432). Interestingly, his poetry style has shifted over the course of his career, from minimalism and brevity to increasing complexity and depth.

Troupe is a prolific writer who has worked in many genres. His first poem, titled "What Is a Black Man?" was published in 1964 in *Paris Match*. His first poetry collection, *Embryo Poems, 1967–1971*, was published in 1972, followed in 1978 by American Book Award winner *Snake-Back Solos: Selected Poems, 1969–1977*. He has published a total of six poetry collections, including his 2000 publication *Transcircularities: New and Selected Poems*. In virtually all of his poetry, music, especially jazz, structures and underpins his writing.

This poet is also well known for work in other genres and media. He has authored *The Inside Story of TV's "Roots"* (1978), which chronicled the television show *Roots,* and *James Baldwin: The Legacy* (1989). Among jazz aficionados, he is acclaimed for his book *Miles Davis: The Autobiography* (1989), which garnered him a second American Book Award. This work later inspired his memoir, *Miles and Me: A Memoir of Miles Davis* (2000), which explores Troupe's friendship with Davis and the influence the musician had on Troupe's life and works. Troupe also received a Peabody Award for writing and coproducing *The Miles Davis Radio Project.*

Among his many accolades, Troupe has received the National Endowment for the Arts award in poetry (1978) and the New York State Council for the Arts fellowship in poetry (1987). He was featured on Bill Moyers's PBS special *The Power of the Word,* and in June 2002 Troupe was named California's first state Poet Laureate. Only four months later, however, amid scandal surrounding falsified claims on his résumé, Troupe resigned the position.

Troupe has led an extended academic teaching career. Most recently, Troupe taught creative writing and American and Caribbean literature at the University of California in San Diego. Troupe also taught creative writing for the Watts Writers' Movement (1966–1968), creative writing and African American literature at the University of California in Los Angeles (1968), creative writing and Third World literature at Ohio University (1969–1972), Third World literature at Richmond College (1972), and writing at Columbia University (1985). He continues to be an active performer and regularly presents his poetry at a variety of colleges, universities, and poetry slams and fairs. Troupe is married to Margaret Porter; the couple have four children: Antoinette, Tymme, Quincy, and Porter.

THEMES AND CONCERNS

Troupe tackles a number of themes and concerns in his work. First and foremost, Troupe's writings are grounded in music, specifically blues, swing, jazz, Latin, and bebop. Growing up in St. Louis, Troupe was exposed to many visiting musical icons, including Dizzy Gillespie, Roy Eldridge, and Louis Armstrong. He grew up listening to Latin music of the countries he lived in at various times and the jazz and classical music his mother loved. Although Troupe experienced a variety of musical genres, blues and Latin music remain at the center of his works. The poem "Follow the North Star Boogaloo" is a prime example of how music has influenced Troupe's writing. This particular poem developed from a conversation among teenage Harlemites on which Troupe eavesdropped. At the same time, Troupe adds his voice into the poem, as well as the voice of history. The voices are separated only by the musical tone of the poem. The poem "The Sound, Breaking Away," from the collection *Avalanche,* is another fine example of his use of internal rhymes and jazz rhythms. Most of all, Troupe was influenced by Miles Davis. Troupe states in his interview with Douglas Turner, "Miles set me on a path that is remarkable in a lot of ways. He's the one that set me on the path to writing and using my imagination, and being creative" (p. 433).

Music infiltrates Troupe's writing in a variety of ways. Troupe's work follows particular rhythms of music, including fast speeds and free-verse lines, and is grounded in oral rhythms, which are a large part of the African American culture. Troupe's experiences growing up in a Baptist church, singing in the church choir, and hearing the language and style of the preacher have all had an impact on his style. For example, the title poem in *Avalanche* reads and sounds like a sermon delivered by a preacher. In *Choruses*, Miles Davis and Muhal Abrams are the subjects of several poems. In 1991, Troupe scripted a film about Thelonious Monk. Troupe has also praised, imitated, or commemorated John Coltrane, Duke Ellington, and Bud Powell in his poems.

Troupe has written about other people, issues, and events as well. *Choruses* discusses the Monica Lewinsky scandal and the Heaven's Gate mass suicide. This same collection pays tribute to athletes Michael Jordan, Sammy Sosa, Mark McGuire, artist George Lewis, and painter Robert Colescott. Troupe also investigates the nature of poetry as performance. This is evidenced in *Avalanche,* wherein the poem "The Architecture of Speech" explores the ways people use language. The same topic is present in several poems in *Embryo.* Likewise, Troupe explores the changing nature of language in the United Stated as different cultures influence one another. *Skulls Along the River* blends myth, history, and the spiritual world with daily activities. Racial politics also plays a role in Troupe's poetry. For example, in "A Response to All You 'Angry White Males,'" Troupe condemns Caucasians for the slaughtering of American Indians and the lynching of African Americans.

Troupe's versatility and broad professional life have made him a well-respected poet who will likely influence generations of African American artists for many years to come.

POETRY COLLECTIONS

Embryo Poems, 1967–1971. New York: Barlenmir, 1972.
Snake-Back Solos: Selected Poems, 1969–1977. New York: I. Reed Books, 1978.
Skulls Along the River. New York: I. Reed Books, 1984.
Weather Reports. New York: Writers and Readers, 1991.
Avalanche. Minneapolis, MN: Coffee House Press, 1996.
Choruses. Minneapolis, MN: Coffee House Press, 1999.
Transcircularities: New and Selected Poems. Minneapolis, MN: Coffee House Press, 2002.

SELECTED ADDITIONAL WORKS

Giant Talk: An Anthology of Third World Writings. Compiler, with Rainer Schulte. New York: Random House, 1975.
The Inside Story of TV's "Roots." New York: Warner Books, 1978.
Miles: The Autobiography. New York: Simon & Schuster 1978.
James Baldwin: The Legacy. Editor. New York: Simon & Schuster, 1989. (Includes Troupe's interview with Baldwin.)
Miles and Me. Berkeley: University of California Press, 2000.

SELECTED RESOURCES FOR FURTHER REFERENCE

"Forecasts." *Publishers Weekly* 246.35 (1999): 78.

Gotera, Vince. "Synecdoche." *North American Review* 288.5 (Sept./Oct. 2003): 50.

Keita, Nzadi. "Quincy Troupe." *American Visions* 8 (1993): 30–33.

"Language Invented, or What? A Panel on Poetry." *Antioch Review* 55.2 (Spring 1997): 193–197.

Spilecki, Susan. "Avalanche" (review). *MELUS: The Journal of the Society for the Study of the Multi-Ethnic Literature of the United States* 23.3 (Fall 1998): 216.

Turner, Douglas. "Miles and Me: An Interview with Quincy Troupe." *African American Review* 36.3 (Fall 2002): 429–434.

Alyce Baker

José García Villa

(1908?–1997)

Filipino, Filipino American

BIOGRAPHY

José García Villa, experimental poet and fiction writer, was born in Manila. He published his first short story in the *Manila Times* as a teenager, although when he went to the University of the Philippines he enrolled first in the College of Medicine and then transferred to the College of Law. Nonetheless, he continued to take classes in the fine arts and was a founder of the university's writers' club. His college writing brought him both notoriety and opportunity: his publication of "Man-Songs" under a pseudonym caused him to be suspended from the club for the "immoral" content of the poems (Davis, p. 306), but his story "Mir-I-Nisa" won a cash prize from the *Philippine Free Press* in 1929, enabling him to move to America. Villa then attended the University of New Mexico, where he founded and edited a literary magazine, *Clay,* and earned his B.A. in 1933. He moved to New York City to pursue graduate study at Columbia University, and he lived the rest of his life there.

Villa's first collection of poems published in the United States was *Have Come, Am Here* (1942), a candidate for the Pulitzer Prize. He received an award from the American Academy of Arts and Letters in 1942 and a Guggenheim fellowship in 1943. His second volume, appropriately titled *Volume Two* (1949), introduced his famous "comma poems." Other awards included a Bollingen Foundation fellowship and a Rockefeller Foundation grant. Several more volumes of poems and short stories appeared through the mid-1970s. He sometimes published under the pseudonym "Doveglion," a blend of "dove," "eagle," and "lion."

During the 1940s, Villa married and fathered two sons, but his marriage was short-lived. He worked briefly as an editor before directing the poetry workshop at the City College of New York from 1952 to 1960. He also served as cultural attaché to the Philippine Mission to the United Nations from 1952 to 1963. He became a vice consul in 1965, serving as an adviser on cultural affairs to the president of the Philippines in the late 1960s.

From 1964 to 1973, Villa was a lecturer at the New School for Social Research and conducted private poetry workshops. He stopped publishing new poems in the 1950s, declaring that he did not want to repeat himself. Instead, he wrote short stories and edited work by Filipino writers, as well as a collection of Edith Sitwell's work. Villa died in 1997 in New York City, survived by his sons and three grandchildren. Although he lived in the United States for sixty-seven years, received a number of American grants and fellowships, and is firmly situated in the ethnic American tradition, it is not clear whether or not José García Villa ever became an American citizen.

THEMES AND CONCERNS

Although Villa's early poetry was not very well-received in the Philippines, when he came to America his work was noticed by such influential poets as e. e. cummings, Marianne Moore, Conrad Aiken, and Edith Sitwell. Cummings's influence can be seen in Villa's playful use of word order, structure, and punctuation. He combines and recombines words, highlighting the multiple meanings possible given any set of words. He also assigns new meanings and possibilities to words in their groupings, as in the eleventh poem of *Poems 55* (1962), where he uses "greens" as a verb, followed by the subject "an infinity" in a clause that begins with the word "there" (p. 27). These seemingly nonsensical phrases add to the metaphysical mood of Villa's poems, presenting us with an idea or an image that we can't quite pin down. Villa continually gives one the feeling that he knows something that is just beyond our grasp.

Villa also developed his own vocabulary to relate his ruminations that are constantly warring with a traditional Catholic theology. Thus Villa continually mentions the "rose" and the "tiger," figures packed with power and symbolism for him, but metaphors that we cannot be sure of understanding. He is preoccupied with the biblical Jacob, who fights with God, and takes on this persona. However, in Villa's world, the tiger or Villa himself often triumphs over God. In his poetry, Villa is quick to point out God's weaknesses, though he portrays these sympathetically. There is at times a role reversal—God brought down to human level, a weak and worried father figure or a very fragile being, while the poet ascends to god level, comforting the Father in his more sympathetic moments. These role reversals appear to come both from a sincere searching and questioning to seek out a relationship with God and from an awe of God's power—a simultaneous respect for God and need to strike down the power of God, of the Catholic Church, or of the father figure. Villa bounces back and forth between his belief in poet as prophet and his humbler human needs and uncertainty; this struggle can be seen in many of the poems in *Poems 55*.

Villa is perhaps best known for his "comma poems," the ultimate result of his punctuation maneuvering. In these poems, Villa places a comma between every single word. Villa attempts to reinvent the comma for his own use, in order to encourage the reader to give each and every word the attention it deserves. Villa wrote many poems in this style, which has had a mixed reception. Some have declared it a brilliant invention for slowing the reader down to spend the requisite time with a poem; others have criticized it for its potential of bringing the reader to the point of losing the sense of the poem. Villa responded to this criticism by publishing several poems in both comma and noncomma versions side by side so that readers could compare and judge for themselves. Villa was also quick to point out, somewhat indignantly, that a reader could always simply ignore the commas. Villa furthered his comma experiments in a number of poems that forgo the words entirely. For example, there is "Centipede Sonnet," consisting entirely of commas; "Sonnet in Polka Dots," composed of capital Os; "The Emperor's New Sonnet," which is a blank page; and "The Bashful One," in which a single comma lurks in the lower left of the page. It is especially in these caprices that the influence of cummings and Villa's desire to take his work to the next level of meaning are evident.

Well known in the mid-twentieth century, Villa's work elicited few readers in the 1980s and 1990s, but the recent increase in attention to Asian American literature has reawakened interest in his enormous influence on writing by Filipinos. Eileen Tabios's 1999 edition of his selected writings won the PEN Oakland Josephine Miles Award, and a collection of his critical writings was published in 2002.

POETRY COLLECTIONS

Many Voices. Manila: Philippine Book Guild, 1939.
Poems by Doveglion. Manila: Philippine Writers' League, 1941.
Have Come, Am Here. New York: Viking, 1942.
Volume Two. New York: New Directions, 1949.
Selected Poems and New. New York: McDowell, Oblensky, 1958.
Poems 55: The Best Poems of José García Villa as Chosen by Himself. Manila: A. S. Florentino, 1962. [Tagalog translation published as *55 Poems.* Trans. Hilario S. Francia. Manila: University of the Philippines Press, 1962.]
The Essential Villa. Manila: A. S. Florentino, 1965.
Makata 3: Poems in Praise of Love—The Best Love Poems of José García Villa. Manila: A. S. Florentino, 1973.
Appassionata: Poems in Praise of Love. New York: King and Cowen, 1979.
The Anchored Angel: Selected Writings by José García Villa. Ed. Eileen Tabios. Foreword by Jessica Hagedorn. New York: Kaya Press, 1999.
The Parlement of Giraffes: Poems for Children—Eight to Eighty. Ed. John Edwin Cowen, with drawings by Villa. Tagalog translation by Larry Francis. Manila: Anvil, 1999.

SELECTED ANTHOLOGIES AND WEB SITES WHERE POETRY APPEARS

Poems by José García Villa. Philippine American Literary House. Online. www.palhbooks.com/villa.htm.

Realuyo, Bino A., ed. *The NuyorAsian Anthology: Asian American Writings on New York City.* Philadelphia, PA: Temple University Press, 1999.

Washburn, Katherine, and John S. Major, eds. *World Poetry: An Anthology of Verse from Antiquity to Our Time.* New York: W. W. Norton, 1998.

SELECTED ADDITIONAL WORKS

Footnote to Youth: Tales of the Philippines and Others. New York: Charles Scribner's Sons, 1933.

A Celebration for Edith Sitwell. Editor. New York: New Directions, 1948.

A Doveglion Book of Philippine Poetry. Editor. Manila: Katha Editions, 1962.

Selected Stories. Manila: A. S. Florentino, 1962.

The New Doveglion Book of Philippine Poetry. Editor. Manila: Anvil, 1993.

The Critical Villa: Essays in Literary Criticism. Ed. Jonathan Chua. Quezon City: Ateneo de Manila University Press, 2002.

SELECTED RESOURCES FOR FURTHER REFERENCE

Davis, Rocío G. "José García Villa (1908–1997)." In *Asian American Poets: A Bio-Bibliographical Critical Sourcebook.* Ed. Guiyou Huang. Westport, CT: Greenwood Press, 2002, 305–310.

Francia, Luis. "Death Comes to Doveglion." *Asiaweek.* Online. www.asiaweek.com/asiaweek/97/0228/feat5.html.

Sitwell, Edith. *The American Genius.* London: John Lehmann, 1951.

Sollors, Werner. *Beyond Ethnicity.* New York: Oxford University Press, 1986.

Tabios, Eileen. "On José García Villa" (acceptance of the PEN Oakland Josephine Miles Award). Online. http://home.jps.net/~nada/villa.htm.

Trudeau, Lawrence J. "José García Villa." In *Asian American Literature: Reviews and Criticism of Works by American Writers of Asian Descent.* Detroit, MI: Gale, 1999, 471–485.

Valeros, Florentino B., and Estrellita V. Gruenberg. *Filipino Writers in English.* Quezon City: New Day, 1987.

Yu, Timothy. "'The Hand of a Chinese Master': José García Villa and Modernist Orientalism" *MELUS: The Journal of the Society for the Study of the Multi-Ethnic Literature of the United States* 29 (forthcoming 2004).

Mary Tasillo

Derek Walcott

(1930–)

West Indian American

Photo by AP/Wide World Photos.

BIOGRAPHY

Derek Walcott has been called one of the most important poets of our time. Born in St. Lucia, an island in the British West Indies, in 1930, Walcott was raised by his mother (his father died when Walcott was one year old) in the capital city of Castries. In the home he shared with his mother (a schoolteacher, seamstress, and amateur actress who used to perform in plays written by his father), his sister, and his twin brother, Roderick, Walcott learned to appreciate literature and drama, the two central concerns of his professional life. His early schooling reinforced his love of the arts; the study of English literature, Greek drama, and Latin occupied much of his time and captured his passionate interest.

Thanks to this passion and support of his family and teachers, Walcott began writing poetry at an early age and has published prolifically every since. He published his first poem at fourteen and self-published his first collection of poems, *25 Poems*, with $200 borrowed from his mother, at the age of eighteen. He won a scholarship to study at the University College of the West Indies in Kingston, Jamaica, in 1950, and he published *Epitaph for the Young, Xll Cantos*, and *Poems* in the year following. His first professionally published collection, *In a Green Night, Poems 1948–60*, was published in 1962, and over a dozen more volumes of poetry have followed since then, including three epic-length poems: the autobiographical *Another Life* (1973), the Homeric-style *Omeros* (1990), and most recently, the lyrical *Tiepolo's Hound* (2000).

While a prolific poet, Walcott is also an accomplished playwright and director. In his first year of university studies, he founded his first theater company, the St. Lucia Arts Guild, and wrote and directed his first full-length play, *Henri Christophe: A Chronicle*. Shortly thereafter, he was commissioned by the Trinidadian government to write another play, *Drums and Colours*. This endeavor secured him a Rockefeller Foundation grant that enabled him to study in New York, where he wrote, directed, and produced several more musicals and dramas. Dedicated not only to producing his own work but also to encouraging the work of other playwrights, Walcott founded the Trinidad Theater Workshop in 1959. The workshop, devoted to arts education and to the production of high-quality art, music, and theater in Trinidad and Tobago, has been continuously operating since its inception. In 1981, Walcott brought his artistic support to the United States, when he founded the Boston Playwrights' Theater to provide playwrights with a space to study their art and to write, direct, and produce new work.

Walcott's poetry and drama have met with high critical praise, perhaps most significantly illustrated in his receipt of the Nobel Prize for literature in 1992. He has also won a MacArthur Foundation "Genius" Award, a Royal Society of Literature Award, and the Queen's Medal of Honor. He was also nominated to serve as Poet Laureate in England, the first West Indian writer to receive this honor. An accomplished painter as well, Walcott's visual art can be seen on many of his books' dust jackets and on canvases worldwide.

Walcott splits his time between Boston, where he teaches English at Boston University, and Trinidad, his adopted home. He has one son and three daughters.

THEMES AND CONCERNS

Walcott's poetry is informed largely by the mixed culture into which he was born. St. Lucia gained independence from Great Britain only recently, in 1979, and Walcott struggled from an early age to define his cultural identity. At home, he spoke Creole and experienced African-inflected culture; at school, due to British occupation, he learned English and experienced European culture, full of the study of white men, English diction, and European subject matter. Pervading Walcott's poetry is what Stephen Breslow calls a "multicultural consciousness," an understanding of the irony that "he is man of letters schooled in the major European traditions while living on islands populated largely by former slaves" (p. 268). The attempt to articulate this understanding, and to straddle these two worlds, is a major concern of his work, and it appears in various forms throughout his poetry and drama.

In one sense, the struggle for cultural identify manifests itself in poems that valorize his beloved Caribbean home. Richly drawn, almost reverently detailed images of the landscape and the sea, as well as integration of the Creole language into predominately English poems, remind the reader that Walcott is one intimately acquainted with and respectful of island life. He further reminds us of this in poems that provide a different version of history from that provided by European and American history books—one with the Caribbean islands and the Caribbean people at its center. Whereas "official" history minimizes the negative impact of colonial expansion, Walcott's poems move these people from the margins of history to its center. In the book-length poem *Omeros*, for instance, which is based stylistically on Homer's epics,

Walcott retells history from a Caribbean vantage point, casting West Indian fishermen as heroes.

Walcott's multicultural perspective is also evident in his darker subject matter. Although using English diction and European forms such as meter and rhyme, at times he spotlights instances of racism and feelings of alienation suffered by non-European people in a colonized state. At other times, he laments his divided loyalties, questioning whether his own position as an English-speaking and English-writing poet will divide him irrevocably from the people of his past. At still other times, he prophesies the end of the superpowers, likening Europe and the United States to the Roman Empire and implying that their reign is coming to an end.

With its multicultural perspective manifesting itself in lush imagery, richly drawn characters, piercing insight, and at times brutal honesty, Walcott's poetry and drama invites readers to share a vision of the world that is neither European nor Caribbean nor English nor Creole. It is, instead, gracefully and vividly all of these at once.

POETRY COLLECTIONS

25 Poems. Port-of-Spain: Guardian Commercial Printery, 1948.
Epitaph for the Young, Xll Cantos. Bridgetown: Barbados Advocate, 1949.
Poems. Kingston, Jamaica: City Printery, 1951.
In a Green Night: Poems 1948–60. London: Cape, 1962.
Selected Poems. New York: Farrar, Straus, & Giroux, 1964.
The Castaway and Other Poems. London: Cape, 1965.
The Gulf and Other Poems. London: Cape, 1969.
Another Life. New York: Farrar, Straus, & Giroux, 1973.
Sea Grapes. New York: Farrar, Straus, & Giroux, 1976.
The Star-Apple Kingdom. New York: Farrar, Straus, & Giroux, 1979.
The Fortunate Traveller. New York: Farrar, Straus, & Giroux, 1981.
Selected Poetry. Ed. Wayne Brown. London: Heinemann, 1981.
Poems of the Caribbean. Illustrated by Romare Bearden. New York: Limited Editions Club, 1983.
Midsummer. New York: Farrar, Straus, & Giroux, 1984.
Collected Poems 1948–1984. New York: Farrar, Straus, & Giroux, 1986.
The Arkansas Testament. New York: Farrar, Straus, & Giroux, 1987.
Omeros. New York: Farrar, Straus, & Giroux, 1990.
The Bounty: Poems. New York: Farrar, Straus, & Giroux, 1997.
Tiepolo's Hound. New York: Farrar, Straus, & Giroux, 2000.

SELECTED ANTHOLOGIES WHERE POETRY APPEARS

Coombs, Orde, ed. *Is Massa Day Dead? Black Moods in the Caribbean.* New York: Doubleday, 1974.
Dathorne, O. R., ed. *Caribbean Verse.* Westport, CT: Heinemann, 1967.

Harper, Michael, and Anthony Walton, eds. *Every Shut Eye Ain't Asleep: An Anthology of Poetry by African Americans Since 1945.* New York: Little, Brown, 1994.

Howes, Barbara, ed. *From the Green Antilles.* New York: Macmillan, 1966.

Walmsley, Anne, ed. *The Sun's Eye: West Indian Writing for Young Readers.* London: Longman, 1989.

SELECTED DRAMA AND NONFICTION

Harry Dernier. Bridgetown: Barbados Advocate, 1952.

Ione: A Play with Music. City: Mona, Jamaica: University College of the West Indies, 1957.

Dream on Monkey Mountain and Other Plays. New York: Farrar, Straus, & Giroux, 1970.

The Joker of Seville and O Babylon! New York: Farrar, Straus, & Giroux, 1978.

Remembrance and Pantomime: Two Plays. New York: Farrar, Straus, & Giroux, 1980.

Three Plays: The Last Carnival; Beef, No Chicken; A Branch of the Blue Nile. New York: Farrar, Straus, & Giroux, 1986.

The Antilles: Fragments of Epic Memory: The Nobel Lecture. New York: Farrar, Straus, & Giroux, 1993.

The Odyssey: A Stage Version. New York: Farrar, Straus, & Giroux, 1993.

Homage to Robert Frost. With Joseph Brodsky and Seamus Heany. New York: Farrar, Straus, & Giroux, 1996.

What the Twilight Says. New York: Farrar, Straus, & Giroux, 1998.

The Haitian Trilogy: Plays: Henri Christophe, Drums and Colours, and The Haytian Earth. New York: Farrar, Straus, & Giroux, 2002.

Walker and the Ghost Dance: Plays. New York: Farrar, Straus, & Giroux, 2002.

SELECTED RESOURCES FOR FURTHER REFERENCE

Bobb, June D. *Beating a Restless Drum: The Poetics of Kamau Brathwaite and Derek Walcott.* Lawrenceville, NJ: Africa World Press, 1998.

Breslow, Stephen. "Derek Walcott: 1992 Nobel Laureate in Literature." *World Literature Today* 67.2 (1993): 267–271.

Brown, Steward, ed. *The Art of Derek Walcott.* Bridgend: Seren Books, 1991.

Burnett, Paula. *Derek Walcott: Politics and Poetics.* Gainesville: University Press of Florida, 2001.

Ferris, William R. "A Multiplicity of Voices: A Conversation with Derek Walcott." *Humanities* 22.6 (2001): 4–10.

Goldstraw, Irma E. *Derek Walcott: An Annotated Bibliography of His Works.* New York: Garland, 1984.

Hamner, R. D., ed. *Critical Perspectives on Derek Walcott.* Pueblo, CO: Passeggiata Press, 1993.

———. *Derek Walcott. Twayne World Authors Series.* New York: Twayne, 1993.

King, Bruce. *Derek Walcott: A Caribbean Life.* Oxford: Oxford University Press: 2000.

Parker, Michael, and Roger Starkey, eds. *Postcolonial Literatures: Achebe, Ngugi, Desai, Walcott.* New York: Palgrave Macmillan, 1995.

Terada, Rei. *Derek Walcott's Poetry.* Boston, MA: Northeastern University Press, 1993.

Thieme, John. *Derek Walcott.* Manchester: Manchester University Press, 1999.

Walcott, Derek, and William Baer. *Conversations with Derek Walcott.* Jackson: University Press of Mississippi, 1996.

Anne M. Dickson

Mitsuye Yamada

(1923–)

Japanese American

BIOGRAPHY

Mitsuye Yamada was born in 1923 while her mother, an Issei (first-generation Japanese American) was visiting Fukuoka, Japan. Yamada immigrated to the United States at the age of three and grew up in Seattle, Washington. Her father, Jack Yasutake, founded Seattle's Senryu Society, or society of Japanese American poets, and was an interpreter for the U.S. Immigration and Naturalization Service. After Pearl Harbor was bombed, Yamada's father was arrested on espionage charges, and shortly thereafter Yamada, along with her mother and brother, moved to the Minidoka Relocation Center, an internment camp, in Idaho.

Yamada's experiences at the internment camp would be a driving force behind her writing and human rights work. Yamada's first book, *Camp Notes and Other Poems,* was written during and immediately following World War II. However, due to the taboo on discussion of the internment camps in the wake of the U.S. victory as well as the difficulty that an Asian American woman writer would experience in trying to find a publisher at that time, *Camp Notes* was not published until 1976. Yamada and her brother were allowed to leave the camp after renouncing any allegiance to the Emperor of Japan, while their mother, a dual citizen, refused to renounce allegiance and therefore remained in the camp until all internees were released. Yamada attended the University of Cincinnati and then New York University, receiving her B.A. in English and art in 1947. In 1950, after marrying research chemist Yoshikazu Yamada, she moved to Irvine, California, where she pursued graduate work. She received her M.A. from the University of Chicago in 1953.

Yamada has led a long academic career, teaching ethnic and children's literature and creative writing at a number of institutions, most recently the University of California, Irvine. She has lectured at workshops and women's conferences and has been involved with organizations such as Amnesty International; the International Women's Writing Guild; the National Women's Political Caucus; the Council for Interracial Books; the American Civil Liberties Union; the Center for the Study of Democratic Institutions; the Academy of American Poets; Poets and Writers; and the Pacific Asian American

Centre, where she served on the board of directors and as chairperson. Yamada also founded the Multicultural Writers of Orange County to support and promote writers of color.

Yamada has received a number of awards, including the Orange County Arts Alliance Literary Arts Award (1980), the Vesta Award for Writing (1982), the Women of Distinction Award (1987), the Women of Achievement Award by the Rancho Santiago Foundation (1991), the Jessie Bernard Wise Women Award (1992), the Paul Delp Peace Award (1994), the Write On, Women! Award (1995), and the Give Women Voice Award (1997).

In addition to her poetry and prose, Yamada has also edited several poetry anthologies and worked on a documentary with Nellie Wong, in which she reads her work and discusses its relationship to her autobiography and experiences in the internment camp. She also used her camp experiences in the exhibit she designed called "The Legacy of Silence—A Japanese American Story," which was displayed in 2000 at the University of California, Irvine, where she was teaching in the Asian American studies department. By telling her own stories along with those of other internees, Yamada hopes to challenge the complacent belief that prejudice is a thing of the past and to educate people to recognize how fragile our freedom is. Her most recent book is *Three Asian American Writers Speak Out on Feminism* (2003), with Merle Woo and Nellie Wong.

THEMES AND CONCERNS

The focus of Yamada's writing has shifted over the years from very personal poetry to essays on social and political issues, the result of her merging her identities as a woman and as an Asian American. Her volumes *Camp Notes and Other Poems* and *Desert Run: Poems and Stories* both address issues of identity as a Japanese and as an American, *Camp Notes* focusing primarily on the internment camp experience and *Desert Run* adding to this topic the complexities of Issei, Nisei, and American identities and family relationships. Yamada uses poems both as a vehicle for self-understanding and for teaching: she has written many autobiographical poems and stories, using her own experiences to illuminate societal realities.

When she began writing intensely personal poetry, Yamada looked to Carolyn Kizer's work as a model for working closely with her personal feelings while portraying events rather than remaining emotionally distanced from painful experiences, as she was initially inclined to do. In the resulting poetry, we face the humiliation that Yamada and others experienced because of prejudice. This humiliation arises from the very act of internment, the way this internment was treated by the media, the reality of the camps and their undermining of the Japanese American lifestyle, and the harassment that other Americans subjected Japanese Americans to outside of the camp.

Yamada illustrates the media portrayals of the camp by telling how a girl boarding a bus obeyed a photographer's command to smile. The incident demonstrates how Japanese Americans' obedience contributed to the myth of voluntary participation in internment. The ideas of obligation and obedience run throughout Yamada's explorations of Japanese Americans' relationship to America as immigrants, as well as throughout her portrayals of family relationships, particularly mother-daughter relationships.

Yamada stresses the importance of confrontation and discussion, of examining and interpreting events. In her poems and stories, we see Japanese Americans engaging with the experiences of other oppressed minorities. One such story, "Mrs. Higashi Is Dead," describes the African American friend of the narrator, who can, to the shock of the narrator's Issei mother, ask bluntly and cavalierly for money from a friend. Through the mother's shock and the subsequent engagement that ensues between mother and daughter, this friend's behavior is compared to that of Japanese Americans in similar financial straits, and both mother and daughter come to a greater understanding of cultural differences and similarities while, through this confrontation, gaining the courage to confront their own conflicts.

Closely tied to cultural conflicts are the challenges of communication with reference to language. Writing of straddling two cultures, Yamada notes the difficulties in translating emotions into words and of translating feelings from one language to another, for there may be no clear translation. Yamada also uses language to demonstrate that at times empathy is impossible in our attempts at cross-cultural understanding, for example in the experience of the writing teacher in "For Laura, Who Still Hears the Geese." The teacher encourages a student to push a poem about her experience of the Holocaust past the clichés that, for the writing teacher, echo the comments she's heard from survivors of Hiroshima. The student comes back with an unforgettable detail, the cries of the geese that the guards were beating as they marched children into the ovens. The teacher can hear the geese; this detail sticks with her, and yet she still does not experience the true focus of the experience—the children—thus highlighting again the challenges of conveying experience through language and the difficulties of experiencing empathy.

Through its focus on language, culture-specific behavior, and the impact of Japanese Americans' internment, Yamada's work encourages reexamination and greater understanding of human rights, peace, and gender issues.

POETRY COLLECTIONS

Camp Notes and Other Poems. San Lorenzon, CA: Shameless Hussy Press, 1976.
Desert Run: Poems and Stories. Lathan, NY: Kitchen Table, 1988.

SELECTED ADDITIONAL WORKS

The Web We Weave: Orange County Poetry Anthology. Editor, with John Brander. Laguna Beach, CA: Literary Arts Press, 1986.
Sowing Ti Leaves: Writings by Multicultural Women. Editor, with Sarie S. Hylkema. New York: Kitchen Table/Women of Color, 1990.
Three Asian American Writers Speak Out on Feminism. With Merle Woo and Nellie Wong. Seattle, WA: Radical Women, 2003.

SELECTED ANTHOLOGIES WHERE POETRY APPEARS

Anzaldúa, Gloria. *Making Face, Making Soul.* San Francisco. CA: Aunt Lute Books, 1990.
Bankier, Joanna, ed. *Women Poets of the World.* New York: Macmillan, 1983.
Harth, Erica. ed. *The Last Witness: Reflections on the Wartime Internment of Japanese Americans.* New York: Palgrave for St. Martin's Press, 2001.
Keenan, Deborah, Roseann Lloyd, and Ruth Thorne-Thomsen, eds. *Looking for Home: Women Writing about Exile.* Minneapolis, MN: Milkweed Editions, 1990.
Kim, Elaine, Lilia V. Villanueva, and Asian Women United of California, eds. *Making More Waves: New Writings by Asian American Women.* Boston, MA: Beacon, 1997.
Lim, Shirley Geok-lin, Mayumi Tsutakawa, and Margarita Donnelly, eds. *The Forbidden Stitch: An Asian American Women's Anthology.* Corvallis, OR: Calyx, 1989.
Moraga, Cherrie L., Johnetta Tinker, and Gloria Anzaldúa. *This Bridge Called My Back: Writings by Radical Women of Color.* New York: Kitchen Table/Women of Color, 1989.

SELECTED RESOURCES FOR FURTHER REFERENCE

Jaskoski, Helen. "A MELUS Interview: Mitsuye Yamada." *MELUS: The Journal of the Society for the Study of the Multi-Ethnic Literature of the United States* 15.1 (1988): 97–108.
Light, Allie, and Irving Saraf. *Mitsuye & Nellie.* New York: Women Make Movies, 1981.
Monura, Gail M. *Frontiers of Asian American Studies: Writing, Research, and Commentary.* Pullman: Washington State University Press, 1989.
Patterson, Anita Haya. "Resistance to Images of Internment: Mitsuye Yamada's Camp Notes." *MELUS: The Journal of the Society for the Study of the Multi-Ethnic Literature of the United States* 23.3 (Fall 1998): 103.
Wooley, Lisa. "Racial and Ethnic Semiosis in Mitsuye Yamada's 'Mrs. Higashi Is Dead.'" *MELUS: The Journal of the Society for the Study of the Multi-Ethnic Literature of the United States* 24.4 (Winter 1999): 77.

Mary Tasillo

Additional Contemporary American Ethnic Poets

Elmaz Abinader
Arab American
b. 1954

Francisco X. Alarcon
Latino
b. 1954

Meena Alexander
East Indian American
b. 1951

Judith Arcana
Jewish American

Himani Bannerji
East Indian American
b. 1942

Stephen Berg
Jewish American

Peter Blue Cloud
American Indian
b. 1935

Vera Borkovec
Slavic American

Kevin Boyle
Irish American

Mei-Mei Brussenbrugge
Asian American
b. 1947

Diane Burns
American Indian
b. 1957

Kathleen Cain
Irish American

Gladys Cardiff
American Indian
b. 1942

Ana Castillo
Latina
b. 1953

Virginia R. Cerenio
Asian American
b. 1955

Eric Chock
Asian American
b. 1950

Chrystos
American Indian
b. 1946

Elizabeth Cook-Lynn
American Indian
b. 1930

Luchi Corpi
Chicana
b. 1945

Toi Derricotte
African American
b. 1941

Jimmie Durham
American Indian
b. 1940

Cornelius Eady
African American
b. 1954

Louise Erdrich
American Indian
b. 1954

Sandra Maria Esteves
Latina

Patrice Gaines
African American
b. 1950

Diana García
Latina

Maria Mazzioto Gillan
Italian American

Keith Gilyard
African American
b. 1952

Kimiko Hahn
Asian American
b. 1955

Additional Contemporary American Ethnic Poets

Nathalie Handal
Arab American
b. 1969

Michael S. Harper
African American
b. 1938

Lance Henson
American Indian
b. 1944

Ha Jin
Asian American
b. 1956

Gayl Jones
African American
b. 1949

X. J. Kennedy
Irish American
b. 1929

Myung Mi Kim
Asian American
b. 1957

Alex Kuo
Asian American

Alan Chong Lau
Asian American
b. 1948

Harold Littlebird
American Indian
b. 1951

Audre Lorde
African American
1934–1992

Wing Tek Lum
Asian American
b. 1946

Haki Madhubuti (aka Don L. Lee)
African American
b. 1942

Cherrie Moraga
Chicana
b. 1952

Aurora Levins Morales
Puerto Rican
Jewish American
b. 1954

Kyoko Mori
Asian American
b. 1957

Thylias Moss
African American
b. 1954

Nila Northsun
American Indian
b. 1951

Alicia Ostriker
Jewish American

Uma Parameswaran
East Indian American
b. 1938

Jay Parini
Italian American
b. 1948

Ricardo Pau-Llosa
Latino
b. 1954

Willie Perdomo
Puerto Rican
b. 1960

Pedro Pietri
Puerto Rican
b. 1944

Miguel Piñero
Nuyorican
1946–1988

Carter Revard
American Indian
b. 1931

Adrienne Rich
Jewish American
b. 1929

Leo Romero
Chicano
b. 1950

Vijay Seshadri
East Indian American
b. 1954

Ntozake Shange
African American
b. 1948

Virgil Suarez
Latino
b. 1962

Arthur Sze
Asian American
b. 1950

Eileen Tabios
Asian American

Kitty Tsui
Asian American
b. 1953

Gayle Two Eagles
American Indian

Gina Valdés
Chicana
b. 1943

Evangelina Vigil-Piñón
Latina
b. 1952

Gerald Vizenor
American Indian
b. 1934

Alice Walker
African American
b. 1944

Roberta Hill Whiteman
American Indian
b. 1947

Nellie Wong
Asian American
b. 1934

Jay Wright
African American
b. 1935

John Yau
Asian American
b. 1950

Kevin Young
African American
b. 1970

Ray Young Bear
American Indian
b. 1950

Index

Index

Index

Jones, LeRoi. *See* Baraka, Amiri
Jordan, June (June Meyer), xxviii; bibliography, 153–54; biography, 151–52; themes and concerns, 152–53. Works: *Living Room,* 153; *Naming Our Destiny,* 153; *Passion: New Poems 1977–1980,* 152; *Things That I Do in the Dark,* 152; *Who Look At Me,* 152
Joy Harjo and Poetic Justice, 136
Joy Harjo and The Real Revolution, 136
Joyce, James, 124
Just Us Books, 106

ka'tsina (kachina), 258
Kavanaugh, Patrick, 124
Kearny Street Writers' Workshop, 127
Kendall, Tim, 209
Kennedy, John F., 46
Kenny, Maurice: bibliography, 157–58; biography, 155–56; themes and concerns, 156–57. Works: *Between Two Rivers,* 156; *Blackrobe,* 156; *Mama Poems,* 156–57
Kerouac, Jack, 37
Kimako's Blues People, 39
King, Martin Luther, Jr., 25, 116
Kinnell, Galway, 9, 135; bibliography, 161–62; biography, 159–60; themes and concerns, 160–61. Works: "The Bear," 160; "Freedom, New Hampshire," 161; "The Porcupine," 160; "Saint Francis and the Sow," 160; "Walking Down the Stairs," 160–61
Kiowa Indians, 199
Kitzinger, Rachel, 123
Kizer, Carolyn, 301

Klallam Indians, 219
Klepfisz, Irena: bibliography, 165–66; biography, 163–64; themes and concerns, 164–65. Works: *Dreams of an Insomniac,* 164; *periods of stress,* 164
Knight, Etheridge, 253; bibliography, 169–70; biography, 167–68; themes and concerns, 168–69. Works: *Belly Song and Other Poems,* 169; *Born of a Woman,* 169; "Dark Prophecy: I Sing of Shine," 169; "The Idea of Ancestry," 168; *Poems from Prison,* 167, 169
Komunyakaa, Yusef: bibliography, 173–74; biography, 171–72; themes and concerns, 172–73. Works: "Autobiography of My Alter-Ego," 172; "The Devil's Workshop," 172; *Dien Cai Dau,* 172; "I Apologize for the Eyes in My Head," 173; *Pleasure Dome,* 172; "Woebegone," 172
KONCH (online periodical), 243
Kono, Juliet, 267
Korelitz, Jean Hanff, 207
Kuo, Alex, 13

Ladies' Home Journal (periodical), 26, 115
Laguna Indians, 17, 258
Laguna Pueblo, 17, 258
Lakota Sioux Reservation, 229
Lamont Poetry Prize, 144, 178, 275
The Language of Life (Moyers), 223
Lannan Foundation, 72, 76
Latin America, 2
Latinadad, 103

Lau, Alan Chong, 144
Laviera, Tato: bibliography, 177; biography, 175; themes and concerns, 175–76
Law, study of the, 102, 199, 246, 291
Lee, Li-Young, 212; bibliography, 180–81; biography, 178–79; themes and concerns, 179–80. Works: *Book of My Nights,* 180; *City in Which I Love You,* 180; "The Cleaving," 180; "Eating Together," 179–80; "The Gift," 179; "Persimmons," 179; *Rose,* 179–80
Leonore Marshall Poetry Prize, 83, 216
Letras de Oro, 2
Lev, Donald, 91
Levertov, Denise, 33
Levine, Philip, 147, 270–71
Lila Wallace–Readers' Digest Writers' Award, 14, 212
Lilith, 92
Lilith (periodical), 235
Lim, Shirley Geok-lin, 64; bibliography, 184–85; biography, 182–83; themes and concerns, 183–84. Works: *Among the White Moon Faces,* 182; "Learning English," 183; "Learning to Love America," 184; *Monsoon History,* 183; "Mr. Tang's Uncles," 182; "Pantoun for Chinese Women," 183; "The Shape of Words," 183; "Walking Around in a Different Language,"183
Listening, theme of, 52
Literary criticism, interest in and practice of, 18, 123, 199–200, 208
Los Angeles, 84, 109, 143

Index

About the Editor and Contributors

ALYCE BAKER has a master's degree in curriculum and supervision from Pennsylvania State University. She is currently attending Indiana University of Pennsylvania, pursuing a Ph.D. in literature and criticism. She has particular interest in twentieth-century African American and Southern writers.

TATIANA BIDO earned a bachelor's degree in English from the University of Central Florida in 2003 and is currently pursuing graduate studies in English there.

ESPERANZA CINTRON is an associate professor of literature and writing at Wayne County Community College in Detroit, Michigan. She is a poet and a founding member of the Sisters of Color Collective.

LINDA CULLUM is the editor of this volume and the supervisor of the entries on American Indian poets. She is an assistant professor of English and the director of the University Writing Center at Kutztown University of Pennsylvania. She has also taught at the Indiana University of Pennsylvania and Lake Superior State University, in Sault Ste. Marie, Michigan. Dr. Cullum is the editor, with Lynne Alvine, of *Breaking the Cycle: Gender, Literacy, and Learning* (Heinemann, 1999) and the author of a number of articles on issues such as American Indian poetry, identity politics in the composition classroom, service learning, and teaching students with physical disabilities.

SUE CZERNY is a librarian at Kutztown University of Pennsylvania, where she is also the liaison to the Native American community for the library's Multicultural Support Center. She holds an M.S. in library science from Drexel University and an M.S. in education from Lehigh University.

ALICE D'AMORE earned her master's degree in English from Kutztown University in May 2003. Between adjuncting, publishing, and applying to doctoral programs, Alice manages to devote her remaining time to her hobbies—books, hikes, and live concerts.

ANNE M. DICKSON is an assistant professor at Kutztown University, where she teaches in the Professional Writing program. She worked for several years as a technical writer while earning her Ph.D. in 19th Century British Literature from Lehigh University. Her research interests include the connections between feminist theory and technical writing pedagogy and representations of race in rhetorical discourse.

HEATHER DRAPER has an M.A. in English from Millersville University of Pennsylvania and is currently completing an M.S. in library science from Kutztown University.

JENNIFER McNAMARA DRESSLER supervised the selection and editing of the entries on poets with Irish, Italian, Jewish, Palestinian, Polish, Czech, and West and East Indian ancestry. Dr. Dressler currently teaches literature and writing in the English department at Kutztown University. She received her M.A. and Ph.D. from Lehigh University in Bethlehem, Pennsylvania. Her fields of scholarly interest include nineteenth-century British literature, medieval literature, and literature relating to her Irish heritage.

AUGUSTINA EDEM DZREGAH is currently an assistant professor of English at the Indiana University of Pennsylvania. Prior to that, she was a tenured English professor at the University of Ghana, Legon. She is a past Fellow of the National Council for Black Studies and has written and presented on Negritude and Black Diaspora poetry, the works of Toni Morrison and Ama Ata Aidoo, and the areas of feminisms, masculinities, and queer theories.

REME A. GREFALDA is the founding editor of *Our Own Voice,* a literary e-zine for Filipinos in the Diaspora. She is a Philippine Palanca Awardee for her historical play *In the Matter of Willie Grayson* and the resident playwright and artistic director of QBd Ink: Friends of the Performing Artist, a community theater group in Washington, DC. A collection of her poetry is published in *Baring More Than Soul* (1997).

RACHAEL GRONER has a Ph.D. in American studies from Purdue University and is an assistant professor at Temple University. She specializes in twentieth-century American and women's literature, cultural studies, and women's studies.

KYLA HEFLIN is a full-time instructor at Colorado University at Colorado Springs. She is pursuing her doctorate in literature and criticism at Indiana University of Pennsylvania. Her areas of interest include women's fiction and film, letters and diaries, and minority literature.

JOSÉ IRIZARRY is an associate professor of American Literature at the University of Puerto Rico in Mayaguez. He was a recipient of a grant from Recovering the U.S. Hispanic Literary Heritage Project for researching the life and works of Pedro Juan Labarthe in English and is currently working on a critical introduction for the reprinting of Labarthe's first novel.

KEVIN MEEHAN is an associate professor of English at the University of Central Florida. He specializes in Caribbean and African American literature, music and literature, literary translation, and multimedia pedagogy.

CECILIA RODRÍGUEZ MILANÉS, herself an accomplished poet and essayist, supervised the contributions on Latino/Latina poets. She is an associate professor of English at the University of Central Florida, specializing in Latino/Latina literature, multiethnic American literature, writing, and women's studies. Dr. Milanés's recent publications include "Negrita," in *Little Havana Blues;* "No Accents Allowed," first published in *The Women's Review of Books* in July 1992; and "A Journey to Voice," in Sandra Kumamoto Stanley's *Other Sisterhoods.* She is currently editing an anthology of Latino literature for the Of Color Series (forthcoming, 2005). She is also the cochair of the NCTE Latino Caucus.

AMY C. O'BRIEN received her Ph.D. from Lehigh University, specializing in Renaissance literature and cultural criticism. Her research interests include women's autobiography and pop culture. She also has experience in the field of public relations. She is an assistant professor of English at Kutztown University.

STACY PAULEY teaches at Bridgewater College in Virginia and was previously on the faculty at Purdue University Calumet (Indiana). She is the coauthor of *Collaborations: Strategies for Readers and Writers* (1992).

ROY PÉREZ is an undergraduate literature, women's studies, and linguistics student at the University of Central Florida. His current research will lead to graduate study in aesthetics, consciousness, and ethnic writing.

JOSEPH REGISTER is founder of *The Bucks County Writer,* a regional literary magazine in Bucks County, Pennsylvania. He is currently a member of the faculty at Harrisburg Area Community College–Lancaster Campus.

LISA TREVIÑO ROY-DAVIS completed her dissertation (2003) on constructions of the self in six Latina writers, including Judith Ortiz Cofer. She lives and writes in Dallas, Texas.

MARY TASILLO graduated from Bennington College and is enrolled in the M.A. program in children's literature at Hollins University. She currently lives in Minneapolis and is an independent student of printmaking, the book arts, the picture book format, and the chocolate cake.

ALICE TRUPE selected and supervised the editing of entries on Asian American poets. She is an associate professor of English and director of the Writing Center at Bridgewater College in the Shenandoah Valley of Virginia. Dr. Trupe's primary teaching responsibilities include courses in writing, linguistics, and young adult literature. Her most recent publication is "Promoting Social Justice in the Young Adult Literature Class: Preparing Pre-Service Teachers to Choose Multicultural Texts," in *Just Literacy: Promoting Justice Through Language and Learning,* edited by John Harmon (2002).

VERONICA WATSON is an associate professor of English and director of the Frederick Douglass Institute at Indiana University of Pennsylvania, where she is also currently serving as dean's associate for the College of Humanities and Social Sciences. Dr. Watson has edited the journal *Making Connections: A Journal for Teachers of Cultural Diversity,* and is co-coordinator of the Indiana County Underground Railroad Project, a historical recovery project documenting the black community and antislavery activities/persons of Indiana County, Pennsylvania. She specializes in the fields of nineteenth-century American literature and contemporary African American literature. Dr. Watson is presently working on a study of white-life novels by African American authors.

JOEL WERLEY holds an M.A. in English from Kutztown University. He is currently teaching in Japan.

BRONWEN WEST is a 2003 graduate of the University of Central Florida with a B.A. in English literature. She is currently pursuing an M.A. in creative writing for poetry and creative nonfiction.